"Preachers and catechists are often limited by a sterile Christian imagination, perhaps on their own part, certainly in their hearers. In *Fulfilled in Christ*, Fr. Roza gives us the means to furnish that imagination with authentic types and symbols from Sacred Scripture and the Fathers of the Church. This will be a great help for sacramental preparation and for the faith-filled celebration of the sacraments."

—*Most Reverend George Lucas, Archbishop of Omaha*

"A marvelous guide to the typology and symbolism of the sacraments found in Scripture and Tradition. Fr. Roza avoids arbitrary and exaggerated claims by a careful methodology that presents the teaching of Scripture, the Liturgy, the Catechism, and the writings of Church Fathers used in the Liturgy of the Hours."

—*Peter S. Williamson, Adam Cardinal Maida Chair*
in Sacred Scripture at Sacred Heart Major Seminary,
Co-editor of the Catholic Commentary on Sacred Scripture

"Years ago, in the course of becoming Catholic, works by Joseph Ratzinger, Jean Danielou, and Henri de Lubac introduced me to the vital riches of typology in Sacred Scripture. Fr. Roza's wonderful book follows in that great tradition and does so with an accessible structure and approach that is deeply informed by the Church Fathers and the *Catechism of the Catholic Church*. Highly recommended for all students of Scripture and sacramental theology!"

—*Carl E. Olson, author of "Opening the Word"*
Scripture column, Our Sunday Visitor *newspaper*

"The Church Fathers, the Liturgy, the Catechism—they all interpret the Scriptures through the lens of typology. And yet contemporary Christians often don't know what to make of the Old Testament. In *Fulfilled in Christ*, Fr. Devin Roza takes what Catholics are most familiar with—the Seven Sacraments—and shows how the Living Tradition finds them prefigured in the pages of the Old Testament. The result is an amazing tool for the renewal of Catholic preaching, teaching, and RCIA. A truly stunning achievement!"

—*Dr. Brant Pitre, Professor of Sacred Scripture,*
Notre Dame Seminary Graduate School of Theology

"Pius IV's *Tridentine Profession of Faith* (1564) taught that the seven sacraments of the New Law were instituted by Jesus Christ, our Lord, for our salvation. *Fulfilled in Christ* shows how this truth of the faith is sustained by a proper understanding of biblical typology. This book is an invaluable resource for understanding the biblical roots of all seven sacraments."

—*Robert Fastiggi, Professor of Systematic Theology,
Sacred Heart Major Seminary*

"One of the most important, and neglected, sources for studying the living Tradition of the Church is the Liturgy. *Fulfilled in Christ* offers an innovative and objective methodology as a remedy to this situation, bringing together in a harmonious and academically solid way Scripture, Liturgy, Patristics, and the teachings of the Church. This book is sure to inspire numerous other studies and will be of great help to academics, pastors, and catechists who wish to share with the faithful the beauty and mystery of the divine life that Christ offers us in his sacraments."

—*Fr. Edward McNamara, LC, Professor of Liturgy and
Dean of Theology at the Pontifical Athenaeum Regina
Apostolorum, Liturgy Specialist for Zenit News Agency*

"In *Fulfilled in Christ* Fr. Roza performs an important service on behalf of readers who are eager to deepen and enrich their understanding of the faith. Through the ancient—but in modern times largely neglected—approach to the interpretation of Sacred Scripture and Tradition called typology, he sheds new light on the sacraments and the Liturgy of the Hours and enhances our appreciation of their role in living a truly Christ-centered life. The result is a book at once scholarly and exciting."

—*Russell Shaw, veteran journalist, author of*
*A*merican Church, Catholic Laity in
the Mission of the Church, *and other works*

"Fr. Roza's *Fulfilled in Christ* is a work of immensely detailed and original scholarship involving Scripture. Like many other works, it seems likely to be a fundamental contribution to all subsequent work in the area, but at the same time open to second thoughts. There will never be a need for second thoughts, however, in the orthodox grounding of *Fulfilled in Christ*."

—*Fr. James Swetnam, S.J., Professor Emeritus,*
Pontifical Biblical Institute

"Typology is misunderstood because it is felt to have a quicksilver quality that allows the text to mean whatever we want it to mean. This is not so, as Fr. Roza tries to demonstrate in two ways. First, he shows how extensively the Catechism relies upon typology to teach doctrine, and second, the examples compiled in the book show the ruled use it has received in Tradition. The believer who uses this as a guide for reading Scripture will be led to discover that the events in the Bible run downhill to pool in the Church's sacraments for our salvation and happiness."

—*David W. Fagerberg, Associate Professor*
of Theology, University of Notre Dame

"Reading the Bible for types of Christ was the heart of the Apostolic Tradition and the source of sacramental theology. Fr. Roza's book will be a godsend to those hoping to re-learn the wisdom of that tradition."

—*William Marshner, Professor of Theology,*
Christendom College

"Typological exegesis of the Holy Bible illuminates the unity of the divine plan of salvation in the Old and New Testaments. In this marvelous book, Fr. Devin Roza shows how typology adheres to the first hermeneutical principle of Dei Verbum 12: 'Be especially attentive to the content and unity of the whole Scripture.' This is a sorely needed study to counter the fragmentation of the Bible."

—*Eduardo Echeverria, Professor of Philosophy*
and Systematic Theology, Sacred Heart Major Seminary

"As the ancient Christian mystagogues knew, one of the keys to being properly disposed to the wonderful graces of the sacraments is the ability to decipher the meaning of the signs (in St. Ambrose, the *ratio sacramentorum*) employed in the liturgical actions. To recognize in the sacramental signs the biblical events to which they give us renewed access is to see (as in a *contemplatio*) the invisible Mystery that lies beneath them. At just the time when the Church is clamoring for a renewal of mystagogy, for the catechetical art of leading others to see the invisible Mystery in the visible signs of the sacraments, Fr. Roza's wonderful book comes along to help us do just that. All practicing and aspiring mystagogues will want to have his indispensable book on their shelves and in their hands. If it is well-used, it may even spell an end to the sad neglect and under-appreciation of these divine mysteries that Christ has so graciously placed in our weak hands."

—*Sean Innerst, Professor of Theology and Catechetics,*
St. John Vianney Theological Seminary, Augustine Institute

"My experience of teaching the art of homiletics to seminarians, deacons, and my brother priests reveals that these good men, in large numbers, remain dedicated to preaching that can make a difference in people's lives. One major and extraordinary obstacle on the whole, however, is that relatively few members of the clergy seem to have the time to discover what remains hidden in the Scriptures. Fr. Roza has given good-intentioned but sadly overburdened pastoral ministers a true gift that will make their homily preparation easier but take them deeper into the Word of God than ever before. Consequently, if they read this book and acquire its treasure, they will preach in a fresh and more stimulating way."

—*Fr. Joseph M. Mele, Secretary for Leadership*
Development, Diocese of Pittsburgh

"*Fulfilled in Christ* is an extraordinary resource and significant aid to priestly formation. As a seminary rector, I read through Fr. Roza's research through the lens of seminary formation and the new evangelization. Considering the damaging effects of secular humanism that have swept through Western culture, experiences of mystery and the divine have been reduced to individualistic and rationalistic interpretations that leave culture devoid of her communal, transcendental calling. Fr. Roza has reintroduced a form of study that illustrates the clear, definitive plan of salvation. He re-proposes the ancient practice of studying Sacred Scripture and Tradition in the context of Jesus' Paschal Mystery as this mystery penetrates the salvific history of man and culture. I therefore encourage priests and seminarians to read *Fulfilled in Christ* as a spiritual work of intellectual study. As a result, I know this will impact fruitful and lively preaching as we catechize the faithful."

—*Fr. James A. Wehner, Rector and President*
of Notre Dame Seminary, New Orleans

"Typology was a staple of patristic interpretation, but has been sadly neglected in modern exegesis. Fr. Roza provides us with an excellent compendium of biblical types that will greatly assist in recovering the typological vision of the Fathers for the contemporary Church."

—John Bergsma, Professor of Sacred Scripture,
Franciscan University of Steubenville

"Fr. Roza's guide to typology is an extremely useful tool for readers of the Bible. The imagery found in the sacred text is rich and profoundly complicated. This clever tool will deeply enrich the prayerful reading and the study of the Word of God."

—Fr. Mitch Pacwa, SJ, author, television host,
Senior Fellow of the St. Paul Center for Biblical Theology

"Fr. Roza's book will prove to be a valuable resource for biblicists, catechists, and religion teachers. First, it is thorough, scanning Sacred Scripture and Sacred Tradition for the key hermeneutical points of reference which often elude treatments of typology—thus reducing such an approach to idiosyncratic. Second, while classically traditional, it breathes a fresh spirit in this very important manner of penetrating not just texts (biblical, liturgical and patrological) but the 'golden thread' of the divine intent which makes this library (*ta biblia*) of Scripture one book with Christ as its center. Third, the revival of this read of Scripture is one small part of a grander renewal of reading Scripture which includes the use of *lectio divina* and is rooted in the teachings of the Second Vatican Council. Looking forward to his subsequent volumes."

—Dcn. Stephen F. Miletic, Professor of Scripture,
Franciscan University of Steubenville

"It is one thing to claim the Catholic Church reveres and cherishes the Bible. It is quite another to demonstrate this as convincingly as Fr. Roza has done in his work *Fulfilled in Christ*. This book is in a class by itself. Like no other resource I've seen, it documents the staggering extent to which the language of Sacred Scripture pervades the language of Sacred Liturgy. Thanks to the author's meticulous research, readers are taken deep into the heart of the Church and her sacramental worship, where the Word of God bears its most abundant fruit. Want to know how the Church understands the Bible, and I mean the whole sweep of salvation history from creation to Christ? This is a wonderful place to start. I wish I had this book on my shelf a long time ago."

—*Curtis Mitch, compiler of the Ignatius Catholic Study Bible*

FULFILLED IN CHRIST

THE SACRAMENTS

A Guide to Symbols and Types
in the Bible and Tradition

FULFILLED IN CHRIST

THE SACRAMENTS

A Guide to Symbols and Types
in the Bible and Tradition

Fr. Devin Roza

Emmaus Academic
Steubenville, Ohio
www.emmausroad.org

Emmaus Academic

Steubenville, Ohio
www.emmausroad.org

A Division of The St. Paul Center for Biblical Theology
Editor-in-Chief: Scott Hahn
1468 Parkview Circle
Steubenville, Ohio 43952

© 2015 Devin Roza, LC
All rights reserved. Published 2015
Printed in the United States of America
20 19 18 17 16 15 1 2 3 4 5 6

Library of Congress Control Number: 2015945481
ISBN: 978-1-941447-31-4

Cover design by Mairead Cameron • Layout by Julie Davis, General Glyphics, Inc., Dallas, Texas

The *nihil obstat* and *imprimatur* are official declarations that a work is considered to be free from doctrinal or moral error. It is not implied that those who have granted the same agree with the content, opinions, or statements expressed.

Nihil Obstat:
Thomas Fox, L.C., Censor Deputatus

Imprimi Potest:
Eduardo Robles Gil, L.C., General Director
September 3, 2014

Imprimatur
† Filippo Iannone
Vicegerent of Rome
From the Vicariate of Rome, January 13, 2015

DEDICATION

For Mom and Dad

Do not think that I have come
to abolish the law and the prophets;
I have come not to abolish them
but to fulfill them.

Matthew 5:17

TABLE OF CONTENTS

FOREWORD

Scott Hahn

In *Fulfilled in Christ: The Sacraments. A Guide to Symbols and Types in the Bible and Tradition*, we find a new look at one of the earliest methods of interpreting Scripture: typology. Bringing together Scripture and the most cherished aspects of our Tradition, Fr. Devin Roza brings us face-to-face with the overarching aspect of God's plan of salvation: for history and for each individual soul. Modern readers who are unfamiliar with typology will be amazed to see that, in the words of Pope Francis, the Church is not merely a "human enterprise," but rather "a love story" (April 24, 2013).

The pervasive nature of typology in the living Tradition of the Church is reflected in a fascinating way in this book, from the authors of the Scripture through the Church Fathers, down to our own day in the Catechism and the liturgy. As demonstrated in this book, the typological understanding of Scripture, unfortunately abandoned by some, has never been abandoned by the Church, who sees in Jesus Christ the fulfillment of God's plan. The Church regards the typological understanding of Scripture as essential to a full understanding of the Word of God (cf. CCC 109–119).

St. Augustine summed up the typological relationship between the Old and New Testaments with the phrase, "The New Testament lies hidden in the Old and the Old Testament is unveiled in the New." Reflecting an understanding of the twofold structure of the Old and New Covenant, typology unveils the ways that the realities and events of the Old Testament prefigure the fulfillment of the New Covenant in Jesus Christ. Typology is the way we read Christ's fulfillment of the Old in the New.

Although typology is little known today, it has been employed since the Church's earliest days. When Jesus accompanied the two disciples on the road to Emmaus, he opened their hearts and minds to see that he himself is the fulfillment of the Old Covenant: "And beginning with Moses and all the prophets, he interpreted to them in all the Scriptures the things concerning himself" (Luke 24:27). The Gospel writers for their part presented Jesus as the typological fulfillment of the Old Covenant: as the new Moses, the new David, the new Solomon, and the new Temple.

In their catechesis, the Church Fathers explained the many ways Christ fulfilled the realities and events of the Old Covenant. They explained that figures, or "types," in the Old Covenant foreshadowed both the mysteries of the life of Christ and the mysteries or sacraments of the New Covenant. The first Christians referred to the sacraments as "mysteries," for it is through the sacraments that we share in the "mystery" of Christ's death and Resurrection. When the Church Fathers explained the mysteries of our salvation in Jesus Christ, they called it *mystagogy* (etymologically, "explaining the mysteries").

Mystagogy is the unveiling of the ways in which everything that was pre-figured in the Old Covenant is fulfilled by the Holy Spirit in the Mystical Body of Christ, *in us*. Enrico Mazza defines mystagogy as "the oral or written explanation of the mystery hidden in the scriptures and celebrated in the liturgy."[1] Mystagogy is the application of typology to the sacraments. What happened to Jesus in the Paschal Mystery is replicated in us by the Holy Spirit in the liturgy and the sacraments. The plan of God did not end when Christ ascended to heaven. In the sacraments, we participate in the Paschal Mystery of Christ's death and Resurrection; in the sacraments, we celebrate and par-ticipate in the mystery of our salvation.

That mystery, and its typological prefiguration, is presented in this book. *Fulfilled in Christ* is a guide to typological or symbolic references to the sacra-ments found in the Scriptures, the Catechism, the liturgy, and the writings of the Church Fathers present in the Liturgy of the Hours. As Fr. Roza explains, these sources have been chosen precisely because the Church considers them authentic witnesses of her living Tradition. The faithful can thus be sure that they can trust the ideas presented here. Scholars will find that a clearly out-lined and objective methodology is employed, which approaches the study of the living Tradition of the Church in a rigorous way (cf. the *Introduction* for more details). The methodology used in this book should be taken into consideration by any theologian or exegete interested in the study of the liv-ing Tradition of the Church.

---

1 *Mystagogy: A Theology of Liturgy in the Patristic Age* (New York: Pueblo Pub. Co, 1989), 2.

Importantly, Fr. Roza's book is quite timely. We are experiencing a call for a renewed emphasis on mystagogy in liturgy and catechesis. Both Pope Benedict and Pope Francis, together with bishops from around the world, have recently called upon the Church to recover a mystagogical understanding of the sacraments. Referring to a recent Synod of Bishops, Pope Benedict wrote: "The Synod Fathers unanimously" called for "a mystagogical approach to catechesis." As well, "the basic structure of the Christian experience calls for a process of mystagogy." Pope Benedict goes on to identify three essential elements of mystagogical catechesis (*Sacramentum Caritatis* 64):

1. It interprets *the rites of the sacraments* in light of *the events of salvation history* in accordance with the Church's living Tradition.
2. It presents the *meaning of the signs* contained in the sacramental rites.
3. It brings out the significance of the rites *for the Christian life* in all its dimensions.

Pope Francis, for his part, recently lamented that many catechetical "manuals and programs have not yet taken sufficiently into account the need for mystagogical renewal" (*Evangelii Gaudium* 166). In doing so, Pope Francis was echoing calls from the bishops around the world to give "more relevance to permanent mystagogy," which should become "true initiation to Christian life through the sacraments" (Proposition 38 from the XIII Ordinary General Assembly of the Synod of Bishops).

What Pope Francis, Pope Benedict, and bishops around the world understand is that sacramental catechesis is an essential part of the new evangelization. The new evangelization is primarily directed to evangelizing the baptized, helping them to understand and appreciate more deeply the divine life that Christ offers us in the sacraments and in his Word. And that means sacramental catechesis of the baptized. In this book, Catholics will find an *indispensable tool for the new evangelization.*

Adult education and RCIA groups will encounter here a rich treasure trove where they can dive into the profound meaning of the sacraments as a real participation in the mysteries of Christ. Catechists and scholars will find a comprehensive and yet succinct volume which makes accessible the beauty of the Church's typological and symbolic understanding of the sacraments, including carefully chosen and compelling excerpts from Church Fathers.

But the appeal of this book is not limited to those working with adult education or RCIA. Pastors will appreciate the fascinating connections between sacraments and Scripture that lend themselves to liturgical preaching. The summaries of the texts referenced are organically organized and theologically solid, allowing even a beginner in the faith to grasp the coherence and completeness of God's plan of salvation and to investigate on their own.

Typological interpretation is especially appropriate today, when so many people have lost the sense of mystery in their faith. Catholics who begin to dig deep into the typology of the sacraments will encounter the mystery of our life in Christ. Fr. Roza's study restores us to the mystery that is at the heart of our faith: the mystery of God's love as it plays out in human history, recorded in the Bible. As Pope Benedict states:

> Mystery is the heart from which our power comes and to which we return to find this center. For this reason I believe that catechesis that we might call mystagogical is very important. Mystagogical also means realistic, referring to our life as people of today. If it is true that the human being's 'measuring stick' for what is just and what is not lies not within but without, in God, it is important that this God is not distant but recognizable, concrete, and that he enter our life and truly be a friend with whom we can speak and who can speak with us.
> *(Lenten Meeting with the Clergy of the Rome Diocese, 2009)*

This is the God who came down from heaven to be with us, to be our intimate friend. In bringing to life the prefiguring of the sacraments, Fr. Roza's complete and accessible book offers a fresh, invigorating means of reading the Scriptures which was present from the earliest Christians—indeed, even Jesus himself—and which is of vital interest to believers today.

ACKNOWLEDGMENTS

I would like to express my gratitude to Fr. Edward McNamara, LC for the fruitful discussions we had at the beginning of this project. I would also like to thank Fr. Nicolas Bossu, LC, Dr. Kathryn Hogan, Dr. Scott Hahn, Fr. Andrew Dalton, LC, Dr. Michael Waldstein, Fr. Cristobal Vilarroig, LC, and Dr. Michael Barber for feedback that in one way or another have enhanced this book. Finally, I would like to especially thank Dr. Andrew Jones, whose help and support made this book possible.

HOW TO USE THIS GUIDE

ORGANIZATION OF THE GUIDE

This book is organized according to sacrament, and presents the types and symbols of each sacrament which are found in the Bible, the Catechism, or the liturgy. Types are presented first, organized according to the order of their occurrence in salvation history. Symbols follow, organized in alphabetical order. Symbols that are also types (such as anointing) are found under both sections respectively, with texts included under one or the other based on whether the text is primarily typological or symbolic.

PRESENTATION OF EACH TYPE OR SYMBOL

Introductory Section

Each type or symbol begins with an introductory section that provides the following information:

• **Old and New Testament Background.** Here are listed references to texts of the Old or New Testament which provide background information regarding the type or symbol in general (i.e. regardless of whether it directly has anything to do with the sacraments). An ample selection of texts have been included to give as full an idea as possible of the ways that the realities or symbols in question have been understood in Scripture. Being familiar with how a symbol or type was used throughout the Scriptures is normally essential to understanding the way it is applied to the sacraments or to other realities of the faith in the writings of the Church Fathers, in the liturgy, or in the Catechism.

• **Catechism Background.** Here are listed references in the Catechism which provide background information regarding the type or symbol in general (i.e. regardless of whether it directly has anything to do with the sacraments). An ample selection of texts have been included. If there are five or more references to the Catechism, those references which are more directly related to the type or symbol as referring to the sacrament are in bold.

• **Type.** Here are listed those references which directly or indirectly affirm that this is a type of the sacrament.

• **Related.** Here are references to related types or symbols found in this book.

Body

Following the introductory section, all references to the respective type or symbol found in the Bible, the Catechism, or the liturgy are organized and summarized. Longer topics are broken up into sections. I have attempted to include all the references to the type or symbol when they are related to the sacrament in question. References that are similar to what is summarized are oftentimes included following *cf.* Texts which are less similar but still closely related are prefaced by *cf. also.* When I have not made an effort to include all texts (usually because they refer to background information), these references are introduced by *cf. for example* or *cf. also for example.*

Occasionally references to types or symbols that do not refer to the sacraments are included when they are important to a proper understanding of the type or symbol as regards the sacrament. For example, the "fruit of the tree of life" prefigures the divine life given in Baptism and the Eucharist (cf. BAPTISM: *Types:* Fruit of the Tree of Life; EUCHARIST: *Types:* Fruit of the Tree of Life). The fruit of the tree of life is at times presented as prefiguring Jesus Christ, the cross, the Scriptures, etc. These texts have *not* been included in this guide, as they do not refer to the sacraments and are not essential for understanding the sacramental references. The opposite occurs with the symbol of the "seal" as regards the Sacrament of Confirmation. It is not easy to properly understand the symbolism of the "seal" without first understanding in general the meanings this symbol takes on in the Scriptures. As such, a wide sampling of texts regarding the non-sacramental symbolism of "seal" have been included and summarized under the subtopic *Seal in General* in CONFIRMATION: *Symbols:* Seal. Similarly, "gift of finest wheat" is a symbol of the Eucharist, but it cannot be understood apart from its Old Testament background. As such, at the beginning of the topic some of the more important aspects of the Old Testament background are summarized.

ADDITIONAL NOTES

The reference text of the Catechism and the liturgy has been the official Latin versions. Three practical consequences of this for the guide are:

1. When typological or symbolic references to the sacraments are found in the Latin original but have been lost in the English translation, "[Latin]" is added to the reference to indicate this.

2. Texts in the English translation of the Liturgy of the Hours that are not found in the Latin original (such as vernacular hymns or the prayers that follow the Psalms) have not been included in the guide.

3. The English translation of the Sacrament of Anointing of the Sick uses a different numbering system than the Latin original. Both the English and Latin numbers are included when they differ.

4. The Second Typical Edition of the Rites of Ordination of a Bishop, of Priests, and of Deacons, uses a different numbering system than the First Typical Edition. Given that the current English translation of the Catechism cites the Rite of Ordination using the numbering scheme of the First Typical Edition, both numbering schemes are always referenced when available, with the Second Typical Edition reference appearing first, followed by the First Typical Edition reference in parenthesis or brackets.

APPENDICES

Finally, at the end of the book are a series of Appendices:

1. *Readings from the Liturgy*—Lists the readings from the Scriptures for each of the sacraments. When a sacrament has a large number of readings available (such as the Eucharist), only those readings most relevant for the topic of symbols and types of the sacraments are included.

2. *Authors of 2nd Readings from the Liturgy of the Hours*—Lists the authors of the second readings of the Liturgy of the Hours which have been included in this volume. They are ordered according to the dates in which they lived.

3. *2nd Readings from the Liturgy of the Hours*—Index of the second readings which are cited in the guide. The reference is given to the reading, followed by a brief summary of the reading, and then finally the symbols or types in which the reading is cited are listed.

4. *Related Christological Titles or Antiphons of the Psalms and Canticles from the Liturgy of the Hours*—Lists the Christological Titles or Antiphons from the Liturgy of the Hours which are in some way related to topics dealt with in this book.

INTRODUCTION

Imagine walking into a church, taking a seat next to the recently baptized Augustine, and listening together with him as St. Ambrose explained the meaning of the sacraments that Augustine had received for the first time just a few days ago at the Easter Vigil. What would it have been like to hear St. Ambrose explain to Augustine and other recently baptized Christians the rich signs and symbols of the rite of Baptism, and the ways Baptism was prefigured by the Crossing of the Red Sea, by the Flood of Noah, and by other moments of salvation history?

While we cannot go back in time and take a seat next to Augustine, we can know what St. Augustine likely heard as he sat at the feet of his great and holy teacher. St. Ambrose baptized St. Augustine in 387, and Ambrose wrote down for posterity his catechesis to the newly baptized sometime between the years 380 and 390.[1] It is safe to suppose that what the converted Augustine heard was quite similar to what we can read there today.

Ambrose's catechetical instructions are entitled *De Mysteriis* and *De Sacramentis*, that is, "On the Mysteries" and "On the Sacraments." In these talks, he explains the symbolism of the rite of Baptism, such as wearing white garments, turning toward the east, and being fully immersed three times in water. He also speaks at length about the ways the sacraments of Christian initiation—especially Baptism and the Eucharist—were prefigured by realities and symbols of the Old Covenant.

Ambrose's typological understanding of Sacred Scripture had a profound effect on Augustine. As Pope Benedict XVI recently wrote: "We know that for Saint Augustine too this passage was at once dramatic and liberating; he came to believe the Scriptures—which at first sight struck him as so disjointed in themselves and in places so coarse—through the very process

---

1 On the dating of *De Mysteriis* and *De Sacramentis*, cf. Craig Alan Satterlee, *Ambrose of Milan's Method of Mystagogical Preaching* (Collegeville, MN: Liturgical Press, 2002), 13–14, 20–30.

of transcending the letter which he learned from Saint Ambrose in typological interpretation, wherein the entire Old Testament is a path to Jess Christ"
(*Verbum Domini* 38).

TYPOLOGY IN THE CHURCH FATHERS
AND IN THE SCRIPTURES

Teaching about the sacraments in light of their Old Testament prefigurations
was not practiced by St. Ambrose alone. Similar catechetical instruction was
done by St. Cyril of Jerusalem, St. John Chrysostom, Theodore of Mopsuestia,
and by St. Augustine himself. This way of teaching the meaning of the sacraments in light of how they fulfill the prefigurations and symbols of the Old
Testament is called "mystagogical catechesis."[2]

While we don't find *systematic* presentations of mystagogical catechesis like Ambrose's until the second half of the fourth century, the *typological
understanding of the sacraments* that is essential to mystagogy is found from
the very beginning of the Church. St. Justin Martyr (100–165), for example,
explains that the offering of fine flour prefigured the Eucharist and considers
Baptism typologically in relation to circumcision (cf. *Dialogue with Trypho*
19 and 41–43). St. Theophilus of Antioch (died c. 183) regards the creation of living beings from water as a prefiguration of the gift of life through
Baptism (cf. *To Autolycus* II, 16). St. Irenaeus (130–202) presents the offering
of sacrifices and of the first fruits as prefigurations of the Eucharist (cf. *Against
Heresies,* IV, 18, 1–5). For St. Clement of Alexandria (150–215), the offering
of bread and wine by Melchizedek prefigures the offering of the Eucharist
(cf. *Stromata* IV, XXV). Tertullian (160–220) considers the hovering of the
Spirit of God over the waters at creation, the angel at the Pool of Bethesda,
the Flood, the Crossing of the Red Sea, and the Water from the Rock, all
to be types of Baptism (*On Baptism,* IV–IX). St. Hippolytus (c. 170–235)
sees in the rivers of Eden that make the earth fertile a prefiguration of the
waters of Baptism, which irrigate the soul and give it divine life (*Sermon on
Epiphany*). Origen (c. 185–254) considers the Crossing of the Red Sea and

---

2 The standard work on mystagogical catechesis in the fourth century is Enrico Mazza, *La Mist-
agogia: Le catechesi liturgiche della fine del quarto secolo e il loro metodo,* 2nd ed. (Roma: CVL, 1996).
The first edition of this work, which lacks the chapter on the mystagogy of St. Augustine, has been
translated into English as *Mystagogy: A Theology of Liturgy in the Patristic Age* (New York: Pueblo
Pub. Co, 1989).

the Crossing of the Jordan to be prefigurations of Baptism, and the Levites and priests of the Old Covenant to be prefigurations of deacons and priests of the New Covenant (cf. *Homily on Joshua* 4, 1). St. Cyprian of Carthage (200–258) sees a prefiguration of the Eucharist in the offering of bread and wine by Melchizedek, in the spiritual drink of Wisdom, and other moments in the Old Covenant (cf. *Epistle* 62). He also sees the Flood and the Crossing of the Red Sea as types of salvation through Baptism (*Epistle* 75). Aphrahat (c. 270–345) presents the second circumcision of the Israelites after crossing the Jordan River as a type of the "second circumcision" of Baptism (cf. *Demonstrations* 11–12). And the list could go on and on.[3]

If the earliest Church Fathers understood the sacraments typologically, it was not by chance—they were following the lead of the authors of the New Testament, and, in fact, of Jesus himself. The First Letter of Peter, for example, presents the salvation of Noah and his family in the ark through water as a prefiguration of Baptism: "God patiently waited in the days of Noah during the building of the ark, in which a few persons, eight in all, were saved through water. This prefigured baptism, which saves you now" (1 Peter 3:20–21 NABRE).[4] St. Paul, for his part, explains the Crossing of the Red Sea as a prefiguration of Baptism. The Israelites, he explains, were "baptized into Moses" when they crossed the Red Sea (1 Corinthians 10:2). Christians are baptized not into Moses but into the one Body of Christ (1 Corinthians 12:13; cf. Galatians 3:27; Romans 6:3).[5] As well, in the letter to the Colossians, St. Paul relates circumcision to Baptism in a way which many scholars consider typological. As circumcision incorporated its recipient into

---

3 An excellent study on the typological understanding of the Church Fathers regarding Baptism, Confirmation, and the Eucharist is *Jean Danielou, The Bible and the Liturgy*, Liturgical Studies (University of Notre Dame Press, 2002). For more on the understanding of typology in general in the Church Fathers, cf. Henri de Lubac, *Medieval Exegesis: The Four Senses of Scripture*, Ressourcement (Grand Rapids, MI – Edinburgh: Eerdmans; T&T Clark, 1998–2009), vols. 1–3, and especially chapter 8 of vol. 2, which deals specifically with typology.

4 Cf. Paul J. Achtemeier, *1 Peter*, Hermeneia (Minneapolis: Fortress Press, 1996), 266–268; and Karen H. Jobes, *1 Peter*, Baker Exegetical Commentary on the New Testament (Grand Rapids, MI: Baker Academic, 2005), 251–256.

5 On 1 Corinthians 10:2, cf. Roy E. Ciampa and Brian S. Rosner, *The First Letter to the Corinthians*, The Pillar New Testament Commentary (Grand Rapids, MI – Cambridge: William B. Eerdmans Publishing Company, 2010), 446–447; and Hans Conzelmann, *1 Corinthians*, Hermeneia (Minneapolis: Fortress Press, 1975), 165–166. On 1 Corinthians 12:13, cf. Joseph A. Fitzmyer, *First Corinthians*, The Anchor Yale Bible 32 (New Haven – London: Yale University Press, 2008), 477–478.

the People of God (cf. Genesis 17:10–14; 34:15; Exodus 12:43–49), Baptism makes its recipient a member of the new People of God, the Body of Christ (cf. Colossians 2:11–13 in light of Galatians 3:27–29 and 1 Corinthians 12:13).[6] Jesus himself spoke typologically of the "bread from heaven," which John's Gospel presents as Eucharistic. In John 6:31–50, Jesus explains that he is the true manna, the true bread from heaven that believers can share in through faith. The manna in the desert prefigured him. In verses 51–58, Jesus applies the same teaching to the Eucharist. He closes the Eucharistic part of his discourse by referring once again to the manna, the bread from heaven: "This is the bread which came down from heaven, not such as the fathers ate and died; he who eats this bread will live forever" (John 6:58). The manna in the desert prefigured Jesus, the Eucharistic bread of life.[7]

Similarly, in the Last Supper, many recent exegetes see in Christ's words a typological reference. Christ takes the cup, gives thanks, and says, "Drink of it, all of you; for this is my blood of the covenant, which is poured out for many for the forgiveness of sins" (Matthew 26:28). By speaking of the "blood of the covenant," Jesus is referring typologically to Exodus 24:8, in which Moses ratified the Sinai Covenant by sprinkling the "blood of the covenant" on the Israelites. As Moses ratified the Old Covenant, now Jesus, the new Moses, ratifies the New Covenant through the "blood of the covenant" offered up in the Last Supper and poured out on the cross.[8] Jesus, by celebrating the Last Supper as a Passover meal (cf. Matthew 26:17; Mark 14:12; Luke 22:7–8), may also be alluding to the blood of the Passover lamb, which saved the Israelites from the destroying angel. As the new and definitive Lamb of

---

6 Cf. N. T. Wright, *Colossians and Philemon*, Tyndale New Testament Commentaries 12 (Downers Grove, IL: InterVarsity Press, 1986), 109–113; and Thomas Kingsmill Abbott, *A Critical and Exegetical Commentary on the Epistles to the Ephesians and to the Colossians*, International Critical Commentary (Edinburgh: T. & T. Clark, 1897), 250–254.

7 Cf. Raymond E. Brown, *The Gospel According to John (I–XII)*, Anchor Yale Bible 29 (New Haven – London: Yale University Press, 2008), 284–294; and Ernst Haenchen, Robert Walter Funk, and Ulrich Busse, *John: A Commentary on the Gospel of John*, Hermeneia (Philadelphia: Fortress Press, 1984), 296. For an alternative interpretation of this passage, but with compatible conclusions, cf. also Francis J. Moloney, *The Gospel of John*, Sacra Pagina Series 4 (Collegeville, MN: The Liturgical Press, 1998), 223–224.

8 Cf. W. D. Davies and D. C. Allison Jr., *A Critical and Exegetical Commentary on the Gospel according to Saint Matthew*, International Critical Commentary (London – New York: T&T Clark International, 2004), 473; Ulrich Luz, *Matthew 21–28: A Commentary*, Hermeneia (Minneapolis, MN: Augsburg, 2005), 380; and D. A. Carson, "Matthew," in *Matthew, Mark, Luke*, The Expositor's Bible Commentary 8 (Grand Rapids, MI: Zondervan Publishing House, 1984), 537.

God, Jesus sees the Last Supper as the fulfillment of what was prefigured in the Passover of the Exodus. His death and Resurrection will be the new Exodus, and, like the old Exodus, will be commemorated in a meal in which the participants partake of the Lamb and are saved from death by its blood.[9]

Of course, the typological understanding of the Old Testament by the New Testament is by no means limited to Baptism and the Eucharist. Leonhard Goppelt famously argued in his doctoral dissertation from 1939 that typology was the principal way Jesus and the New Testament authors understood and interacted with the Old Testament. In the New Testament, Jesus is presented as the New Adam, the New Moses, the New David, the New Solomon, the New Jonas, and the true Son of Man. The Gospel of John presents Jesus as the true Passover Lamb of God and the fulfillment of the institutions of the Old Covenant. What each of these realities of the Old Testament pointed to, Jesus is in its fullness.[10]

Similarly, Jesus likely saw the Church as the fulfillment of the Old Covenant People of God. Most scholars argue, for example, that Jesus chose twelve apostles as a reference to the twelve tribes of Israel. The new community that he was founding would be the fullness of what God had prepared for in the twelve tribes of the Old Covenant.[11]

Typology was essential to Jesus's and the early Church's understanding of Christ, the Church, and the sacraments. Does this hold true for the current teachings of the Catholic Church? What is typology and what is its role according to the Catholic Church? There is no better place to ask that question than the Catechism of the Catholic Church.

---

9 On the allusion to the Lamb of the Passover meal, cf. R. T. France, *The Gospel of Matthew*, The New International Commentary on the New Testament (Grand Rapids, MI: Eerdmans, 2007), 993–995; and Davies and Allison, *A Critical and Exegetical Commentary on the Gospel according to Saint Matthew*, 474.

10 Cf. Leonhard Goppelt, *Typos: The Typological Interpretation of the Old Testament in the New* (Grand Rapids, MI: Eerdmans, 1982). Scholars since have refined and developed the seminal insights of Goppelt. For a recent example of how scholars see the New Testament's use of the Old Testament and the role of typology, cf. G. K. Beale and D. A. Carson, eds., *Commentary on the New Testament Use of the Old Testament* (Grand Rapids, MI – Nottingham: Baker Academic; Apollos, 2007), and its accompanying volume, G. K. Beale, *Handbook on the New Testament Use of the Old Testament: Exegesis and Interpretation* (Grand Rapids, MI: Baker Academic, 2012).

11 Cf. Joel Marcus, *Mark 1–8*, Anchor Yale Bible 27 (New Haven – London: Yale University Press, 2008), 266–267; and Adela Yarbro Collins, *Mark: A Commentary on the Gospel of Mark*, Hermeneia (Minneapolis, MN: Fortress Press, 2007), 215–217.

Typology in the Catechism of the Catholic Church

The Literal and the Spiritual Sense

The Catechism of the Catholic Church introduces typology in the "Senses of Scripture" (cf. CCC 115–119) and teaches that two basic senses of Scripture can be distinguished: the literal sense and the spiritual sense.

The *literal sense* is the sense conveyed by the words of Scripture. This is the sense that is studied by exegesis, and all other senses are based on the literal sense (CCC 116). To discover the meaning of the words of Scripture, it is necessary to seek out the "sacred authors' intention," taking into account "the conditions of their time and culture, the literary genres in use at that time, and the modes of feeling, speaking, and narrating then current" (CCC 110). Not to be confused with an overly literalistic interpretation of the Scriptures, the literal sense is the meaning of the words and expressions as they were meant to be understood by the author, taking into account the rules that govern different literary forms of writing, such as a historical narration, poetry, apocalyptic visions, the use of metaphoric or symbolic language, etc. For example, the Catechism notes that the account of creation in seven days is symbolic, intending not to communicate scientific truths about the Big Bang but theological truths about God alone as Creator of the world, the value of work, the importance of the Sabbath rest, and so on (CCC 337–349; cf. also 290–299). To understand the literal sense of Scripture it is essential to seek out what the original sacred author intended to assert in light of the ways of speaking and writing in use at that time.

But Sacred Scripture is not just a human text. As a divinely inspired text, the words of Scripture also have God as their author, and "all that the inspired authors or sacred writers affirm should be regarded as affirmed by the Holy Spirit' (*Dei Verbum* 11)" (CCC 107). To correctly interpret Scripture, then, it must be "'read and interpreted in light of the same Spirit by whom it was written' (*Dei Verbum* 12 § 4)" (CCC 111). The Church suggests three criteria to read and interpret the Scriptures in light of their divine authorship: (1) Be attentive to the content and unity of the whole Scripture, (2) read the Scriptures within the living Tradition of the whole Church, and (3) be attentive to the analogy of faith, that is, the coherence of the truths of faith amongst themselves (CCC 111–114; cf. *Dei Verbum*).[12] These three criteria provide the proper context to interpret Scripture and should be taken into account when trying to determine the literal sense of a passage.[13]

Most modern commentaries on the Bible are centered principally or even exclusively on the literal sense. But the literal sense is not the only valid sense of Scripture. The spiritual sense is also present: "Thanks to the unity of God's plan, not only the text of Scripture but also the realities and events about which it speaks can be signs" (CCC 117). The spiritual sense is itself subdivided into the allegorical, moral, and anagogical senses (CCC 115).[14] This distinction between the literal and spiritual meaning of Scripture is essential to understanding what typology is, and deserves some explanation.

The Catechism here distinguishes the meaning of *the text* from the meaning of *the realities and events about which it [the text] speaks*. The meaning of *the text* is the "literal sense." However, the Catechism here states that not only the text, but the realities and events themselves which are recounted in Scripture have meaning and are "signs." The meaning of *the realities and events* is the "spiritual sense" of Scripture. It is possible that realities and events themselves have meaning, the Catechism explains, "thanks to the unity of God's plan."

The real difference between the literal and spiritual senses of the Scriptures is the difference between the meaning of the text and of the realities signified by the text. Now, every book ever written has a literal sense, regardless of whether that literal meaning regards history, science, faith, etc. Only one

---

12 For more on the literal sense of Scripture, cf. Second Vatican Ecumenical Council, Dogmatic Constitution on Divine Revelation *Dei Verbum*, 11–12; Pius XII, Encyclical Letter *Divino afflante Spiritu* (30 September 1943), 23–24 and 34–41: AAS 35 (1943), 310 and 314–317; Benedict XVI, Post-Synodal Apostolic Exhortation *Verbum Domini*, 37–38: AAS 102 (2010), 716–718; Pontifical Biblical Commission, *The Interpretation of the Bible in the Church* (Vatican City: Libreria Editrice Vaticana, 1993), II, B, 1.

13 The Catechism defines the literal sense in paragraph 116, cross-referencing paragraphs 110–114, which includes the three criteria to read the Scripture in light of the Spirit by whom it was written. This would seem to imply that for the Catechism the study of the literal sense of Scripture is incomplete if divine inspiration is not taken into account.

14 While this book concentrates on typology, referred to in CCC 115 and 117 as the *allegorical sense*, a word can be said here about the moral and the anagogical sense. As with typology, the moral and anagogical sense considers the meaning of the realities themselves which are signified by the literal sense of Scripture. While typology considers their meaning with relation to the fulfillment of God's plan in Jesus Christ, the *moral sense* considers the realities described by Scripture in relation to our lives (often applied in homilies), and the *anagogical sense* considers their meaning with respect to eternal life (cf. CCC 117 and St. Thomas Aquinas, *Summa Theologiæ* I, q. 1, art. 10).

book in all of history, however, has a spiritual sense: the Bible, because only in the Bible do we find that the very realities and events signified by the words have themselves a deeper meaning, a meaning signified by God himself in his plan of salvation. Only God can write a love story with realities and events. He wrote that love story in his plan of salvation and told it in the Bible.

This distinction between the meaning of the text and the meaning of the realities and events is illustrated by an example from the Catechism "The crossing of the Red Sea is a sign or type of Christ's victory and also of Christian Baptism (Cf. 1 Cor. 10:2)" (CCC 117). The book of Exodus contains the crossing of the Red Sea. After the tenth plague, the death of the firstborn sons, Pharaoh finally gives the Israelites permission to leave Egypt (cf. Exodus 12:29–32). Moses leads them out and they flee into the wilderness, toward the Red Sea (cf. Exodus 13:17–22). Almost immediately, however, Pharaoh changes his mind, and leads his army out to pursue the Israelites (cf. Exodus 14:1–14). The Egyptians catch up to Moses and the Israelites at the Red Sea. The Israelites are terrified, fearing that the Egyptians will either kill or enslave them once again. But the Lord has other plans. God instructs Moses to stretch out his hand over the sea, and as Moses does so, the waters divide and the Israelites pass through the sea on dry ground. The Egyptians pursue them, but their chariots get stuck. As the last Israelite finishes the crossing, dawn breaks. Moses stretches out his hand once again and the waters return to their normal depth, destroying Pharaoh's army and saving the Israelites (cf. Exodus 14:21–31).

These events as recounted in the Scriptures are of great significance: they are often remembered within the Old Testament itself, and every Jewish family annually remembers and relives them through the celebration of the Passover. But the Catechism teaches us that the importance of the crossing of the Red Sea goes beyond that of the historical rescue of the Israelites from slavery. In God's plan, it was an event which also prefigured the even greater salvation that God would give the world through the death and Resurrection of Jesus Christ. In saving the Jewish people from slavery, God was pointing forward to what he would later do through the new Exodus that his Son, Jesus Christ, would bring about on the cross.

The Gospel of Luke makes this connection explicit. Eight days after revealing for the first time to his apostles that he must suffer, die, and be raised from the dead, Jesus took Peter, James, and John up a mountain with him to pray. There he was transfigured before them, revealing his divine glory. The three apostles see Moses and Elijah in glory speaking with the transfigured Jesus. What most interests us here, however, is *what* they were talking about. The topic of their conversation, the Evangelist informs us, was "his *exodus* that he was going to accomplish in Jerusalem" (Luke 9:31 NABRE, emphasis mine). Moses and Elijah, representing the law and the prophets, speak with Jesus about the exodus (in Greek, *exodos*) that his death and Resurrection would bring about in Jerusalem. The Exodus of the Old Covenant prepared and prefigured the Exodus of Jesus Christ. Not only Christ's victory was prefigured by the Exodus, however, but also Christian Baptism. As we have already seen, St. Paul alluded to this in 1 Corinthians 10:2. As the Israelites passed from slavery to freedom through water and were baptized into Moses, the Christian passes from the slavery of sin to the freedom of the Spirit through the waters of Baptism, being baptized into the Body of Christ, the Church. The Catechism explains: "We can acquire a more profound understanding of events by recognizing their significance in Christ" (CCC 117). The event of the Exodus, when understood in light of Christ, takes on a new and deeper meaning.

Note that the original inspired human author or authors of the Book of Exodus almost certainly had no idea that the Exodus from Egypt prefigured the future events of the "exodus" of Jesus Christ in his victory on the cross and in Baptism. What the inspired human author understood and signified were the events surrounding the Exodus of the Israelites from Egypt. This is the literal sense.

These events, however, were part of God's plan of salvation history. In God's plan, *these very events* signified a future fullness in Christ, in whom "God recapitulates all of his history of salvation on behalf of men" (CCC 430). Man writes and signifies with words. God signifies not only with words, but also with realities and events—the spiritual sense.

If the spiritual sense is the meaning *of the realities and events* of salvation history in God's plan, is it really a meaning *of Scripture*? The Catechism answers in the affirmative (cf. CCC 115–117). As Creator, properly speaking only God can signify through realities and events, and in the Scriptures that is precisely what he does. God speaks through both the words (the literal sense) and the realities which are signified by the words (the spiritual sense). Through the divine authorship of Scripture, the meaning of the realities signified by the words is fused and joined in a mysterious way to the meaning of the words, while retaining a distinct meaning. The spiritual sense is thus truly a sense of Scripture. In the literal sense, the human author and God signify with words; in the spiritual sense, God signifies with the very realities signified by the words. Thus, the spiritual sense is based on the literal sense and presupposes it as its indispensable foundation.[15]

The literal and the spiritual sense together are integral to the full understanding of Scripture: "The profound concordance of the four senses guarantees all its [Scripture's] richness to the living reading of Scripture in the Church" (CCC 115). By reading the Scriptures with both the literal and the spiritual senses, they reciprocally enlighten one another. The proper understanding of one complements and enriches the understanding of the other. Limiting ourselves to one or the other would be depriving ourselves of part of the banquet God has left us in his living Word.

God's Plan, the Unity of the Old and New Testaments, and Typology

The spiritual sense, the Catechism tells us, is present in Scripture thanks to the unity of God's plan (CCC 117). From creation, God has had a saving plan, a plan that culminated in Jesus Christ (cf. CCC 280). The Father's plan was to gradually form the "family of God," giving men a share in his own divine life (CCC 759). From Adam and Eve, to Abraham, to Moses and the people of Israel, God progressively enlarged his family. Finally, in Jesus Christ, he revealed "the plan of the mystery hidden for ages in God . . . that through the Church the manifold wisdom of God might now be made known" (Ephesians 3:9–10; cf. CCC 1066). In Jesus Christ, the family of God became a worldwide family, the Church. The Church Fathers called this plan the "economy of salvation." It is oftentimes also called the "history of salvation" or simply, "God's plan."

God's plan, played out in salvation history, demonstrates the unity of the Old and New Testaments. Because God has a plan that he realizes in history, the realities and events which Scripture speaks about can have a meaning in that plan above and beyond what the human authors of the texts of Scripture

---

15 For more on how the spiritual sense is truly a sense of Scripture, cf. Michael Waldstein, "Analogia Verbi: The Truth of Scripture in Rudolf Bultmann and Raymond Brown," *Letter & Spirit* 6 (2010): 93–140, especially p. 128–129; and the Pontifical Biblical Commission's document, *The Interpretation of the Bible in the Church*, II, B, 2.

had in mind. God can use realities and events to point forward to the salvation that Jesus Christ would bring in its fullness. This meaning of Scripture is the "typological sense" (called the "allegorical sense" in number 117 of the Catechism). The Catechism presents typology as *the* key that unlocks the unity of the Old and New Testaments. The Catechism dedicates three paragraphs to explaining how the Old and the New Testaments relate to each other, and all three paragraphs are centered on typology (cf. CCC 128–130; cf. also CCC 1093–1095).

Typology, the Catechism states, "discerns in God's works of the Old Covenant prefigurations of what he accomplished in the fullness of time in the person of his incarnate Son" (CCC 128). Reading the Scripture typologically means reading "the Old Testament in the light of Christ crucified and risen" (CCC 129). The Catechism further elaborates: "Typology indicates the dynamic movement toward the fulfillment of the divine plan" (CCC 130). According to the Catechism, if we want to understand how the Old and New Testaments of Scripture form a unity—the Bible—we must learn to read the Scriptures typologically.

The Fulfillment of God's Plan

As we have seen, the Catechism explains that the Old and New Testaments form a unity through typology (CCC 128–130). These same paragraphs from the Catechism also explain an essential aspect of typology—fulfillment. In Jesus Christ, God's plan came to its fulfillment. God's works of the Old Covenant prefigured what he accomplished in the "fullness of time" in Jesus Christ (CCC 128). As such, typology "indicates a dynamic movement toward the fulfillment of the divine plan," and the stages of salvation history that came before the fulfillment in Jesus Christ were "intermediate stages"[16] (CCC 130). The type always points forward to something greater that will come in a fullness given in Jesus Christ.[17] As such, it is not enough for two realities in Scripture to be similar or to follow a certain pattern for us to speak

---

16 The Catechism also reminds us that the Old Testament retains its own intrinsic value as Revelation (CCC 129), and the realities and events have their own value in God's plan (apart from their typological meaning) (CCC 130).

17 A sort of typology was present already within the Old Testament, in which, for example, Joshua was presented as a new Moses and the return from exile as a new Exodus. Cf. Michael A Fishbane, *Biblical Interpretation in Ancient Israel* (Clarendon, 1988), 350–379. Nevertheless, the aspect of fulfillment, essential to Christian typology, is missing.

about typology. Christian typology goes beyond the recognition of patterns in God's saving plan to include the fulfillment in Jesus Christ as an essential aspect, where the reality prefigured is far greater than the prefiguration.

Completing the Picture

Not only realities, events, and deeds prefigure the fullness which was revealed in Jesus Christ, but also "the deeds, words, and symbols of the first covenant" prefigure the newness of Christ (CCC 1094). Some examples of symbols that prefigure the fullness given in Christ are "circumcision, anointing and consecration of kings and priests, laying on of hands, sacrifices, and above all Passover. The Church sees in these signs a prefiguring of the sacraments of the New Covenant" (CCC 1150; cf. also CCC 1151–1152).

Finally, while types are principally found in the Old Covenant, the Catechism mentions some prefigurations found in the New Covenant as well. For example, the blood and water from the side of Christ are types[18] of Baptism and the Eucharist (CCC 1225). Similarly, the miracles of the multiplication of the loaves prefigure[19] the abundance of the bread of the Eucharist (cf. CCC 1335). In both these cases, a physical reality found in the New Testament prefigures a greater spiritual gift given in the sacraments.

Defining Typology

While the Catechism refers often to typology, it never actually gives a definition of typology.[20] In light of the summary we have seen of the most important numbers of the Catechism dealing with typology, however, the following definition can be inferred (cf. CCC 117, 128–130, 1093–1094, 1150–1152, 1225, and 1335):[21]

---

18 The Latin reads: "Sanguis et aqua quae de aperto Iesu crucifixi exiverunt latere, typi sunt Baptismi et Eucharistiae . . ." (CCC 1225).

19 The Latin reads: ". . .superabundantiam praefigurant unius huius panis Eucharistiae Eius." (CCC 1335).

20 Note that the glossary of terms included in some editions of the Catechism is not officially part of the Catechism and "does not participate in the approval of the text of the Catechism given in the Apostolic Constitution *Fidei despositum* of John Paul II" (Prefatory Note to the Glossary).

21 For a summary of recent scholarly debate about the definition of typology, cf. Beale, *Handbook on the New Testament Use of the Old Testament*, 13–25. The reluctance of the Catechism to define typology, together with the apparent tension between certain texts of the Catechism regarding what typology is (compare CCC 128 and 1225 for example), may reflect the fact that there is currently a debate among theologians regarding the definition of typology. This definition seeks to reflect the understanding of the Catechism regarding typology insofar as it can be inferred from the

> Typology is the discernment of realities, events, deeds, words, symbols, or signs in the Bible that foreshadow the fulfillment of God's plan in Jesus Christ.

The following are brief comments on each section of the above definition to sum up what we have seen so far.

• *The discernment.* Typology *discerns* in the works of God prefigurations of what is to come in the person of Jesus Christ. More than a scientific study that follows mathematical rules, discernment implies a work of faith, with openness to the Holy Spirit and the living Tradition of the Church (cf. CCC 128 and below: "The Goal of This Book").

• *Realities, events, deeds, words, symbols, or signs.* Typology goes beyond the literal sense of Scripture, discerning in faith what those very realities described by the Scriptures signify in God's divine plan.

• *In the Bible.* Given that it is precisely the literal sense of Scripture that describes the realities, events, etc. of God's saving plan, the spiritual meaning of Scripture must always be founded on the literal sense. Also, while types are principally present in the Old Covenant, they can occasionally be found in the New Covenant.

• *Foreshadows the fulfillment of God's plan in Jesus Christ.* Typology presupposes the unity of God's plan that finds its fullness in Jesus Christ. When the Bible is read in light of Jesus Christ, certain realities signified by the text are seen to point forward to a fullness made present in Christ.

RECENT RESERVATIONS

Typology has been the constant way of reading the Scriptures of the authors of the New Testament themselves, of the Church Fathers from the earliest times, and of the Catholic Church up to the present day. And yet, the use of typology has been in large part abandoned by many Bible scholars. While practically all scholars recognize that typology played an essential role in the way the New Testament authors understood the Old Testament, most modern commentators of the Bible have reservations about applying such a methodology to the study of the Scriptures, and limit themselves to the study of the literal sense of the text.

---

texts of the Catechism themselves.

One reason for the movement away from typology in Bible exegesis has been a desire to be objective and scientific. Studying the literal sense of the biblical text allows for the application of methods and tools used in the study of any literary work, historical period, etc. Examples of methods useful in discovering the literal sense of the text include the historical critical method, the narrative method, and linguistic studies. All of these tools and methods are useful for discovering the meaning of the biblical text. Methods like the historical critical method have much to say about the meaning of a text, but have little or nothing to say about the meaning of God's plan. At most they can say what a certain author thought about God's plan, and not what the realities themselves signify. But typology concerns the meaning of the realities signified by the text, a meaning present in God's plan. To return to our previous example, methods like the historical critical method or the narrative method can illuminate the way that the authors of the Pentateuch understood Israel's exodus from Egypt, but not the role that it has in God's plan preparing the way for Jesus Christ's definitive exodus through his death and Resurrection. For the study of typology, exegetical methods must be complemented with other, theological methods.

A second reason many scholars have reservations about typology is that some of the prefigurations proposed by the Church Fathers seem subjective, exaggerated, or strange. St. Cyprian of Carthage (200–258), for example, suggests that Noah's getting drunk on wine prefigures the Eucharist (cf. *Epistle* 62)! Similarly, the Church Fathers at times don't distinguish properly between allegory and typology. In typology, realities (even symbolic realities like the anointing of prophets, priests, and kings) prefigure future greater realities; in allegory, realities symbolize ideas or concepts. While typology is horizontal, allegory is vertical. Allegory of course has its valid uses, such as Plato's *Allegory of the Cave*, but as a method of interpretation, it is especially prone to subjectivity. Many modern authors are skeptical whether typology can be studied in a way that avoids such dangers.

The Goal of This Book

The idea for this book came about as a result of considering these difficulties. How can typology be studied in a way that is objective and that avoids the excesses sometimes present in the past? How can one discern prefigurations of the fulfillment of God's plan in Jesus Christ in a way that is not only useful for one's personal relationship with God, but that can also be confidently shared with others as trustworthy and authentic?

Different answers have been given to this question in recent times. Some have suggested limiting ourselves to those types that are explicitly present in the Scriptures. The constant use of typology in the New Testament, however, gives the impression that for the first Christians, reading the realities of the Scriptures in light of Christ was a way of understanding that permeated their faith, and should thus be considered more as an example of how Christians understand God's plan than as an exhaustive compendium.

Another answer has been to enumerate principles that can be applied to discern whether a type is valid or not. One important principle, for example, is that the spiritual sense of Scripture is based on the literal sense (cf. CCC 116). By applying this and other principles, one can discern with a certain level of confidence that a type is or is not part of God's plan, or at the very least, that it is or is not compatible with Revelation. This approach corresponds to the recommendation of Vatican II to read the Scriptures while being attentive to the analogy of faith, that is, the inner coherence of the truths of faith among themselves and within the whole plan of Revelation (cf. *Dei Verbum* 12 and CCC 90, 114). While this type of discernment is praiseworthy and important, this book takes a different approach.

The approach of this book is based on another recommendation of Vatican II: that of reading the Scriptures within "'the living Tradition of the whole Church' (*Dei Verbum* 12)" (CCC 113). The Catechism's explanation is worth quoting at length:

> According to a saying of the Fathers, Sacred Scripture is written principally in the Church's heart rather than in documents and records, for the Church carries in her Tradition the living memorial of God's Word, and it is the Holy Spirit who gives her the spiritual interpretation of the Scripture ("according to the spiritual meaning which the Spirit grants to the Church" (Origen, *Hom. in Lev.* 5, 5: PG 12, 454D; CCC 113).

The authentic understanding of God's Word, of his plan that culminates in Jesus Christ, is found in the living Tradition of the Church. One way to discern which prefigurations are a part of God's plan is to ask what the living Tradition of the Church understands as prefigurations of the fulfillment of God's plan in Jesus Christ.

The validity and importance of studying typology through the living Tradition of the Church is indicated by the Catechism itself, which states, "The Church, as early as apostolic times (cf. 1 Cor. 10:6, 11; Heb. 10:1; 1 Pet. 3:21), and then *constantly in her Tradition*, has illuminated the unity of the divine plan in the two Testaments *through typology*" (CCC 128, emphasis mine).

But what is Tradition? Vatican II teaches that "Tradition transmits *in its entirety* the Word of God which has been entrusted to the apostles by Christ the Lord and the Holy Spirit" (*Dei Verbum* 9, emphasis mine; cf. CCC 81). All that God has revealed in Jesus Christ is transmitted in the living Tradition of the Church. *Tradition* is thus very different from *traditions*. *Tradition* in the singular (and uppercase) refers to the handing on of the entirety of the Word of God; *traditions* in the plural (and lowercase) refer to human traditions which can change over time. Sacred Scripture and Sacred Tradition together constitute the sacred deposit of the faith (*depositum fidei*).[22]

Where is the living Tradition of the Church found? One of the most important witnesses to Sacred Tradition is the liturgy. The Catechism states, "Liturgy is a constitutive element of the holy and living Tradition (Cf. DV 8)" (CCC 1124). This theological truth was summed up by Prosper of Aquitaine, a contemporary of St. Augustine, in the phrase, *Legem credendi lex statuat supplicandi*. Literally: "The law of prayer establishes the law of faith." Theologians shortened it to *Lex orandi, lex credendi*, which means, "The law of prayer is the law of faith." The Catechism rephrases it aptly: "The Church believes as she prays" (cf. CCC 1124).

The liturgy of the Church has always been one of the essential ways the Church bears witness to the faith received and faithfully transmits the Word of God to future generations. As St. Irenaeus put it in the second century, "Our way of thinking is attuned to the Eucharist, and the Eucharist in turn confirms our way of thinking" (*Against Heresies*, IV, 18, 5, cited in CCC 1327).

---

22 Cf. CCC 84. For more on the meaning of Tradition and the difference between Tradition and traditions, cf. Yves Congar, *The Meaning of Tradition* (San Francisco: Ignatius Press, 2004).

As a constitutive element of Tradition, the Catechism invites the faithful to seek the spiritual understanding of the Scriptures in the liturgy. After explaining how the Old and New Covenants are united through typology (CCC 1094), the Catechism continues: "For this reason the Church, especially during Advent and Lent and above all at the Easter Vigil, re-reads and re-lives the great events of salvation history in the 'today' of her liturgy. But this also demands that catechesis help the faithful to open themselves to this spiritual understanding of the economy of salvation as the Church's liturgy reveals it and enables us to live it" (CCC 1095). It is in the liturgy where we understand and live out today the typological fulfillment of salvation history in Jesus Christ.[23]

Apart from the liturgy, the Magisterium of the Church provides an authentic interpretation to the Word of God as it is handed down in the living Tradition of the Church (cf. CCC 85–86). The Catechism of the Catholic Church is a faithful presentation of the living Tradition of the Church (cf. *Fidei Depositum* 3–4 and CCC 11), and has much to say about typology. It makes up part of the ordinary Magisterium of Pope John Paul II, and is a "sure and authentic reference text for teaching Catholic doctrine" (*Fidei Depositum* 4).

Finally, the Church Fathers are also "timely witnesses" to the living Tradition of the Church (CCC 688). As "timely" witnesses, the Church Fathers are always relevant for discerning the living Tradition of the Church. As with the writings of any theologian, however, discernment is necessary to leave aside those texts which are not authentic representations of the living Tradition of the Church.[24]

This book seeks to answer, in as objective fashion as possible, this question: What do the Scriptures and the living Tradition of the Church present as prefigurations of the fulfillment of God's plan in Jesus Christ? While ideally such a study could be done of all prefigurations, it would be almost never-ending. As such, this book limits its scope to the prefigurations of the

---

23 Cf. chapter 4 of Congar, *The Meaning of Tradition*; and Cipriano Vagaggini, *Theological Dimensions of the Liturgy* (Collegeville, MN: Liturgical Press, 1976). For a study on the relationship between the liturgy and the Word of God from a pastoral perspective, cf. Scott Hahn, *Letter and Spirit* (New York: Doubleday, 2005).

24 For a summary by the Pontifical Biblical Commission of the positive and negative aspects of the interpretation of the Scriptures found in the Church Fathers, cf. *The Interpretation of the Bible in the Church*, III, B, 2.

sacraments. It is my hope to eventually publish other volumes that will cover other prefigurations (of Christ, of the Church and Mary, and so forth).

It was also necessary to limit the scope of the texts covered, as regards the liturgy, the Magisterium of the Church, and the Church Fathers. In order to keep the study as objective as possible and limit it to authentic representations of the living Tradition of the Church, the writings of the Church Fathers are considered only when they are present in the Liturgy of the Hours. An ample selection of texts from the Church Fathers and other writers is included in the Office of Readings of the Liturgy of the Hours. Through their inclusion in the Liturgy of the Hours, the Church has made her own such texts as authentic expressions of the living Tradition handed down from the apostles.

Within the liturgy, it was also necessary to limit the scope of this work. The following texts have been included, covering the principal liturgical texts of the Roman Rite of the Catholic Church:

1. The Liturgy of the Hours[25]
2. The Rites of the Seven Sacraments:
    a. The Rite of Baptism[26]
    b. The Rite of Confirmation[27]
    c. The Roman Missal (i.e. the Eucharist)[28]
    d. The Rite of Penance[29]
    e. Pastoral Care of the Sick: Rites of Anointing and Viaticum[30]

---

25 Cf. *The Liturgy of the Hours: According to the Roman Rite* (New York: Catholic Book Publishing Corp., 1975). For the Latin edition, cf. *Liturgia Horarum: Iuxta Ritum Romanum*, 3rd ed. (Vatican City: Libreria Editrice Vaticana, 2000).

26 Cf. *The Rites of the Catholic Church: Study Edition* (Collegeville, MN: Liturgical Press, 1990), vol. I, 1–468. For the Latin edition, cf. *Ordo Initiationis Christianae Adultorum*, Editio typica (Vatican Polyglot Press, 1972) (currently out of print), and *Ordo Baptismi Parvulorum*, Editio typica altera (Vatican City: Libreria Editrice Vaticana, 2003).

27 Cf. *The Rites of the Catholic Church: Study Edition*, vol. I, 469–516. For the Latin edition, cf. *Ordo Initiationis Christianae Adultorum* (currently out of print).

28 Cf. *The Roman Missal*, Third Typical Edition (Washington, D.C.: United States Conference of Catholic Bishops, 2011). For the Latin edition, cf. *Missale Romanum*, Editio Typica Tertia (Vatican City: Libreria Editrice Vaticana, 2008).

29 Cf. *The Rites of the Catholic Church: Study Edition*, vol. I, 517–630. For the Latin edition, cf. *Ordo Paenitentiae* (Vatican City: Vatican Polyglot Press, 1974) (currently out of print).

30 Cf. *The Rites of the Catholic Church: Study Edition*, vol. I, 759–908. For the Latin edition, cf. *Ordo Unctionis Infirmorum Eorumque Pastoralis Curae* (Vatican City: Vatican Polyglot Press, 1972) (currently out of print).

f. Rites of Ordination of a Bishop, of Priests, and of Deacons[31]

g. The Rite of Marriage[32]

3. The Lectionary[33]

4. Suggested Readings for the Sacraments[34]

5. The Rite of Blessing of Oils and Consecrating the Chrism[35]

6. The Rite of Blessing of the Pontifical Insignia[36]

Apart from the Roman Rite, the other rites of the Church (such as the Byzantine or Coptic Rite), also contain a wealth of typological and symbolic references. It is my hope that others can complement this book with similar studies of other Rites, which are also authentic representations of the living Tradition of the universal Church.

Finally, as regards the Magisterium of the Church, I have restricted the scope of this work to the Catechism of the Catholic Church[37]. As an authentic representation of the living Tradition of the Church that seeks to summarize the faith which has been handed down, it is an excellent source to discover what prefigurations the Church proposes to the faithful as authentic understandings of God's plan brought to fulfillment in Jesus Christ. Ideally such a study could be extended to other documents of the Magisterium. Nevertheless, the Catechism contains a representative summary of the Church's understanding of typology.

---

31 Cf. *Rites of Ordination of a Bishop, of Priests, and of Deacons*, Second Typical Edition (ICEL, 2003). For the Latin edition, cf. *De Ordinatione Episcopi, Presbyterorum et Diaconorum*, Editio typica altera (Vatican City: Libreria Editrice Vaticana, 1990). Given that the current English tranlsation of the *Catechism of the Catholic Church* uses the now out of date numbering scheme of the First Typical Edition of the Rites of Ordination, references are always given to both numbering schemes when they are available, with the Second Typical Edition reference appearing first, followed by the First Typical Edition reference in parenthesis or brackets. The First Typical Edition can be consulted in *The Rites of the Catholic Church: Study Edition*, vol. II, 3–86.

32 Cf. *The Rites of the Catholic Church: Study Edition*, vol. I, 715–758. For the Latin edition, cf. *Ordo Celebrandi Matrimonium*, Editio typica altera (Vatican City: Libreria Editrice Vaticana, 2008).

33 Cf. *Lectionary for Mass*, Second Typical Edition (1998–2002). For the Latin edition, cf. *Ordo Lectionum Missae*, Editio typica altera (Vatican City: Libreria Editrice Vaticana, 1988).

34 As found in *The Rites of the Catholic Church: Study Edition*.

35 Cf. Ibid. vol. I, 699–714.

36 Cf. Ibid., vol. II, 88.

37 Cf. *Catechism of the Catholic Church*, 2nd Edition (Vatican City – Washington, DC: Libreria Editrice Vaticana; USCCB, 2000). For the Latin edition, cf. *Catechismus Catholicae Ecclesiae* (Vatican City: Libreria Editrice Vaticana, 1997).

While studying examples of typology, it soon became clear that it is oftentimes difficult if not at times impossible to distinguish between typology
and symbolism. As we have seen, in fact, oftentimes symbols themselves act
as types. In light of this difficulty, I decided to widen this study to include
not only types but also symbols of the sacraments, including those which are
clearly not typological.[38]

Insofar as I have been able, rather than impose a certain vision of typology or symbolism, my intention has been to let the Bible, the Catechism,
and the liturgy decide both what types and symbols should be included and
what meaning they have.[39] For example, the decision to include types from
the New Testament, as well as the decision to include symbolic realities as
types, was based entirely on the fact that texts in the Catechism and the liturgy explicitly refer to types in the New Testament and to symbols as types.

My hope is that by taking such an approach, this index may be useful for
inductive study of typology in the living Tradition of the Church. An inductive study begins with particular examples. By studying multiple particular
examples, an inductive study hopes to eventually infer and draw out conclusions. It is the opposite of a *deductive study*, which begins with general
principles or rules and seeks to logically apply those principles to particular cases. As an inductive study, this book hopes to present to the reader
all the available references to typology of the sacraments in the Bible, the
Catechism, and the liturgy, allowing the texts themselves to decide both what
types to include as well as what those types mean. Nevertheless, when texts
were unclear regarding whether some reality is a type or not, I have sought
to judge in light of the somewhat broad definition of typology given above.[40]

---

38 By symbol is meant an image or thing that stands for something else and that conveys more
than its literal meaning. Symbols normally carry multiple meanings simultaneously within a cultural
context. They partially unveil that which is signified, and convey mystery without dispelling it (making the use of symbols to speak about supernatural realities particularly apt). Metaphors and similes
function very much like symbols do and in this book will be considered symbols. The Bible is rich
in symbols, metaphors, etc. For a recent study, including a discussion of the meaning of symbol and
related terms, cf. Leland Ryken, Jim Wilhoit, and Tremper Longman, eds., *Dictionary of Biblical
Imagery* (Downers Grove, IL: InterVarsity Press, 1998).

39 A work of this scope necessarily involves some interpretation. While I have striven to be as
faithful as possible to the meaning and language of the texts, I am well aware that some texts could
be interpreted or classified differently.

40 Cf. *Defining Typology.*

It is my hope that this book will encourage a revival of mystagogical catechesis of the sacraments. I also hope that this book might be useful for scholars who wish to study typology and symbolism of the sacraments as understood by the Church, as well as exegetes and theologians who hope to study the Scriptures within the living Tradition of the Church. Finally, I pray that this book facilitates for many a refreshing encounter with the living Lord in his sacraments, where the salvation he won for us by his cross and Resurrection is made present today.

ABBREVIATIONS

Biblical Abbreviations

Gen.	Genesis	Isa.	Isaiah
Exod.	Exodus	Jer.	Jeremiah
Lev.	Leviticus	Lam.	Lamentations
Num.	Numbers	Bar.	Baruch
Deut.	Deuteronomy	Ezek.	Ezekiel
Josh.	Joshua	Dan.	Daniel
Judg.	Judges	Hos.	Hosea
Ruth	Ruth	Joel	Joel
1 Sam.	1 Samuel	Amos	Amos
2 Sam.	2 Samuel	Obad.	Obadiah
1 Kings	1 Kings	Jon.	Jonah
2 Kings	2 Kings	Mic.	Micah
1 Chron.	1 Chronicles	Nah.	Nahum
2 Chron.	2 Chronicles	Hab.	Habakkuk
Ezra	Ezra	Zeph.	Zephaniah
Neh.	Nehemiah	Hag.	Haggai
Tob.	Tobit	Zech.	Zechariah
Jth.	Judith	Mal.	Malachi
Esther	Esther	1 Macc.	1 Maccabees
Job	Job	2 Macc.	2 Maccabees
Ps.	Psalms	Matt.	Matthew
Prov.	Proverbs	Mark	Mark
Eccles.	Ecclesiastes	Luke	Luke
Song	Song of Solomon	John	John
Wisd.	Wisdom	Acts	Acts of the Apostles
Sir.	Sirach	Rom.	Romans

1 Cor.	1 Corinthians	Philem.	Philemon
2 Cor.	2 Corinthians	Heb.	Hebrews
Gal.	Galatians	James	James
Eph.	Ephesians	1 Pet.	1 Peter
Phil.	Philippians	2 Pet.	2 Peter
Col.	Colossians	1 John	1 John
1 Thess.	1 Thessalonians	2 John	2 John
2 Thess.	2 Thessalonians	3 John	3 John
1 Tim.	1 Timothy	Jude	Jude
2 Tim.	2 Timothy	Rev.	Revelation
Titus	Titus		

Liturgical Abbreviations

Sources

CCC	Catechism of the Catholic Church
LH	Liturgy of the Hours
OUI	Ordo Unctionis Infirmorum
PCS	Pastoral Care of the Sick
RB	Rite of Baptism for Several Children
RBOC	Rite of Blessing of Oils and Rite of Consecrating the Chrism
RC	Rite of Confirmation
RCIA	Rite of Christian Initiation of Adults
RM	Roman Missal
RMat	Rite of Matrimony
RO	Rites of Ordination of a Bishop, of Priests, and of Deacons (2nd Typical Edition)
ROB	Rite of Ordination of a Bishop
ROD	Rite of Ordination of a Deacon
ROP	Rite of Ordination of a Priest
RP	Rite of Penance

Liturgical Seasons

Adv	Advent
CT	Christmas time
BE	From January 2nd to Epiphany
AE	After Epiphany to Baptism
AAW	After Ash Wednesday
OT	Ordinary time
Lent	Lent
HW	Holy Week
ET	Easter time

Hours

OR	Office of Readings
MP	Morning Prayer (Laudes)
DP	Daytime Prayer
MM	Midmorning Prayer
MD	Midday Prayer
MA	Midafternoon Prayer
EP	Evening Prayer or Evening Prayer I
EP2	Evening Prayer II
NP	Night Prayer

Elements within the Hours

1R	First reading
2R	Second reading
Ant1	Antiphon of Psalm 1
Ant2	Antiphon of Psalm 2
Ant3	Antiphon of Psalm 3
Cant	Antiphon of the Canticle
CantZech	Antiphon of the Canticle of Zechariah
Magn	Antiphon of the Magnificat
Psalter	The Four-Week Psalter (of Ordinary Time if not specified otherwise)
Resp	Responsory
Title1	Christological Title of Psalm 1
Title2	Christological Title of Psalm 2
Title3	Christological Title of Psalm 3

2ND READINGS OF THE LITURGY OF THE HOURS

CCL	Corpus Christianorum, Series Latina
CSEL	Corpus Scriptorum Ecclesiasticorum Latinorum
Ch.	Chapter
PG	Patrologia Graeca
PL	Patrologia Latina
PLS	Patrologia Latina Supplement
SC	Sources Chrétiennes

MONTHS

Jan	January
Feb	February
Mar	March
Apr	April
Aug	August
Sep	September
Oct	October
Nov	November
Dec	December

DAYS OF THE WEEK

Mo	Monday
Tu	Tuesday
We	Wednesday
Th	Thursday
Fr	Friday
Sa	Saturday
Su	Sunday

BAPTISM

Definition: The first of the seven sacraments and the "door" which gives access to the other sacraments. Baptism is the first and chief sacrament of forgiveness of sins because it unites us with Christ, who died for our sins and rose for our justification. Baptism, Confirmation, and Eucharist constitute the "sacraments of initiation" by which a believer receives the remission of original and personal sin, begins a new life in Christ and the Holy Spirit, and is incorporated into the Church, the Body of Christ. The rite of Baptism consists in immersing the candidate in water, or pouring water on the head, while pronouncing the invocation of the Most Holy Trinity: the Father, the Son, and the Holy Spirit (Glossary of the Catechism of the Catholic Church).

TYPES

WATERS AT CREATION

OT Background: Gen. 1:2; Ps. 29:3; 33:6–7; 104:30
NT Background: Matt. 3:16; Mark 1:10; Luke 3:22; John 1:32; 2 Cor. 3:6
Catechism Background: 694; 1218
Type: CCC 1218; RM, Easter Vigil, Blessing of Baptismal Water, 46; LH, OT.15.Mo, 2R: St. Ambrose, On the Mysteries, 8–11: SC 25 bis, 158–160
Related: BAPTISM: *Types*: Dove; Crossing of the Red Sea; Crossing of the Jordan River; *Symbols*: Dove; Fountain of Water; Immersion; Second Birth

• As the Spirit of God hovering over the waters of the first creation (*cf.* Gen. 1:2) made them the source of life and fruitfulness and gave them even then the power to sanctify, so the Holy Spirit hovering over the waters of

Baptism makes them the source of the new creation (*cf.* CCC 1218; 1224; RM, Easter Vigil, Blessing of Baptismal Water, 46).

- As the Spirit of God hovered over the waters and was active in the first creation, so he hovers over the waters and is active in Baptism (LH, OT.15.Mo, 2R: St. Ambrose, On the Mysteries, 8–11: SC 25 bis, 158–160).
- The new creation, the justification conferred through faith and Baptism (CCC 1987), is even greater than the first creation (RM, Easter Vigil, Prayer after the 1st reading, 24; RM, Easter Vigil, Blessing of Water, 54; CCC 1994; 349; 420).
- The same Spirit which hovered over the waters of creation also hovered over Christ at his baptism (Matt. 3:16; Mark 1:10; Luke 3:22; John 1:32), as a prelude to the new creation (CCC 1224; *cf. also* LH, Baptism of the Lord, 2R: St. Gregory of Nazianzus, Oratio 39 in Sancta Lumina, 14–16.20: PG 36, 350–351.354.358–359).

Rivers of Eden

OT Background: Gen. 2:10–15; Ps. 1:3; Ezek. 47; Amos 5:24
NT Background: John 7:38–39; Rev. 22:1
Type: LH, CT.AE.Tu, 2R: St. Hippolytus, Sermon on the Epiphany, 2.6–8.10: PG 10, 854.858–859.862
Related: Baptism: *Types:* Fruit of the Tree of Life; *Symbols*: Fountain of Water

- As the rivers of Eden irrigated Paradise, making the earth fertile, so the waters of Baptism irrigate the soul, giving it divine life (LH, CT.AE.Tu, 2R: St. Hippolytus, Sermon on the Epiphany, 2.6–8.10: PG 10, 854.858–859.862).

Fruit of the Tree of Life[1]

OT Background: Gen. 2:9; 3:22–24; Prov. 3:18; 11:30; 13:12; 15:4; Isa. 65:22 (LXX); Ezek. 47:12
NT Background: Rom. 5:12–21; Rev. 2:7; 22:2, 14, 19
Catechism: 374–379; 390; 396; 1008; **1129**; **1134**; 1147; **1279**; **2074**; 2688; 2821; 2847

---

1 The topic of the fruit of the tree of life as prefiguring the cross, Jesus Christ, or the Scriptures is common. Here are presented only those texts that explicitly or implicitly refer to Baptism.

Type: LH, Lent.AAW[=2, 4].Fr, MP, 4th intercession; LH, Lent. HW.Su[=Mo, Tu, We, Th], MP, 4th intercession; LH, ET.2.Th, MP, 4th intercession

Related: BAPTISM: *Types:* Rivers of Eden; *Symbols:* Second Birth; EUCHARIST: *Types:* Fruit of the Tree of Life; Wisdom's Banquet; *Symbols:* Banquet

- The fruit of the sacraments is a share in the divine life in Jesus Christb (CCC 1129; 1134).
- The fruit of Baptism includes birth into new life in Christ (CCC 1279; *cf. also* CCC 2074, which cites John 15:5).
- Those reborn in Baptism may enjoy the abundance of fruits from the tree of life (LH, Lent.AAW[=2, 4].Fr, MP, 4th intercession; LH, Lent. HW.Su[=Mo, Tu, We, Th], MP, 4th intercession; *cf. also* LH, Triumph of the Cross [Sep 14], 2R: St. Andrew of Crete, Oratio 10 in Exaltatione sanctae crucis: PG 97, 1018–1019.1022–1023).
- The flaming sword barred access to the tree of life. The blood of Christ quenched those flames, and those reborn in Baptism now have the way open for them to return to their native land, paradise, from which they had been exiled (LH, Lent.4.Th, 2R: St. Leo the Great, Sermo 15, De passione Domini, 3–4: PL 54, 366–367).

Liturgy of the Hours

No one, however weak, is denied a share in the victory of the cross. No one is beyond the help of the prayer of Christ. His prayer brought benefit to the multitude that raged against him. How much more does it bring to those who turn to him in repentance?

Ignorance has been destroyed, obstinacy has been overcome. The sacred blood of Christ has quenched the flaming sword that barred access to the tree of life. The age-old night of sin has given place to the true light.

The Christian people are invited to share the riches of paradise. All who have been reborn have the way open before them to return to their native land, from which they had been exiled. Unless indeed they close off for themselves the path that could be opened before the faith of a thief.

The business of this life should not preoccupy us with its anxiety and pride, so that we no longer strive with all the love of our heart to be like our Redeemer, and to follow his example. Everything that he did or suffered was for our salvation: he wanted his body to share the goodness of its head.

LH, Lent.4Th, 2R: St. Leo the Great,
Sermo 15, De passione Domini, 3–4: PL 54, 366–367

FLOOD

OT Background: Gen. 6:5–9:17; Job 22:11; 27:20; Ps. 18:16; 29:10; 42:7; 69:1–2, 14; 88:16–18; 89:8–9; 93:3; 124:2–5; Wisd. 10:4; Sir. 44:17–18; Isa. 43:2; 54:9; Ezek. 14:12–20; Dan. 9:26; Jon. 2:3; Nah. 1:8; 2:6

NT Background: Matt. 24:37–41; Luke 6:46–49; 17:26–27; Heb. 11:7; 1 Pet. 3:20–21; 2 Pet. 2:4–10; Rev. 12:15

Catechism Background: 701; 1094; 1219–1220

Type: 1 Pet. 3:20–21; CCC 701; 1094; 1219–1220; RM, Easter Vigil, Blessing of the baptismal water, 46; LH, OT.15.Mo, 2R: St. Ambrose, On the Mysteries, 8–11: SC 25 bis, 158–160

Related: BAPTISM: *Types:* Dove; *Symbols:* Dove; Immersion

• As Noah and his family were saved through water (Gen. 7:1–4), so through Baptism the Christian is saved (1 Pet. 3:20–21; LH, Lent.2.Su, MP, 3rd intercession; LH, Lent.4.Su, MP, 3rd intercession).

The Word of God

For Christ also died for sins once for all, the righteous for the unrighteous, that he might bring us to God, being put to death in the flesh but made alive in the spirit; in which he went and preached to the spirits in prison, who formerly did not obey, when God's patience waited in the days of Noah, during the building of the ark, in which a few, that is, eight persons, were saved through water. Baptism, which corresponds to this, now saves you, not as a removal of dirt from the body but as an appeal to God for a clear conscience, through the resurrection of Jesus Christ, who has gone into heaven and is at the right hand of God, with angels, authorities, and powers subject to him.

1 Pet. 3:18–22

- The waters of Baptism are a new and greater flood than the flood in the times of Noah. While the flood in the times of Noah destroyed the human race, the flood of the waters of Baptism recall the dead sinner to life (LH, CT.AE.We, 2R: St. Proclus of Constantinople, Sermo 7 in sancta Theophania, 1–3: PG 65, 758–759).
- As the flood wiped out sin from the earth (Gen. 6:5–7, 11–13), so Baptism washes sin from the soul of the baptized (1 Pet. 3:21; LH, OT.15.Mo, 2R: St. Ambrose, On the Mysteries, 8–11: SC 25 bis, 158–160; *cf. also* BAPTISM: *Symbols:* Washing).
- As Noah's family passed through the waters of death to a new life, so in the waters of Baptism the Christian is buried with Christ, dying to sin, and rises with him to new life (CCC 1219–1220; *cf.* BAPTISM: *Symbols:* Immersion).
- In the flood the same water both destroyed vice and restored virtue; so in Baptism the same water both destroys sin and gives divine life (RM, Easter Vigil, Blessing of Baptismal Water, 46, quoted in CCC 1219).
- Baptism brings an end to the flood (*cf.* BAPTISM: *Types:* Dove).

DOVE

OT Background: Gen. 1:2; 8:8–12
NT Background: Matt. 3:16; 10:16; Mark 1:10; Luke 3:22; John 1:32
Catechism Background: 535; 701
Type: LH, Baptism of the Lord, 2R: St. Gregory of Nazianzus, Oratio 39 in Sancta Lumina, 14–16.20: PG 36, 350–351.354.358–359; LH, OT.15.Mo, 2R: St. Ambrose, On the Mysteries, 8–11: SC 25 bis, 158–160; LH, OT.15.We, 2R: St. Ambrose, On the Mysteries, 19–21.24.26–38: SC 25 bis, 164–170; LH, CT.AE.Mo, 2R: St. Peter Chrysologus, Sermo 160: PL 52, 620–622; LH, ET.4.Mo, 2R, Resp
Related: BAPTISM: *Types:* Flood; *Symbols:* Dove

Note: The dove is presented as both a type and a symbol in texts related to Baptism. Cf. BAPTISM: Symbols: Dove for texts which speak of the dove as a symbol.

- The dove which announced the end of the flood (Gen. 8:11) prefigured the true dove, the Holy Spirit, which came down upon Christ at his baptism and announced that the world's shipwreck was at an end forever (LH, CT.AE.Mo, 2R: St. Peter Chrysologus, Sermo 160: PL 52, 620–622; similar is LH, Baptism of the Lord, 2R: St. Gregory of Nazianzus, Oratio 39 in Sancta Lumina, 14–16.20: PG 36, 350–351.354.358–359; CCC 701 seems to imply this as well; cf. also Gen. 1:2).
- The dove prefigures the mystery of Baptism in multiple ways (LH, OT.15. Mo, 2R: St. Ambrose, On the Mysteries, 8–11: SC 25 bis, 158–160 and LH, OT.15.We, 2R: St. Ambrose, On the Mysteries, 19–21.24.26–38: SC 25 bis, 164–170):
  - As the dove announced the end of the flood, so it was a dove that descended on Christ in Baptism, and that descends on the baptized with the gift of peace.
  - As the dove brought back a wooden olive branch, so the gift of peace came through the wood of the cross.
  - The Holy Spirit's descent on Christ in the form of a dove reminds us of the dove from the flood and makes clear that the flood was a type of Baptism.
- As the dove offered a sign of peace at the end of the flood, so the Holy Spirit descends upon the baptized to give the gift of peace (LH, ET.4.Mo, 2R, Resp).
- The dove in the days of the flood with the olive branch in its mouth prefigured the fragrance of the good odor of Christ (LH, CT.AE.We, 2R: St. Proclus of Constantinople, Sermo 7 in sancta Theophania, 1–3: PG 65, 758–759).

CIRCUMCISION

Definition: The rite prescribed in Judaism and other cultures which involves cutting off the foreskin of a male. Circumcision was a sign of the covenant between God and his people Israel and prefigured the rite of Christian initiation in Baptism. Jesus was circumcised eight days after his birth in accord with Jewish law (Glossary of the Catechism of the Catholic Church).

OT Background: Gen. 17:9–14, 23–27; 34:15, 22; Exod. 4:26; 12:43–49; Lev. 12:3; Deut. 10:16; 30:6; Jer. 4:4; 9:25–26

NT Background: Luke 1:59; 2:21; John 7:22–23; Acts 7:8; 15:5–29; Rom. 2:25–29; 4:11–12; Gal. 5:3; Phil. 3:3; Col. 2:11–13; 3:11

Catechism Background: 527; 1150

Type: Col. 2:11–13; CCC 527; 1150; LH, Lent.1.We, 2R: Aphrahat, Dem. 11, On Circumcision, 11–12: PS 1, 498–503; LH, ET.2.Su, 2R: St. Augustine, Sermo 8 in octava Paschae 1.4: PL 46, 838.841

Related: BAPTISM: *Types:* Crossing of the Jordan River; CONFIRMATION: *Symbols:* Seal

• As circumcision incorporated its recipient into the People of God (*cf.* Gen. 17:10–14; 34:15; Exod. 12:43–49), Baptism makes its recipient a member of the new People of God, the Body of Christ, the Church (CCC 527 and Col. 2:11–13 in light of Gal. 3:27–29, 1 Cor. 12:13, CCC 1267, and 1271).

Catechism of the Catholic Church

Jesus' *circumcision*, on the eighth day after his birth (Cf. Luke 2:21), is the sign of his incorporation into Abraham's descendants, into the people of the covenant. It is the sign of his submission to the Law (Cf. Gal. 4:4) and his deputation to Israel's worship, in which he will participate throughout his life. This sign prefigures that "circumcision of Christ" which is Baptism (Cf. Col. 2:11–13).

CCC 527

• As circumcision was the sign of the Old Covenant, the "circumcision of Christ" brought about in Baptism is the sign of the New Covenant (Col. 2:11–13; CCC 527; *cf. also* CCC 1150).
• The circumcision of the Israelites upon crossing the Jordan (Josh. 5:1–9) is a type of Baptism called a "second circumcision" (LH, Lent.1.We, 2R: Aphrahat, Dem. 11, On Circumcision, 11–12: PS 1, 498–503):

- As Joshua circumcised the people of Israel upon crossing the Jordan (Josh. 5:1–9), Jesus circumcises the heart of believers beside the true Jordan, the waters of Baptism.
- While Joshua used a knife of stone, Jesus circumcises the heart of baptized believers with the sword of his word (*cf.* Heb. 4:12).
- *Cf. also* BAPTISM: *Types:* Crossing of the Jordan River.
- Baptism as a sign of faith was prefigured by circumcision (LH, ET.2.Su, 2R: St. Augustine, Sermo 8 in octava Paschae 1.4: PL 46, 838.841).

CROSSING OF THE RED SEA

OT Background:

Crossing of the Red Sea: Exod. 14:15–15:21; Deut. 11:4; Josh. 2:10; 4:23; 24:6–7; Jth. 5:13; Ps. 33:7; 78:53; 106:9, 22; 114:3–5; 136:13–15; Wisd. 10:18–19; 19:7–8; Isa. 51:10; 63:11; 1 Macc. 4:9

Egypt: Lev. 19:34; Deut. 5:12–15; 15:12–15; 16:9–12; 24:17–22; 2 Kings 18:19–25; Isa. 30:1–3; 30:7; 31:1–7; 36:4–10; Jer. 42–43; Ezek. 23; 29:3–5; Hos. 7:11–12

Pharaoh: Exod. 5:2; 9:16–17; 1 Sam. 6:6; 2 Kings 18:19–25; Ps. 136:15; Isa. 36:4–10; Ezek. 29:3; 31:18

NT Background:

Crossing of the Red Sea: Acts 7:36; 1 Cor. 10:1–4; Heb. 11:29

Egypt: Heb. 11:23–29; Rev. 11:8

Pharaoh: Rom. 9:17; Heb. 11:24

Other: Luke 9:31; Rom. 6:4–6, 16–23

Catechism Background: 117; 130; 431; **1094**; 1220–**1221**

Type: 1 Cor. 10:1–4; CCC 117; 1094; 1221; RM, Easter Vigil, 1st and 2nd Prayer after the 3rd reading, 26; RM, Easter Vigil, Blessing of the baptismal water, 46; LH, OT.10.We, 2R: Origen, Homily on Joshua, 4, 1: PG 12, 842–843; LH, OT.13.Th, 2R: St. Jerome, Sermon on Ps. 41 addressed to newly baptized: CCL 78, 542–544; LH, OT.15.Tu, 2R: St. Ambrose, On the Mysteries, 12–16.19: SC 25 bis, 162–164; LH, Lent.2.Mo, 2R: St. John Chrysostom, Cat. 3, 24–27: SC 50, 165–167; LH, ET.2.Th, 2R: St. Gaudentius of Brescia, Tract. 2: CSEL

68, 30–32; LH, ET.3.Mo, 2R: St. Bede the Venerable, Commentary on 1 Pet., Ch. 2: PL 93, 50–51

Related: BAPTISM: *Types:* Pillar of Cloud and Fire; Crossing of the Jordan

• The Israelites were "baptized into Moses" when they crossed the Red Sea (1 Cor. 10:2), and this took place as an "example" (*typos* in Greek) for us. Christians are baptized not into Moses, but into the one Body of Christ (1 Cor. 12:13; *cf.* Gal. 3:27; Rom. 6:3).

• Baptism frees from the "slavery" of sin (Rom. 6:4–6, 16–23; RB, 49, B).

• As the People of God passed through the waters of death to a new life, so in the waters of Baptism the Christian is buried with Christ, dying to sin, and rises with him to new life (*cf.* BAPTISM: *Symbols:* Immersion; Second Birth).

• As God freed his people from physical slavery in Egypt through the crossing of the Red Sea, he frees the Christian from the slavery of sin through the waters of Baptism (CCC 1221; RM, Easter Vigil, Blessing of the baptismal water, 46; LH, OT.15.Tu, 2R: St. Ambrose, On the Mysteries, 12–16.19: SC 25 bis, 162–164; LH, Lent.2.Mo, 2R: St. John Chrysostom, Cat. 3, 24–27: SC 50, 165–167; LH, ET.1.Su, 1R, Prayer; LH, ET.3.Mo, 2R: St. Bede the Venerable, Commentary on 1 Peter, Ch. 2: PL 93, 50–51).

The Eucharistic Celebration

O God, who caused the children of Abraham to pass dry-shod through the Red Sea, so that the chosen people, set free from slavery to Pharaoh, would prefigure the people of the baptized … look now, we pray, upon the face of your Church and graciously unseal for her the fountain of Baptism. May this water receive by the Holy Spirit the grace of your Only Begotten Son, so that human nature, created in your image and washed clean through the Sacrament of Baptism from all the squalor of the life of old, may be found worthy to rise to the life of newborn children through water and the Holy Spirit.

RM, Easter Vigil, Blessing of Baptismal Water, 46

• The Red Sea prefigures the sacred font of Baptism, and "the nation delivered from slavery foreshadows the Christian people" who, reborn in Baptism, obtain "the privilege of Israel" (RM, Easter Vigil, 2nd Prayer after the 3rd reading, 26).

- As the Israelites were set free from slavery to Pharaoh, so the baptized are set free from slavery to sin (RM, Easter Vigil, Blessing of the Baptismal Water, 46).

- As Pharaoh and his army were defeated in the waters of the Red Sea, so the devil is defeated in the waters of Baptism (LH, OT.13.Th, 2R: St. Jerome, Sermon on Ps. 41 addressed to newly baptized: CCL 78, 542–544; LH, Lent.2.Mo, 2R: St. John Chrysostom, Cat. 3, 24–27: SC 50, 165–167; *cf. also* RM, Easter Vigil, 1st Prayer after the 3rd reading, 26; LH, Lent. HW.Th, 2R: St. Melito of Sardis, Easter homily, 65–71: SC 123, 95–101).

- The Egyptians symbolize the sins which oppressed us. As they were destroyed in the Red Sea, so our sins were destroyed in Baptism (LH, ET.3.Mo, 2R: St. Bede the Venerable, Commentary on 1 Pet., Ch. 2: PL 93, 50–51; LH, Lent.2.Mo, 2R: St. John Chrysostom, Cat. 3, 24–27: SC 50, 165–167; *cf. also* RM, Easter Vigil, Easter Proclamation, 19; LH, Lent.HW.Th, 2R: St. Melito of Sardis, Easter homily, 65–71: SC 123, 95–101).

- While God freed one people bringing them through the waters of the Red Sea, now through the waters of Baptism he brings salvation to all nations (RM, Easter Vigil, 1st Prayer after the 3rd reading, 26).

- Renouncing the world, the baptized leave Egypt (LH, Psalter.1.Su, EP2, Title2).

- As the People of God abandoned Egypt and its gods, so the baptized abandon idolatry (LH, OT.10.We, 2R: Origen, Homily on Joshua, 4, 1: PG 12, 842–843).

- As those freed by Moses sang a song of triumph to the Lord after they had crossed the Red Sea and Pharaoh's army had been destroyed, so the baptized should give fitting thanks to God that their sins have been forgiven and they have received the gifts of heaven (LH, ET.3.Mo, 2R: St. Bede the Venerable, Commentary on 1 Pet., Ch. 2: PL 93, 50–51).

- Those who (through Baptism) have escaped the power of Egypt and Pharaoh, who is the devil, can partake of the table of the Lord (LH, ET.2.Th, 2R: St. Gaudentius of Brescia, Tract. 2: CSEL 68, 30–32).

PILLAR OF CLOUD AND FIRE

OT Background:

Preceding: Exod. 13:21–22; 14:19–25; 40:36–37; Num. 9:17; 10:34; 14:14; Neh. 9:12; Ps. 78:14; Wisd. 18:3

Overshadowing / Presence: Exod. 16:10; 19:9, 16; 20:21; 24:15–18; 33:9–10; 34:5; 40:34–38; Lev. 16:2, 13; Num. 9:15; 11:25; 12:5–6; 16:42; Deut. 4:11; 5:22; 31:15–16; 2 Sam. 22:12; 1 Kings 8:10–12; 2 Chron. 5:13–6:1; Ps. 18:11; 97:2; 99:7; 104:3; 105:39; Wisd. 19:7; Sir. 24:4; Isa. 4:5; 19:1; Lam. 2:1; 3:44; Ezek. 1:4; 10:3–4; Dan. 7:13; 2 Macc. 2:8

NT Background:

Preceding: 1 Cor. 10:1–2

Overshadowing / Presence: Matt. 17:5; 24:30; 26:64; Mark 9:7; 13:26; 14:62; Luke 1:35; 9:34–35; 21:27; Acts 1:9; 1 Thess. 4:17; Rev. 1:7

Catechism Background: 554; 659; **697**; 707; **1094**; 2058

Type: 1 Cor. 10:1–2; CCC 1094; RM, Easter Vigil, Easter Proclamation, 19; LH, OT.15.Tu, 2R: St. Ambrose, On the Mysteries, 12–16.19: SC 25 bis, 162–164; LH, CT.AE.Fr, 2R: St. Maximus of Turin, Sermo 100, De sancta Epiphania 1, 3: CCL 23, 398–400, in reference to 1 Cor. 10:1–2; LH, ET.3.Mo, 2R: St. Bede the Venerable, Commentary on 1 Pet., Ch. 2: PL 93, 50–51

Related: BAPTISM: *Types:* Crossing of the Red Sea; *Symbols:* Illumination / Light / Candle; Immersion

• As the Israelites were baptized into Moses in the cloud and in the sea, the Christian is baptized into Christ in the Holy Spirit and in water (1 Cor. 10:1–2; *cf. also* John 3:5).

• The cloud / pillar of fire prefigured salvation by Baptism (CCC 1094; 1 Cor. 10:1–2).

• The pillar of fire prefigured Baptism in multiple ways (LH, CT.AE.Fr, 2R: St. Maximus of Turin, Sermo 100, De sancta Epiphania 1, 3: CCL 23, 398–400 in reference to 1 Cor. 10:1–2):

  ▪ As the pillar of fire preceded the Israelites through the sea, so Christ in the pillar of his body goes through the waters of Baptism before the Christian people, showing them the way.

- As the pillar of fire provided light to those who followed it, so now it provides light in the hearts of believers.
- As the pillar of fire made firm the pathway through the waters, so now in the waters of Baptism it strengthens the footsteps of faith.

• As the cloud overshadowed the People of God when they crossed the Red Sea, and as the Holy Spirit overshadowed Mary at the Annunciation (cf. Luke 1:35), so does the cloud of the Holy Spirit overshadow the neophyte in Baptism (LH, OT.15.Tu, 2R: St. Ambrose, On the Mysteries, 12–16.19: SC 25 bis, 162–164).

• In the Easter Vigil celebration, the Exsultet (or "Easter Proclamation") compares at length the Easter Candle (which symbolizes the light of Christ) with the pillar of fire. While the typology refers primarily to the Resurrection of Christ, in the context of the Easter Vigil as a whole and the use of similar types and symbols in the same celebration to refer to Baptism, the Easter Candle may be understood to refer secondarily to salvation by Baptism as well[2] (the following references are to RM, Easter Vigil, Easter Proclamation, 19):

- The Easter Candle itself calls to mind the pillar of fire. The Easter Candle enters down the main aisle of the Church, with the Church in darkness, as the pillar of fire led the Israelites through the Red Sea in darkness (RM, Easter Vigil, 15–17). The Easter Candle is referred to both as "the light of Christ" (RM, Easter Vigil, 14–15) as well as a "pillar, which glowing fire. . . ."

---

2 For example:

The crossing of the Red Sea is said to be a type of both the Resurrection (RM, Easter Vigil, Easter Proclamation, 19) and of Baptism (RM, Easter Vigil, 46), using almost identical language.

• The Resurrection of Christ is said to "wash" away sin (RM, Easter Vigil, Easter Proclamation, 19), an image usually used for Baptism.

• In the entrance procession, the Easter Candle leading the way is said to symbolize the pillar of fire as a type of the light of Christ (RM, Easter Vigil, Easter Proclamation, 19). Before the rite of Baptism within the Easter Vigil, another procession takes place, also led by the Easter Candle (RM, Easter Vigil, 39), to the font of Baptism, possibly signifying that the neophytes are being led there by the "pillar of fire," where they will be saved through water.

More examples could be given, but the message seems to be that the redemption won by Christ's death and Resurrection is given to the catechumen in Baptism, where the baptized participate in Christ's death and Resurrection (cf. RM, Easter Vigil, last part of 46; Rom. 6:3–5; Col. 2:12; cf. also CCC 117.1 where the crossing of the Red Sea is said to be a type of both Christ's victory and of Baptism; BAPTISM: *Types:* Crossing of the Red Sea; *Symbols:* Immersion).

- "This is the night" (referring both to Passover night and to the night of the Resurrection of Christ) "that with a pillar of fire banished the darkness of sin."
- "This is the night" (referring both to Passover night and to the night of the Resurrection of Christ) "of which it is written: the night shall be as bright as day, dazzling is the night for me, and full of gladness" (*cf.* Ps. 139:12).
- As the light of the Easter Candle is shared among believers without diminishing, so the light of Christ is shared without diminishing in brightness.

The Eucharistic Celebration

These then are the feasts of Passover, in which is slain the Lamb, the one true Lamb, whose Blood anoints the doorposts of believers.

This is the night, when once you led our forebears, Israel's children, from slavery in Egypt and made them pass dry-shod through the Red Sea. This is the night that with a pillar of fire banished the darkness of sin. This is the night that even now, throughout the world, sets Christian believers apart from worldly vices and from the gloom of sin, leading them to grace and joining them to his holy ones. . . .

O love, O charity beyond all telling, to ransom a slave you gave away your Son! O truly necessary sin of Adam, destroyed completely by the Death of Christ! O happy fault that earned so great, so glorious a Redeemer!

O truly blessed night, worthy alone to know the time and hour when Christ rose from the underworld!

RM, Easter Vigil, Easter Proclamation, 19

- As the pillar of cloud and fire led the way for the Israelites, so the light of the grace of Christ leads the baptized on their way to the heavenly homeland, protecting them from darkness (LH, ET.3.Mo, 2R: St. Bede the Venerable, Commentary on 1 Pet., Ch. 2: PL 93, 50–51).

• The Liturgy of the Hours correlates 1 Cor. 10:1–2, in which St. Paul remembers how the Israelites were baptized into Moses when they passed through the Red Sea, and Exod. 40:32–34, in which Moses and Aaron wash themselves before entering the Tent of Meeting, where the cloud descends and covers the Tent with the glory of the Lord (LH, Lent.3.Sa, 1R, Resp [1 Cor. 10:1–2; Exod. 40:32–34]).

WATER OF MARAH

OT Background: Exod. 4:9; 7:17–24; 15:22–26; Num. 5:18–27; 2 Kings 2:19–21; Sir. 38:5

NT Background: James 3:11–12; 1 John 5:6–8; Rev. 8:8–11; 16:3–6

Type: LH, OT.15.Tu, 2R: St. Ambrose, On the Mysteries, 12–16.19: SC 25 bis, 162–164

Related: BAPTISM: *Types:* Water from the Side of Christ; *Symbols:* Fountain of Water

• As Moses sweetened the bitter water through wood (*cf.* Exod. 15:22–26; Sir. 38:5), so the waters of Baptism are consecrated by the power and proclamation of the cross of Christ (LH, OT.15.Tu, 2R: St. Ambrose, On the Mysteries, 12–16.19: SC 25 bis, 162–164).

CROSSING OF THE JORDAN RIVER

OT Background: Gen. 32:10; Num. 32:5, 21, 29; 33:51–56; 35:10–11; Deut. 4:21–22; 9:1–3; 11:31–32; 12:10–11; 27:2–4, 12; 31:2, 12–13; 32:47; Josh. 1:2, 11; 3:1–5:12; 7:7; Jth. 5:15

NT Background: Matt. 3:13; Mark 1:9; Luke 4:1

Catechism Background: 535; 1222; 1223

Type: CCC 1222; LH, OT.10.We, 2R: Origen, Homily 4, 1: PG 12, 842–843; HL, Lent.1.We, 2R: Aphrahat, Dem. 11, On Circumcision, 11–12: PS 1, 498–503

Related: BAPTISM: *Types:* Circumcision; Crossing of the Red Sea; Pillar of Cloud and Fire

• As the Israelites received the gift of the promised land by passing through the Jordan (*cf.* Josh. 3:1–5:2), the People of God receive the gift of eternal life by passing through the waters of Baptism (CCC 1222).

- The passage of the Jordan is a type of Baptism in multiple ways (LH, OT.10. We, 2R: Origen, Homily on Joshua, 4, 1: PG 12, 842–843):
  - As the People of God passed through the Jordan River into the promised land, so the baptized pass through the waters of Baptism into the promised land of the Church and of heaven.
  - The passage of the Jordan River was accompanied by great signs, such as the waters parting (Josh. 3:14–17). The promise to those who pass the Jordan River by the Sacrament of Baptism is even greater: the promise of a passage to heaven.
  - As Moses handed the Israelites on to Joshua before crossing the Jordan (*cf.* Deut. 31:7), so the neophyte is handed on to Jesus as he crosses the waters of Baptism to be guided on the rest of his journey.
- As Joshua led the Israelites across the Jordan River into the promised land, so Jesus leads the People of God through the waters of Baptism (called the "true Jordan") into the land of the living (LH, Lent.1.We, 2R: Aphrahat, Dem. 11, On Circumcision, 11–12: PS 1, 498–503; *cf. also* BAPTISM: *Types:* Circumcision).

HOLY OF HOLIES

OT Background: Exod. 26:33–34; Lev. 16; 1 Kings 6:16, 19–32; 8:6–11; 2 Chron. 3:8–14; 5:7–14; Ps. 68:17; Ezek. 41:4; 45:3–4

NT Background: Matt. 27:51; Mark 15:38; Luke 23:45; Heb. 6:19–20; 9:1–28; 10:19–22

Catechism Background: 433

Type: Heb. 10:19–22; LH, OT.15.Su, 2R: St. Ambrose, On the Mysteries, 1–7: SC 25 bis, 156–158

Related: BAPTISM: *Types:* Fruit of the Tree of Life; *Symbols*: Second Birth

- Jesus, as high priest, entered once and for all into the Holy of Holies, and opened the way for us to enter through his flesh, having been washed clean in Baptism (Heb. 10:19–22; *cf. also* Heb. 6:19; 9:1–28; Matt. 27:51; Mark 15:38; Luke 23:45).
- The catechumen enters into the Holy of Holies where he is baptized (LH, OT.15.Su, 2R: St. Ambrose, On the Mysteries, 1–7: SC 25 bis, 156–158).

The Liturgy of the Hours

Open then your ears. Enjoy the fragrance of eternal life, breathed on you by means of the sacraments. We explained this to you as we celebrated the mystery of "the opening" when we said: *Effetha, that is, be opened.* Everyone who was to come for the grace of baptism had to understand what he was to be asked, and must remember what he was to answer. This mystery was celebrated by Christ when he healed the man who was deaf and dumb, in the Gospel which we proclaimed to you.

After this, the holy of holies was opened up for you; you entered into the sacred place of regeneration. Recall what you were asked; remember what you answered. You renounced the devil and his works, the world and its dissipation and sensuality. Your words are recorded, not on a monument to the dead but in the book of the living. . . .

You entered to confront your enemy, for you intended to renounce him to his face. You turned toward the east, for one who renounces the devil turns toward Christ and fixes his gaze directly on him.

LH, OT.15.Su, 2R: St. Ambrose,
On the Mysteries, 1–7: SC 25 bis, 156–158

ANOINTING OF PRIESTS, PROPHETS, AND KINGS

Definition: A symbol of the Holy Spirit, whose "anointing" of Jesus as Messiah fulfilled the prophecies of the Old Testament. Christ (in Hebrew *Messiah*) means the one "anointed" by the Holy Spirit. Anointing is the sacramental sign of Confirmation, called Chrismation in the Churches of the East. Anointings form part of the liturgical rites of the catechumenate, and of the Sacraments of Baptism and Holy Orders (Glossary of the Catechism of the Catholic Church).

OT Background:

Temple and related: Gen. 28:18–22; 31:13; 35:14; Exod. 29:21, 36; 30:22–33; 40:9–11; Lev. 7:10–11; 8:10–11, 30; Num. 7:1, 10, 84, 88; Sir. 35:6; Dan. 9:24

Priest: Exod. 28:41; 29:7, 21, 29; 30:30–33; 40:12–15; Lev. 4:3, 5, 16; 6:20, 22; 7:12, 36; 8:12, 30; 10:7; 16:32; 21:10, 12; Num. 3:3; 35:25; 1 Chron. 29:22; Ps. 133:2; Sir. 45:15; Zech. 4:14; 2 Macc. 1:10

King: Judg. 9:8, 15; 1 Sam. 2:10, 35; 9:16; 10:1; 12:3, 5; 15:1, 17; 16:1–13; 24:6, 10; 26:9, 11, 16, 23; 2 Sam. 1:14, 16; 2:4, 7; 3:39; 5:3, 17; 12:7; 19:10, 21; 22:51; 23:1; 1 Kings 1:34, 39, 45; 5:1; 19:15–16; 2 Kings 9:1–13; 11:12; 23:30; 1 Chron. 11:3; 14:8; 29:22; 2 Chron. 6:42; 22:7; 23:11; Ps. 2:2; 18:50; 20:6; 28:8; 45:7–8; 84:9; 89:20, 38, 51; 132:10, 17; Sir. 46:13, 19; 48:8; Isa. 11:2; 45:1; Lam. 4:20; Dan. 9:25–26; Hos. 8:10; Hab. 3:13; Zech. 4:14

Prophet: 1 Kings 19:16; 1 Chron. 16:22; Ps. 105:15; Isa. 61:1

Suffering Servant: Isa. 42:1

Other: Ps. 23:5; 133:2; Isa. 61:1, 3

NT Background:

Jesus Christ: Luke 4:16–21; John 1:41; 4:25; Acts 4:26–27; 10:38; Heb. 1:9

Believers / Other: John 9:6, 11; 2 Cor. 1:21–22; 2:14–16; Eph. 1:13–14; 1 Pet. 2:5, 9; 1 John 2:20, 27; Rev. 1:6; 3:18; 5:10; 20:6

Catechism Background: 91; 436; 438; 486; 690; **695**; **698**; 782; **783–786**; **1141**; 1148; **1150–1151**; 1183; 1189; **1216**; **1241–1242**; **1268**; **1273**; 1279; 1289–1290; **1291**; **1293–1296**; **1297**; 2769; 2782

Type: CCC 1150; 1291 in light of 1150, 698, and 1268; RBOC 25

Related: CONFIRMATION: *Symbols:* Anointing; HOLY ORDERS: *Types:* Anointing of Priests, Prophets, and Kings; *Symbols:* Anointing; *cf. also* discussion at CONFIRMATION: *Types.*

Note: *The anointing of priests, prophets, and kings is primarily a type of Jesus, the Christ (i.e. "the anointed one"; cf. CCC 436. A small sampling of texts referring to this are included below). Nevertheless, sacramental anointing is also presented as foreshadowed by the anointing of priests, prophets, and kings, insofar as the baptized participate in the anointing of Christ (cf. CCC 783–786; 1150; RBOC 25; RM, Chrism Mass, Collect; cf. also LH, ET.1.Fr, 2R: St. Cyril of Jerusalem, Jerusalem Catecheses, 21:1–3, Mystagogica 3, 1–3: PG*

33, 1087–1091; LH, ET.3.Mo, 2R: St. Bede the Venerable, Commentary on 1 Pet., Ch. 2: PL 93, 50–51). For a discussion of whether the anointing of priests, prophets, and kings is best understood as foreshadowing the Sacraments of Baptism or Confirmation, cf. CONFIRMATION: *Types.*

Anointing is both a symbol and a type. CCC 1150 discusses "signs" which "prefigure" the sacraments, mentioning among them "anointing and consecration of kings and priests." In these cases it is not easy, and sometimes probably impossible, to distinguish too sharply between symbolism and typology. Presented here are texts which speak primarily of anointing as a type, or texts which are closely related to the types of anointing, even if they also speak of symbolism. For texts which speak of anointing as a symbol, cf. CONFIRMATION: *Symbols: Anointing.*

- The anointing of prophets, priests, and kings (*cf. OT Background* above) prefigured the anointing of Christ as prophet, priest, and king (*cf. for example* RBOC 2; *cf. also* Luke 4:16–21; CCC 436; 2579; LH, OT.12.Su, 2R: Faustus Luciferanus, Treatise on the Trinity, 39–40: CCL 69, 340–341).
- The anointing and consecration of priests and kings in the Old Covenant prefigures the sacramental anointing of believers in the Sacrament of Baptism (CCC 1150; 1241; 1291; *cf. also* 1 Pet. 2:9–10; CCC 698; 1152; 1268; LH, ET.3.Mo, 2R: St. Bede the Venerable, Commentary on 1 Pet., Ch. 2: PL 93, 50–51).
- The consecratory prayer of the chrism oil used for Baptism, Confirmation, and Holy Orders (RBOC 25; *cf. also* CCC 1241):
  - Remembers from the history of salvation:
    - the creation of the world, when God created "fruit bearing trees" (*cf.* Gen. 1:12, 29; 2:9), among which the olive tree, whose fruit gives the oil for the holy chrism;
    - the prophet David who sung of the "life and joy that the oil would bring us in the sacraments of your love";
    - the olive branch which the dove brought back to Noah (*cf.* Gen. 8:11), announcing the gift of peace and foreshadowing a greater gift to come (*cf. also* LH, CT.AE.Mo, 2R: St. Peter Chrysologus, Sermo 160: PL 52, 620–622);
    - the washing with water of Aaron and his anointing as priest by Moses (*cf.* Exod. 40:12–15), which foreshadowed a greater reality

to come (*cf.* HOLY ORDERS: *Types*: Anointing of Priests, Prophets, and Kings);

- that God has anointed for himself priests, kings, prophets and martyrs with chrism (the name of which, we are reminded, comes from Jesus Christ) (*cf. OT Biblical Background* above);
- the anointing of Jesus in the Jordan, in which the Spirit came down in the form of a dove (*cf.* Matt. 3:16; Mark 1:10; Luke 3:22; John 1:32) and the prophecy of David was fulfilled that Christ would be "anointed with the oil of gladness beyond his fellow men" (*cf.* Ps. 45:7).

▪ And asks God that those anointed with this holy oil, chrism of salvation:

- become temples of God's glory (*cf. also* RM, Ritual Masses, For the Conferral of Confirmation, A, Collect);
- be radiant with the goodness of life that has its source in him;
- receive royal, priestly, and prophetic honor;
- be clothed with incorruption.

- Baptismal anointing signifies the participation in the prophetic, priestly, and kingly anointing of Jesus Christ (CCC 1241–1242; 1291; RB 62; RBOC 2; 25, 2nd form; *cf. also* 1 Pet. 2:9; CCC 783–786; 1216; RM, Chrism Mass, Collect; RBOC 25, 1st form; LH, ET.1.Fr, 2R: St. Cyril of Jerusalem, Jerusalem Catecheses, 21:1–3, Mystagogica 3, 1–3: PG 33, 1087–1091).

- The baptized is anointed as priest (LH, OT.15.Th, 2R: St. Ambrose, On the Mysteries, 29–30.34–35.37.42: SC 25 bis, 172–178 in reference in part to Ps. 133:2; LH, Leo the Great [Nov 10], 2R: Leo the Great, Sermo 4, 1–2: PL 54, 148–149, quoted in CCC 786; CCC 1216 citing St. Gregory of Nazianzus, Oratio 40, 3–4: PG 36, 361C; *cf. also* LH, Baptism of the Lord, MP, 6th intercession; LH, Psalter.1.Tu, MP, 2nd intercession, which speak of a "royal priesthood").

- As kings, the Christians rule over their bodies after having surrendered their souls to God; as priests, they offer to God a pure conscience and unblemished sacrifices on the altar of their heart (LH, Leo the Great [Nov 10], 2R: Leo the Great, Sermo 4, 1–2: PL 54, 148–149).

- The anointing in Confirmation "is the sign of consecration" (CCC 1294 in light of CCC 436 which speaks of the consecration of kings, priests, and occasionally prophets by anointing; *cf.* discussion at CONFIRMATION: *Types*).

HEALING OF NAAMAN

OT Background: 2 Kings 5:1–14
NT Background: Luke 4:27
Type: LH, OT.15.Tu, 2R: St. Ambrose, On the Mysteries, 12–16.19: SC 25 bis, 162–164; LH, OT.15.We, 2R: St. Ambrose, On the Mysteries, 19–21.24.26–38: SC 25 bis, 164–170
Related: BAPTISM: *Types:* Healing at the Sheep Gate Pool; *Symbols:* Immersion; Washing

- As Naaman was cured by washing in the waters of the Jordan (*cf.* 2 Kings 5:1–14), so the baptized is cured in the waters of Baptism (LH, OT.15.Tu, 2R: St. Ambrose, On the Mysteries, 12–16.19: SC 25 bis, 162–164).
- As the waters of the Jordan cleansed Naaman of leprosy not due to their intrinsic power but the grace of God, so the waters of Baptism cleanse the soul of sin not due to their intrinsic power but the grace of God (LH, OT.15.Tu, 2R: St. Ambrose, On the Mysteries, 12–16.19: SC 25 bis, 162–164).
- While Naaman dipped seven times in the Jordan (*cf.* 2 Kings 5:14) to be cleansed under the old law, the baptized is dipped three times in the name of the Trinity under the new law (LH, OT.15.We, 2R: St. Ambrose, On the Mysteries, 19–21.24.26–38: SC 25 bis, 164–170).

HEALING AT THE SHEEP GATE POOL

NT Background: John 5:2–9
Type: LH, OT.15.We, 2R: St. Ambrose, On the Mysteries, 19–21.24.26–38: SC 25 bis, 164–170
Related: BAPTISM: *Types:* Healing of Naaman

- As the angel of the Lord would come and heal one of the sick at the Sheep Gate pool (*cf.* John 5:7), so Jesus comes and heals the baptized in the waters of Baptism. This healing points forward to the sanctifying power of water at Baptism (LH, OT.15.We, 2R: St. Ambrose, On the Mysteries, 19–21.24.26–38: SC 25 bis, 164–170).

Opening of the Ears and Mouth

OT Background: Ps. 37:30; 71:8, 23; Wisd. 10:20–21; Isa. 29:18; 35:5–6; 42:18; 43:8; 53:7; Ezek. 3:26–27; 24:27; 33:22; Mic. 7:16–20

NT Background: Mark 7:31–37; *cf. also* Matt. 9:32–34; 11:5; 12:22; 15:30–31; Mark 9:17–29; Luke 1:22, 64; 7:22; 11:14; 24:32; Acts 8:32

Catechism Background: 1151; 1504

Type: RCIA 197–199; RB 65; LH, OT.15.Su, 2R: St. Ambrose, On the Mysteries, 1–7: SC 25 bis, 156–158

Related: Baptism: *Symbols:* Illumination / Light / Candle

• As Jesus opened the ears and mouth of the deaf and dumb man (*cf.* Mark 7:31–37), so he opens the ears and mouth of the catechumens in preparation for Baptism (LH, OT.15.Su, 2R: St. Ambrose, On the Mysteries, 1–7: SC 25 bis, 156–158) that they may receive the Word and proclaim it (RCIA 197–199; RB 65; *cf. also* Luke 24:32; CCC 108; RCIA 94H).

• The Church solemnly prays on Good Friday for catechumens, that God "may open wide the ears of their inmost hearts and unlock the gates of his mercy," and that having been forgiven through Baptism they may be one with Jesus Christ (RM, Good Friday, Solemn Intercessions, 13).

Water from the Side of Christ

OT Background: Zech. 12:10–13:1

NT Background: John 19:34–37; 1 John 5:6–8

Catechism Background: 478; 694; 766; 1225

Type[3]: CCC 1225; RM, Easter Vigil, Blessing of the baptismal water, 46

Related: Baptism: *Symbols:* Fountain of Water; Washing; Eucharist: *Types:* Blood from the Side of Christ; Water from the Rock

• The piercing of Christ's side fulfilled the prophecy of Zechariah that "They shall look on him whom they have pierced" (John 19:37 in reference to Zech. 12:10). The text of Zechariah continues shortly thereafter stating: "On that day there shall be a fountain opened for the house of David and the inhabitants of Jerusalem to cleanse them from sin and uncleanness"

---

3 Paragraph 1225 of the Catechism is relevant to the question of whether types are limited to the Old Testament, or whether there are types in the New Testament as well. Here is the pertinent phrase in the Latin text: "Sanguis et aqua quae de aperto Iesu crucifixi exiverunt latere, typi sunt Baptismi et Eucharistiae, vitae novae sacramentorum" (CCC 1225; *cf. also* CCC 1335).

(Zech. 13:1). The liturgy relates this prophecy of Zechariah to the water and the blood flowing from the side of Christ (LH, OT.33.Sa, 1R, Resp which explicitly correlates Zech. 13:1 and Zech. 14:8 with John 19:34). The importance given by the Gospel of John to the water and the blood flowing from the side of Christ (*cf.* John 19:35) may be at least in part related to this prophecy of Zechariah (*cf. also* 1 John 5:6–8 and BAPTISM: *Symbols:* Fountain of Water).

- The water and blood flowing from Christ's side on the cross (John 19:34–35) are types of the life-giving Sacraments of Baptism (*cf.* John 3:5) and the Eucharist (*cf.* John 6:53–54) (CCC 1225), which continually give new life to the Church and thus symbolize her birth (CCC 766; RB 54, B; LH, Lent.HW.Fr, 2R: St. John Chrysostom, Catecheses 3, 13–19: SC 50, 174–177; *cf. also* LH, OT.23.Fr, 2R: Bl. Isaac of Stella, Sermo 11: PL 194, 1728–1729; LH, Baptism of the Lord, EP2, Resp may be a reference to Baptism and the Eucharist as symbolized by the blood and water).

- Christ spoke of his death as a "baptism" with which he had to be baptized (Mark 10:38; Luke 12:50). The waters which flowed from his side at his death can thus be understood as having fulfilled his desire of being "baptized." [4] Through this "baptism" on the cross, Christ opened up the saving fountain of Baptism to all people (CCC 1225).

- The three witnesses in Baptism: the water, the blood, and the Spirit, are one (1 John 5:8). In Baptism, the "water" united to the power of the cross of Christ ("the blood") and to the Holy "Spirit" gives eternal life through faith (LH, OT.15.We, 2R: St. Ambrose, On the Mysteries, 19–21.24.26–38: SC 25 bis, 164–170 in reference to 1 John 5:6–8; *cf. also* LH, ET.7.We, 1R, Resp which correlates 1 John 5:6 and Zech. 13:1).

- The pierced side of Christ and his Sacred Heart are the wellspring of the Church's sacraments (RM, Sacred Heart of Jesus, Preface in reference to John 19:34 and Isa. 12:3; LH, Sacred Heart, 2R: St. Bonaventure, On the Tree of Life, 29–30.47: Opera Omnia 8, 79; *cf. also* LH, Common of the Dedication of a Church, EP [=EP2], 3rd intercession).

---

4 The image of Christ being "baptized" by the water from his side seems to be implied but is not made explicit by CCC 1225.

The Liturgy of the Hours

It was a divine decree that permitted one of the soldiers to open his sacred side with a lance. This was done so that the Church might be formed from the side of Christ as he slept the sleep of death on the cross, and so that the Scripture might be fulfilled: *They shall look upon him whom they have pierced* (Zech. 12:10). The blood and water which poured out at that moment were the price of our salvation. Flowing from the secret abyss of our Lord's heart as from a fountain, this stream gave the sacraments of the Church the power to confer the life of grace, while for those already living in Christ it became the spring of living water welling up to life everlasting.

Arise then, beloved of Christ! Imitate the dove *that nests in a hole in the cliff* (*cf.* Song 2:14), keeping watch at the entrance *like the sparrow that finds a home* (*cf.* Ps. 84:3). There, like the turtle-dove hide your little ones, the fruit of your chaste love. Press your lips to the fountain, *draw water from the wells of your Savior* (*cf.* Isa. 12:3); for *this is the spring flowing out of the middle of paradise, dividing into four rivers* (*cf.* Gen. 2:10), inundating devout hearts, watering the whole earth and making it fertile.

LH, Sacred Heart, 2R: St. Bonaventure,
On the Tree of Life, 29–30.47: Opera Omnia 8, 79

- The blood and water which flow from Christ's side are a sign of the mysteries of human rebirth (RM, Masses and Prayers for Various Needs and Occasions, For Holy Church, 11, A, Prayer over the Offerings).
- From the pierced side of Christ flowed forth a stream of immortality, blood and water for the world's cleansing (LH, Triumph of the Cross [Sep 14], 2R: St. Andrew of Crete, Oratio 10 in Exaltatione sanctae crucis: PG 97, 1018–1019.1022–1023).
- While from Adam's side was born a woman who, being tricked, was to become the death-bearer, from Christ's side came forth a fountain of life that regenerates the world in Baptism and feeds the reborn in the Eucharist

(LH, OT.19.Mo, 2R: Theodoret of Cyr, On the Incarnation, 26–27: PG 75, 1466–1467).

SYMBOLS

ANOINTING

Cf. BAPTISM: *Types:* Anointing of Priests, Prophets, and Kings; Confirmation: *Symbols*: Anointing.

BAPTISM OF FIRE

OT Background:

Purifying or Testing: Num. 31:22–23; Jth. 8:27; Ps. 66:12; Sir. 2:5; Isa. 6:6–7; 43:2; Jer. 6:29; Ezek. 24:12; Zech. 13:9; Mal. 3:2–3

Divine fire in the heart: Jer. 20:9

Consuming sacrifices: Lev. 9:24; Judg. 6:21; 1 Kings 18:24, 38; 1 Chron. 21:26; 2 Chron. 7:1; 2 Macc. 2:10

God / Theophany: Gen. 15:17; Exod. 3:2; 19:18; 24:17; Deut. 4:11–15, 24, 33, 36; 5:4, 22–26; 9:3, 10; 10:4; 2 Sam. 22:13; Ps. 18:12–14; 29:7; 50:3; Isa. 10:17; 33:14, 27; 66:15; Ezek. 1:27; 8:2; Dan. 7:9–10; Amos 5:6; Zech. 2:5 (*cf. also* BAPTISM, *Types*, Pillar of Cloud and Fire, OT Background)

NT Background:

Baptism of Fire: Matt. 3:11; Luke 3:16; possibly Mark 10:38; Luke 12:49–50

Baptism of Holy Spirit: Matt. 3:11; Mark 1:8; Luke 3:16; John 1:33; Acts 1:5; 2:3–4; 11:16; 1 Cor. 12:13

Divine fire in the heart: Luke 12:49; 1 Thess. 5:19

Purifying or Testing: Mark 9:49; 10:38; 1 Cor. 3:10–15; 1 Pet. 1:7; 4:12; Rev. 3:18

God / Jesus / Holy Spirit as a Fire: Matt. 3:11; Luke 3:16; 12:49–50; Acts 2:3–4; 7:30; Heb. 12:18, 29; 1 Thess. 5:19; 2 Thess. 1:7; Rev. 1:14; 2:18; 4:5; 19:12

Catechism Background: 536; 678; 696; 718; **1127;** 1147; 1189; **1225;** 1258–1259; 2583; 2671; 2804

Related: BAPTISM: *Types:* Pillar of Cloud and Fire; *Symbols:* Illumination / Light / Candle; CONFIRMATION: *Symbols:* Fire

- John the Baptist proclaimed that Jesus would baptize with the Holy Spirit and with fire (Matt. 3:11; Luke 3:16; LH, Baptism of the Lord, EP, Ant2; LH, ET.7.We, EP, Magn; LH, OT.15.We, 2R, Resp [Matt. 3:11; Isa. 1:16, 17, 18]; *cf. also* Mark 1:8; John 1:33; Acts 1:5; 11:16; 1 Cor. 12:13; CCC 678).

- In Baptism the words of John the Baptist are fulfilled. The faithful are (LH, ET.6.Mo, 2R: Didymus of Alexandria, On the Trinity, 2, 12: PG 39, 667–674):

  - cleansed by both water and a spiritual fire;
  - recast as in a furnace by spiritual water;
  - and hardened by spiritual fire.

The Liturgy of the Hours

Visibly, through the ministry of priests, the font gives symbolic birth to our visible bodies. Invisibly, through the ministry of angels, the Spirit of God, whom even the mind's eye cannot see, baptizes into himself both our souls and bodies, giving them a new birth.

Speaking quite literally, and also in harmony with the words "of water and the Spirit," John the Baptist says of Christ: "He will baptize you with the Holy Spirit and with fire." Since we are only vessels of clay, we must first be cleansed in water and then hardened by spiritual fire—for God "is a consuming fire." We need the Holy Spirit to perfect and renew us, for spiritual fire can cleanse us, and spiritual water can recast us as in a furnace and make us into new men.

LH, ET.6.Mo, 2R: Didymus of Alexandria,
On the Trinity, 2, 12: PG 39, 667–674

- Jesus Christ burned away man's guilt by fire and the Holy Spirit (LH, Baptism of the Lord, MP, Ant3).

- Jesus compares his death (and Resurrection?) to a baptism (Luke 12:50; *cf.* Mark 10:38; Rom. 6:3–4), right after saying he came to cast fire on the earth (Luke 12:49).

- The saints were saved by passing through fire (i.e. their struggles) and through water (LH, St. Denis [Oct 9], 2R, Resp).
- God sent down visible fire for Gideon (Judges 6:21) and Elijah (1 Kings 18:38–39) to consume their sacrifice; in the baptized an invisible fire is at work (LH, OT.15.We, 2R: St. Ambrose, On the Mysteries, 19–21.24.26–38: SC 25 bis, 164–170; *cf. also* CCC 696; 2583).
- The baptized receives the "flame of faith" (RB 64; *cf. also* BAPTISM: *Symbols:* Illumination / Light / Candle).
- John the Baptist proclaimed the judgment of the Last Day, and in this context, the baptism of fire (Matt. 3:7–12; *cf.* CCC 678).

DEW FROM ABOVE

OT Background: Gen. 2:6 (Hebrew); 27:28, 39; Exod. 16:13–15; Num. 11:9; Deut. 32:2–3; 33:13 (Hebrew), 28; Judg. 6:37–40; Job 36:26–28; Ps. 110:3; 133:3; Prov. 3:20; 19:12; Song 5:2; Sir. 18:16; 24:3; 43:22; Isa. 18:4; 26:19; 45:8; Hos. 14:5; Mic. 5:7; Hag. 1:10; Zech. 8:12

NT Background: 1 Cor. 3:6–8

Related: BAPTISM: *Types:* Dove; *Symbols:* Fountain of Water; EUCHARIST: *Types:* Manna

- The dew from above is the Holy Spirit, given to believers in Baptism (LH, Pentecost, 2R: St. Irenaeus, Treatise Against Heresies, Book 3, 17, 1–3: SC 34, 302–306):
  - who are like dry flour that cannot become dough (and thus bread) without water from heaven;
  - who are like parched ground which cannot yield a harvest without water from heaven (similar to Hag. 1:9);
  - who are like a waterless tree that cannot bear fruit without water from heaven (*cf. also* RM, Votive Masses, 9, A, Prayer after Communion);
  - the dew of God (the Advocate) protects the believer from being scorched by the devil (the Accuser), who was cast down to the earth like lightning (in reference to Luke 10:18).

DOVE

OT Background: Gen. 1:2; 8:8–12
NT Background: Matt. 3:16; 10:16; Mark 1:10; Luke 3:22; John 1:32; Acts
10:37–38
Catechism Background: 535; 701
Related: BAPTISM: *Types:* Flood; Dove

*Note: The dove is presented as both a type and a symbol in texts related to
Baptism. Cf. BAPTISM: Types:* Dove *for texts which speak of the dove as a type.*

* At Christ's baptism, the Holy Spirit descended upon him in the form of
a dove (*cf.* Matt. 3:16; Mark 1:10; Luke 3:22; John 1:32). The dove thus
symbolizes the Holy Spirit who comes down and remains in the hearts of
the baptized (CCC 701; 535; *cf. also* Gen. 1:2).
* The dove bears public witness at Christ's baptism that he is the anointed
of God, as the presence of the Spirit is upon him (CCC 535; LH, Baptism
of the Lord, MP, Ant1; RM, Baptism of the Lord, Preface; *cf. also* Acts
10:37–38).
* By making himself visible in the figure of a dove and fire, the Holy Spirit
manifested that those who are full of him should practice both the virtue of
simplicity as well as that of zeal (LH, OT.8.Su, 2R: St. Gregory the Great,
Moral Reflections on Job, Book 1, 2.36: PL 75, 529–530.543–544; *cf.*
Matt. 10:16).

FOUNTAIN OF WATER

OT Background: Gen. 2:10; Esther 10:6; 11:10; Ps. 36:8–9; 46:4; 65:9;
84:6; 107:35; Prov. 8:24; 10:11; 13:14; 14:27; 16:22; 18:4; Sir. 21:13;
Isa. 12:3; 30:25; 33:21; 35:7; 41:18; 43:19–20; 48:18; 49:10; 55:1;
59:19–20; 66:12; Jer. 2:13; 17:13; 31:9; Bar. 3:12; Ezek. 47:1–12;
Hos. 13:15; Joel 3:18; Nah. 1:4; Zech. 13:1 (*cf.* 12:10); 14:8
NT Background: John 4:10–14; 7:37–39; 19:34; Rom. 8:26; 2 Pet. 2:17; 1
John 5:8; Rev. 7:17; 21:6; 22:1–2, 17
Catechism: **694**; 728; 1011; 1220; **1225**; 1287; 1584; **2561**; **2652**
Related: BAPTISM: *Types:* Water from the Side of Christ; EUCHARIST:
Types: Wisdom's Banquet; Water from the Rock; Blood from the Side
of Christ; *Symbols:* Bread and Wine / Nourishment

The Fountain of Water is the Holy Spirit

- The fountain of water which Christ promised believers is the Holy Spirit living in their hearts (John 7:37–39; CCC 1287; 728; LH, Lent.3.Su, 2R: St. Augustine, Treatise on John, Tract. 15, 10–12.16–17: CCL 36, 154–156; LH, ET.7.We, 2R: Vatican II, Lumen Gentium 4.12; LH, Psalter.3.Fr, MP, 3rd intercession; *cf. also* reference to "living water" in LH, OT.10.Tu, 2R: St. Ignatius of Antioch, Letter to the Romans, 6, 1–9, 3: Funk 1, 219–223).

The Word of God

On the last day of the feast, the great day, Jesus stood up and proclaimed, "If any one thirst, let him come to me and drink. He who believes in me, as the scripture has said, 'Out of his heart shall flow rivers of living water.'" Now this he said about the Spirit, which those who believed in him were to receive; for as yet the Spirit had not been given, because Jesus was not yet glorified.

John 7:37–39

- The Holy Spirit comes into the soul like a fountain, and the soul is immersed in it, receiving treasures and virtues (LH, St. Mary Magdalene de Pazzi [May 25], 2R: St. Mary Magdalene de Pazzi, On Revelation and On Trials, Mss. III, 186.264; IV, 716: Opere di S. M. Maddalene de Pazzi, Firenze, 1965, 4, pp. 200.269; 6, p. 194).
- As all things need water, and its effects are different in each, so the Holy Spirit, the living water, is needed by all, but his effects are unique in each person (LH, ET.7.Mo, 2R: St. Cyril of Jerusalem, Catechetical Instruction 16, De Spiritu Sancto 1, 11–12.16: PG 33, 931–935.939–942).
- God himself is the fountain of water: the Father (Jer. 2:13), the Son (Bar. 3:12), and the Holy Spirit (John 4:14) (LH, OT.13.Th, 2R: St. Jerome, Sermon on Ps. 41 addressed to newly baptized: CCL 78, 542–544).

Christ, the Living Water, Flows from Mary as from a Fountain

- In the Incarnation, Mary is the temple of the Son of God and the fountain from which living water (Jesus Christ) flowed (LH, Our Lady of Fatima

[May 13], 2R: St. Ephrem the Syrian, Sermo 3, De diversis: Opera Omnia, III, syr. et. lat., Rome 1743, 607).

The Fountain of Water Flows from Christ

* Jesus Christ is the source of the living water which satisfies our thirst (LH, OT.13.Su, 2R: Pope Paul VI, Homily, November 29, 1970).
* Christ himself is the fountain, and he who drinks from the fountain drinks God himself and is united to him (LH, OT.21.Th, 2R: St. Columban, Instr. 13, De Christo fonte vitae, 2–3: Opera, Dublin 1957, 118–120).
* All grace, and the life itself of the People of God, flow from Christ to his Body, the Church, as from its fountain and head (CCC 957).
* At the well, Jesus offered the Samaritan woman to drink of the living water which he would give (John 4:10–14; LH, Lent.3.Su, 2R: St. Augustine, Treatise on John, Tract. 15, 10–12.16–17: CCL 36, 154–156; *cf. also* LH, Lent.3.Su, 2R, Resp [John 7:37–39; 4:13]).
* In his death on the cross, "the Spring" suffered thirst (CCC 556, which quotes St. Augustine, Sermo 78, 6: PL 38, 492–493 in reference to John 19:28; *cf. also* LH, Lent.HW.Sa, 2R, Resp which speaks of the death of Christ, the fountain of living water).
* The divine water that Christ offers us to drink is that which flowed out of his side on the cross, and springs up in he who drinks it to eternal life (LH, OT.33.Th, 2R: St. Gregory of Nyssa, Commentary on the Song of Songs, Ch. 2: PG 44, 802; *cf.* LH, St. Peter Canisius [Dec 21], 2R: St. Peter Canisius, Epistulae et Acta [edit. O. Brunsberger], I, Friburgi Brisgoviae, 1896, pp. 53–55; *cf. also* BAPTISM: *Types:* Water from the Side of Christ).
* In Christ's baptism, the infinite river and unfathomable fountainhead was baptized in a small river. He is the fountain of life and of healing (LH, CT.AE.Tu, 2R: St. Hippolytus, Sermon on the Epiphany, 2.6–8.10: PG 10, 854.858–859.862; *cf. also* LH, CT.AE.We, 2R: St. Proclus of Constantinople, Sermo 7 in sancta Theophania, 1–3: PG 65, 758–759).
* When a Christian draws from Christ the inspiration of his thoughts and inclinations, he draws forth pure water which also purifies (LH, OT.12.Tu, 2R: St. Gregory of Nyssa, On Christian Perfection: PG 46, 283–286).

The Fountain Gives Birth to the Sacraments

- The pierced side of Christ is the wellspring of the Church's sacraments, opened so that all might draw water joyfully from the springs of salvation (RM, Sacred Heart, Preface, which rephrases Isa. 12:3; *cf. also* BAPTISM: *Types:* Water from the Side of Christ).
- The fountain flowing from the side of Christ gave the sacraments the power to confer the life of grace, and for those already living in Christ, this stream became a spring of living water welling up to eternal life (LH, Sacred Heart, 2R: St. Bonaventure, On the Tree of Life, 29–30.47: Opera Omnia 8, 79).
- The Body of Christ (the Church) is the temple from which the source of living water springs forth (CCC 1179; *cf.* Rev. 21:10; 22:1–2; Ezek. 47:1–12).
- From Christ's side came forth a fountain of life that regenerates the world in Baptism and feeds the reborn in the Eucharist (LH, OT.19.Mo, 2R: Theodoret of Cyr, On the Incarnation, 26–27: PG 75, 1466–1467).

Especially to Baptism

- Baptism is a fountain, unsealed by God to wash clean human nature and give it new life through water and the Spirit (RM, Easter Vigil, Blessing of Baptismal Water, 46).
- Descending into the waters of baptism in the Jordan, Christ sanctified the waters of Baptism (LH, Baptism of the Lord, 2R: St. Gregory of Nazianzus, Oratio 39 in Sancta Lumina, 14–16.20: PG 36, 350–351.354.358–359).

The Liturgy of the Hours

Christ is bathed in light; let us also be bathed in light. Christ is baptized; let us go down with him, and rise with him. . . . He comes to sanctify the Jordan for our sake and in readiness for us; he who is spirit and flesh comes to begin a new creation through the Spirit and water. . . . Jesus rises from the waters; the world rises with him. The heavens like Paradise with its flaming sword, closed by Adam for himself and his descendants, are rent open. The Spirit comes to him as to an equal, bearing witness to his Godhead. A voice bears witness to him from heaven, his place of origin. The Spirit descends in bodily form like the dove that so long ago announced the ending of the flood and so gives honor to the body that is one with God.

LH, Baptism of the Lord, 2R: St. Gregory of Nazianzus,
Oratio 39 in Sancta Lumina, 14–16.20:
PG 36, 350–351.354.358–359

- At the Easter Vigil, as the newly baptized return to their seats, the faithful sing, "I saw water flowing from the Temple, from its right-hand side, alleluia; and all to whom this water came were saved and shall say: Alleluia, alleluia" (*cf.* Ezek. 47:1–2) (*cf.* RM, Easter Vigil, Renewal of Baptismal Promises, Antiphon, 56; *cf. also* Rev. 22:1–2; RCIA 153B, 3rd intercession; 154B).
- The fountain of life pouring from Christ's side regenerates the world by its two streams: the water of Baptism which gives new life, and the blood of the Eucharist which nourishes those already reborn (LH, Sacred Heart, 2R: Saint Bonaventure, On the Tree of Life, 29–30.47: Opera Omnia 8, 79).
- When Baptism is administered by someone who is unworthy, the gift of Christ is not profaned. The grace given flows clear through him, keeping its purity, "and reaches the fertile earth" (CCC 1584, quoting St. Augustine, In Jo. ev. 5, 15: PL 35, 1422).
- The baptized are lambs who have come to the fountain of water and are full of light; they are the great multitude standing before the throne of the Lamb, dressed in white and with palms in their hands (LH, ET.1.Th, 2R, Resp in reference to Rev. 7:9; *cf. also* Baptism: *Symbols:* White Garment / Wedding Garment).
- The river of God, given in Baptism, inundates us with gifts (LH, OT.25.Sa, 2R: St. Hilary, Discourse on Psalm 64, 14–15: CSEL 22, 245–246 in reference to Ezek. 47; Ps. 46:4, 65:9; John 4:14, 7:38–39).
- Water springing up from the earth symbolizes life (CCC 1220; *cf.* Ps. 36:9) and purification, gifts given in Baptism (RM, Appendices, Appendix II: Rite for the Blessing and Sprinkling of Water, 2; *cf. also* Baptism: *Symbols:* Washing).

The Fountain Nourishes Us in the Eucharist

- To receive the Eucharist with faith is to drink at the fountain of water, to find the hidden treasure (LH, St. Peter Julian Eymard [Aug 2], 2R: St. Peter

Julian Eymard, *La Présence réelle*, vol. 1, Paris, 1950, pp. 270–271 and 307–308).

• Jesus Christ is the fountain of water. The Christian is invited to eat and drink of him in the Eucharist, in the Word of God, and in the love of wisdom (LH, OT.21.We, 2R: St. Columban, Instr. 13, De Christo fonte vitae, 1–2: Opera, Dublin 1957, 116–118; *cf.* EUCHARIST: *Types:* Wisdom's Banquet).

• At the Eucharistic Celebration, the faithful are renewed at the wellspring of salvation (RM, Commons, Common of Holy Men and Women, For a Nun, Prayer after Communion; *cf. also* RM, Votive Masses, 2, Prayer after Communion), and the Eucharistic presence of Christ becomes as a spring of water welling up to eternal life (RM, Votive Masses, The Most Precious Blood of Our Lord Jesus Christ, Prayer after Communion; *cf. also* EUCHARIST: *Types:* Water from the Rock; Blood from the Side of Christ).

The Fountain Can Be Drunk through the Word of God and Prayer

• God's word is like the living spring, the rock struck in the desert. This spring quenches thirst and is never exhausted (LH, OT.6.Su, 2R: St. Ephrem, Commentary on the Diatessaron, 1, 18–19: SC 121, 52–53).

• Ordained ministers are called to lead the People of God to the living waters of prayer: the Word of God, the liturgy, the life of grace, and the "Today" of God in everyday situations (CCC 2686).

Believers Can Share the Fountain with Others

• Believers (and in a special way a bishop) are called to drink from Christ, and when the river in their hearts overflow, their voices lifts up to preach Jesus Christ and their words can become a source of pure water for others (LH, St. Ambrose [Dec 7], 2R: St. Ambrose, Letter 2, 1–2.4–5.7: PL [edit. 1845] 879, 881).

The Fountain Is in Heaven

• The beatific vision in heaven will be the ever-flowing wellspring of happiness, peace, and communion with God and men (CCC 1045). Even in this life we should flee in spirit from things of the world and drink from the fountain of life (LH, Lent.2.Sa, 2R: St. Ambrose, On Flight from the

World, Ch. 6, 36; 7, 44; 8, 45; 9, 52: CSEL 32, 192.198–199.204; *cf. also* RCIA 94K).

• The Holy Spirit prays in us, inspiring in us a longing for heaven (*cf.* Rom. 8:26), where the fountain of life will satisfy our thirst (LH, OT.29.Fr, 2R: St. Augustine, Letter to Proba 130, 14, 27–15, 28: CSEL 44, 71–73).

• In Baptism the believer has been sprinkled with dew from the fountain and has become light in a world of darkness; in heaven he will drink from the fountain itself, and will see light itself (LH, OT.34.Tu, 2R: St. Augustine, Treatise on John, Tract. 35, 8–9: CCL 36, 321–323).

The Liturgy of the Hours

Let us long for our heavenly country, let us sigh for our heavenly home, let us truly feel that here we are strangers. What shall we then see? Let the Gospel tell us: "In the beginning was the Word and the Word was with God and the Word was God." You will come to the fountain, with whose dew you have already been sprinkled. Instead of the ray of light which was sent through slanting and winding ways into the heart of your darkness, you will see the light itself in all its purity and brightness. It is to see and experience this light that you are now being cleansed.

LH, OT.34.Tu, 2R: St. Augustine, Treatise on John, Tract. 35, 8–9: CCL 36, 321–323

ILLUMINATION / LIGHT / CANDLE

OT Background:

God is light / dwells in light: 2 Sam. 22:13; Ps. 27:1; 50:2; 94:1; 104:2; Wisd. 7:26–29; Isa. 51:4; Ezek. 1:4, 27–28; 8:2; 10:4; Dan. 2:22; Hos. 6:5; Hab. 3:4

God gives light: Num. 6:25; 2 Sam. 22:29; Job 22:28; 29:3; Ps. 4:6; 18:28; 19:8; 27:1; 31:16; 36:9; 43:3; 67:1; 80:3, 7, 19; 94:1; 118:27; 119:105, 130, 135; Prov. 6:23; Wisd. 18:1–4; Sir. 34:17; Isa. 42:16; 60:1, 19–20; Bar. 1:12; Ezek. 43:2; Dan. 9:17; Mic. 7:8–9; Mal. 4:2

Living / walking in the light: Job 18:5–6; Ps. 89:15; 90:8; Wisd. 5:6; Sir. 50:29; Isa. 2:5; 9:2; Bar. 3:14; 4:2; 5:9

Light of God's People: Exod. 34:29–30, 35; 2 Sam. 23:4; Job 11:17; Ps. 34:5; 37:6; 97:11; 112:4; Prov. 4:18; 13:9; Eccles. 8:1; Sir. 32:16; Isa. 42:6; 49:6; 58:8–10; 60:1–5; Dan. 12:3

Light of things: Gen. 1:2–5; 23:4; Esther 10:6; 11:11; Job 24:13–16; Prov. 15:30; Wisd. 7:10; Sir. 42:16; Bar. 3:20, 33

Other: 2 Sam. 21:17; 1 Kings 11:36; 15:4; 2 Kings 8:19; 2 Chron. 21:7; Tob. 14:10; Job 21:17; Ps. 132:17; Prov. 20:27; 21:4; 24:20; Dan. 10:6

NT Background:

Light of Christ / God: Matt. 17:2–5; Luke 2:32; John 1:4–9; 3:19; 8:12; 9:5; 12:35–36, 46; Eph. 5:14; 1 Tim. 6:16; James 1:17; 1 John 1:5; Rev. 21:23; 22:5

Light of God's People: Matt. 5:14–16; 13:43; 25:1; Luke 12:35; 16:8; John 5:35; 12:36; Acts 13:47; Rom. 2:19; Eph. 5:8; Phil. 2:15; 1 Thess. 5:5

Living / walking in the light: Matt. 4:16; 6:22; Luke 1:78–79; 11:34–36; John 3:19–21; 8:12; 9:5; 11:9–10; 12:35–36, 46; Acts 26:18, 23; 2 Cor. 3:7–8; Eph. 5:9; Col. 1:12–13; Heb. 6:4; 10:32; 1 Pet. 2:9; 1 John 1:7–10; 2:8–11; Rev. 21:24; 22:5

Light of the Gospel: 2 Cor. 4:4–6; Eph. 1:17–18; 2 Pet. 1:19

Light of angels: Matt. 28:3; Luke 2:9; Rev. 18:1

Public knowledge: Matt. 10:27; Mark 4:21–22; Luke 8:16–17; 12:3; Eph. 5:11–13

Catechism: 736; 1147; **1165–1168**; **1216**; 1236; **1243**; 1268; 1458; 1584

Related: BAPTISM: *Types:* Pillar of Cloud and Fire; *Symbols:* White Garment / Wedding Garment; PENANCE: *Symbols:* Coming to the Light

• Jesus Christ, who is "Light from Light" (*cf.* Nicene Creed), was baptized by John in the Jordan and has appeared to us (LH, CT.AE.We, 2R, Resp; LH, CT.AE.Tu, 2R: St. Hippolytus, Sermon on the Epiphany, 2.6–8.10: PG 10, 854.858–859.862) as a new light for all ages (LH, Baptism of the Lord, OR, Ant2 [Latin]).

• Through his death and Resurrection ("the Paschal Mystery"), eternal light is ushered in for those who believe in Christ, the eternal light of the day which never ends, the "mystical Passover." Through the liturgy and through the life of grace we participate in this eternal "today" (CCC 1165, which quotes

St. Hippolytus, De pasch. 1–2: SC 27, 117; *cf. also* CCC 1166–1168; RM, The Presentation of the Lord, Blessing of the Candles, 5, especially the 2nd form; LH, ET.1.We, 2R: Easter homily by an ancient author, Sermo 35, 6–9: PL 17 [ed. 1879], 696–697; LH, ET.5.Su, 2R: St. Maximus of Turin, Sermo 53, 1–2.4: CCL 23, 214–216).

- In Baptism, the People of God escape from the darkness of sin (Egypt), and pass through the water of Baptism led by the light of Christ (the pillar of fire) on their journey toward the light of our heavenly home (LH, ET.3.Mo, 2R: St. Bede the Venerable, Commentary on 1 Pet., Ch. 2: PL 93, 50–51; *cf. also* BAPTISM: *Types:* Crossing of the Red Sea; Pillar of Cloud and Fire).
- Christ, the column of fire, gives light to the hearts of believers (LH, CT.AE. Fr, 2R: St. Maximus of Turin, Sermo 100, De sancta Epiphania 1, 3: CCL 23, 398–400).
- In Baptism, the neophyte descends into the water, into the night of the death of Christ, and ascends from the water into the light of the Resurrection (LH, ET.1.Th, 2R: St. Cyril of Jerusalem, Jerusalem Catecheses, 20:4–6, Mystagogica 2, 4–6: PG 33, 1079–1082).
- At his baptism, Jesus Christ manifested himself and in so doing illuminated us (LH, Baptism of the Lord, MP, 2nd intercession).
- In Christ, the light of the world, the baptized become sons of the light, and even light himself (CCC 1216 in reference to John 1:9, 1 Thess. 5:5, Heb. 10:32, and Eph. 5:8). They are to live as "children of the light" (RB 64; RCIA 168B; *cf. also* CCC 736, LH, ET.4.Mo, 2R: St. Basil the Great, On the Holy Spirit, Ch. 15, 35–36: PG 32, 130–131).
- In Christ, the baptized are the light of the world (CCC 1243; 782; 898; 2105; LH, Baptism of the Lord, 2R: St. Gregory of Nazianzus, Oratio 39 in Sancta Lumina, 14–16.20: PG 36, 350–351.354.358–359; *cf.* Matt. 5:14; Phil. 2:15).
- The baptized receive the "light of Christ" (RB 64). They have been called out of darkness into the light of Christ (CCC 1268, in reference to 1 Pet. 2:9; RB 49, A; *cf. also* LH, Christmas, 2R: St. Leo the Great, Sermo 1 in Nativitate Domini, 1–3: PL 54, 190–193).
- The baptized is "bathed in light" (RB, 47, 1st intercession; LH, Baptism of the Lord, 2R: St. Gregory of Nazianzus, Oratio 39 in Sancta Lumina, 14–16.20: PG 36, 350–351.354.358–359).

- The baptized is "resplendent as the sun, radiant in his purity" (LH, CT.AE. Tu, 2R: St. Hippolytus, Sermon on the Epiphany, 2.6–8.10: PG 10, 854.858–859.862).
- Baptism is referred to as "illumination" because the baptized have been enlightened by hearing the Word of God (CCC 1236) and by catechesis (LH, ET.3.We, 2R: St. Justin, First Apology, 61: PG 6, 419–422, quoted in CCC 1216). The baptized are called to live by "the light of faith" (RB 70).
- The baptized are lambs who have come to the fountain of water and are full of light; they are the great multitude standing before the throne of the Lamb, dressed in white and with palms in their hands (LH, ET.1.Th, 2R, Resp in reference to Rev. 7:9; *cf. also* BAPTISM: *Symbols:* Fountain of Water; White Garment / Wedding Garment).
- In Baptism the believer has been sprinkled with dew from the fountain and has become light in a world of darkness; in heaven he will drink from the fountain itself, and will see light itself (LH, OT.34.Tu, 2R: St. Augustine, Treatise on John, Tract. 35, 8–9: CCL 36, 321–323).
- The candle, lit from the Easter candle, signifies that Christ has enlightened the baptized (RB 64; CCC 1216; 1243).
- In Baptism, the eyes of the blind are opened (LH, Baptism of the Lord, EP [=EP2], 4th intercession; compare BAPTISM: *Types:* Opening of the Ears and Mouth).
- Those who embark on a path of catechesis to receive Baptism are invited to walk in the light of Christ (RCIA 52A).
- The power of the Sacrament of Baptism is comparable to light—even if it should pass through (i.e. be administered by) "defiled beings, it is not itself defiled" (CCC 1584, quoting St. Augustine, In Jo. ev. 5, 15: PL 35, 1422).

IMMERSION

OT Background: Gen. 7:6–7; Ps. 42:7; 69:1–2, 15; 88:7; Lam. 3:54–58; Jon. 2:3–7

NT Background: Matt. 3:16; Mark 1:10; 10:38–39; Luke 12:50; Acts 8:38; Rom. 6:3–11; 1 Cor. 12:13; Gal. 3:27; Col. 2:12; 1 Pet. 3:18–22

Catechism: 537; 562; **628**; 790; 985; **1002–1003**; 1010; **1214**; 1220; 1225; **1227**; **1239**; 1243; 1258–1259; **1262**; 1278; 1523; 1681–1682; 1987–1988; 2017

Related: BAPTISM: *Types:* Flood; Crossing of the Red Sea; *Symbols:* Liberation; Second Birth; Washing

- Immersion into water in Baptism symbolizes and brings about our participation in the death and Resurrection of Christ (Rom. 6:3–5; Col. 2:12; CCC 628; 790; 985; 1002–1003; 1010; 1214; 1227; 1239; 1523; 1681–1682; 2017; RM, Easter Vigil, 46; RM, Easter Vigil, 55; RM, ET.3.Sa, Entrance Antiphon; RM, ET.5.Sa, Entrance Antiphon; RM, Ritual Mass for the Conferral of Baptism, A, Collect; LH, OT.19.Tu, 2R: Theodoret of Cyr, On the Incarnation, 28: PG 75, 1467–1470; LH, Dec31, 2R: St. Leo the Great, Sermo 6 in Nativitate Domini, 2–3, 5: PL 54, 213–216; LH, Baptism of the Lord, 2R: St. Gregory of Nazianzus, Oratio 39 in Sancta Lumina, 14–16.20: PG 36, 350–351.354.358–359; LH, Lent.HW.Tu, 2R: St. Basil, On the Holy Spirit, Ch. 15, 35: PG 32, 127–130; LH, Lent. HW.Tu, 2R, Resp [Rom. 6:3, 5, 4]; LH, Lent.HW.Sa, 2R, Prayer; LH, ET.2.Su, 2R: St. Augustine, Sermo 8 in octava Paschae 1.4: PL 46, 838.841; LH, ET.1.Th, 2R: St. Cyril of Jerusalem, Jerusalem Catecheses, 20:4–6: PG 33, 1079–1082; LH, ET.2.Mo, 2R: Pseudo-Chrysostom, Ancient Easter Homily: PG 59, 723–724; LH, ET.2.We, 2R: St. Leo the Great, Sermo 12 de Passione, 3, 6–7: PL 54, 355–357; LH, ET.2.Sa, 2R: Vatican II, Sacrosanctum Concilium 5–6; LH, OT.15.We, 2R: St. Ambrose, On the Mysteries, 19–21.24.26–38: SC 25 bis, 164–170; LH, Office for the Dead, MP, 2nd intercession; LH, Lent.1[=3, 5].Su, MP, 2nd intercession; LH, Lent.HW.Sa, MP, 6th intercession; LH, Lent.HW.Sa, DP, Prayer; LH, Lent.HW.Sa, EP, Prayer; LH, ET.6.Fr, EP, After the Ascension, 6th intension).

- By immersion into the water of Baptism, the baptized participates in the baptism of Jesus, is reborn of water and the Spirit and is adopted as a son or daughter of God (CCC 537).

- Water of the sea can symbolize death, and thus the mystery of the cross. In Baptism it symbolizes our participation in the death of Christ (CCC 1220).

- Immersion symbolizes and brings about both death and purification (with regard to sin) and regeneration and renewal (through a new birth in the Holy Spirit) (CCC 1262 in reference to Acts 2:38 and John 3:5; Rom. 6:3–8; Col. 2:11–15).

- Descending into the font of Baptism as into a tomb, we die to sin; rising from the water, we are reborn in the Spirit (LH, ET.4.Mo, 2R: St. Basil the Great, On the Holy Spirit, Ch. 15, 35–36: SC 17 bis, 364–370; cf. CCC 1220 for water as a symbol of death).

- The old Adam is buried in the waters of Baptism; the new man is born in grace (LH, Lent.1.Th, 2R: St. Asterius of Amasea, Homily 13: PG 40, 355–358.362).

- We rise with Christ in Baptism through faith (RM, Blessings at the End of Mass, Easter Time).

- As Baptism symbolizes the death and Resurrection of Christ, which happened only once, it likewise is only given once (LH, Lent.HW.Tu, 2R: St. Basil, On the Holy Spirit, Ch. 15, 35: PG 32, 127–130; cf. also CCC 1272).

- Immersion in the waters of Baptism points to the washing away of sin (LH, ET.4.Mo, 2R, Resp).

- Triple immersion or pouring water three times over the head of the candidate symbolizes and brings about "entry into the life of the Most Holy Trinity through configuration to the Paschal mystery of Christ" (CCC 1239; cf. CCC 1240; cf. also LH, OT.15.We, 2R: St. Ambrose, On the Mysteries, 19–21.24.26–38: SC 25 bis, 164–170).

- Being plunged into the water and rising three times symbolizes the three days which Christ spent in the tomb before rising (LH, ET.1.Th, 2R: St. Cyril of Jerusalem, Jerusalem Catecheses, 20:4–6, Mystagogica 2, 4–6: PG 33, 1079–1082).

- In Baptism our sin is buried in the water (CCC 1216, citing St. Gregory of Nazianzus, Oratio 40, 3–4: PG 36, 361C).

LIBERATION

OT Background:

From slavery in Egypt: Exod. 4:23; 5:1; 6:6, 11; 7:2, 16; 8:1, 20; 9:1, 13, 28; 10:3; 14:21–15:21; 18:10; Lev. 26:13; Deut. 5:6; Jer. 2:20

From exile: Ps. 126:1; Isa. 45:13; 49:9; 52:2; 61:1; Jer. 28:2–4; 30:8; 2 Macc. 1:27

God freeing captives: Job 12:18; Ps. 68:6; 102:20; 107:14; 116:16; 142:7; 146:7; Isa. 42:7; 61:1; Jer. 30:8; Ezek. 34:27; Nah. 1:13; Zech. 9:11

Through wisdom: Wisd. 1:6; 6:15; 12:2; 16:14; Sir. 6:18–31

Through death: Tob. 3:6, 13

Other: Ezek. 13:20; 30:18; Dan. 3:25; Hos. 11:4

NT Background:

Through Christ: Luke 4:18; 13:12–16; John 8:32–36; 11:44

Through faith: Acts 13:39

From sin / death / the Mosaic law: Acts 2:24; Rom. 6:3–7, 18–22; 7:6; 8:2, 21; Gal. 3:27–4:7; 5:1; Rev. 1:5

Power to loose: Matt. 16:19; 18:18; John 20:21–23

Other: Acts 7:34; 12:6–10, 17; 13:39

Catechism: 553; 979; **1221;** 1237; **1282;** 1446; 1673; 1990

Related: BAPTISM: *Types:* Crossing the Red Sea; *Symbols:* Washing; PENANCE: *Symbols:* Liberation

- Through Baptism we are united to Christ in his death and Resurrection; through union with his death we are freed from the slavery to sin (Rom. 6:3–7).
- Through Baptism the believer becomes a part of the Body of Christ, in which there is neither slave nor free, but children of God (Gal. 3:27–4:7).
- As God liberated the people of Israel from slavery to Pharaoh by leading them through the Red Sea, so he has liberated the People of God through Baptism (CCC 1221; RM, Easter Vigil, 1st and 2nd Prayer after the 3rd reading, 26; RM, Easter Vigil, Blessing of the baptismal water, 46; LH, ET.3.Mo, 2R: St. Bede the Venerable, Commentary on 1 Pet., Ch. 2: PL 93, 50–51).
- As God freed the people of Israel from the persecution of Pharaoh, so through Baptism he frees all nations (RM, Easter Vigil, 1st Prayer after the 3rd reading, 26).
- By entering into Christian life through Baptism, we gain access to true freedom (CCC 1282), that of the children of God, and throw off our old slavery (LH, CT.AE.Tu, 2R: St. Hippolytus, Sermon on the Epiphany, 2.6–8.10:

PG 10, 854.858–859.862; LH, OT.13.Sa, 2R: St. Cyril of Jerusalem, Catechetical Instruction, 1, 2–3.5–6: PG 33, 371.375–378).

- Baptism frees us from the chains of sin (LH, OT.19.Sa, 2R: St. Pacian, Sermon on Baptism, 6–7: PL 13, 1093–1094; RCIA 174B, 3rd intercession).

- Through the Sacraments of Baptism and Penance, the Church uses "the keys of the Kingdom of heaven received from Jesus Christ" to forgive sins (Roman Catechism I, 11, 4, quoted in CCC 979; cf. CCC 553; 1446; Matt. 16:19; 18:18; John 20:21–23).

- The baptized promises to renounce sin so as to live in the freedom of the children of God (RM, Easter Vigil, Renewal of Baptismal Promises, 55).

- By his baptism in the Jordan, Christ freed us from the slavery to the serpent (LH, Baptism of the Lord, EP, Ant2).

- Baptism frees from slavery to Satan, the source of sin and death, and places the baptized under the reign of Christ (RCIA 175B).

- The simple exorcism which is performed in the baptismal rite points to how Baptism signifies "liberation from sin and from its instigator the devil" (CCC 1237; 1673).

Seal

OT Background:

Used Literally: Gen. 38:18, 25; 41:42; Exod. 28:11, 21, 36; 39:6, 14, 30; 1 Kings 21:8; Neh. 9:38; 10:1; Tob. 7:14 (RSV = Tob. 7:13 NAB, NRSV); 9:5; Esther 3:10, 12; 8:2, 8, 10; Sir. 38:27; 42:6; Jer. 32:10–11, 14, 44; Dan. 6:17; 14:11, 14, 17; 2 Macc. 2:5

Used Symbolically: Gen. 4:15; Deut. 32:34; Job 9:7; 14:17; 37:7; 38:14; 41:15; Song 4:12; 8:6; Wisd. 2:5; Sir. 22:27; 32:5–6; Isa. 8:16; 29:11–12; Jer. 22:24; Ezek. 9:4–6; Dan. 8:26; 9:24; 12:4, 9; Hag. 2:23

NT Background: Matt. 27:66; John 3:33; 6:27; Acts 2:1–4, 38; Rom. 4:11; 8:29; 1 Cor. 9:2; 2 Cor. 1:21–22; Eph. 1:13–14; 4:30; 2 Tim. 2:19; Rev. 5:1–10; 6:1–12; 7:2–5, 8; 8:1; 9:4; 10:4; 13:16–17; 14:9, 11; 16:2; 19:20; 20:3–4; 22:10

Catechism Background: 188; 190; 197; **698**; 837; **1121**; 1183; 1216; 1272–1274; 1280; 1293; **1295**–1296; 1297; 1300; 1303–1305; 1317; 1320; 1523; 1955

Related: BAPTISM: *Types*: Circumcision; Anointing of Priests, Prophets, and Kings; CONFIRMATION: *Symbols*: Anointing; Sign of the Cross; PENANCE: *Symbols*: Seal; HOLY ORDERS: *Types:* Anointing of Priests, Prophets, and Kings; *Symbols*: Anointing; Seal; MATRIMONY: *Symbols*: Seal

Note: The seal of Confirmation perfects the seal of Baptism (cf. CCC 1303; 1318) to such an extent that when Baptism and Confirmation are celebrated together, only one anointing, that of Confirmation, is given (cf. RCIA 319; 326). Because of this, symbolisms of "seal" related to either Baptism or Confirmation are presented under CONFIRMATION: Symbols: Seal.

SECOND BIRTH[5]

OT Background: Gen. 6:2, 4; Exod. 4:22–23; Deut. 14:1; 32:5; 32:8 (LXX); 2 Sam. 7:14; Job 1:6; Ps. 73:15; 82:6; Wisd. 18:13; Sir. 36:17; Isa. 53:10; Jer. 3:19; 31:20; Hos. 1:10; 2:1–2; 11:1

NT Background: Matt. 5:9, 45; Luke 6:35; 20:36; John 1:12–13; 3:5; 11:52; Acts 17:28–29; Rom. 6:3–11; 8:14–16; 9:8, 26; 1 Cor. 12:13; 2 Cor. 6:18; Gal. 3:25–4:7; Eph. 5:1; Phil. 2:15; Titus 3:4–7; Heb. 2:10; 12:5–7; 1 Pet. 1:3–5 (compare with 1 Pet. 3:21–22); 1:23–25; 2 Pet. 1:4; 1 John 3:1–2, 10; Rev. 21:7

Catechism: 1; 52; 169; 270; 422; 441–445; 505; 537; 556; 591; 654; 683; 690; 693; 694; 720; 736; 784; 980; 1110; 1129; 1141; **1213**; **1215**; 1250; 1257; 1262; 1263; **1265**; 1270; 1271; 1279; 1355; 1426; 1682–1683; 1709; 1996; 1997; 2009; 2021; 2026; 2345; 2639; 2717; 2740; 2769; 2782–2785; 2790; 2798; 2803; 2825

Related: BAPTISM: *Types*: Fruit of the Tree of Life; *Symbols:* Immersion; EUCHARIST: *Types*: Fruit of the Tree of Life

---

5 Baptism as "rebirth," "second birth," "divine adoption," etc., is by far the most common way of referring to that which is both symbolized and realized sacramentally in Baptism. Oftentimes references in passing to the "reborn" or those "born anew," etc., are made. In order to be as complete as possible, I have included almost all such references. Based on the constant, common, and close association in the Scriptures, the Catechism, and the Liturgy between rebirth and Baptism, such references have been supposed to be referring to rebirth through Baptism, even when Baptism is not explicitly mentioned. The references are organized according to what is said about those "reborn," etc. As these titles are so common, the end result also serves as a theological summary of the topic of divine adoption (and thus of Baptism) in general.

God's Plan to Gather Humanity into His Family

- God sent his Son in the fullness of time to redeem us so we might receive adoption as sons and daughters of God (Gal. 4:4–5; CCC 422; RM, CT, Weekdays of Christmas Time, Saturday, Entrance Antiphon)

- God, "in a plan of sheer goodness," has wished to gather together all men "into the unity of his family, the Church," as adopted children in his Son (CCC 1; *cf. also* CCC 441 for the use of "son of God" in the Old Testament, which cites Deut. 14:1; 32:8 [LXX]; Job 1:6; Exod. 4:22; Hos. 2:1; 11:1; Jer. 3:19; Sir. 36:11; Wisd. 18:13; 2 Sam. 7:14; Ps. 82:6.).

- Through the mystery of the Incarnation, the faithful are able to be born again of God (RM, St. Joachim and St. Anne [July 26], Prayer after Communion).

- The new birth of Baptism is "in God the Father, through his Son, in the Holy Spirit. For those who bear God's Spirit are led to the Word, that is, to the Son, and the Son presents them to the Father, and Father confers incorruptibility on them" (St. Irenæus, Dem. ap. 7: SCh 62, 41–42 cited in CCC 683).

By the Death and Resurrection of Christ

- The baptized are given a new life by being united to Christ's death and Resurrection (Rom. 6:3–11; CCC 1239; *cf. also* BAPTISM: *Symbols: Immersion*).

- By the one sacrifice offered once for all, Christ gained for himself a people by adoption (RM, OT.21.Su, Collect; RM, Masses and Prayers for Various Needs and Occasions, 17, Prayer over the Offerings).

- God confers the gift of new birth through the Resurrection of Jesus Christ (1 Pet. 1:3–5; RM, Solemn Blessings at the End of Mass, Easter Time, 1st blessing; RM, Appendices, Appendix II: Rite for the Blessing and Sprinkling of Water, Outside Easter Time, Hymn).

- Through the sacrifice of Christ on the cross and Paschal Mystery, the Church "is wondrously reborn" (RM, Easter Sunday, Mass during the Day, Prayer over the Offerings, 73).

Through Water and the Spirit in Baptism

• Through Baptism we are reborn in water and the Spirit (John 3:1–6; Titus 3:4–7; CCC 537; 694; 720; 1215; 1257; 1262; 2790; RM, Easter Vigil, Blessing of the baptismal water, 46; RM, Easter Vigil, Renewal of Baptismal Promises, Concluding Prayer, 55; RM, Eucharistic Prayer I, 87; RM, Ritual Masses, I, 3, A, Commemoration of the Newly Baptized, d; RM, Ritual Masses, I, 4, A, Solemn Blessing at the End of Mass, 1st blessing; RB 53; 56; 62; 70; RC 25; 33; RM, Baptism of the Lord, 1st Collect; RM, ET.3.Tu, Collect; LH, OT.15.We, 2R: St. Ambrose, On the Mysteries, 19–21.24.26–38: SC 25 bis, 164–170; LH, OT.15.Th, 2R: St. Ambrose, On the Mysteries, 29–30.34–35.37.42: SC 25 bis, 172–178; LH, OT.19. Fr, 2R: St. Pacian, Sermon on Baptism, 5–6: PL 13, 1092–1093; LH, CT.AE.Tu, 2R: St. Hippolytus, Sermon on the Epiphany, 2.6–8.10: PG 10, 854.858–859.862; LH, Baptism of the Lord, EP [=MP, EP2], Prayer; LH, Lent.5.Th, 2R: Vatican II, Lumen Gentium 9; LH, ET.2.Su, EP2, 4th intercession; LH, ET.3.We, 2R: St. Justin, First Apology, 61: PG 6, 419–422 in reference to John 3:5; LH, ET.6.Mo, 2R: Didymus of Alexandria, On the Trinity, 2, 12: PG 39, 667–674; RCIA 204).

The Liturgy of the Hours

You were told before not to believe only what you saw. This was to prevent you from saying: Is this the great mystery that eye has not seen nor ear heard nor man's heart conceived? I see the water I used to see every day; does this water in which I have often bathed without being sanctified really have the power to sanctify me? Learn from this that water does not sanctify without the Holy Spirit.

You have read that the three witnesses in baptism—the water, the blood and the Spirit—are one. This means that if you take away one of these the sacrament is not conferred. What is water without the cross of Christ? Only an ordinary element without sacramental effect. Again, without water there is no sacrament of rebirth: Unless a man is born again of water and the Spirit he cannot enter into the kingdom of God. The catechumen believes in the cross of the Lord with

which he too is signed, but unless he is baptized in the name
of the Father, and of the Son and of the Holy Spirit he cannot
receive the forgiveness of sins or the gift of spiritual grace.

The Syrian Naaman bathed seven times under the old
law, but you were baptized in the name of the Trinity. You
proclaimed your faith in the Father—recall what you did—
and the Son and the Spirit. Mark the sequence of events. In
proclaiming this faith you died to the world, you rose again to
God, and, as though buried to sin, you were reborn to eternal
life. Believe, then, that the water is not without effect.

*LH, OT.15.We, 2R: St. Ambrose,
On the Mysteries, 19–21.24.26–38: SC 25 bis, 164–170*

* Our first birth was through water; our second birth in Baptism is through
  water and the Spirit (CCC 694).
* The same Spirit through whom Jesus Christ was conceived and brought
  forth is the author of our second, spiritual birth (LH, Dec17, 2R: St. Leo
  the Great, Letter 31, 2–3: PL 54, 791–793; LH, Lent.4.Th, 2R: St. Leo the
  Great, Sermo 15, De passione Domini, 3–4: PL 54, 366–367; LH, ET.5.Fr,
  2R: Blessed Isaac of Stella, Sermo 42: PL 194, 1831–1832; LH, OT.13.Fr,
  2R: St. Augustine, On the Predestination of the Saints, 15, 30–31: PL 44,
  981–983).

Through Faith

* Baptism and faith are inseparable and we are saved through them (Mark
  16:15–16; CCC 977; 1236). Baptism is "the sacrament of faith," the sacramental entry into the life of faith (CCC 1236; 1226; 1249; 1253; 1258; *cf.
  also* CCC 1229; 977–978).
* In Baptism we enter into the faith of the Church, and this faith offers us
  eternal life (CCC 168; RCIA 50).
* The baptized are "justified by faith." This justification occurs "in Baptism,"
  where they are reborn into the Body of Christ, the Church (CCC 1271).
* Through faith we prepare ourselves for rebirth through Baptism. In Baptism
  the soul is reborn through faith (LH, OT.13.Sa, 2R: St. Cyril of Jerusalem,
  Catechetical Instruction, 1, 2–3.5–6: PG 33, 371.375–378).
* This new birth is "in the Holy Spirit through faith" (CCC 505).

Adopted as Children of God

- The baptized, having been reborn in Baptism, is a child of God (Gal. 3:27–4:7 [*cf. also* Rom. 8:15; 1 John 3:1]; CCC 1997; 2782; 2798; LH, ET.1.We, 2R: Easter homily by an ancient author, Sermo 35, 6–9: PL 17 [ed. 1879], 696–697; LH, ET.1.Th, 2R: St. Cyril of Jerusalem, Jerusalem Catecheses, 20:4–6, Mystagogica 2, 4–6: PG 33, 1079–1082; LH, ET.6.Mo, 2R: Didymus of Alexandria, On the Trinity, 2, 12: PG 39, 667–674; RM, Masses for the Dead, I, E, 1, Collect; RCIA 154B; 182; *cf.* CCC 683; LH, ET.4.Mo, 2R: St. Basil the Great, On the Holy Spirit, Ch. 15, 35–36: SC 17 bis, 364–370; *cf. also* RM, Ritual Masses, I, 3, A, Collect; RM, OT.19. Su, Collect; RM, St. Jerome Emiliani [Feb 8], Collect; LH, OT.19.Mo, 2R: Theodoret of Cyr, On the Incarnation, 26–27: PG 75, 1466–1467).
- The baptized becomes a son of God in the Son of God, Jesus Christ, and participates in his divine life (*cf.* CCC 1265; 1129; LH, CT.AE.Tu, 2R: St. Hippolytus, Sermon on the Epiphany, 2.6–8.10: PG 10, 854.858–859.862; LH, Dec31, 2R: St. Leo the Great, Sermo 6 in Nativitate Domini, 2–3, 5: PL 54, 213–216; LH, ET.1.Fr, 2R: St. Cyril of Jerusalem, Jerusalem Catecheses, 21:1–3, Mystagogica 3, 1–3: PG 33, 1087–1091; *cf. also* CCC 1; 52; 654; LH, OT.29.Sa, 2R: St. Peter Chrysologus, Sermo 117: PL 52, 520–521; LH, OT.33.Fr, 2R: St. John Eudes, On the Kingdom of Jesus, Pars 3, 4: Opera Omnia 1, 310–312).
- The waters of Baptism are the "waters of new birth" (RCIA 175B; *cf. also* RC 24).
- As adopted children of God, the baptized are able to share in the prayer of Jesus (CCC 2717; 2740; *cf.* Rom. 8:15–17).
- The Christian is able to truly pray the "Our Father" (CCC 2769; 1243; 2782–2783; 2798; RB 68; RCIA 178–180; LH, OT.11.Mo, 2R: St. Cyprian, On the Lord's Prayer, 8–9: CSEL 3, 271–272).

The Liturgy of the Hours

Here, then, is the grace conferred by these heavenly mysteries, the gift which Easter brings, the most longed for feast of the year; here are the beginnings of creatures newly formed: children born from the life-giving font of holy Church, born anew with the simplicity of little ones, and crying out with the evidence of a clean conscience. Chaste fathers and inviolate mothers accompany this new family, countless in number, born to new life through faith. As they emerge from the grace giving womb of the font, a blaze of candles burns brightly beneath the tree of faith. The Easter festival brings the grace of holiness from heaven to men. Through the repeated celebration of the sacred mysteries they receive the spiritual nourishment of the sacraments. Fostered at the very heart of holy Church, the fellowship of one community worships the one God, adoring the triple name of his essential holiness, and together with the prophet sings the psalm which belongs to this yearly festival: This is the day the Lord has made; let us rejoice and be glad. And what is this day? It is the Lord Jesus Christ himself, the author of light, who brings the sunrise and the beginning of life, saying of himself: I am the light of day; whoever walks in daylight does not stumble. That is to say, whoever follows Christ in all things will come by this path to the throne of eternal light.

LH, ET.1.We, 2R: Easter homily by an ancient author,
Sermo 35, 6–9: PL 17 [ed. 1879], 696–697

- The baptized descends with Christ into the water of the Jordan, and arising, is reborn. He hears the words of the Father, "This is my beloved Son" (CCC 535; *cf. also* RM, Baptism of the Lord, 1st Collect).
- Jesus was "reborn sacramentally" and "born in mystery" ("renatus est sacramentis . . . per mysterium generatus") in the Jordan River[6] to sanctify and

6 Theologically this image could be problematic if misunderstood as affirming that Jesus was "adopted" at the moment of his baptism (the heresy of Adoptionism). This is not, however, what is being affirmed by St. Maximus (fifth century), who shortly thereafter states that "Christ the Lord does all these things: in the column of fire he went through the sea before the sons of Israel; so now, in the column of his body, he goes through baptism before the Christian people" (compare with Jude 5 in the Nestle Aland 28th Edition, which reads: "Jesus, who saved a people out of the land of Egypt . . ." [Ἰησοῦς λαὸν ἐκ γῆς Αἰγύπτου σώσας]).

This description implies that St. Maximus believed in the eternal pre-existence of "Christ the Lord," an idea incompatible with Adoptionism. Although calling "Christ the Lord" the "column of fire" that went before the Israelites is not as theologically precise as speaking of "the Son," the use of "Christ the Lord" indicates this is not an Adoptionist text (*cf. also* BAPTISM: *Types:* Pillar of Cloud and Fire).

The idea of Christ being "born in mystery" in the Jordan River could also be understood in light of CCC 537, which states that Jesus anticipated his death and Resurrection through his baptism in

purify the waters and lead the way (LH, CT.AE.Fr, 2R: St. Maximus of Turin, Sermn 100, De sancta Epiphania 1, 3: CCL 23, 398–400; *cf. also* RCIA 168B).

• The baptized are added to the number of God's adopted children (RM, Celebration of the Passion of the Lord, Solemn Intercessions, IV; CCC 1279).

• The baptized become a "'partaker of the divine nature' (2 Cor. 5:17; 2 Pet. 1:4; *cf.* Gal. 4:5–7)" (CCC 1265; *cf.* CCC 460). They partake of the divine nature by being conformed to Christ (CCC 1129; LH, Christmas, 2R: St. Leo the Great, Sermo 1 in Nativitate Domini, 1–3: PL 54, 190–193).

• As Father, God cares for the needs of his adopted children and forgives their sins (CCC 270; *cf.* 2 Cor. 6:18; Matt. 6:32; *cf. also* RCIA 97D; 97E).

• This gift of divine adoption is a completely free gift, apart from any merits (LH, OT.13.Fr, 2R: St. Augustine, On the Predestination of the Saints, 15, 30–31: PL 44, 981–983), something made particularly clear in the Baptism of infants (CCC 1250; 1996).

• Those born in slavery to "ancient sin" are brought through the waters of regeneration to become adopted children (RM, Lent.4.Su, Preface).

• The baptized are called to live as "children of the light" (RCIA 168B; *cf. also* BAPTISM: *Symbols:* Illumination / Light / Candle).

• Through filial adoption the Christian is given the ability to follow Christ's example and is made capable of doing good (CCC 1709). Through the grace of adoption, those reborn in Baptism are made co-heirs with Christ and can merit through his gift (CCC 2009; 2026; *cf.* Rom. 8:15–17; Titus 3:4–7).

• By means of the spirit of adoption as children the believer in some way already "sees" God by participating in the life of the Son (LH, Adv.3.We, 2R: St. Irenaeus, Treatise Against Heresies, Book 4, 20, 4–5: SC 100, 634–640).

New Creation

• Baptism brings about a new creation (2 Cor. 5:17–18 in light of Rom. 6:3 and Gal. 3:27; Gal. 6:15 in light of Col. 2:11–12; Titus 3:5; CCC 1999; *cf. also* CCC 281, 536–537, 1224; LH, Christmas, 2R: St. Leo the Great, Sermo 1 in Nativitate Domini, 1–3: PL 54, 190–193; LH, Jan3, MP [=EP],

---

the Jordan. The Resurrection could be compared to a second birth, which Jesus anticipates "in mystery" when he rises up out of the waters of the Jordan River.

Prayer [Latin]; LH, Baptism of the Lord, 2R: St. Gregory of Nazianzus, Oratio 39 in Sancta Lumina, 14–16.20: PG 36, 350–351.354.358–359; LH, ET.5.Mo, 2R: St. Gregory of Nyssa, Oratio 1 in Christi resurrectionem: PG 46, 603–606.626–627; LH, ET.6.Mo, 2R: Didymus of Alexandria, On the Trinity, 2, 12: PG 39, 667–674).

- The baptized, having been reborn, is made new, or become a "new creature" (CCC 1265), or a "new man," or is born "to new life" (*cf.* LH, St. George [Apr 23], 2R: St. Peter Damian, Sermo 3, De sancto Georgio: PL 144, 567–571; LH, OT.19.Fr, 2R: St. Pacian, Sermon on Baptism, 5–6: PL 13, 1092–1093; RM, ET.3.Sa, Collect; RM, ET.5.Su, Collect; RCIA 174B, 4th intercession; 175A; 175B).

- The catechumen may choose a new name. One of the following readings may be chosen for the ceremony of the giving of the new name: Gen. 17:1–7 ("Your name shall be Abraham."), Isa. 62:1–5 ("You will be called by a new name"), Rev. 3:11–13 ("I will write on him . . . my own new name"), Matt. 16:13–18 ("You are Peter"), or John 1:40–42 ("You shall be called Cephas" (RCIA 200–202; CCC 2156).

- The old Adam is buried in the waters of Baptism; the new man is born in grace (LH, Lent.1.Th, 2R: St. Asterius of Amasea, Homily 13: PG 40, 355–358.362).

- The transformation of the water into wine at the wedding at Cana (John 2:1–11) symbolizes the transformation of the old covenant into the new. As the water is transformed into wine from within, in a hidden way, so the baptized is changed from within in a hidden way by rebirth as a child of God (LH, CT.AE.Sa, 2R: Faustus of Riez, Sermo 5, de Epiphania 2: PLS 3, 560–562).

- Those reborn in Baptism die to their old life of sin and are born to a new life, like a runner who changes direction (LH, Lent.HW.Tu, 2R: St. Basil, On the Holy Spirit, Ch. 15, 35: PG 32, 127–130).

- The baptized receive the seed of eternal life (RM, Appendices, V, 11, 4a; LH, OT.19.Fr, 2R: St. Pacian, Sermon on Baptism, 5–6: PL 13, 1092–1093; *cf.* 1 Cor. 3:6–9).

- Through the rebirth of Baptism, all sins are washed away, original and personal, as well as any punishment for sins (CCC 1263; *cf. also* RM, Eucharistic Prayer I, 87; RCIA 161). Through the new birth of Baptism one becomes "'holy and without blemish' just as the Church herself, the

Bride of Christ, is 'holy and without blemish'" (CCC 1426, citing Eph. 1:4 and 5:27; *cf. also* BAPTISM: *Symbols:* Washing).

- Those reborn in Baptism become a "temple of the Holy Spirit" (CCC 1265; 1279; 1 Cor. 6:19; LH, Christmas, 2R: St. Leo the Great, Sermo 1 in Nativitate Domini, 1–3: PL 54, 190–193; RCIA 94A; 97H) and through the Spirit can bear great fruit (CCC 736; LH, OT.25.Sa, 2R: St. Hilary, Discourse on Psalm 64, 14–15: CSEL 22, 245–246).

- The baptized, by their second birth and their anointing of the Holy Spirit, are consecrated to be a holy priesthood (CCC 784 citing Rev. 1:6; CCC 1141 citing 1 Pet. 2:4–5; CCC 1279).

- All those reborn in Christ are a chosen race and a royal priesthood (RM, Lent.5.Sa, Collect).

- Through the grace of adoption, the baptized are chosen to be children of light (RM, OT.13.Su, Collect; LH, Psalter.1.We, MP, Prayer; RCIA 94C).

- Even here on earth, those reborn through Baptism receive greater honor than the angels (LH, ET.6.Mo, 2R: Didymus of Alexandria, On the Trinity, 2, 12: PG 39, 667–674).

- This new life given in the waters of Baptism is spiritual (RB 54).

Incorporate into the Body of Christ, the Church

- By rebirth in Baptism the faithful are incorporated into the Body of Christ (which, in many of the following passages, is also explicitly referred to as the Church) (1 Cor. 12:13; Gal. 3:27–28; Col. 1:18; CCC 1213; 1279; RCIA 24; LH, OT.13.Th, 2R: St. Jerome, Sermon on Ps. 41 addressed to newly baptized: CCL 78, 542–544; RCIA 97A; 97B; 97G; LH, Adv.2.Sa, 2R: Bl. Isaac of Stella, Sermo 51: PL 194, 1862–1863, 1865; LH, ET.5.Fr, 2R: Blessed Isaac of Stella, Sermo 42: PL 194, 1831–1832; LH, Pentecost, 2R: St. Irenaeus, Treatise Against Heresies, Book 3, 17, 1–3: SC 34, 302–306; LH, CT.BE.Mo, 2R [Latin Edition: Jan 2]: St. Basil the Great, On the Holy Spirit, Ch. 26, Nn. 61, 64: PG 32, 179–182.186).

- The Church herself is established ("sancta fundata est Ecclesia") through the rebirth and renewal of Baptism and through the Eucharist (LH, Lent. HW.Fr, 2R: St. John Chrysostom, Catecheses 3, 13–19: SC 50, 174–177; *cf.* BAPTISM: *Types:* Water from the Side of Christ).

- The first birth brings children into the world, while the second birth in Baptism gives increase to the Church (RM, Ritual Mass for the Celebration of Marriage, A, Preface).
- There is a sacramental bond of unity among those reborn as Christians in Baptism (CCC 1271).
- Through rebirth in Baptism God has united many nations (RM, ET.1.Th, Collect), uniting Gentiles and Jews (LH, Lent.5.Th, 2R: Vatican II, Lumen Gentium 9).
- By the outpouring of the grace of adoption, God gives increase to the children of the promise of Abraham (RM, Easter Vigil, Prayer after the 2nd reading [Gen. 22:1–18], 25) and to the Patriarchs (RM, Easter Vigil, Prayer after the 4th reading [Isa. 54:5–14], 27).
- All those reborn obtain "the privilege of Israel by merit of faith" and partake of the Spirit (RM, Easter Vigil, Prayer after the 3rd reading [Exod. 14:15–15:1], 26).
- The Church is called to live in a "spirit of adoption" and thus render God undivided service (RM, Easter Vigil, Collect after the Glory, 32).
- Having been reborn, the baptized share in the mission of the Church (CCC 1213; 1270).
- The baptized is given access to the other sacraments (CCC 1213). Those reborn in Baptism who believe the faith and live in accordance with the teachings of Christ can participate in the Eucharist (LH, ET.3.We, 2R: St. Justin, First Apology, 61: PG 6, 419–422; LH, ET.3.Su, 2R: St. Justin Martyr, First Apology, 66–67: PG 6, 427–431).

Born of the Church as Mother

- As the faithful receive their new life through the Church, she is their mother. God alone, however, is the author of their salvation (CCC 169; cf. Rev. 12:17).
- The children born from the fruitful marriage between Christ and the Church are nurtured in the womb of the Church and born of Christ at the font of Baptism (LH, OT.19.Fr, 2R: St. Pacian, Sermon on Baptism, 5–6: PL 13, 1092–1093; cf. also LH, Adv.2.Sa, 2R: Bl. Isaac of Stella, Sermo 51: PL 194, 1862–1863, 1865).

- Reborn through the Church in Baptism, Christians become living temples of Christ (LH, Dedication of St. John Lateran [Nov 9], 2R: St. Caesarius of Arles, Sermo 229, 1–3: CCL 104, 905–908).
- The baptized are children in Christ and the new offspring of the Church (LH, ET.2.Su, 2R: St. Augustine, Sermo 8 in octava Paschae 1.4: PL 46, 838.841; LH, ET.2.We, 2R: St. Leo the Great, Sermo 12 de Passione, 3, 6–7: PL 54, 355–357).
- This new life is virginally conceived, as it is entirely the Spirit's gift to man (CCC 505 citing John 1:13).
- As mother, the Church accompanies those born sacramentally in her womb throughout their life, until surrendering them at the end of their lives "into the Father's hands" (CCC 1683).

Fulfillment in Eternal Life

- The fulfillment of the new birth begun at Baptism is in heaven, where the baptized will be definitively conformed to Christ and clothed with the nuptial garment (CCC 1682; cf. also BAPTISM: Symbols: White Garment / Wedding Garment).
- Even now those reborn share in the blessings of rebirth and resurrection (LH, Christ the King, 2R: Origen, On Prayer, 25: PG 11, 495–499).
- The Transfiguration of Christ prefigures our full adoption to sonship in heaven (RM, The Transfiguration of the Lord, Collect, understood in light of the Preface and Communion Antiphon of the same Mass; idem for LH, Transfiguration of the Lord, EP [=OR, MP, EP2], Prayer).
- The faithful are reborn as citizens of heaven (RM, Ritual Mass For the Second Scrutiny, Collect; LH, OT.29.Sa, 2R: St. Peter Chrysologus, Sermo 117: PL 52, 520–521).
- Those who did not approach the fountain of rebirth will stand on the left hand (of Christ on judgment day), with their sins clinging to them like a goatskin (LH, OT.13.Sa, 2R: St. Cyril of Jerusalem, Catechetical Instruction, 1, 2–3.5–6: PG 33, 371.375–378).
- Those who have received divine adoption "look forward in confident hope to the rejoicing of the day of resurrection" (RM, ET.3.Su, Collect).
- Baptized children have been adopted as children of God, and those who die are already in heaven (RM, Masses for the Dead, For the Funeral of a Baptized Child, 1, Collect).

- God opens "wide the gates of the heavenly Kingdom to those reborn" in Baptism (RM, ET.3.Tu, Collect; LH, ET.3.Tu, MP [=EP], Prayer).
- Those reborn in Baptism have had the "way open before them to return to their native land, from which they had been exiled" (LH, Lent.4.Th, 2R: St. Leo the Great, Sermo 15, De passione Domini, 3–4: PL 54, 366–367).
- God through the regenerating power of Baptism confers "heavenly life" and renders the baptized "capable of immortality by justifying them" (RM, ET.5.Sa, Collect).

The Liturgy of the Hours

No one, however weak, is denied a share in the victory of the cross. No one is beyond the help of the prayer of Christ. His prayer brought benefit to the multitude that raged against him. How much more does it bring to those who turn to him in repentance.

Ignorance has been destroyed, obstinacy has been overcome. The sacred blood of Christ has quenched the flaming sword that barred access to the tree of life. The age-old night of sin has given place to the true light.

The Christian people are invited to share the riches of paradise. All who have been reborn have the way open before them to return to their native land, from which they had been exiled. Unless indeed they close off for themselves the path that could be opened before the faith of a thief.

LH, Lent.4.Th, 2R: St. Leo the Great,
Sermo 15, De passione Domini, 3–4: PL 54, 366–367

SIGN OF THE CROSS

Cf. CONFIRMATION: *Symbols*: Sign of the Cross

TURNING TOWARDS THE EAST

OT Background: Gen. 2:8; Num. 2:3; Isa. 60:19; Ezek. 43:1–5; Zech. 14:4; Mal. 4:2

NT Background: Matt. 24:27; Mark 16:2; Luke 1:78–79; John 1:9; 8:12; 1 John 1:5; Rev. 22:16

Catechism: 1240

Related: BAPTISM: *Symbols:* Illumination / Light / Candle

- Having renounced Satan facing west, where the sun sets, the catechumen turns toward the east, where the sun rises, a symbol of turning toward Christ, and professes his faith (LH, OT.15.Su, 2R: St. Ambrose, On the Mysteries, 1–7: SC 25 bis, 156–158).
- Turning to the east symbolizes looking to Christ, the Dayspring, the sun of righteousness, and walking in the light of faith (LH, Lent.4.Mo, 2R: Origen, Homily on Leviticus, 9, 5.10: PG 12, 515.523).
- In the Eastern Catholic liturgies, the catechumen turns toward the east and is baptized (CCC 1240).

WASHING

OT Background:[7] Exod. 30:20–21; 40:32; Lev. 8:5–6; 14:8–9; 15:1–33; 16:3–4; Ps. 51:1–2, 7–10; Isa. 1:16–20; 4:3–4; Ezek. 16:3–9; 36:24–29; Zech. 13:1 (*cf.* 12:10)

NT Background: John 2:6; 9:7–15; 13:10; Acts 22:16; 1 Cor. 6:11; Eph. 5:25–27; Titus 3:5; Heb. 10:22; 1 Pet. 3:20–21; Rev. 7:14; 22:14

Catechism: 1148; **1215**; 1216; **1227**; 1228; 1425; 1617; 1987; 2813

Related: BAPTISM: *Types:* Healing of Naaman; Healing at the Sheep Gate Pool; *Symbols:* Fountain of Water; Immersion; Liberation; Second Birth; White Garment / Wedding Garment; PENANCE: *Symbols:* Washing

Through the Saving Grace of Christ

- It is the sanctifying power of the death of Christ (RM, Palm Sunday, Preface; RM, Baptism of the Lord, Prayer over the Offerings; RM, Good Friday, Hymn Crux Fidelis, 20) and of the Resurrection which washes sins away (RM, Easter Vigil, Easter Proclamation, 19) (*cf. also* PENANCE: *Symbols:* Washing).

---

7 This topic is too broad to include a wide selection of references to background texts. A sampling of some of the more significant references to the topic of washing are included.

- We are cleansed by the saving baptism of the Passion (RM, St. James Apostle [July 25], Prayer over the Offerings; *cf.* Luke 12:50).
- The cross of Christ transforms water into a spiritual bath that is "sweet, ready for the giving of grace" (LH, OT.15.Tu, 2R [Latin]: St. Ambrose, On the Mysteries, 12–16.19: SC 25 bis, 162–164).
- In Baptism, the neophyte is spiritually cleansed by water sprinkled from the hyssop that was sanctified when it touched Christ's lips on the cross (LH, St. Cyril of Jerusalem [Mar 18], 2R: St. Cyril of Jerusalem, Catechetical Instruction 3, 1–3: PG 33, 426–430).
- Christ cleansed the Church offering himself up to make her holy with a bath of water accompanied by the life giving word (LH, Lent.1[=3, 5].Mo, EP, 2nd intercession [Latin]).
- In Christ's baptism in the Jordan he washed away the sin of the world (LH, CT.AE.Mo, 2R: St. Peter Chrysologus, Sermo 160: PL 52, 620–622) and sanctified the water of Baptism (LH, CT.AE.Fr, 2R: St. Maximus of Turin, Sermo 100, de sancta Epiphania 1, 3: CCL 23, 398–400).

Sins are Washed Away

- Baptism washes sin away (Acts 22:16; RM, All Souls' Day, Mass 2, Prayer over the Offerings; RBOC 25; LH, Baptism of the Lord, 2R: St. Gregory of Nazianzus, Oratio 39 in Sancta Lumina, 14–16.20: PG 36, 350–351.354.358–359 explaining Ps. 51:2.7; LH, OT.19.Fr, 2R: St. Pacian, Sermon on Baptism, 5–6: PL 13, 1092–1093; LH, OT.19.Sa, 2R: St. Pacian, Sermon on Baptism, 6–7: PL 13, 1093–1094; LH, Lent.HW.Tu, 2R: St. Basil, On the Holy Spirit, Ch. 15, 35: PG 32, 127–130 in reference to Ps. 51:7; LH, ET.1.Th, 2R: St. Cyril of Jerusalem, Jerusalem Catecheses, 20:4–6, Mystagogica 2, 4–6: PG 33, 1079–1082; LH, ET.3.Mo, 2R: St. Bede the Venerable, Commentary on 1 Pet., Ch. 2: PL 93, 50–51; LH, ET.3.We, 2R: St. Justin, First Apology, 61: PG 6, 419–422 in reference to Isa. 1:16–20 being used as a reading for Baptism; LH, ET.4.Mo, 2R, Resp).
- The neophyte is washed clean by the waters of Baptism (1 Cor. 6:11; Eph. 5:25–27; CCC 1425; RCIA 204; RM, Easter Vigil, Prayer after the 6th reading, 29; RM, Easter Vigil, 46; RM, ET.2.Su, Collect; RM, Pentecost, Vigil Mass, 1st Prayer after the 3rd reading, 7; RM, All Souls' Day, Mass 2, Prayer over the Offerings; RM, Masses for the Dead, For the Funeral, D, Prayer over the Offerings; RM, Masses for the Dead, On the

Anniversary, During Easter Time, Prayer over the Offerings; RM, Masses for the Dead, Various Commemorations, B, 7, Collect; RM, Ritual Masses, For the Conferral of Baptism, A, Intercessions of Eucharistic Prayer III; LH, Baptism of the Lord, EP, Magn; LH, CT.AE.Tu, 2R: St. Hippolytus, Sermon on the Epiphany, 2.6–8.10: PG 10, 854.858–859.862).

- The crimson stains of sin are washed away in the saving waters of Baptism, leaving the baptized white as wool (LH, Lent.HW.Su, 2R: St. Andrew of Crete, Oratio 9 in Ramos Palmarum: PG 97, 990–994; *cf. also* BAPTISM: *Symbols:* White Garment / Wedding Garment).

- Through the new birth of Baptism one becomes "'holy and without blemish' just as the Church herself, the Bride of Christ, is 'holy and without blemish'" (Eph. 1:4 and 5:27, cited in CCC 1426).

- Having been cleansed in the baptismal font, the baptized can offer himself up as a sacrifice to God in the Tent of Christ, which is the Church (LH, St. George [Apr 23], 2R: St. Peter Damian, Sermo 3, De sancto Georgio: PL 144, 567–571).

- The martyr Pudens in Carthage was washed in a baptism of blood when he was covered with his own blood, devoured by lions (LH, Saints Perpetua and Felicity [Mar 7], 2R: From the story of the death of the holy martyrs of Carthage, Chap. 18, 20–21: edit. van Beek, Noviomagi, 1936, pp. 42.46–52).

Baptism as a Bath

- Baptism is a bath (Eph. 5:26; Titus 3:5; CCC 1216; 1227; 1228; 1291; 537; 1617; 1587; LH, ET.3.We, 2R [Latin]: St. Justin, First Apology, 61: PG 6, 419–422) because it washes (CCC 1216 citing St. Gregory of Nazianzus, Oratio 40, 3–4: PG 36, 361C), it purifies, justifies and sanctifies (CCC 1227; *cf.* 1 Cor. 6:11; Titus 3:5).

- The bath of Baptism gives life (Titus 3:5–7; CCC 1228; LH, Lent.1[=3, 5].Sa, MP, 1st intercession [Latin]; LH, ET.3.Su, 2R [Latin]: St. Justin Martyr, First Apology, 66–67: PG 6, 427–431; LH, OT.13.Sa, 2R [Latin]: St. Cyril of Jerusalem, Catechetical Instruction, 1, 2–3.5–6: PG 33, 371.375–378).

- The bath of Baptism strengthens the footsteps of faith (LH, CT.AE.Fr, 2R: St. Maximus of Turin, Sermo 100, De sancta Epiphania 1, 3: CCL 23, 398–400).

- Through the bath of Baptism Christians are united in Christ Jesus like different grains of wheat that become one loaf of bread (LH, Pentecost, 2R [Latin]: St. Irenaeus, *Treatise Against Heresies*, Book 3, 17, 1–3: SC 34, 302–306).
- Baptism is a nuptial bath in which Christ washes the Church to present her to himself as a spotless Bride ready for the wedding feast (Eph. 5:26–27; CCC 1617).

- In this bath of regeneration the baptized is divinized, made an adopted son of God, co-heir with Christ (LH, CT.AE.Tu, 2R [Latin]: St. Hippolytus, *Sermon on the Epiphany*, 2.6–8.10: PG 10, 854.858–859.862).
- Through the bath of Baptism and Penance sin is washed clean (LH, Common of Apostles, MP, 5th intercession [Latin]; LH, Conversion of St. Paul [Jan 25], MP, 5th intercession [Latin]; LH, Chair of Peter [Feb 22], MP, 5th intercession [Latin]; LH, St. Philip and St. James [May 3], MP, 5th intercession [Latin]; LH, St. Andrew [Nov 30], MP, 5th intercession [Latin]).

WEDDING FEAST

cf. BAPTISM: *Symbols*: White Garment / Wedding Garment.

WHITE GARMENT / WEDDING GARMENT

OT Background:[8]

God's garments: Ps. 93:1; 104:1–2; Dan. 7:9

God clothes: Gen. 3:21; Ezek. 16:8–10

Liturgical garments: Exod. 28:42–43; 39:27–29; Lev. 16:3–4, 32; 2 Sam. 6:14; 1 Chron. 15:27; 2 Chron. 6:41; Ps. 132:9

Righteousness / wisdom as a garment: 2 Chron. 6:41; Job 29:14; Ps. 51:7; 132:9; Sir. 6:29–31; Isa. 1:18; 59:17; 61:3, 10

Other: Exod. 24:8; Eccles. 9:8; Song 1:5, 15; 8:5 (LXX); Isa. 52:1; Zech. 3:3–5; 1 Macc. 2:10–11

NT Background:

Jesus' garments: Matt. 17:2; Mark 9:3; Luke 9:29

---

8 Clothing imagery abounds throughout Scripture, to indicate both holiness and sinfulness. A sampling of some of the more significant references to the topic of white garments or garments related to salvation are included here.

Garments of the righteous: Matt. 13:43; 22:11–13; Rom. 13:12, 14; 1 Cor. 15:53; Gal. 3:27; Eph. 4:22–24; Col. 3:9–10; Rev. 3:4–5, 18; 4:4; 6:11; 19:8, 14; 21:2; 22:14

Angels' garments: Matt. 28:3; Mark 16:5; Luke 24:4; Acts 10:30; Rev. 7:9–14; 15:6

Catechism: 1216; **1243**; 1244; 1304; 2839

Related: BAPTISM: *Symbols:* Illumination / Light / Candle; Washing; CONFIRMATION: *Symbols:* Seal

- The baptized have "put on Christ" or been "clothed in Christ" (Gal. 3:27; CCC 124; RB 63; LH, OT.13.Th, 2R: St. Jerome, Sermon on Ps. 41 addressed to newly baptized: CCL 78, 542–544; LH, ET.1.Fr, 2R: St. Cyril of Jerusalem, Jerusalem Catecheses, 21:1–3, Mystagogica 3, 1–3: PG 33, 1087–1091; LH, ET.2.Su, 2R: St. Augustine, Sermo 8 in octava Paschae 1.4: PL 46, 838.841 in reference to Gal. 3:27–28 and Rom. 13:14)
- The white garment symbolizes the wedding garment worn by the Bride to the marriage supper of the Lamb (CCC 1244; LH, St. Cyril of Jerusalem [Mar 18], 2R: St. Cyril of Jerusalem, Catechetical Instruction 3, 1–3: PG 33, 426–430; *cf.* Rev. 21:2).

The Liturgy of the Hours

Let the heavenly angels rejoice! Let those who are to be wedded to a spiritual spouse prepare themselves. . . . Through a sincere faith prepare yourselves so that you may be free to receive the Holy Spirit. Through your penance begin to wash your garments; then, summoned to the spouse's bedchamber, you will be found spotless.

Heralds proclaim the bridegroom's invitation. All mankind is called to the wedding feast, for he is a generous lover. Once the crowd has assembled, the bridegroom decides who will enter the wedding feast. This is a figure for baptism.

Give your name at his gate and enter. I hope that none of you will later hear the words: "Friend, how did you enter without a wedding garment?" Rather may all of you hear the words: "Well done, my good and faithful servant. . . . Enter into the joy of your Lord."

Up to this point in the history of salvation you have stood outside the gate. Now I hope you will all hear the words: "The king has brought me into his chambers. My soul rejoices in my God. He has clothed me in the garment of salvation and in the cloak of joy. He has made me a bridegroom by placing a crown on my head. He has made me a bride by adorning me with jewels and golden ornaments." . . .

My brothers, this is a truly great occasion. Approach it with caution. You are standing in front of God and in the presence of the host of angels. The Holy Spirit is about to impress his seal on each of your souls. You are about to be pressed into the service of a great king.

LH, St. Cyril of Jerusalem (Mar 18),
2R: St. Cyril of Jerusalem,
Catechetical Instruction 3, 1–3: PG 33, 426–430

- The fulfillment of the new birth begun at Baptism is in heaven, where the baptized will be definitively conformed to Christ and clothed with the nuptial garment (CCC 1682; *cf. also* CCC 1617; RM, ET.1.Sa, Collect; RM, ET.6.Fr, 1st Collect; RM, St. Aloysius Gonzaga [June 21], Prayer over the Offerings).
- The white garment signifies the dignity of one who shares in Christ's divine life (RB 63; *cf. also* CCC 1003–1004).
- The white garment of Baptism symbolizes that the baptized (LH, OT.15. Th, 2R: St. Ambrose, On the Mysteries, 29–30.34–35.37.42: SC 25 bis, 172–178):
  - has "cast off the clothing of sin and put on the chaste covering of innocence" (in reference to Ps. 51:7);
  - has been made clean in terms of the law, having been sprinkled in the blood of the Lamb, as Moses purified the people by sprinkling them with the blood of the lamb (*cf.* Exod. 24:8);
  - has been made clean in terms of the Gospel, being united to Christ whose garments became white as snow when he revealed the glory of his resurrection (*cf.* Matt. 17:2, Mark 9:3, and Luke 9:29);
  - has been made whiter than snow through the forgiveness of sins (in reference to Isa. 1:18)

- has been made beautiful through grace, in spite of the frailty of nature and in spite of sin (in reference to Song 1:5; 8:5 [LXX]);
- has become the object of love of Christ (in reference to Song 1:15), who put on "filthy garments" (in reference to Zech. 3:3–5) so that his beloved Church might be clothed in white.

- The baptized are lambs who have come to the fountain of water and are full of light; they are the great multitude standing before the throne of the Lamb, dressed in white and with palms in their hands (LH, ET.1.Th, 2R, Resp in reference to Rev. 7:9–14; *cf. also* BAPTISM: *Symbols:* Fountain of Water; Illumination / Light / Candle).
- Baptism clothes in the garment of immortality (LH, OT.19.Mo, 2R: Theodoret of Cyr, On the Incarnation, 26–27: PG 75, 1466–1467; RCIA 97E; LH, Baptism of the Lord, EP, Magn [Latin]; RM, ET.1.Sa, Collect; RM, ET.6.Fr, 1st Collect; *cf.* 1 Cor. 15:53).
- The baptized themselves, having been washed white in Baptism, are the garments which should be spread before Christ in his entry into Jerusalem (LH, Lent.HW.Su, 2R: St. Andrew of Crete, Oratio 9 in Ramos Palmarum: PG 97, 990–994).

The Liturgy of the Hours

So let us spread before his feet [Christ's feet as he enters Jerusalem on Palm Sunday], not garments or soulless olive branches, which delight the eye for a few hours and then wither, but ourselves, clothed in his grace, or rather, clothed completely in him. We who have been baptized into Christ must ourselves be the garments that we spread before him. Now that the crimson stains of our sins have been washed away in the saving waters of baptism and we have become white as pure wool, let us present the conqueror of death, not with mere branches of palms but with the real rewards of his victory. Let our souls take the place of the welcoming branches as we join today in the children's holy song: "Blessed is he who comes in the name of the Lord. Blessed is the king of Israel."

LH, Lent.HW.Su, 2R: St. Andrew of Crete,
Oratio 9 in Ramos Palmarum: PG 97, 990–994

- In Baptism the indelible spiritual mark, or "character," which is imprinted on the soul is compared to being "clothed" with power from on high so as to be Christ's witness (CCC 1304 in reference to Luke 24:48–49).
- The baptized is called to put on the various "garments" of the virtues, to leave aside the garments of the old man and strive to put on the new man (LH, St. George [Apr 23], 2R: St. Peter Damian, Sermo 3, De sancto Georgio: PL 144, 567–571 in reference to 2 Chron. 6:41; *cf. also* Ps. 73:6; Mal. 2:16; Eph. 4:22–24; Col. 3:9–10).
- The sacrament "veils our shame" and thus is called "clothing" (CCC 1216, citing St. Gregory of Nazianzus, Oratio 40, 3–4: PG 36, 361C).

CONFIRMATION

Definition: One of the ensemble of the sacraments of initiation into the Church, together with Baptism and Eucharist. Confirmation completes the grace of Baptism by a special outpouring of the gifts of the Holy Spirit, which seal or "confirm" the baptized in union with Christ and equip them for active participation in the worship and apostolic life of the Church (Glossary of the Catechism of the Catholic Church).

TYPES

Note: The Catechism of the Catholic Church presents Confirmation as a fulfillment of the promises announced by the prophets "that the Spirit of the Lord would rest on the hoped-for Messiah for his saving mission (Cf. Isa. 11:2; 61:1; Luke 4:16–22)" (CCC 1286). This Spirit would in turn be communicated to the whole messianic people (cf. CCC 1287, which cites Ezek. 36:25–27 and Joel 3:1–2). This promise was fulfilled "first on Easter Sunday and then more strikingly at Pentecost (Cf. John 20:22; Acts 2:1–4)" (CCC 1287).

The Sacrament of Confirmation, practiced from apostolic times through the laying on of hands to impart the gift of the Spirit, perpetuates the grace of Pentecost (cf. CCC 1288, which cites Acts 8:15–17, 19:5–6, and Heb. 6:2).

Although the Sacrament of Confirmation fulfills the promises announced by the prophets in the Old Testament, the Bible, the Catechism, and the liturgy do not present the Sacrament of Confirmation as being prefigured by types. St. Thomas Aquinas explains why there are no types of the Sacrament of Confirmation in the Old Testament: "Confirmation is the sacrament of the fullness of grace: wherefore there could be nothing corresponding to it in the Old Law, since 'the Law brought nothing to perfection' (Heb. 7:19)" (Summa Theologiæ III, Q. 72, a. 1, ad. 2).

The closest thing to a type with respect to Confirmation is the anointing of priests, prophets, and kings in the Old Testament. The Catechism, however, relates this more directly with the anointing of Baptism (cf. CCC 1241–1242 and 783–784, for example) than with that of Confirmation, and oftentimes speaks of the baptized as priests, prophets, and kings. The character imparted in Baptism, prefigured by the anointing of priests, prophets, and kings in the Old Testament, is brought to perfection through the anointing of Confirmation. In light of these considerations, this type is presented under BAPTISM: *Types*: Anointing of Priests, Prophets, and Kings.

SYMBOLS

ANOINTING

Definition: A symbol of the Holy Spirit, whose "anointing" of Jesus as Messiah fulfilled the prophecies of the Old Testament. Christ (in Hebrew *Messiah*) means the one "anointed" by the Holy Spirit. Anointing is the sacramental sign of Confirmation, called Chrismation in the Churches of the East. Anointings form part of the liturgical rites of the catechumenate, and of the Sacraments of Baptism and Holy Orders (Glossary of the Catechism of the Catholic Church; *cf. also* Chrism; Christ; Jesus Christ; Messiah).

OT Background:

Temple and related: Gen. 28:18–22; 31:13; 35:14; Exod. 29:21, 36; 30:22–33; 40:9–11; Lev. 7:10–11; 8:10–11, 30; Num. 7:1, 10, 84, 88; Sir. 35:6; Dan. 9:24

Priest: Exod. 28:41; 29:7, 21, 29; 30:30–33; 40:12–15; Lev. 4:3, 5, 16; 6:20, 22; 7:12, 36; 8:12, 30; 10:7; 16:32; 21:10, 12; Num. 3:3; 35:25; 1 Chron. 29:22; Ps. 133:2; Sir. 45:15; Zech. 4:14; 2 Macc. 1:10

King: Judg. 9:8, 15; 1 Sam. 2:10, 35; 9:16; 10:1; 12:3, 5; 15:1, 17; 16:1–13; 24:6, 10; 26:9, 11, 16, 23; 2 Sam. 1:14, 16; 2:4, 7; 3:39; 5:3, 17; 12:7; 19:10, 21; 22:51; 23:1; 1 Kings 1:34, 39, 45; 5:1; 19:15–16; 2 Kings 9:1–13; 11:12; 23:30; 1 Chron. 11:3; 14:8; 29:22; 2 Chron. 6:42; 22:7; 23:11; Ps. 2:2; 18:50; 20:6; 28:8; 45:7–8; 84:9; 89:20, 38, 51; 132:10, 17; Sir. 46:13, 19; 48:8; Isa. 11:2; 45:1; Lam. 4:20; Dan. 9:25–26; Hos. 8:10; Hab. 3:13; Zech. 4:14

Prophet: 1 Kings 19:16; 1 Chron. 16:22; Ps. 105:15; Isa. 61:1

Suffering Servant: Isa. 42:1

Other: Exod. 19:6; Lev. 14:15–18, 26–29; Deut. 11:13–14; 32:13; Judg. 9:9; 2 Sam. 12:20; 2 Chron. 28:15; Ruth 3:3; Tob. 6:8 (RSV = Tob. 6:9 NAB, NRSV); 11:8; Jth 10:3; 16:8 (RSV = Jth 16:7 NAB, NRSV); Job 29:6; Ps. 23:5; 92:10; 104:15; 133:2; Prov. 27:9; Eccles. 9:8; Song 1:3–4; 4:10; Isa. 1:6; 61:3, 6; Ezek. 16:9; 28:14; 36:25–26; Dan. 13:17; Joel 2:24; Amos 6:6

NT Background:

Jesus Christ: Mark 14:8; 16:1; Luke 4:16–21; 7:38, 46; John 1:41; 4:25; 11:2; 12:3; Acts 4:26–27; 10:38; Heb. 1:9

Believers / Other: Matt. 6:17; Mark 6:13; Luke 10:34; John 9:6, 11; Rom. 15:16; 2 Cor. 1:21–22; 2:14–16; Eph. 1:13–14; James 5:14–15; 1 Pet. 2:5, 9; 1 John 2:20, 27; Rev. 1:6; 3:18; 5:10; 20:6

Catechism Background: 91; **436**; 453; 486; 690; **695**; 698; 713–714; 727; 739; 745; 782; 783–786; 901; 1141; 1148; **1150–1151**; 1183; 1189; 1216; 1237; **1241–1242**; **1289–1292**; **1293–1296**; **1297**; **1300**; 1320; 1682; 2579; 2672; 2769; 2782

Related: BAPTISM: *Types:* Anointing of Priests, Prophets, and Kings; HOLY ORDERS: *Types:* Anointing of Priests, Prophets, and Kings

Note: Anointing is presented as both a type and a symbol. CCC 1150 speaks of "signs" which "prefigure" the sacraments, mentioning among them "anointing and consecration of kings and priests." It is not easy, and sometimes probably impossible, to distinguish too sharply between symbolism and typology in this and similar cases, and it should not be forgotten that the primary typological meaning refers to the anointing of Jesus Christ, in which the baptized and confirmed participate. Presented here are texts which speak primarily of anointing as a symbol. Cf. also BAPTISM: Types: Anointing of Priests, Prophets, and Kings and HOLY ORDERS: Types: Anointing of Priests, Prophets, and Kings.

Anointing of Confirmation

• The anointing with oil in Confirmation signifies the gift of the Holy Spirit (CCC 695; 1241; 1289; 1300; RC 22; 27; 58, Prayer after Communion; RC 59, Prayer after Communion; RM, Ritual Masses, For the Conferral of Confirmation, A, Prayer after Communion; LH, ET.1.Fr, 2R: St. Cyril of Jerusalem, Jerusalem Catecheses, 21:1–3, Mystagogica 3, 1–3: PG 33,

1087–1091; LH, OT.19.Fr, 2R: St. Pacian, Sermon on Baptism, 5–6: PL 13, 1092–1093)

- The anointing with oil in Confirmation signifies the gift of the Holy Spirit, through whom the believer participates more deeply in the life of Christ ("the anointed one") (CCC 695; 1241; 1291 in the context of 1289; LH, ET.1.Fr, 2R: St. Cyril of Jerusalem, Jerusalem Catecheses, 21:1–3, Mystagogica 3, 1–3: PG 33, 1087–1091; RM, Chrism Mass, Collect; *cf. also* CCC 739; 782–786; 1682).

- The anointing with oil in Confirmation "highlights the name 'Christian,' which means 'anointed' and derives from that of Christ himself whom God 'anointed with the Holy Spirit' (Acts 10:38)" (CCC 1289).

- The anointing with chrism expresses "the effect of the giving of the Holy Spirit. Signed with the perfumed oil, the baptized receive the indelible character, the seal of the Lord, together with the gift of the Spirit that conforms them more closely to Christ and gives them the grace of spreading 'the sweet odor of Christ'" (RC 9; *cf. also* CONFIRMATION: *Symbols:* Seal).

- The anointing in Confirmation (LH, ET.1.Fr, 2R: St. Cyril of Jerusalem, Jerusalem Catecheses, 21:1–3, Mystagogica 3, 1–3: PG 33, 1087–1091):
  - gives a likeness to Christ in his glory;
  - makes believers "anointed ones" who have received the sign of the Holy Spirit; it is of them that the Scriptures said, "Touch not my anointed ones" (1 Chron. 16:22);
  - signifies the Holy Spirit who anointed Christ after his baptism;
  - gives a share in the life of Christ through the "oil of gladness," i.e. the Holy Spirit who gives spiritual joy;
  - acts as the "instrument" through which the believer receives the Holy Spirit;
  - and symbolically anoints the body and truly sanctifies the soul by the "holy and life-giving Spirit."

The Liturgy of the Hours

We became "the anointed ones" when we received the sign of the Holy Spirit. Indeed, everything took place in us by means of images, because we ourselves are images of Christ. Christ bathed in the river Jordan, imparting to its waters the fragrance of his divinity, and when he came up from them the Holy Spirit descended upon him, like resting upon like. So we also, after coming up from the sacred waters of baptism, were anointed with chrism, which signifies the Holy Spirit. . . .

Christ's anointing was not by human hands, nor was it with ordinary oil. On the contrary, having destined him to be the Savior of the whole world, the Father himself anointed him with the Holy Spirit. . . .

The oil of gladness with which Christ was anointed was a spiritual oil; it was in fact the Holy Spirit himself, who is called "the oil of gladness" because he is the source of spiritual joy. But we too have been anointed with oil, and by this anointing we have entered into fellowship with Christ and have received a share in his life. Beware of thinking that this holy oil is simply ordinary oil and nothing else. After the invocation of the Spirit it is no longer ordinary oil but the gift of Christ, and by the presence of his divinity it becomes the instrument through which we receive the Holy Spirit. While symbolically, on our foreheads and senses, our bodies are anointed with this oil that we see, our souls are sanctified by the holy and life-giving Spirit.

LH, ET.1.Fr, 2R: St. Cyril of Jerusalem, Jerusalem Catecheses,
21:1–3, Mystagogica 3, 1–3: PG 33, 1087–1091

- Through the oil of Confirmation, Jesus draws Christians after him to breathe the fragrance of the Resurrection (LH, OT.15.Th, 2R: St. Ambrose, On the Mysteries, 29–30.34–35.37.42: SC 25 bis, 172–178 in reference to Song 1:3–4 and 4:11).
- The lives of the confirmed are called to give off the sweet aroma of Christ (CCC 1294, which quotes 2 Cor. 2:15).
- The Holy Spirit is poured out in Confirmation to strengthen believers and to anoint them to be more like Christ the Son of God (RC 24).
- The anointing of Confirmation is a "spiritual anointing" (RM, Ritual Masses, For the Conferral of Confirmation, Prayer over the Offerings).

Anointing with Chrism in General

• Chrism is used in the Sacraments of Confirmation and Holy Orders (or in the anointing of Baptism if Confirmation is not celebrated together with Baptism) (CCC 1241–1242).

• The chrism oil (myron) is a sacramental sign of the seal of the gift of the Holy Spirit (CCC 1183; 1241; 1295).

• Anointing with chrism signifies consecration (CCC 1294; RM, Chrism Mass, Collect), especially as a priest, prophet, or king (CCC 1297; cf. Baptism: *Types:* Anointing of Priests, Prophets, and Kings; Holy Orders: *Types:* Anointing of Priests, Prophets, and Kings).

• The anointing with chrism in Confirmation perfects the conformity to Jesus Christ given in Baptism (RM, Ritual Masses, For the Conferral of Baptism, A, Prayer over the Offerings).

• The anointing of the Holy Spirit gives interior knowledge of the truth which comes from God (1 John 2:20; LH, OT.6.Fr, 2R: St. Augustine, Tractates on the first letter of John, 4: PL 35, 2008–2009, citing 1 John 2:20).

• Those anointed with chrism are made temples of God's glory (RBOC 25; cf. Baptism: *Types:* Anointing of Priests, Prophets, and Kings).

• Anointing with chrism signifies the salvation which Christ gives (RB 50; 62; RBOC 24; 25; RC 59, Prayer over the Gifts).

• Anointing with chrism signifies radiance from the salvation which comes from Christ (RBOC 25).

• In the prayer of consecration of the chrism in the liturgy of Antioch, the bishop prays that the chrism be for all who are signed with it: "holy myron, priestly myron, royal myron, anointing with gladness, clothing with light, a cloak of salvation, a spiritual gift, the sanctification of souls and bodies, imperishable happiness, the indelible seal, a buckler of faith, and a fearsome helmet against all the works of the adversary" (CCC 1297 quoting the liturgy of Antioch).

Other Symbolisms of Anointing in General

• As there is no distance between oil and the anointed skin, so there is no difference between Christ and the Holy Spirit, with whom he is anointed, and thus one who comes to Christ "must first encounter the oil" of the Holy

Spirit (St. Gregory of Nyssa, De Spiritu Sancto, 16: PG 45, 1321 A–B cited in CCC 690).

- The consecration of virgins is called a "spiritual anointing" (*cf. for example* RM, Ritual Masses, For the Consecration of Virgins, Addition to the Eucharistic Prayer II).
- Anointing signifies the joy or blessings which come from God (sometimes called the "oil of gladness") (*cf. for example* Ps. 45:7; Isa. 61:3; Heb. 1:9; CCC 1293 which cites Deut. 11:14, Ps. 23:5 and 104:15; RM, Baptism of the Lord, Preface; RM, Our Lord Jesus Christ King of the Universe, Preface; LH, ET.1.Fr, 2R: St. Cyril of Jerusalem, Jerusalem Catecheses, 21:1–3, Mystagogica 3, 1–3: PG 33, 1087–1091; LH, Dedication of St. Mary Major [Aug 5], 2R: St. Cyril of Alexandria, Homily delivered at the Council of Ephesus, 4: PG 77, 991.995–996; RBOC 25; *cf. also for example* LH, OT.4.Mo, 2R: St. Hilary of Poitiers, Commentary on the Psalms, Ps. 132 [Ps. 133]: PLS 1, 244–245).
- Anointing signifies strength or the strengthening power of Christ (*cf. for example* RBOC 22; 25, 2nd form; RB 50; CCC 1020; 1293–1294; RC 24).
- Anointing signifies cleansing (anointing before and after a bath) (*cf. for example* CCC 1293–1294; 2 Sam. 12:20; Ruth 3:3; Jth. 10:3; Ezek. 16:9; Dan. 13:17; Matt. 6:17).
- Anointing signifies healing and comfort (*cf. for example* CCC 1293 which cites Isa. 1:6 and Luke 10:34; CCC 1294; 2 Chron. 28:15; Tob. 6:8 [RSV = Tob. 6:9 NAB, NRSV]; 11:8; Mark 6:13; John 9:6, 11; *cf. also* ANOINTING OF THE SICK, *Symbols:* Anointing).
- Anointing signifies radiance with beauty, health, strength (*cf. for example* CCC 1293; Jth. 16:8 (RSV = Jth. 16:7 NAB, NRSV); Ps. 104:15; Eccles 9:8).
- Anointing signifies limbering (*cf. for example* CCC 1293).
- Anointing signifies abundance and blessing from God (*cf. for example* Deut. 11:13–14; 32:13; Judg. 9:9; Job 29:6; Ps. 23:5; 92:10; 133:2; Joel 2:24).

FIRE

OT Background:

God / theophany: Gen. 15:17; Exod. 3:2; 19:18; 24:17; Deut. 4:11–15, 24, 33, 36; 5:4, 22–26; 9:3, 10; 10:4; Ps. 29:7; 50:3; Isa. 10:17; 33:14;

66:15; Ezek. 1:27; 8:2; Dan. 7:9–10; Amos 5:6; Zech. 2:5 (*cf. also* Baptism, *Types,* Pillar of Cloud and Fire, OT Background)

Consuming sacrifices: Lev. 9:24; Judg. 6:21; 1 Kings 18:24, 38; 1 Chron. 21:26; 2 Chron. 7:1; 2 Macc. 2:10

Purifying or testing: Num. 31:22–23; Jth. 8:27; Ps. 66:12; Sir. 2:5; Isa. 6:6–7; 43:2; Jer. 6:29; Ezek. 24:12; Zech. 13:9; Mal. 3:2

Other: Gen. 3:24; Prov. 16:27; Isa. 5:24; 33:11; Jer. 5:14; 20:9; 23:29

NT Background:

God / Jesus Christ / Holy Spirit: Matt. 3:11; Luke 3:16; 12:49–50; Acts 2:3–4; 7:30; Heb. 12:18, 29; 1 Thess. 5:19; 2 Thess. 1:7; Rev. 1:14; 2:18; 4:5; 19:12

Purifying or testing: Mark 9:49; 1 Cor. 3:10–15; 1 Pet. 1:7; 4:12; Rev. 3:18

Other: Luke 12:49; James 3:5–6

Catechism Background: 696; 718; **1127**; 1147; 1189; 2583; 2671

Related: Baptism: *Types:* Pillar of Cloud and Fire; *Symbols:* Baptism of Fire; Illumination / Light / Candle; Eucharist: *Types:* Holocaust of Elijah

Fire and Pentecost

- The Holy Spirit came down upon the disciples in tongues of fire the morning of Pentecost (Acts 2:3–4; RM, Eucharistic Prayer I, Proper Form of Communicantes for Pentecost; LH, Pentecost, EP2, Magn; *cf. also* CCC 696).

- On Pentecost, God manifested the New Covenant in the fire of the Spirit (RM, Pentecost, Vigil Mass, Extended Form, Prayer after the 2nd Reading).

- As God gave the Law on Mount Sinai in fire and lightning, so he manifested the New Covenant in the fire of the Spirit on Pentecost (RM, Pentecost, Vigil Mass, Extended Form, Prayer after 2nd Reading; *cf.* Exod. 19:16–20; Acts 2:3).

- Jesus says he came to "cast fire upon the earth" (Luke 12:49), referring to the Holy Spirit (CCC 696) and to the fire of divine charity in the hearts of believers (*cf.* LH, Sacred Heart, EP, Magn; LH, Triumph of the Cross [Sep 14], MP, 6th intercession).

Confirmation as Reception of the Fire of the Holy Spirit

- At Confirmation the Holy Spirit is given, who at Pentecost set the hearts of the disciples on fire with love (RC 33, 3rd petition; cf. Acts 2:3–4; cf. also RC 7).
- At Confirmation the faithful ask that the fire of the Holy Spirit's love be kindled in the hearts of those confirmed (RC, Alleluia Verses, 5).
- At Confirmation the bishop may wear red vestments (RC 57). This is normally understood to symbolize the fire of the Holy Spirit (cf. Acts 2:1–4).[1]
- The confirmed become more like Christ, who was anointed by the Holy Spirit and sent out on his public ministry to set the world on fire (RC 22; cf. Luke 12:49).

Other Related Symbolisms of Fire

- Fire symbolizes the transforming power of the Holy Spirit's actions (CCC 696; 1127; cf. also 1 Thess. 5:19; Acts 2:3–4; CCC 718).

The Catechism of the Catholic Church

Celebrated worthily in faith, the sacraments confer the grace that they signify (Cf. Council of Trent [1547]: DS 1605; DS 1606). They are *efficacious* because in them Christ himself is at work: it is he who baptizes, he who acts in his sacraments in order to communicate the grace that each sacrament signifies. The Father always hears the prayer of his Son's Church which, in the epiclesis of each sacrament, expresses her faith in the power of the Spirit. As fire transforms into itself everything it touches, so the Holy Spirit transforms into the divine life whatever is subjected to his power.

CCC 1127

- As the fire from heaven came down to consume the sacrifice of Elijah on Mount Carmel (cf. 1 Kings 18:38), so the fire of the Holy Spirit transforms

---

1 To my knowledge there are no official Church documents explaining the symbolism of the colors of the liturgical vestments. For the general regulations regarding the colors to be used at different times in the liturgical calendar, cf. GIRM 345–347.

what he touches (CCC 696; *cf. also* EUCHARIST: *Types*: Holocaust of Elijah).

• The Holy Spirit himself is compared to a fire in whom the believer participates (Acts 2:3–4; 1 Thess. 5:19; RM, Lent.2.Th, Collect; RM, St. Francis de Sales [Jan 24], Prayer over the Offerings; RM, St. Alphonsus Liguori [Aug 1], Prayer over the Offerings; RM, Ritual Masses, For Perpetual Profession, A, Prayer after Communion; RM, Masses and Prayer for Various Needs and Occasions, 39, Collect; RM, Votive Masses, 9, C, Prayer over the Offerings; LH, Lent.2.Th, MP, Prayer; LH, Lent.2.Th, EP, Prayer; LH, ET.1.Su, EP, 2nd intercession; LH, ET.2.Th, 2R: St. Gaudentius of Brescia, Tract. 2: CSEL 68, 30–32; LH, ET.3[=5].Su, EP2, 2nd intercession; LH, Pentecost, EP, Hymn; LH, Psalter.3.Su, EP, 3rd intercession; LH, St. George [Apr 23], 2R: St. Peter Damian, Sermo 3, De sancto Georgio: PL 144, 567–571; LH, St. Catherine of Siena [Apr 29], 2R: St. Catherine of Siena, Dialogue on Divine Providence, Ch. 167, Gratiarum actio ad Trinitatem: ed. lat., Ingolstadii 1583, f. 290v–291; LH, St. Philip Neri [May 26], 2R, Prayer; LH, St. Bonaventure [July 15], 2R [Latin]: St. Bonaventure, Journey of the Mind to God, Ch. 7, 1.2.4.6: Opera Omnia, 5, 312–313; LH, St. Anthony Claret [Oct 24], 2R: St. Anthony Mary Claret, L'egoismo vinto, Romae 1869, 60; LH, St. John Damascene [Dec 4], 2R: St. John Damascene, Statement of Faith, Ch. 1: PG 95, 417–419; *cf. also* LH, St. Pancras [May 12], 2R: St. Bernard, Sermo 17 in psalmum Qui habitat, 4, 6: Opera Omnia 4, 489–491).

• Fire signifies divine love in the heart of believers (Luke 12:49; 1 Thess. 5:19; CCC 2617; 2717; RM, Lent.3.Su, Preface; RM, Sacred Heart, Prayer after Communion; RM, Easter Vigil, 10; RM, Conversion of St. Paul [Jan 25], Prayer after Communion; RM, St. John Bosco [Jan 31], Collect; RM, St. Catherine of Siena [Apr 29], Collect; RM, St. Mary Magdalene de'Pazzi [May 25], Collect; RM, St. Philip Neri [May 26], Collect; RM, St. Barnabas [June 11], Prayer over the Offerings; RM, St. Maximilian Kolbe [Aug 14], Prayer after Communion; RM, Assumption of the Blessed Virgin Mary [Aug 15], Mass during the Day, Prayer over the Offerings; RM, St. Bernard [Aug 20], Collect; RM, St. Rose of Lima [Aug 23], Collect; RM, St. Francis Xavier [Dec 3], Prayer after Communion; RM, Commons, Common of Martyrs, Outside Easter Time, For Several Martyrs, 5, Prayer over the Offerings, 2nd option; RM, Commons, Common of Pastors, For a Pope or for a Bishop, 1, Prayer after Communion; RM, Commons, Common of Holy Men and Women, For Monks and Religious, For an Abbot, Prayer over the Offerings; RM, Masses and Prayer for Various Needs and Occasions, 29, Collect; RC 33; LH, Lent.1.Fr, 2R: St. Aelred, From the Mirror of Love, Book 3, 5: PL 195, 582; LH, ET.2[=4, 6].Mo, MP, 4th intercession; LH, Pentecost, EP, Hymn; LH, OT.2.Fr, 2R: Diadochus of Photice, Treatise on Spiritual Perfection, Ch. 12.13.14: PG 65, 1171–1172; LH, Psalter.1.Su, EP, 3rd intercession; LH, OT.28.Tu, 2R: St. Columban, Instruction on Compunction, 12, 2–3: Opera, Dublin 1957, pp. 112–114; LH, St. Justin Martyr [June 1], EP, Magn; LH, St. Camillus de Lellis [July 14], 2R: S. Cicatelli, Vita del P. Camillo de Lellis, Viterbo 1615; LH, St. Mary Magdalene [July 22], 2R: St. Gregory the Great, Homily on the Gospels 25, 1–2.4–5: PL 76, 1189–1193; LH, St. Hedwig [Oct 16], 2R: Life of St. Hedwig, Acta Sanctorum Octobris 8 [1853], 201–202; LH, St. Paul of the Cross [Oct 19], 2R: St. Paul of the Cross, Letter 1, 43; 2, 440.825; LH, St. Anthony Claret [Oct 24], 2R: St. Anthony Mary Claret, L'egoismo vinto, Romae 1869, 60; LH, St. Charles Borromeo [Nov 4], 2R: St. Charles Borromeo, Sermon given during the last synod he attended, Acta Ecclesiae Mediolanensis, Mediolani 1599, 1177–1178).

- Fire signifies zeal for God (Jer. 20:9; Luke 12:49; LH, OT.8.Su, 2R: St. Gregory the Great, Moral Reflections on Job, Book 1, 2.36: PL 75, 529–530.543–544; *cf. also* RM, St. Teresa of Jesus [Oct 15], Collect; RM, Ritual Masses, For the Consecration of Virgins, Solemn Blessing, 3rd prayer; LH, Lent.AAW.Fr, 2R: St. John Chrysostom, Supp., Homily 6 De precatione: PG 64, 462–466).

- Fire symbolizes the light of Christ (RM, Easter Vigil, 14–17; *cf.* BAPTISM: *Symbols*: Illumination / Light / Candle; *Types*: Pillar of Cloud and Fire).

LAYING ON OF HANDS

OT Background:

Appointing for ministry: Num. 8:10–16; 27:18–23; Deut. 34:9

Filling with the spirit of wisdom: Deut. 34:9

Blessing: Gen. 48:13–18; Ps. 139:5; Sir. 50:20–21

NT Background:

Blessing: Matt. 19:13–15; Mark 10:13, 16; Rev. 1:17

Giving the Holy Spirit: Acts 8:14–19; 9:17; 19:5–6; Heb. 6:2 (*cf.* CCC 1288)

Healing: Matt. 9:18; Mark 5:23; 6:5; 7:32; 8:23–25; 16:18; Luke 4:40; 13:13; Acts 5:12; 9:12, 17; 14:3; 28:8; James 5:14–15

Ordaining for ministry: Acts 6:6; 13:3; 1 Tim. 4:14; 5:22; 2 Tim. 1:6

Catechism Background: 699; 1150; 1288; 1289; **1299;** 1300; 1315; 1320; 1668

Related: CONFIRMATION: *Symbols:* Anointing; HOLY ORDERS: *Types:* Laying on of Hands; *Symbols:* Laying on of Hands

Laying On of Hands in Confirmation

• The laying on of hands "represents the biblical gesture by which the gift of the Holy Spirit is invoked" (RC 9; *cf.* Acts 8:14–17; 19:5–6; RC 22; 25; CCC 1288; 1315).

• The laying on of hands signifies the outpouring of the Holy Spirit (CCC 699; 1299–1300; RC 25).

• The laying on of hands signifies the invocation of the gifts of the Holy Spirit (RC 25; CCC 1299).

• The ordinary minister of the Sacrament of Confirmation is the bishop, "so that there will be a clearer reference to the first pouring forth of the Holy Spirit on Pentecost" (*cf.* Acts 2.1–4), for "after the apostles were filled with the Holy Spirit, they themselves gave the Spirit to the faithful through the laying on of hands" (RC 7; *cf.* Acts 8:17; 19:5–6).

• Through the imposition of hands in Confirmation, in a certain way the grace of Pentecost is perpetuated in the Church (CCC 1288; *cf.* Acts 2:3–4; 8:14–19; 19:5–6).

Other Symbolisms of Laying On of Hands

• Laying on of hands signifies healing (Matt. 9:18; Mark 5:23; 6:5; 7:32; 8:23–25; 16:18; Luke 4:40; 13:13; Acts 5:12; 9:12, 17; 14:3; 28:8; CCC 699).

• Laying on of hands signifies blessing (Gen. 48:13–18; Ps. 139:5; Sir. 50:20–21; Matt. 19:13–15; Mark 10:13, 16; Rev. 1:17; CCC 699; 1668–1670; *cf. also* the many instances of Solemn Blessings and Prayers over the People in the RM).

• Laying on of hands signifies ordaining for ministry (cf. HOLY ORDERS: *Types:* Laying on of Hands).

SEAL

OT Background:

Used Literally: Gen. 38:18, 25; 41:42; Exod. 28:11, 21, 36; 39:6, 14, 30; 1 Kings 21:8; Neh. 9:38; 10:1; Tob. 7:14 (RSV = Tob. 7:13 NAB, NRSV); 9:5; Esther 3:10, 12; 8:2, 8, 10; Sir. 38:27; 42:6; Jer. 32:10–11, 14, 44; Dan. 6:17; 14:11, 14, 17; 2 Macc. 2:5

Used Symbolically: Gen. 4:15; Deut. 32:34; Job 9:7; 14:17; 37:7; 38:14; 41:15; Song 4:12; 8:6; Wisd. 2:5; Sir. 22:27; 32:5–6; Isa. 8:16; 29:11–12; Jer. 22:24; Ezek. 9:4–6; Dan. 8:26; 9:24; 12:4, 9; Hag. 2:23

NT Background: Matt. 27:66; John 3:33; 6:27; Acts 2:1–4, 38; Rom. 4:11; 8:29; 1 Cor. 9:2; 2 Cor. 1:21–22; Eph. 1:13–14; 4:30; 2 Tim. 2:19; Rev. 5:1–10; 6:1–12; 7:2–8; 8:1; 9:4; 10:4; 13:16–17; 14:9, 11; 16:2; 19:20; 20:3–4; 22:10

Catechism Background: 188; 190; 197; **698**; 837; **1121**; 1183; 1216; 1272–1274; 1280; 1293; **1295**–1296; 1297; 1300; 1303–1305; 1317; 1320; 1523; 1955

Related: BAPTISM: *Types:* Circumcision; Anointing of Priests, Prophets, and Kings; *Symbols:* Seal; CONFIRMATION: *Symbols:* Anointing; Sign of the Cross; PENANCE: *Symbols:* Seal; HOLY ORDERS: *Types:* Anointing of Priests, Prophets, and Kings; *Symbols:* Anointing; Seal; MATRIMONY: *Symbols:* Seal

Note: The seal of Confirmation perfects the seal of Baptism (cf. CCC 1303; 1318) to such an extent that when Baptism and Confirmation are celebrated together, only one anointing, that of Confirmation, is given (cf. RCIA 319; 326). Because of this, symbolisms of "seal" related to either Baptism or Confirmation are presented here, as is the subtopic "Seal in General."

Seal in General

• A seal symbolizes the person it represents (CCC 1295; cf. also Gen. 41:42; Esther 3:10, 12; 8:2, 8, 10).

• A seal is a sign of ownership of an object, and was used to mark soldiers and slaves with the seal of their leader or owner (CCC 1295 which cites Gen.

38:18; 41:42; Deut. 32:34; *cf. also* CCC 1296; LH, St. Cyril of Jerusalem [Mar 18], 2R: St. Cyril of Jerusalem, Catechetical Instruction 3, 1–3: PG 33, 426–430; Ezek. 9:4–6; Rev. 7:2–4; 9:4 where the mark of God indicates his ownership and protection, in contrast with Rev. 13:16–17; 14:9, 11; 16:2; 19:20; 20:4 where the worshippers of the beast receive his mark).

* A seal indicates protection, either by a physical seal (Sir. 42:6; 2 Macc. 2:5; Matt. 27:66; *cf. also* Deut. 32:34 and Rev. 20:3 where a physical seal is presented symbolically) or by a non-physical seal (Gen. 4:15; Ezek. 9:4–6; Rev. 7:2–5; 9:4; CCC 1296).

* A seal is a sign of belonging to a beloved (*cf.* Song 8:6).

* A seal is used to authenticate a juridical act or document (CCC 1295 which cites 1 Kings 21:8; Isa. 29:11; Jer. 32:10; *cf. also* Dan. 6:17) or symbolically a person, his righteousness, etc. (John 3:33; 6:27; Rom. 4:11; 1 Cor. 9:2).

* A seal represents a promise or guarantee (2 Cor. 1:21–22; Eph. 1:13–14; 4:30).

* Covenants are "sealed" (CCC 2060; 1624; 1639; Neh. 9:38; 10:1; RM, Ritual Masses, For the Celebration of Marriage, A, Addition to the Eucharistic Prayer III; *cf. also* CCC 1621; 1642; LH, OT.16.Mo, 1R, Resp [2 Cor. 1:21–22; Deut. 5:2, 4]).

* A scroll can be sealed, requiring the seals to be broken to be opened (Isa. 29:11–12; Dan. 8:26; 12:4, 9; Rev. 5:1–10; 6:1–12; 8:1; 22:10; LH, St. Jerome (Sep 30), 2R: St. Jerome, Prologue of the Commentary on Isaiah, 1.2: CCL 73, 1–3 in reference to Isa. 29:11–12).

* Circumcision of the flesh was a physical seal of the Old Covenant, no longer present in the New Covenant, in which God circumcises the hearts of believers (LH, Lent.1.We, 2R: Aphrahat, Dem. 11, On Circumcision, 11–12: PS 1, 498–503; *cf.* Rom. 4:11; BAPTISM: *Types*: Circumcision; *cf. also* LH, ET.2.Su, 2R [Latin]: St. Augustine, Sermo 8 in octava Paschae 1.4: PL 46, 838.841).

* The martyrs sealed their witness to the faith in their blood (RM, St. Boniface [June 5], Collect; RM, The Passion of St. John the Baptist, Prayer over the Offerings; LH, Beheading of John the Baptist [Aug 29], 2R: St. Bede the Venerable, Homily 23: CCL 122, 354.356–357).

* The proclamation of faith in the Father, the Son, and the Holy Spirit are called three "heads" or "chapters" which fit together to form the "seal" of Baptism (*cf.* CCC 190 which quotes St. Irenaeus, Demonstratio apostolicae

praedicationis 100: SCh 62, 170; *cf. also* CCC 837; 1274). In this case, each of the "heads" or "chapters" of the seal are needed as a sign of recognition of the Christian (*cf.* CCC 188; 197).

• The moral truth is impressed in man's heart like wax that has received a seal from the image on a ring (CCC 1955 quoting St. Augustine, De Trin. 14, 15, 21: PL 42, 1052).

The Seal in the Trinity

• The Father is the source of the stamp, the Son is the stamp, and the Holy Spirit is the seal (LH, CT.BE.Mo, 2R [Latin Edition: Jan 2]: St. Basil the Great, On the Holy Spirit, Ch. 26, Nn. 61, 64: PG 32, 179–182.186; *cf. also* Rom. 8:29).

• Christ was marked with the Father's seal (John 6:27; CCC 1296).

Seal Gives the Holy Spirit

• Christians are sealed by God (2 Cor. 1:21–22) in the Holy Spirit (Eph. 1:13–14; 4:30) (CCC 1296; LH, ET.1.Fr, 2R, Resp [Eph. 1:13–14; 2 Cor. 1:21–22] [=LH, OT.8.Th, 2R, Resp]; *cf. also* RM, Eucharistic Prayer for Various Needs III, Preface; LH, OT.16.Mo, 1R, Resp [2 Cor. 1:21–22; Deut. 5:2, 4]; LH, ET.1.Fr, 2R: St. Cyril of Jerusalem, Jerusalem Catecheses, 21:1–3, Mystagogica 3, 1–3: PG 33, 1087–1091).

• The seal is a gift of the Holy Spirit (RC 27; CCC 1300; 1320; *cf. also* CCC 1183; 1295; 1304; RCIA 115).

• The seal, especially of Confirmation, is associated with the reception of the gifts of the Holy Spirit (*cf.* CCC 1303 citing St. Ambrose, De myst. 7, 42: PL 16, 402–403; LH, OT.15.Th, 2R: St. Ambrose, On the Mysteries, 29–30.34–35.37.42: SC 25 bis, 172–178).

• The Christian is sealed by God the Father and confirmed by Christ, who pours the pledge of the Holy Spirit into the Christian's heart (LH, OT.15. Th, 2R [Latin]: St. Ambrose, On the Mysteries, 29–30.34–35.37.42: SC 25 bis, 172–178).

• When a soul is sealed with the "blood of the Word and of the slain Lamb" the Holy Spirit comes to that soul, in fact "that very blood urges it to come, although the Spirit moves itself and desires to come" (LH, St. Mary Magdalene de Pazzi [May 25], 2R: St. Mary Magdalene de Pazzi,

On Revelation and On Trials, Mss. III, 186.264; IV, 716: Opere di S. M. Maddalene de Pazzi, Firenze, 1965, 4, pp. 200.269; 6, p. 194).

- The anointing of Baptism seals the new life in the believer (CCC 1523; *cf.* BAPTISM: *Symbols*: Second Birth).

- In Baptism, the seal of the Holy Spirit is impressed on the believer's soul (LH, St. Cyril of Jerusalem [Mar 18], 2R: St. Cyril of Jerusalem, Catechetical Instruction 3, 1–3: PG 33, 426–430; LH, Lent.1.Th, 2R: St. Asterius of Amasea, Homily 13: PG 40, 355–358.362).

- Baptism is the seal of faith prefigured by circumcision (LH, ET.2.Su, 2R [Latin]: St. Augustine, Sermo 8 in octava Paschae 1.4: PL 46, 838.841; *cf.* BAPTISM: *Types*: Circumcision).

Configures to Christ

- The seal, or sacramental character, imprinted by the Holy Spirit indelibly configures the Christian to Christ (CCC 698; 1121; 1272 which cites Rom. 8:29; 1317; RC 22; *cf. also* LH, St. Cyril of Jerusalem [Mar 18], 2R: St. Cyril of Jerusalem, Catechetical Instruction 3, 1–3: PG 33, 426–430). This seal is given in Baptism and perfected in Confirmation (RM, Ritual Masses, For the Conferral of Baptism, A, Prayer over the Offerings).

- Given the indelible character of the seal of Baptism, Confirmation, and Holy Orders, these seals can never be erased or repeated (CCC 1121; 1271–1272; 1280; 1304; 1582).

- In Baptism, Confirmation, and Holy Orders the seal is imparted through the Sign of the Cross and the anointing with oil (RC 59; *cf. also* CCC 1293; BAPTISM: *Types*: Anointing of Priests, Prophets, and Kings; *Symbols*: Anointing; Sign of the Cross; CONFIRMATION: *Symbols*: Sign of the Cross; HOLY ORDERS: *Types:* Anointing of Priests, Prophets, and Kings; *Symbols*: Anointing).

- The seal is the sign of God's Lordship (CCC 1216 quoting St. Gregory of Nazianzus, Oratio 40, 3–4: PG 36, 361C). It marks our total belonging to Christ (CCC 1296).

- Being marked with the supernatural seal, the Christian is easily recognized by the Master (LH, OT.13.Sa, 2R: St. Cyril of Jerusalem, Catechetical Instruction, 1, 2–3.5–6: PG 33, 371.375–378).

- The love of Christ is like a seal, which marks the soul of the believer and makes the soul love like Christ loves (LH, OT.18.Th, 2R: Baldwin, bishop of Canterbury, Tract. 10: PL 204, 513–514.516 in reference to Song 8:6 and 1 Pet. 2:21).

Configures to the Church

• The seal, or sacramental character, imprinted by the Holy Spirit indelibly configures the Christian to Christ and to the Church, giving a share in Christ's priesthood and making one a more perfect member of the Church according to different states or functions (CCC 1121; RC 22).
• The seal is a consecration to the service of the Church (CCC 1121). It marks the enrollment of the Christian in the service of Christ forever (CCC 1296; *cf. also* LH, St. Cyril of Jerusalem [Mar 18], 2R: St. Cyril of Jerusalem, Catechetical Instruction 3, 1–3: PG 33, 426–430).

For Liturgy and for Witness

• The seal is a consecration for divine worship (CCC 1121; 1280) in the holy liturgy of the Church (CCC 1273).
• The seal is "a positive disposition for grace" (CCC 1121).
• The seal of the Holy Spirit enables Christians to live out their baptismal priesthood by "holy lives and practical charity (Cf. Lumen Gentium 10)" (CCC 1273) and gives him or her the "'power to profess faith in Christ publicly and as it were officially (*quasi ex officio*)' (St. Thomas Aquinas, STh III, 72, 5, ad 2)" (CCC 1305).
• The seal of the Holy Spirit enrolls the believers into the army of the Great King (LH, St. Cyril of Jerusalem [Mar 18], 2R [Latin]: St. Cyril of Jerusalem, Catechetical Instruction 3, 1–3: PG 33, 426–430).
• The seal of Confirmation gives special strength "for the combat of this life" (CCC 1523).
• The seal of the Holy Spirit that the Christian receives on the forehead is that same sign of the Emperor that the martyrs of past times joyfully wore; indeed we fight under the same King that they merited to fight for and conquer under (LH, St. Cristopher Magallanes [May 21], 2R [Latin]: St. Caesarius of Arles, Sermo 225, 1–2: CCL 104, 888–889).
• The seal of the Holy Spirit, especially in Confirmation, gives a special strength "to spread and defend the faith by word and action as true witnesses of Christ, to confess the name of Christ boldly, and never to be

ashamed of the Cross (Cf. Council of Florence [1439]: DS 1319; Lumen Gentium 11; 12)" (CCC 1303).

• The indelible spiritual mark, or "character," which is imprinted on the soul is compared to being "clothed" with power from on high so as to be Christ's witness (CCC 1304 in reference to Luke 24:48–49).

• The seal is a promise and guarantee of divine protection (CCC 1121; 1216 quoting St. Gregory of Nazianzus, Oratio 40, 3–4: PG 36, 361C), especially "in the great eschatological trial (Rev. 7:2–3; 9:4; Ezek. 9:4–6)" (CCC 1296).

For Eternal Life

• The seal, especially in Baptism, marks the Christian for eternal life (Eph. 1:13–14; 4:30; CCC 1274; cf. also 2 Cor. 1:21–22; CCC 1296; RM, Eucharistic Prayer I, 95; LH, St. Ephrem [June 9], 2R: St. Ephrem, Sermo 3, de fine et admonitione, 2.4–5: ed. Lamy, 3, 216–222).

• To obtain eternal life, the Christian must keep the seal undefiled (LH, OT.32.Tu, 2R [Latin]: From a homily written in the second century, Ch. 8, 1–9, 11: Funk 1, 152–156). Those who do not guard their seal will be condemned to eternal damnation (LH, OT.32.Mo, 2R [Latin]: From a homily written in the second century, Ch. 3, 1–4, 5; 7, 1–6: Funk 1, 149–152).

SIGN OF THE CROSS[2]

Definition: A sign in the form of a cross made by the Christian as a prayer honoring the Blessed Trinity, "in the name of the Father and of the Son and of the Holy Spirit" (Glossary of the Catechism of the Catholic Church).

OT Background: Gen. 4:15; Ezek. 9:4–6
NT Background: Matt. 28:19; 1 Cor. 1:21–22; Eph. 1:13–14; 4:30; Rev. 7:2–8; 9:4; 14:1; 22:4–5
Catechism: 617; 786; 1161; **1235**; **1303**; 1320; 1668; 2157; 2166
Related: CONFIRMATION: *Symbols*: Anointing; Seal

---

2 Note that this topic deals with the "sign of the cross" and not with the "cross as a sign." Occasionally texts in the liturgy speak of the "sign of the cross" but are referring to the "cross as a sign."

In General

- The Sign of the Cross "signifies the grace of the redemption Christ won for us by his cross" (CCC 1235).
- The Sign of the Cross is used by Christians to begin their day, their prayers, and their activities (CCC 2157; 2166; *cf.* LH, Our Lady of Lourdes [Feb 11], 2R: St. Marie Bernadette Soubirous, Ep. Ad P. Gondrand, 1861: *cf.* A. Ravier, Les écrits de sainte Bernadette, Paris 1961, pp. 53–59).
- The Sign of the Cross strengthens the believer in temptations and in difficulties (CCC 2157; *cf.* LH, Our Lady of Lourdes [Feb 11], 2R: St. Marie Bernadette Soubirous, Ep. Ad P. Gondrand, 1861: *cf.* A. Ravier, Les écrits de sainte Bernadette, Paris 1961, pp. 53–59).
- The Sign of the Cross, especially in Baptism, marks the Christian for eternal life (*cf.* RM, Eucharistic Prayer I, 95; CONFIRMATION: *Symbols: Seal*).

For Catechumens

- At the beginning of the path toward Christian Initiation, the Sign of the Cross on the forehead marks the neophyte with the imprint of Christ (RCIA 54–55; *cf. also* CCC 1235; 617). A cross may also be presented to them to signify this reality (RCIA 57).
- At that time, the Sign of the Cross may additionally be made over the ears ("that you may hear the voice of God"), the eyes ("that you may see the glory of God"), the lips ("that you may respond to the word of God"), the heart ("that Christ may dwell there by faith"), and the shoulders ("that you may bear the gentle yoke of Christ") (RCIA 56).
- The signing of the catechumens with the cross of Christ symbolizes the grace of redemption won for us by the cross (CCC 1235), protection by the power of the cross (RCIA 57A), and the call to follow in the footsteps of Christ (RCIA 57B).

In Confirmation

- Christians are "signed" with the seal of the Holy Spirit (RM, Eucharistic Prayer for Various Needs III, Preface).
- Anointing the forehead in the form of the cross with chrism is part of the essential rite of Confirmation. Together with the laying on of the hands, it

signifies being sealed with the gift of the Holy Spirit. In the East, the other sense organs are anointed as well (CCC 1320; 1300; *cf.* RC 27).

- Those confirmed are anointed with the oil of salvation, which signs them with the cross of Christ (RC 59).
- Having received the Sign of the Cross on the forehead, the confirmed must witness to the suffering, death, and Resurrection of Christ before all the world and reflect the goodness of Christ in their life (RC 22).
- Having been signed with the cross and anointed in Confirmation, the Church prays that the confirmed offer themselves to God in union with Christ and merit a greater outpouring of the Holy Spirit (RM, Ritual Masses, For the Conferral of Confirmation, B, Prayer over the Offerings).
- Christians wear on their foreheads the sign of their king (LH, St. Cristopher Magallanes [May 21], 2R: St. Caesarius of Arles, Sermo 225, 1–2: CCL 104, 888–889).
- The Sign of the Cross makes the reborn into kings, sharing in the one kingship of Christ. This kingship is lived out through service with Christ, especially of the poor and suffering, and through the governance of the body in obedience to God (CCC 786, which quotes St. Leo the Great, Sermo 4, 1: PL 54, 149; *cf.* LH, Leo the Great [Nov 10], 2R: Leo the Great, Sermo 4, 1–2: PL 54, 148–149).
- Soldiers of Christ should arm themselves with a spiritual helmet (*cf.* Eph. 6:17) so that the sign of God on their foreheads may be preserved intact (LH, St. Stanislaus [Apr 11], 2R: St. Cyprian, Letter 58, 8–9.11: CSEL 3, 663–666).
- The cross on the forehead is part of the armor of a soldier of God, and serves as a defense (LH, ET.4.Tu, 2R: St. Peter Chrysologus, Sermo 108: PL 52, 499–500; compare with Eph. 6:10–20).
- The forehead of Christians is marked with the name of God (CCC 2159 in reference to Rev. 14:1; 2:17 and in the context of speaking about the Sign of the Cross [*cf.* CCC 2157]).

EUCHARIST

Definition: The ritual, sacramental action of thanksgiving to God which constitutes the principal Christian liturgical celebration of and communion in the paschal mystery of Christ. The liturgical action called the Eucharist is also traditionally known as the Holy Sacrifice of the Mass. It is one of the seven sacraments of the Church; the Holy Eucharist completes Christian initiation. The Sunday celebration of the Eucharist is at the heart of the Church's life (Glossary of the Catechism of the Catholic Church).

TYPES

FRUIT OF THE TREE OF LIFE[1]

OT Background: Gen. 3:9, 22–24; Prov. 3:18; 11:30; 13:12; 15:4; Isa. 65:22 (LXX); Ezek. 47:12

NT Background: John 6:27, 33, 35, 39–40, 44, 47–58; 15:1, 4–5, 8; Rom. 5:12–21; Rev. 2:7; 22:2, 14, 19

Catechism Background: 374–379; 390; 396; 1008; **1129**; **1134**; 1147; **1366**; **1391**; **2074**; 2688; 2821; 2847

Type: LH, St. Albert the Great (Nov 15), 2R: St. Albert the Great, Commentary on Luke 22, 19: Opera Omnia, Paris 1890–1899, 23, 672–674

Related: BAPTISM: *Types:* Fruit of the Tree of Life; EUCHARIST: *Types:* Wisdom's Banquet; Blood from the Side of Christ; *Symbols*: Banquet; Bread from Heaven / Bread of Life / Bread of Angels

• The Eucharist is the fruit of the tree of life. He who receives the Eucharist with sincere faith will never taste death (LH, St. Albert the Great [Nov 15],

---

1 The topic of the fruit of the tree of life as prefiguring the cross, Jesus Christ, or the Scriptures is common. Here are presented only those texts that explicitly or implicitly refer to the Eucharist.

2R: St. Albert the Great, Commentary on Luke 22, 19: Opera Omnia, Paris 1890–1899, 23, 672–674; *cf.* John 6:51–58).

- The fruit of the sacraments is a share in the divine life in Jesus Christ (*cf. for example* CCC 1129; 1134).

- As a memorial, the Eucharist applies the fruit of the sacrifice of Christ (CCC 1366), that is, life in Christ (CCC 1391, which cites John 6:56–57; *cf.* CCC 2074, which cites John 15:5).

- The Church prays that the gifts of bread and wine in the Eucharistic Celebration may bear fruit in eternal happiness (RM, ET.2[=4, 6].Mo, Prayer over the Offerings [=RM, ET.3.Su, Prayer over the Offerings; RM, ET.3[=5].Tu, Prayer over the Offerings]).

- The Church prays that those who eat here below of the bread of life might be allowed to eat as victors from the tree of life in paradise (RM, Commons, Common of Martyrs, II, A, 1, Prayer after Communion).

GIFTS OF ABEL

OT Background: Gen. 4:1–16, 25
NT Background: Matt. 23:35; Luke 11:51; Heb. 11:4; 12:24; 1 John 3:12
Catechism Background: 58; 2569
Type: RM, Eucharistic Prayer I, 93
Related: EUCHARIST: *Types*: Offering of the First Fruits; *Symbols*: Banquet

- In the Eucharistic Celebration, the priest prays that God may be pleased to accept the gifts of the consecrated bread and wine as he once was pleased to accept the gifts of his servant Abel the just (RM, Eucharistic Prayer I, 93; *cf.* Gen. 4:4; Heb. 11:4).

- The Church prays that God might accept the offerings (of bread and wine) from his faithful servants and make them holy, as he once accepted the gifts of Abel (RM, OT.16.Su, Prayer over the Offerings).

OFFERING OF MELCHIZEDEK

OT Background: Gen. 14:17–20; Ps. 110:4
NT Background: Heb. 5:1–10; 6:13–7:22
Catechism Background: 58; **1333**; **1350**; 1359; **1544–1545**
Type: CCC 1333; 1350; 1544 (in light of CCC 1545); RM, Eucharistic Prayer 93; RO 162 (=ROP 25)

Related: HOLY ORDERS: *Types*: High Priest; Melchizedek; *Symbols*: Presentation of the Paten and Chalice

- Melchizedek prefigures the priesthood of Christ (Heb. 5:1–10; 6:13–7:22; CCC 1544, citing Heb. 5:10; 6:19–20; Gen. 14:18; *cf. also* LH, Lent.4.Mo, 2R, Resp [Heb. 6:20; 7:2, 3]; LH, Lent.5.Su, 2R, Resp [Heb. 6:20; John 1:29]; LH, Lent.5.We, 1R, Resp [Heb. 6:19–20; 7:24–25]; LH, Lent.5.Th, 1R, Resp [Gen. 14:18; Heb. 7:3; Ps. 110:5; Heb. 7:16]; LH, Lent.5.Fr, 1R, Resp [Heb. 5:5, 6; 7:20, 21]; LH, OT.12.Su, 2R: Faustus Luciferanus, Treatise on the Trinity, 39–40: CCL 69, 340–341; LH, OT.12.Su, 2R, Resp; LH, Corpus Christi, EP2, Ant1; Psalter.2.Su, EP2, Ant1).
- The priesthood of Christ, prefigured by Melchizedek (CCC 1544), is made present in the Church through the ministerial priesthood (CCC 1545) by means of participation in the one priesthood of Christ (CCC 1546–1547; *cf.* HOLY ORDERS: *Types:* Melchizedek).
- Melchizedek, who offered bread and wine, prefigures Christ, who offered bread and wine (LH, Lent.5.Th, 1R, Resp [Gen. 14:18; Heb. 7:3; Ps. 110:5; Heb. 7:16]; LH, Corpus Christi, EP2, Ant1).
- The Church prays that the consecrated bread and wine may be accepted by God as once he was pleased to accept the offering of his high priest, Melchizedek (RM, Eucharistic Prayer I, 93).
- The offering by the king-priest Melchizedek of bread and wine (*cf.* Gen. 14:17–20) prefigures the offering of bread and wine by the Church (CCC 1333, which cites Gen. 14:18 and RM, Eucharistic Prayer I, 93; *cf.* CCC 1350).

The Catechism of the Catholic Church

At the heart of the Eucharistic celebration are the bread and wine that, by the words of Christ and the invocation of the Holy Spirit, become Christ's Body and Blood. Faithful to the Lord's command the Church continues to do, in his memory and until his glorious return, what he did on the eve of his Passion: "He took bread. . . ." "He took the cup filled with wine. . . ." The signs of bread and wine become, in a way surpassing understanding, the Body and Blood of Christ; they continue also to signify the goodness of creation. Thus in the

Offertory we give thanks to the Creator for bread and wine (Cf. Ps. 104:13–15), fruit of the "work of human hands," but above all as "fruit of the earth" and "of the vine"—gifts of the Creator. The Church sees in the gesture of the king-priest Melchizedek, who "brought out bread and wine," a prefiguring of her own offering (Gen. 14:18; *cf.* Roman Missal, EP I [Roman Canon] 95).

CCC 1333

- The offering of bread and wine in the Offertory "takes up the gesture of Melchizedek and commits the Creator's gifts into the hands of Christ who, in his sacrifice, brings to perfection all human attempts to offer sacrifices" (CCC 1350; *cf.* CCC 1359).
- At the ordination of priests and deacons, the responsorial psalm may be Ps. 110:1, 2, 3, 4, with the antiphon "Christ the Lord, a priest for ever in the line of Melchizedek, offered bread and wine." (Lectionary 772; RO 349).
- As newly ordained priests are being vested, the faithful sing Psalm 110 with the following antiphon: "Christ the Lord, a priest forever according to the order of Melchizedek, offered bread and wine" (RO 162 [=ROP 25]).
- The Catechism closely relates Melchizedek's prefiguring the priesthood of Christ with Christ's single offering (citing Heb. 10:4), the sacrifice of the cross. This may be presenting the single offering of Melchizedek in the Bible (Gen. 14:18) as a type of the single offering of Christ, which is made present in the Eucharist (*cf.* CCC 1544–1545).
- On the feast of Corpus Christi and in Votive Masses of the Most Holy Eucharist the first reading may be Gen. 14:18–20, in which Melchizedek offers bread and wine to God (Lectionary 169; 976).
- On the feast of Corpus Christi and in Votive Masses of the Most Holy Eucharist the responsorial psalm may be Ps. 110:1, 2, 3, 4, in which the Lord swears an oath: "You are a priest forever in the line of Melchizedek" (Ps. 110:4), implicitly relating the offering of the priest Melchizedek with the the Eucharist (Lectionary 169; 978).

SACRIFICE OF ABRAHAM

OT Background: Gen. 22:1–18; 26:4–5; 2 Chron. 20:7; Neh. 9:7–8; Sir. 44:20; Isa. 41:8; 1 Macc. 2:52

NT Background: John 1:29; 3:16; 8:56; 19:17; Acts 3:25; Rom. 4:11, 16–18, 20–22; 8:32; Heb. 11:17–19; James 2:21–24; 1 John 4:9

Catechism Background: 144–146; 165; 332; 422; 706; 1080; 1819; 2570–2571; **2572**; 2592

Type: RM, Eucharistic Prayer I, 93

Related: EUCHARIST: *Types*: Gifts of Abel; Offering of Melchizedek; Passover / Passover Lamb; HOLY ORDERS: *Symbols*: Father

- The sacrifice of Abraham of his only son, Isaac, prefigures the sacrifice of the Father of his only son, Jesus Christ (*cf. for example* CCC 2572; LH, OT.5.Tu, 2R, Resp [John 19:16–17; Gen. 22:6]; *cf. also for example* Gal. 3:16; Heb. 11:19; CCC 706; RM, Easter Vigil, 25). The one sacrifice of Christ is made present in the Eucharistic sacrifice of the Church (*cf. for example* CCC 1545; *cf.* EUCHARIST: *Types*: Passover / Passover Lamb).
- The Church prays that as God was pleased to accept the sacrifice of Abraham, our father in faith, so he may also accept the offering of the Eucharistic Body and Blood of Christ (RM, Eucharistic Prayer I, 93).

PASSOVER / PASSOVER LAMB

Definition: Jesus' saving death and its memorial in the Eucharist is associated with the Jewish feast of Passover (or Pasch) commemorating the deliverance of the Jewish people from death by the blood of the lamb sprinkled on the doorposts in Egypt, which the angel of death saw and "passed over." Hence Jesus is acknowledged in the New Testament as the Lamb of God, who takes away the sins of the world; he is the Paschal Lamb, the symbol of Israel's redemption at the first Passover. The Eucharist celebrates the new Passover, in which Jesus "passes over" to his Father by his death and Resurrection, thus anticipating the final Passover of the Church in the glory of the Kingdom (Glossary of the Catechism of the Catholic Church).

OT Background:

Passover / Lamb: Exod. 12:1–51; 13:3–5, 8; 34:25; Lev. 23:4–8; Num. 9:1–14; 28:16; Deut. 16:1–8; Josh. 5:10; 2 Kings 23:21–23; 2 Chron. 30:1–5, 13–21; 35:1–19; Ezra 6:19–20; Isa. 53:7; Jer. 11:19; Ezek. 45:21

Memorial: Exod. 13:8; Deut. 5:3 (cf. Deut. 2:14); Judg. 2:1; 6:8–10; 10:11–12; Amos 2:10

NT Background:

The Last Supper and the Passover memorial: Matt. 26:17–30; Mark 14:12–26; Luke 22:7–20; 1 Cor. 11:23–26; *cf. also* Heb. 7:24, 27

Jesus the Lamb: John 1:29, 36; 19:36; Acts 8:32; 1 Cor. 5:7–8; 1 Pet. 1:18–19; Rev. 5:6, 8, 12–13; 6:1, 16; 7:9–10, 14, 17; 8:1; 12:11; 13:8, 11; 14:1, 4, 10; 15:3; 17:14; 19:7, 9; 21:9, 14, 22–23, 27; 22:1, 3

Other: Mark 10:45; Luke 2:41; John 2:13, 23; 6:4, 51; 11:55; 12:1; 13:1; 18:28; 19:14; Heb. 11:28

Catechism Background:

The Passover: 130; 583; 608; 1081; 1093; 1150–1151; 1164; 1334; 2574; *cf. also* 2170

Jesus as Lamb: 523; 536; 602; **608; 613; 719; 757; 796; 865; 869; 1045; 1137–1138; 1244; 1329; 1602; 1612; 1618; 1642; 2159; 2618; 2642; 2665**

Christ's Passover: 112; 243; 429; 444; 498; **512**; 530; 542; 556; 560; 570–572; 585; 613; 618; 631; 638; 642; 654–655; 671; 731; 793; 1067; 1094; 1115; 1130; 1164–1165; 1168; 1170; 1225; 1239; 1260; 1337; 1449; 1505; 1621; 1670; 2175; 2719; 2746–2748; 2812

The Eucharist as memorial of Christ's Passover: 559; 610–611; 1067; 1076; **1085; 1088; 1099; 1103–1104; 1139; 1166; 1171; 1173–1174; 1182; 1200; 1244; 1323; 1324; 1330; 1333; 1337; 1341; 1344; 1347; 1357–1358; 1362–1372; 1380; 1382; 1394; 1402–1403; 1409; 1517; 1621; 2175; 2177; 2659; 2746**

The Passover / Passover lamb as a type of the Eucharist: 1096 (in light of 1093); 1150–1152; 1189; **1334; 1339–1340; 1363–1364**; *cf. also* 2175

The Passover of the Body of Christ, the Church: 675–677; 793; 1173; 1340; 1680–1683; 1685; 1689

Type: CCC 1096 (in light of 1093); 1150–1152; 1189; 1334; 1339–1340; 1363–1364; RM, Easter Vigil, 19; Lectionary 976; LH, Lent.HW.Fr, 2R: St. John Chrysostom, Catecheses 3, 13–19: SC 50, 174–177; LH, ET.1.Sa, 2R, Resp [Luke 22:19; Exod. 12:27]; LH, ET.2.Th, 2R: St. Gaudentius of Brescia, Tract. 2: CSEL 68, 30–32; LH, ET.5.Th, 2R: St. Gaudentius of Brescia, Tract. 2: CSEL 68, 26.29–30

Related: EUCHARIST: *Types:* Animal Sacrifices; Manna

The Feast of the Jewish Passover

• The Passover feast of the Old Covenant commemorates the astonishing actions of God, gives him thanks for them, perpetuates their remembrance, and teaches new generations to conform their conduct to them (CCC 1164).

• Some significant aspects of the celebration of the Passover:
   ▪ The Passover lamb was to be a year old lamb, without blemish (*cf.* Exod. 12:5).
   ▪ The lamb was sacrificed on the fourteenth of the month of Abib (Nisan) at twilight (*cf.* Exod. 12:6).
   ▪ The blood of the lamb was put on the doorposts and lintel of the house (*cf.* Exod. 12:7).
   ▪ The lamb was to be wholly consumed that night (Exod. 12:8–10; 34:25) together with unleavened bread and herbs.
   ▪ The unleavened bread eaten at Passover "commemorates the haste of the departure that liberated them from Egypt" (CCC 1334; *cf.* Exod. 12:8, 34, 39; Deut. 16:3).
   ▪ The Passover lamb was the symbol of the redemption of Israel (CCC 608, citing Exod. 12:3–14; *cf.* Exod. 12:26–27; 13:3, 5, 8).
   ▪ The "cup of blessing" (*cf.* 1 Cor. 10:16) at the end of the Jewish Passover celebration symbolized "the messianic expectation of the rebuilding of Jerusalem" (CCC 1334).

• Foreigners were allowed to eat of the Passover lamb only after receiving circumcision (*cf.* Exod. 12:43–49).

• Every time Israel celebrates Passover it does so as a memorial, according to the biblical understanding of memorial, that is, it understands that the Exodus events become in a certain way present and real (CCC 1363; *cf.* below *The Passover as memorial prefigured the Eucharist*).

Jesus, the Lamb of God, and His Passover

• Jesus Christ is the Passover Lamb, the Lamb of God who takes away the sins of the world (*cf. for example* John 1:29, 36; 19:36; CCC 523; 536; 602; 608; 613; RM, The Order of the Mass, 8; 45; 47; 49; RM, The Nativity of St. John the Baptist [June 24], Vigil Mass, Prayer after Communion; for other references in general to Christ as Lamb of God *cf. for example* CCC 719;

757; 796; 865; 869; 1045; 1137–1138; 1244; 1329; 1602; 1612; 1618; 1642; 2159; 2618; 2642; 2665; RM, Dec 18, Entrance Antiphon; RM, The Nativity of St. John the Baptist [June 24], Mass during the Day, Preface; RM, The Passion of St. John the Baptist [Aug 29], Preface; RM, The Immaculate Conception of the Blessed Virgin Mary [Dec 8], Preface; RM, The Holy Innocents [Dec 28], Entrance Antiphon; RM, Votive Masses, 12, Preface; RM, Votive Masses, 12, Prayer after Communion).

- The Passion, crucifixion, death, burial, descent into hell, Resurrection, and Ascension of Christ are the Paschal mystery, the Passover of Jesus Christ (*cf. for example* CCC 512; RM, Easter Vigil, 25; for other references in general to the Passover of Jesus Christ in the Catechism *cf.* Catechism Background above).
- Jesus Christ "gives new meaning to the deeds and signs of the Old Covenant, above all to the Exodus and the Passover [Cf. Luke 9:31; 22:7-20], for he himself is the meaning of all these signs" (CCC 1151).
- The Passover of Jesus Christ (i.e. his death and Resurrection) was prefigured by the ancient Passover and the paschal lamb (*cf. for example* LH, Lent. HW.Th, 2R: St. Melito of Sardis, Easter homily, 65–71: SC 123, 95–101; LH, ET.1.Mo, 2R: St. Melito of Sardis, Easter Homily, Ch. 2–7, 100–103: SC 123, 60–64.120–122; LH, ET.2.Mo, 2R: Pseudo-Chrysostom, Ancient Easter Homily: PG 59, 723–724).
- There is nothing more marvelous than the world's creation, "except that, at the end of the ages, Christ our Passover has been sacrificed" (RM, Easter Vigil, Prayer after the first reading [Gen. 1:1–2:2]).
- Jesus is the true Lamb of God, slain in the feasts of Passover, whose blood anoints the doorposts of believers (RM, Easter Vigil, 19).
- Jesus Christ brought the Paschal Mystery to completion by bestowing the Holy Spirit at Pentecost (*cf. for example* RM, ET, Pentecost, At the Mass during the Day, Preface).

The Passover (In General) Prefigured the Eucharist

- The liturgical celebration of Passover prefigured the sacraments of the New Covenant (CCC 1150; *cf. also* 1093; 1096).
- Jesus chose the time of the Passover to give his disciples his Body and Blood in the Eucharist (CCC 1339, which cites Matt. 26:17–29; Mark 14:12–25; Luke 22:7–20; 1 Cor. 11:23–26).

- Jesus celebrated the Last Supper in the course of the Passover meal (*cf. for example* Matt. 26:17–19; Mark 14:12, 14, 16; Luke 22:7–8, 11, 13, 15; LH, Holy Thursday, MP, Magn; LH, Corpus Christi, MM, Ant). By doing so, he gave the Jewish Passover its definitive meaning (CCC 1340; *cf. also* RM, Eucharistic Prayer for Reconciliation I, 3; LH, Corpus Christi, 2R: St. Thomas Aquinas, Opusculum 57, in festo Corporis Christi, lect. 1–3).

- At the Last Supper, Jesus anticipated his "passing over" to the Father by his death and Resurrection, the new Passover. This new Passover is celebrated in the Eucharist, which fulfills the Jewish Passover (CCC 1340; *cf. also* CCC 1402; 1409).

- Jesus used the rite of breaking of bread, "part of a Jewish meal when as master of the table he blessed and distributed the bread, above all at the Last Supper" (CCC 1329, citing Matt. 14:19; 15:36; 26:26; Mark 8:6, 19; 1 Cor. 11:24; *cf.* CCC 1355; EUCHARIST: *Symbols:* Breaking of Bread). At the Last Supper, Jesus "gave a new and definitive meaning to the blessing of bread and the cup" of the Passover (CCC 1334; *cf. also* CCC 1355; EUCHARIST: *Symbols:* Bread and Wine / Nourishment).

- The liturgical celebration of the Church takes up the signs and symbols of the rites of Passover. "Integrated into the world of faith and taken up by the power of the Holy Spirit," they "become bearers of the saving and sanctifying action of Christ" (CCC 1189).

- The Lord's paschal sacrifice is celebrated with the unleavened bread of sincerity and truth, tossing out the leaven of malice, for the effect of receiving the Body and Blood of Christ "is to change us into what we receive" (LH, ET.2.We, 2R: St. Leo the Great, Sermo 12 de Passione, 3, 6–7: PL 54, 355–357; *cf.* 1 Cor. 5:7–8 and the Old Covenant background in Exod. 12:8, 34, 39; Deut. 16:3).

- In Votive Masses of the Most Holy Eucharist the first reading may be Exod. 12:21–27, in which Moses gives instructions on how to celebrate the Passover. Seeing the blood of the Lamb on the lintel and the doorposts, the Lord will pass over that door and they will be saved (Lectionary 976).

The Passover Lamb Prefigured the Eucharistic Lamb of God

- As Lamb of God, Jesus was prefigured by the Passover lamb, "the symbol of Israel's redemption at the first Passover (Isa. 53:7, 12; *cf.* Jer. 11:19; Exod. 12:3–14; John 19:36; 1 Cor. 5:7)" (CCC 608; *cf.* CCC 613).

- The lamb of Passover prefigured the Eucharist (LH, Lent.HW.Fr, 2R: St. John Chrysostom, Catecheses 3, 13–19: SC 50, 174–177):
  - The blood of the Passover lamb was able to save the Jews because it was a sign of the Lord's blood.
  - The angel of death passed over the doors with the prefigurative blood of the Passover lamb on them; how much more will the devil pass by those believers who have the true blood on their lips, which are the doors of the temple of Christ.
  - The blood from the side of Christ, the Lamb, symbolizes the Eucharist, which nourishes the faithful (*cf. also* EUCHARIST: *Types:* Blood from the Side of Christ).

The Liturgy of the Hours

If we wish to understand the power of Christ's blood, we should go back to the ancient account of its prefiguration in Egypt. "Sacrifice a lamb without blemish," commanded Moses, "and sprinkle its blood on your doors." If we were to ask him what he meant, and how the blood of an irrational beast could possibly save men endowed with reason, his answer would be that the saving power lies not in the blood itself, but in the fact that it is a sign of the Lord's blood. In those days, when the destroying angel saw the blood on the doors he did not dare to enter, so how much less will the devil approach now when he sees, not that figurative blood on the doors, but the true blood on the lips of believers, the doors of the temple of Christ.

If you desire further proof of the power of this blood, remember where it came from, how it ran down from the cross, flowing from the Master's side. The gospel records that when Christ was dead, but still hung on the cross, a soldier came and pierced his side with a lance and immediately there poured out water and blood. Now the water was a symbol of baptism and the blood, of the holy Eucharist. The soldier pierced the Lord's side, he breached the wall of the sacred temple, and I have found the treasure and made it my own. So also with the lamb: the Jews sacrificed the victim and I have been saved by it.

LH, Lent.HW.Fr, 2R: St. John Chrysostom, Catecheses 3, 13–19: SC 50, 174–177

- In the Eucharistic Celebration, "fulfilling the sacrifices of the Fathers, is offered the true Lamb, Jesus Christ your Son" (RM, Commons, Common of the Blessed Virgin Mary, II, Prayer over the Offerings).
- At the Last Supper, Jesus offered himself as the unblemished Lamb (RM, The Order of the Mass, 61; RM, The Presentation of the Lord [Feb 2], Prayer over the Offerings).
- The Eucharist is the flesh and blood of the Lamb (LH, ET.5.Th, 2R: St. Gaudentius of Brescia, Tract. 2: CSEL 68, 26.29–30).
- In the Eucharistic Celebration, in the presence of the Eucharist the faithful proclaim, "Lamb of God, you take away the sins of the world, have mercy on us . . . grant us peace" (RM, The Order of the Mass, 130).
- In the Eucharistic Celebration, the priest elevates the Eucharist and proclaims, "Behold the Lamb of God, behold him who takes away the sins of the world. Blessed are those called to the supper of the Lamb" (RM, The Order of the Mass, 132).
- In the Eucharistic sacrifice, the Passover Lamb whose Passion unlocked the gates of heaven is presented to God the Father (RM, Ritual Masses, III, Prayer over the Offerings).
- The Eucharist is the banquet of the heavenly Lamb (RM, The Nativity of St. John the Baptist [June 24], Mass during the Day, Prayer after Communion).

The Passover as Memorial Prefigured the Eucharist

- Every time Israel celebrates Passover, it understands that the Exodus events become in a certain way present and real (CCC 1363; *cf. for example* Exod. 13:8 and its interpretation in Mishnah Pesachim 10:5E; other verses that speak of future generations as having been present at past events of salvation history are for example Deut. 5:3 [compare with 2:14], Judg. 2:1, 6:8–10, 10:11–12, and Amos 2:10). Similarly, the Eucharist as memorial makes present the death and Resurrection of Jesus Christ, i.e. his Passover, where the work of redemption is carried out (CCC 1362; 1364; *cf. also* CCC 559).

- The Liturgy of the Hours associates the institution of the Eucharistic memorial in Luke 22:19 with Exod. 12:27, in which, at the end of the Passover celebration, the child asks his father about the meaning of the rite, and the father responds, "It is the sacrifice of the Lord's passover, for he passed over the houses of the people of Israel in Egypt, when he slew the Egyptians but spared our houses" (LH, ET.1.Sa, 2R, Resp [Luke 22:19; Exod. 12:27]).

- The Eucharist is the sacrifice of the saving Passover, which the faithful join in after having escaped from the power of Egypt and of Pharaoh, who is the devil (LH, ET.2.Th, 2R: St. Gaudentius of Brescia, Tract. 2: CSEL 68, 30–32).

- The Eucharist celebrates the Passover of the Lord, that is, the Lord's passing. In the Eucharist the Lord passes into the bread and wine and they become his Body and Blood (LH, ET.5.Th, 2R: St. Gaudentius of Brescia, Tract. 2: CSEL 68, 26.29–30).

- Jesus transformed the Last Supper with his apostles "into the memorial of his voluntary offering to the Father for the salvation of men: 'This is my body which is given for you.' 'This is my blood of the covenant, which is poured out for many for the forgiveness of sins'" (CCC 610, quoting Luke 22:19, Matt. 26:28, and citing 1 Cor. 5:7; *cf.* CCC 1085; 1323; *cf. also for example* LH, Holy Thursday, EP, 1st intercession; for a more complete list of references from the Catechism to the Eucharistic Celebration as a memorial, *cf.* Catechism Background above).

- As a memorial, the Eucharist re-presents (i.e. makes present) the once-for-all sacrifice of Jesus Christ on the cross and applies its fruit (CCC 1366–1367, citing among others 1 Cor. 11:23 and Heb. 7:24, 27). In this offering, the whole Church is united with the one offering of Jesus Christ (CCC 1369–1372).

- The Eucharist is the memorial of the sacrifice of Christ (*cf. for example* CCC 1085; 1323; 1362–1372; RM, The Sacred Paschal Triduum, Thursday of the Lord's Supper, 15; 26; RM, OT.2.Su, Prayer over the Offerings; RM, OT.17.Su, Prayer after Communion; RM, Corpus Christi, Collect; RM, The Order of the Mass, 60; 61; 92; 105; 113; 122; RM, Eucharistic Prayer for Reconciliation I, 7; RM, Eucharistic Prayer for Reconciliation II, 7; RM, Eucharistic Prayer for Use for Masses for Various Needs, I [=II, III, IV], 7; RM, St. John Neumann [Jan 5], Prayer after Communion; RM, St. Augustine [Aug 28], Prayer over the Offerings; RM, Ritual Masses, I, 4, A,

Prayer over the Offerings; RM, Ritual Masses, X, 2, Preface; RM, Masses and Prayers for Various Needs and Occasions, I, 1, C [=E], Prayer over the Offerings; RM, Masses and Prayers for Various Needs and Occasions, I, 17, B, Prayer over the Offerings; RM, Votive Masses, 2, Prayer over the Offerings; RM, Votive Masses, 3; 5; LH, Holy Thursday, EP, Prayer; LH, Corpus Christi, EP [=EP2], 2nd intercession; LH, Corpus Christi, EP [=MP, OR, EP2], Prayer; LH, St. Bridget [July 23], 2R: St. Bridget, Oratio 2: Revelationum S. Birgittae libri, 2, Romae 1628, p. 408–410; LH, St. Albert the Great [Nov 15], 2R: St. Albert the Great, Commentary on Luke 22, 19: Opera Omnia, Paris 1890–1899, 23, 672–674; *cf. also* Catechism Background above).

The Eucharist Celebrates the Paschal Mystery of Christ

- The liturgy is the celebration of the Paschal Mystery of Christ (*cf. for example* CCC 1067; 1076; 1085; 1104; 1166; 1171; 1173; 1182; 1200; 1344; 1621; 1670; 2177; 2659; RM, Ash Wednesday, Blessing and Distribution of Ashes; RM, Lent.1.Su, Preface; RM, ET.3[=5].We, Prayer over the Offerings [=RM, ET.4.Su, Prayer over the Offerings; RM, ET.4[=]6.Tu, Prayer over the Offerings]; RM, Faithful Departed [Nov 2], 1, Prayer after Communion; RM, Masses for the Dead, I, D, Prayer after Communion [=RM, Masses for the Dead, II, C, Prayer after Communion]; LH, ET.2.Sa, 2R: Vatican II, Sacrosanctum Concilium 5–6; LH, OT.3.Su, 2R: Vatican II, Sacrosanctum Concilium 7–8.106).

- By gift of God the faithful celebrate the paschal mysteries on earth (RM, ET.4.Mo, Collect).

- The liturgy prays that the faithful might partake unceasingly of the paschal mysteries, persevering in the sacraments of their rebirth (RM, Lent. HW.We, Prayer over the People).

- The liturgy prays that the faithful might be conformed to the paschal mysteries (RM, ET.5.Fr, Collect).

- In the Eucharistic Celebration, the priest prays that God may constantly accomplish the Paschal Mysteries within the faithful (RM, ET.5.Su, Collect).

- The Eucharist is the paschal Sacrament (*cf. for example* RM, Easter Vigil, 67; RM, ET.1.Mo, Prayer after Communion; RM, ET.2.Su, Prayer after Communion; RM, ET.2[=4, 6].Th, Prayer after Communion; RM, ET.3[=5].Mo, Prayer after Communion; RM, ET.6.Su, Prayer after

Communion; *cf. also* RM, Eucharistic Prayer for Use for Masses for Various Needs, I [=II, III, IV], 7; RM, Faithful Departed [Nov 2], 1, Prayer after Communion; RM, Commons, Common of the Blessed Virgin Mary, IV, Prayer after Communion; RM, Masses for the Dead, I, C, Prayer after Communion).

- The Eucharist is the paschal banquet (*cf. for example* RM, Lent.HW.Th, Chrism Mass, 12; RM, Ritual Masses, IV, 1 [=2], A [=B], Preface).
- In the liturgy are celebrated the paschal festivities (*cf. for example* RM, Lent.2.Su, Prayer over the Offerings; RM, Lent.4.Th, Collect; RM, Lent. HW.Mo, Prayer after Communion; RM, ET.7.Sa, Collect).
- In the Sacred Paschal Triduum, the Church "solemnly celebrates the greatest mysteries of our redemption, keeping by means of special celebrations the memorial of her Lord, crucified, buried, and risen" (RM, The Sacred Paschal Triduum, 1; *cf. also* RM, Preface I of Lent).

The Eucharist and the Soul's Final Passover

- At the Last Supper, Jesus anticipated his "passing over" to the Father by his death and Resurrection, the new Passover. This new Passover is celebrated in the Eucharist, "which fulfills the Jewish Passover and anticipates the final Passover of the Church in the glory of the kingdom" (CCC 1340; *cf.* CCC 677; 1344; 1402). In this "final Passover" of the Church, the Church will pass through a final trial that will shake the faith of many, and will enter the glory of the kingdom only after having followed "her Lord in his death and Resurrection (Cf. Rev. 19:1–9)" (CCC 677; *cf.* 675).
- The Eucharist, sacrament of Christ's Passover (i.e. his death, Resurrection, and Ascension) has particular importance and meaning at the time of death, the moment of the soul's "passing over" (i.e. "Passover") to the Father. The Eucharist is "the seed of eternal life and the power of resurrection, according to the words of the Lord: 'He who eats my flesh and drinks my blood has eternal life, and I will raise him up on the last day' (John 6:54)" (CCC 1524; *cf.* John 13:1; CCC 1392; *cf. also* CCC 512; EUCHARIST: *Symbols:* Bread for the Journey / Daily Bread / Viaticum).
- The ancient Passover was a symbol of the Passover of Jesus Christ. The faithful are reminded that the Passover of Jesus Christ is itself symbolic, for this Passover (in which they are about to share) points to that eternal Passover, when the faithful will share with the Word the new wine in the kingdom of

his Father (LH, Lent.5.Sa, 2R: St. Gregory of Nazianzus, Oratio 45, 23–24: PG 36, 654–655).

- By celebrating the Paschal Mystery of Christ in a worthy manner, Christians hope to "pass over at last to the eternal paschal feast" (RM, Lent.1.Su, Preface; *cf. for example* RM, Easter Vigil, 9; 10; *cf. also for example* RM, Easter Vigil, 61; 68; RM, Easter Sunday, At the Mass during the Day, 76; RM, Ritual Masses, VIII, 2, A, Hanc igitur, a).

Offering of the First Fruits

OT Background: Exod. 23:16, 19; 34:22, 26; Lev. 2:14; 23:10–14; Num. 15:20–21; 18:12–13; Deut. 18:4; 26:10; 2 Kings 4:42; 2 Chron. 31:5; Neh. 10:35–37; Jth. 11:13; Prov. 3:9; Sir. 35:8–11; 45:20–21; Jer. 2:3; Ezek. 44:30

NT Background: Rom. 8:23; 11:16; 1 Cor. 15:20–23; 16:15; Eph. 5:2; Heb. 10:1, 14; James 1:18; Rev. 14:4

Catechism Background: 528; 655; 735; 991; 1046; **1171**; **1334**; **1391**; 1832

Type: LH, OT.2.Sa, 2R: St. Irenaeus, Against Heresies, Book 4, 18, 1–2.4.5: SC 100, 596–598.606.610–612; LH, OT.18.Sa, 2R: St. Irenaeus, Against Heresies, Book 4, 17, 4–6: SC 100, 590–594

Related: EUCHARIST: *Types*: Gifts of Abel; *Symbols*: Bread and Wine / Nourishment

- In the Old Covenant, the bread and wine were offered up to God among the fruits of the earth "as a sign of grateful acknowledgment to the Creator" (CCC 1334).
- Jesus Christ taught his disciples to offer to God the first fruits of creation. He did this by taking bread and the cup, fruit of the creation, and saying, "This is my body," and "This is my blood." He taught them that this was the sacrifice of the new covenant. In this sacrifice, the Church offers to God the first fruits and fulfills Malachi's prophecy that a pure sacrifice would be offered everywhere to his name (LH, OT.18.Sa, 2R: St. Irenaeus, Against Heresies, Book 4, 17, 4–6: SC 100, 590–594, citing Mal. 1:10b–11).

The Liturgy of the Hours

Moreover, he instructed his disciples to offer to God the first fruits of creation, not because God had any need, but so that they themselves should not be unproductive and ungrateful. This is why he took bread, a part of his creation, gave thanks and said: "This is my body." In the same way he declared that the cup, an element of the same creation as ourselves, was his blood; He taught them that this was the new sacrifice of the new covenant. The Church has received this sacrifice from the apostles; throughout the world she offers to God, who feeds us, the first fruits of his own gifts, under the new covenant. It was foretold by Malachi, one of the twelve prophets, in the words: "I take no pleasure in you, says the Lord Almighty, and no sacrifice will I accept from your hands. For, from the rising of the sun to its setting, the Gentiles glorify my name, and in every place incense and a spotless sacrifice are offered to my name; my name is great among the Gentiles, says the Lord Almighty" (Mal. 1:10b–11).

LH, OT.18.Sa, 2R: St. Irenaeus, Against Heresies, Book 4, 17, 4–6: SC 100, 590–594

- The Church alone lifts up to God in the Eucharist the pure offering of the first fruits of his creation. While in the Old Covenant these oblations were done by slaves, now they are offered up by sons (LH, OT.2.Sa, 2R: St. Irenaeus, Against Heresies, Book 4, 18, 1–2.4.5: SC 100, 596–598.606.610–612).
- When the faithful receive the Body of Christ, "they proclaim to one another the Good News that the first fruits of life have been given" (CCC 1391, quoting Fanqîth, Syriac Office of Antioch, Vol. I, Commun., 237 a–b; *cf.* RM, Mass and Prayers for Various Needs and Occasions, 33, B, Prayer over the Offerings).
- The liturgical celebration of the feasts surrounding the mystery of the Incarnation (Annunciation, Christmas, Epiphany) communicates the first fruits of the Paschal mystery (CCC 1171).

BLOOD OF THE COVENANT

OT Background: Exod. 6:6–7; 24:8; Lev. 16:15–16; Jer. 31:31–34; Zech. 9:11

NT Background: Matt. 26:28; Mark 14:24; Luke 22:20; 1 Cor. 11:25; Heb. 9:18–21; 12:24; 13:20

Catechism Background: 610; 613; **781**; 1339; 1365; 1846; **2060**; 2260

Type: Matt. 26:28; Luke 22:20; CCC 781; 1330; Lectionary 168; 976

Related: EUCHARIST: *Types*: Passover / Passover Lamb; Animal Sacrifices

- At the Last Supper, Jesus Christ took the cup of wine and said, "This is my blood of the [new] covenant, which is poured out for many for the forgiveness of sins," alluding to Exod. 24:8 and Jer. 31:31. The allusion to Exod. 24:8 is usually considered typological: as Moses ratified the Old Covenant by sprinkling the Israelites with the "blood of the covenant," so now Jesus ratifies the New Covenant (*cf.* Jer. 31:31) by giving his disciples the "blood of the covenant," offered up through the Last Supper and shed during his crucifixion (*cf.* Matt. 26:28; Mark 14:24; Luke 22:20; 1 Cor. 11:25; Heb. 9:18–21; CCC 781; *cf. also* Heb. 12:24; 13:20; CCC 610; 613; 1365; 2060; RM, Eucharistic Prayer I, 90 and parallels; LH, The Most Precious Blood of Our Lord Jesus Christ, OR, Ant1).
- God chose the Israelite people and made a covenant with them as a preparation for and a figure of the new and perfect covenant which would be ratified in the blood of Christ (CCC 781).
- In the celebration of the Eucharist, the faithful "celebrate anew the sprinkling" of the blood of Jesus, "the Mediator of the New Covenant" (RM, Votive Masses, The Most Precious Blood of Our Lord Jesus Christ, Prayer over the Offerings; *cf.* Exod. 24:8; Jer. 31:31).
- On the feast of Corpus Christi and in Votive Masses of the Most Holy Eucharist, the first reading may be Exod. 24:3–8, in which Moses ratified the Old Covenant by sprinkling the Israelites with "the blood of the covenant" (Lectionary 168; 976).
- On the Feast of Corpus Christi, the first reading of the Liturgy of the Hours is Exod. 24:1–11, and its Responsory is John 6:48–52 (LH, Corpus Christi, 1R, Resp [John 6:48–52]).

Animal Sacrifices

OT Background:[2]

Examples of animal sacrifices: Gen. 4:4; 22:13; 31:54; 46:1; Exod. 3:18; 5:3, 8, 17; 8:8; 29:1; Lev. 1, 3–7, 16; Deut. 12:5–14; 1 Sam. 9:12; 15:15, 21; 16:2–5; 2 Sam. 15:12; 1 Kings 3:3–4; 8:62–63; 19:21; 2 Chron. 7:4–5

Acceptable animal sacrifices: Ps. 4:5; 50:14, 23; 51:19; 54:6; 56:12; 107:22; 116:13, 17; Sir. 45:20–21

Animal sacrifices are insufficient: 1 Sam. 15:21–22; Ps. 40:6–8; 51:16–17; 69:30–31; Prov. 15:8; 21:3, 27; Eccles. 5:1; Isa. 1:11–17; Jer. 6:20; 7:21–28; 14:12; Hos. 6:6; Amos 5:22–24; Mic. 6:6–8; Mal. 1:10–12; 2:13

Acceptable sacrifices performed by Gentiles: Isa. 19:21; Mal. 1:11

NT Background: Matt. 5:23–24; 9:13; 12:7; 26:28; Mark 12:33; 14:24; Luke 22:20; John 1:29; Rom. 12:1; 15:16; 1 Cor. 10:14–21; Eph. 5:2; Phil. 2:17; 4:18; 2 Tim. 4:6; Heb. 5:1–3; 7:27; 8:3; 9:9–10:18; 11:4; 12:24; 13:10, 15–16; 1 Pet. 2:5

Catechism Background: 28; **522**; **614**; **1330**; 1350; 1359–1361; 1362–1372; 1383; 1540; 1544–1545; 1589; 2099–2100; **2643**

Type: CCC 1330; 2643; LH, Lent.5.Tu, 2R: St. Leo the Great, Sermo 8 de passione Domini, 6–8: PL 54, 340–342; LH, Lent.5.Fr, 2R: St. Fulgentius of Ruspe, Treatise on Faith Addressed to Peter, Ch. 22, 62: CCL 91 A, 726.750–751; LH, OT.2.Sa, 2R: St. Irenaeus, Against Heresies, Book 4, 18, 1–2.4.5: SC 100, 596–598.606.610–612; LH, Corpus Christi, 2R: St. Thomas Aquinas, Opusculum 57, in festo Corporis Christi, lect. 1–3; LH, OT.18.Sa, 2R [Latin]: St. Irenaeus, Against Heresies, Book 4, 17, 4–6: SC 100, 590–594

Related: EUCHARIST: *Types*: Gifts of Abel; Sacrifice of Abraham; Blood of the Covenant; Holocaust of Elijah; Passover / Passover Lamb; *Symbols*: Altar / Table

Animal Sacrifices Prefigured the Sacrifice of Christ

• The animal sacrifices of the Old Covenant foreshadowed the offering which the only Son of God in his human nature offered for our sake (LH,

---

2 Only a small sampling of texts dealing with sacrifices are presented here.

Lent.5.Fr, 2R: St. Fulgentius of Ruspe, Treatise on Faith Addressed to Peter, Ch. 22, 62: CCL 91 A, 726.750–751; *cf. also for example* LH, Lent.5.Mo, 2R: St. John Fisher, Commentary on the Psalms 129: Opera omnia, edit. 1579, p. 1610).

- Jesus Christ is the Lamb of God whose sacrifice takes away the sins of the world (*cf.* John 1:29; EUCHARIST: *Types*: Passover / Passover Lamb).

- While in the Old Covenant priests had to offer up sacrifices every day, Jesus Christ offered himself to God once and for all (*cf. for example* Heb. 7:27; 9:12–14, 24–28; 10:1–18).

- Jesus Christ gave himself up for us as a fragrant offering to God (*cf. for example* Eph. 5:2; RM, Ritual Masses, For Religious Profession, For Perpetual Profession, A, Preface).

- The sacrifice of Christ completes and surpasses all other sacrifices (CCC 614 citing Heb. 10:10; *cf. also for example* CCC 1350; 1540; 1544; 1939; 2100).

- All the rituals and sacrifices of the Old Covenant converge on Christ and were part of God's preparation for the coming of his Son (CCC 522; *cf. also for example* LH, Lent.2.We, 2R: St. Irenaeus, Against Heresies, Book 4, 14, 2–3; 15, 1: SC 100, 542.548).

Prefigured the Eucharist

- At the Last Supper, Jesus Christ took the cup of wine and said, "This is my blood of the [new] covenant, which is poured out for many for the forgiveness of sins," alluding to Exod. 24:8 and Jer. 31:31. The allusion to Exod. 24:8 is usually considered typological: as Moses ratified the Old Covenant by sprinkling the Israelites with the "blood of the covenant" taken from the sacrifice of animals, so now Jesus ratifies the New Covenant (*cf.* Jer. 31:31) by giving his disciples the "blood of the covenant," his own blood, offered up through the Last Supper and his crucifixion. (*cf.* Matt. 26:28; Mark 14:24; Luke 22:20; 1 Cor. 11:25; Heb. 9:18–21; *cf.* EUCHARIST: *Types*: Blood of the Covenant).

- St. Paul compares and contrasts the sacrifices and sacred meals of Jews, pagans, and Christians (1 Cor. 10:14–21). Implicit in the comparison is that the "table of the Lord" (1 Cor. 10:21) through which Christians participate in the body and blood of Christ (1 Cor. 10:16) is also an altar, as is the case for the table / altar of the Israelites (1 Cor. 10:18; *cf. also* Ezek. 40:39–43;

41:22; 44:16; Mal. 1:7, 12) and of the pagans (1 Cor. 10:20–21) (*cf. also* Matt. 26:26–28; Mark 14:22–24; Luke 22:19–20; John 6:51; 1 Cor. 11:23–29; Heb. 13:10; EUCHARIST: Symbols: Altar / Table).

- The Eucharist, the memorial of Christ's sacrifice, completes and surpasses all the sacrifices of the Old Covenant (CCC 1330; *cf. also* CCC 1350; 1359).
- The sacrifice of the Passover lamb prefigured the one offering of the Lamb of God, made present in the Eucharistic sacrifice (*cf.* EUCHARIST: *Types:* Passover / Passover Lamb).
- The Eucharist fulfills what was foreshadowed in the sacrifices of the Old Covenant (LH, Lent.5.Tu, 2R: St. Leo the Great, Sermo 8 de passione Domini, 6–8: PL 54, 340–342):
  - In the Eucharist all people everywhere can celebrate, "in a sacrament made perfect and visible, what was carried out in the one temple of Judea under obscure foreshadowings."
  - In the New Covenant, through the cross of Christ, there is "a more distinguished order of Levites, a greater dignity for the rank of elders, a more sacred anointing for the priesthood."
  - The one offering of the Lamb of God, of Christ's body and blood, fulfills all the different sacrificial offerings of the Old Covenant.

The Liturgy of the Hours

How marvelous the power of the cross; how great beyond all telling the glory of the passion: here is the judgment-seat of the Lord, the condemnation of the world, the supremacy of Christ crucified.

Lord, you drew all things to yourself so that the devotion of all peoples everywhere might celebrate, in a sacrament made perfect and visible, what was carried out in the one temple of Judea under obscure foreshadowings.

Now there is a more distinguished order of Levites, a greater dignity for the rank of elders, a more sacred anointing for the priesthood, because your cross is the source of all blessings, the cause of all graces. Through the cross the faithful receive strength from weakness, glory from dishonor, life from death.

The different sacrifices of animals are no more; the one offering of your body and blood is the fulfillment of all the different sacrificial offerings, for you are the true "Lamb of God: you take away the sins of the world." In yourself you bring to perfection all mysteries, so that as there is one sacrifice in place of all other sacrificial offerings, there is also one kingdom gathered from all peoples.

LH, Lent.5.Tu, 2R: St. Leo the Great, Sermo 8 de passione Domini,
6–8: PL 54, 340–342

- While under the old law the flesh of calves and goats were offered, under the new law Christ himself is set before the faithful as food (LH, Corpus Christi, 2R: St. Thomas Aquinas, Opusculum 57, in festo Corporis Christi, lect. 1–3).

- The Lord Jesus taught that the Church was to offer an oblation throughout the whole world as a pure sacrifice, acceptable to God. The Church alone offers this pure oblation to the Creator, when it offers bread from the earth which become the Eucharist, made of two elements, one heavenly and one earthly. This is a fulfillment of the old sacrifices (LH, OT.2.Sa, 2R: St. Irenaeus, Against Heresies, Book 4, 18, 1–2.4.5: SC 100, 596–598.606.610–612):

  - Moses taught that the Israelites were to offer the first fruits of creation. Now the Church offers the first fruits of bread and wine in thanksgiving.

  - There were oblations and sacrifices among the people of Israel. Now, in the Church, only the kind of oblation has changed: while the oblations of Israel were offered by slaves, the oblation of the Church is offered by sons.

The Liturgy of the Hours

The oblation of the Church, which the Lord taught was to be offered throughout the whole world, has been regarded by God as a pure sacrifice, and is acceptable to him. . . . It is not oblations as such that have met with disapproval. There were oblations of old; there are oblations now. There were sacrifices among the people of Israel; there are sacrifices in the Church. Only the kind of oblation has been changed: now it is offered by freemen, not by slaves. There is one and the same Lord, but the character of an oblation made by slaves is distinctive, so too that of an oblation made by sons: their oblations bear the mark of freedom.

. . . The Church alone offers this pure oblation to the Creator when it makes its offering to him from his creation, with thanksgiving. We offer him what is his, and so we proclaim communion and unity and profess our belief in the resurrection of flesh and spirit. Just as bread from the earth, when it receives the invocation of God, is no longer common bread but the Eucharist, made up of two elements, one earthly and one heavenly, so also our bodies, in receiving the Eucharist, are no longer corruptible, for they have the hope of resurrection.

LH, OT.2.Sa, 2R: St. Irenaeus, Against Heresies, Book 4, 18, 1–2.4.5: SC 100, 596–598.606.610–612

• In the Old Covenant, God demanded faith, obedience, and righteousness, not sacrifices and holocausts, as he said through the prophet Hosea: "I desire mercy and not sacrifice, the knowledge of God, rather than burnt offerings" (Hos. 6:6). In the New Covenant, Jesus taught that the new sacrifice is the offering of the bread and the cup, which he declared to be his Body and Blood. The Church has received this sacrifice from the apostles and offers it to God throughout the world, fulfilling the prophecy of Mal. 1:10b–11 that the sacrifices of the Old Covenant would cease and a pure sacrifice would be offered up throughout the world (LH, OT.18.Sa, 2R [Latin]:[3] St. Irenaeus, Against Heresies, Book 4, 17, 4–6: SC 100, 590–594).

---

3 The current English translation of the Liturgy of the Hours (1975) omits a part of this reading found in the Latin Liturgy of the Hours which contains typological references. The following text appears immediately after the citation of Mal. 1:10b–11: "manifestíssime significans per haec quóniam prior quidem pópulus cessábit offérre Deo; omni autem loco sacrifícium offerétur ei, et hoc purum; nomen autem eius glorificátur in géntibus." In English: "With these words he most clearly manifested that the sacrifices of the people of an earlier time would cease, and that in every place a sacrifice would be offered to him, a pure sacrifice, and that his name would be glorified among the nations" [my translation].

- By confessing their sins before celebrating the Eucharist, the faithful make sure that their sacrifice is pure, and fulfill the words of the Lord: "In every place and time a pure sacrifice is offered to me"[4] (*cf.* Mal. 1:11) (LH, OT.14.We, 2R: Didache 9, 1 – 10, 6; 14, 1–3: Funk 2, 19–22.26; *cf. also* LH, Corpus Christi, MP, 4th intercession; LH, OT.18.Sa, 2R: St. Irenaeus, Against Heresies, Book 4, 17, 4–6: SC 100, 590–594).
- St. Fulgentius of Ruspe compares and contrasts the animal sacrifices of the Old Covenant and the Eucharistic sacrifice of the New Covenant (LH, Lent.5.Fr, 2R: St. Fulgentius of Ruspe, Treatise on Faith Addressed to Peter, Ch. 22, 62: CCL 91 A, 726.750–751):
    - In the Old Covenant, patriarchs, prophets, and priests offered animal sacrifices in God's honor. In the New Covenant, the Church ceaselessly offers the sacrifice of bread and wine to God.
    - The animal sacrifices foreshadowed the offering of the flesh and blood of Christ for sins. The Eucharistic sacrifice is thanksgiving for and memorial of the flesh and blood which Christ offered to God.
    - The animal sacrifices pointed in sign to what was to be given to the faithful. In the Eucharistic sacrifice, the faithful see plainly what has already been given to them.
    - The animal sacrifices foretold the death of the Son of God for sinners. In the Eucharistic sacrifice, Christ is proclaimed as already slain for sinners.
- The Eucharistic liturgy at times implicitly presents the sacrifice of Christ made present in the Eucharist as the fulfillment of the sacrifices of the Old Covenant (*cf. for example* RM, Eucharistic Prayer I, 92–93).
- The sacrifices of the sons of Aaron in the tabernacle where shadows of the good things to come (*cf.* RO 159 [=ROP 22]).
- The Eucharist is *the* "sacrifice of praise" and the "pure offering" to the glory of God's name (CCC 2643, citing Mal. 1:11. Italics in the original).
- The liturgy correlates Isa. 19:21, the prophecy that Egypt will recognize the Lord and offer sacrifices and offerings, with Luke 13:29, Christ's promise

---

4 Although there is no direct reference to animal sacrifices in this text, the presentation of the Eucharistic sacrifice as the fulfillment of the prophecy of Malachi 1:11, 14 implicitly compares the Eucharistic sacrifice offered throughout the world with the sacrifice in the Temple of Jerusalem, and may have been understood typologically in that respect by the author of the Didache.

that people will come from east and west, north and south, and sit at table in the Kingdom of God (LH, Adv.1.Fr, 1R, Resp [Isa. 19:21; Luke 13:29]).

- The Eucharist is oftentimes called by titles such as "holy sacrifice of the Mass," "sacrifice of praise," "spiritual sacrifice," "pure and holy sacrifice," and similar, which may be understood as implicitly referring to the Eucharist as a fulfillment of the sacrifices of the Old Covenant (*cf. for example* CCC 1330).

- The priest, who shares in Christ's priesthood, "causes sacrifices to rise to the altar on high" (CCC 1589, quoting St. Gregory of Nazianzus, Oratio 2, 71, 74, 73: PG 35, 480–481).

- The altar around which the Church gathers is at the same time altar of sacrifice and table of the Lord (CCC 1383; *cf.* EUCHARIST: *Symbols*: Altar / Table).

- The Eucharist is an unbloody sacrifice (CCC 1369).

Other

- God prefers the following to animal sacrifices:
  - obedience (1 Sam. 15:21–22; Ps. 40:6–8; Jer. 7:21–23);
  - the sacrifice of a humble and contrite heart (Ps. 51:16–17; *cf.* LH, OT.14.Su, 2R: St. Augustine, Sermo 19, 2–3: CCL 41, 252–254);
  - praising God in song and magnifying him in thanksgiving (Ps. 69:30–31);
  - approaching the house of God to listen (Eccles. 5:1);
  - righteousness and justice (Prov. 21:3; Amos 5:22–24; *cf. also for example* Prov. 15:8; 21:7; Isa. 1:11–17);
  - mercy and the knowledge of God (Hos. 6:6; *cf.* Matt. 9:13; 12:7);
  - doing justice, loving kindness, and walking humbly with God (Mic. 6:6–8);
  - loving God with all the heart, all the understanding, all the strength, and loving one's neighbor as oneself (Mark 12:33).

- The sacrifice which is truly pleasing to God is the sacrifice of one's self in Christ (*cf. for example* LH, ET.4.Tu, 2R: St. Peter Chrysologus, Sermo 108: PL 52, 499–500; *cf. also for example* LH, St. Polycarp [Feb 23], 2R: Letter on the Martyrdom of St. Polycarp by the Church of Smyrna, Ch. 13, 2–15, 2).

- Prayer in Christ fulfills the prefigurations of the animal sacrifices of the Old Covenant (*cf. for example* LH, Lent.3.Th, 2R: Tertullian, Treatise on Prayer, 28–29: CCL 1, 273–274; *cf. also for example* LH, OT.28.Su, 2R: St. Cyril of Alexandria, Commentary on Haggai, Ch. 14: PG 71, 1047–1050).
- Christians are to present their bodies as living sacrifices, holy and acceptable to God (Rom. 12:1).
- The offering of the Gentile Christians (probably referring to their conversion and life in Christ) is offered by St. Paul to Christ (Rom. 15:16).
- Paul compares the offering of his life in the service of the Gospel and/or his martyrdom to a sacrificial offering (2 Tim. 4:6; *cf. also* Phil. 2:17; Eph. 5:2; Rom. 12:1).
- The gifts which the Philippians sent to Paul were "a fragrant offering, a sacrifice acceptable and pleasing to God" (Phil. 4:18).
- Through Christ, Christians continually "offer up a sacrifice of praise to God, that is, the fruit of lips that acknowledge his name" (Heb. 13:15).
- Doing good and sharing what one has are sacrifices pleasing to God (Heb. 13:16).
- As a holy priesthood, Christians are called "to offer spiritual sacrifices acceptable to God through Jesus Christ" (1 Pet. 2:5).

Manna

OT Background: Exod. 16:4, 8, 12–15, 19–21; 31–35; Num. 11:6–9; 21:5; Deut. 8:3, 16; Josh. 5:11–12; 1 Kings 19:4–8; Neh. 9:15, 20; Ps. 78:24–25; 105:40; Wisd. 16:20

NT Background: Matt. 4:4; Luke 4:4; John 6:31–35, 41, 48–51, 58; 1 Cor. 10:1–22; Heb. 9:4; Rev. 2:17

Catechism Background: 1094; 1150; 1331; **1334**; 1338; 1355; 1392; 1406; **2837**; 2861

Type: John 6:48–51, 58; CCC 1094; 1334; 2837; Lectionary 167; 976; 978; RM, Eucharistic Prayer II, 101; LH, OT.15.Fr, 2R: St. Ambrose, On the Mysteries, 43.47–49: SC 25 bis, 178–180.182; LH, Lent.2.Mo, 2R: St. John Chrysostom, Cat. 3, 24–27: SC 50, 165–167; LH, St. Albert the Great [Nov 15], 2R: St. Albert the Great, Commentary on Luke 22, 19: Opera Omnia, Paris 1890–1899, 23, 672–674

Related: BAPTISM: *Symbols*: Dew from Above; EUCHARIST: *Types:* Fruit of the Tree of Life; Bread for the Journey of Elijah; Wisdom's Banquet; *Symbols:* Bread from Heaven / Bread of Life / Bread of Angels; Medicine of Immortality

- The manna of heaven prefigured Jesus Christ (*cf. for example* John 6:32; LH, Lent.2.Tu, 1R, Resp [Wisd. 16:20; John 6:32]; LH, ET.2[=4, 6].Th, MP, 4th intercession).
- The manna in the desert prefigured the Eucharist (John 6:48–51, 58; CCC 1094, citing John 6:32; 1 Cor. 10:1–6; *cf.* RM, Votive Masses, The Most Holy Eucharist, Entrance Antiphon [Ps. 78:23–25]; LH, ET.3.Th, 2R, Resp [John 6:48–52]; LH, Corpus Christi, EP, Ant3; LH, Corpus Christi, EP [=EP2], 4th intercession; LH, Corpus Christi, 1R, Resp [John 6:48–52]; LH, Corpus Christi, MP, Ant1; LH, Corpus Christi, MP, Ant3; LH, Corpus Christi, MP, 5th intercession; *cf. also* LH, Psalter.2.We, EP, 3rd intercession).
- The manna (as bread of angels) prefigured the Eucharist (RM, Votive Masses, The Most Holy Eucharist, Entrance Antiphon [Ps. 78:23–25]; LH, Lent.2.Mo, 2R: St. John Chrysostom, Cat. 3, 24–27: SC 50, 165–167).
- Moses raised his hands to heaven and brought down the bread of angels, manna; the new Moses, Jesus Christ, lifts his hands to heaven and gives the food of eternal life (LH, Lent.2.Mo, 2R: St. John Chrysostom, Cat. 3, 24–27: SC 50, 165–167).
- The Eucharist is in many ways superior to the manna (LH, OT.15.Fr, 2R: St. Ambrose, On the Mysteries, 43.47–49: SC 25 bis, 178–180.182):
  - Those who daily ate the manna, the bread of angels, all died in the desert. The one who eats the bread from heaven of the Eucharistic receives eternal life, and will never die, because it is the Body of Christ.
  - The manna in the desert fell from heaven. The Eucharistic manna is above heaven.
  - The manna in the desert was from heaven. The Eucharistic manna is the Lord of heaven.
  - The manna in the desert would go bad after one day. The Eucharistic manna cannot go bad, and communicates incorruptibility to all who receive it with reverence.
  - The manna was a shadow. The Eucharistic manna is reality.

- The manna in the desert pointed to God's sweetness: bread of angels, of many flavors, cooked to perfection. The Eucharist is even greater: the healthiest food imaginable, fruit of the tree of life, cause of love and of union, gift of self. In the Eucharist the desire of the Israelites in the desert to eat flesh is fulfilled, and a deeper union would be impossible to imagine (LH, St. Albert the Great [Nov 15], 2R: St. Albert the Great, Commentary on Luke 22, 19: Opera Omnia, Paris 1890–1899, 23, 672–674).
- The manna in the desert was a figure of the Eucharist. That is why St. Paul says that our fathers ate the same spiritual food and drank the same spiritual drink (cf. 1 Cor. 10:3–4), for they ate the figure of the true spiritual food and drink (LH, OT.15.Sa, 2R: St. Ambrose, On the Mysteries, 52–54.58: SC 25 bis, 186–188.190).
- As the dew descended upon the earth and left behind the manna from heaven (cf. Exod. 16:13–15; Num. 11:9), so the Holy Spirit descends like the dewfall upon the gifts of bread and wine, leaving behind the true Manna from heaven of the Eucharist (RM, Eucharistic Prayer II, 101).
- As God sent the Israelites the bread of "this day" in the manna (cf. Exod. 16:19–21), so it is fitting that Eucharistic liturgy be celebrated each day, in which the faithful participate in the "this day" of Christ's Resurrection (CCC 2837, citing Exod. 16:19–21; cf. Acts 13:33; Ps. 118:24).
- In the Passover supper, the unleavened bread recalls (among other things) the manna in the desert, which taught Israel to live by the bread of the Word of God. In the Eucharist, Jesus Christ gave a new and definitive meaning to the blessing of the bread of the Passover meal (CCC 1334, citing Deut. 8:3; cf. EUCHARIST: Types: Passover / Passover Lamb).
- In Votive Masses of the Most Holy Eucharist, the first reading may be Exod. 16:2–4, 12–15, in which God promises to rain down bread from heaven as their daily bread (Lectionary 976).
- On the feast of Corpus Christi and in Votive Masses of the Most Holy Eucharist, the first reading may be Deut. 8:2–3, 14b–16a, in which Moses reminds the Israelites that in their journey through the desert God gave them manna so that they might know that they live not by bread alone, but by every word that comes forth from the mouth of God (Lectionary 167; 976).
- In Votive Masses of the Most Holy Eucharist, the responsorial psalm may be Ps. 78, with response of Ps. 78:24, in which the psalmist remembers

how God gave the Israelites bread from heaven (Lectionary 978; *cf. also* RM, Votive Masses, The Most Holy Eucharist, Entrance Antiphon [Ps. 78:23–25]).

• On the Eighteenth Sunday in Ordinary Time, Year B, the first reading is Exod. 16:2–4, 12–15 in which the Lord gives Israel bread to eat in the form of manna. The Gospel is John 6:24–35 (Lectionary 113).

Bread of the Presence / Cereal Offerings

OT Background:

Bread of the Presence: Exod. 25:23–30; 26:35; 35:13; 37:16; 39:36; Lev. 24:5–9; Num. 4:7; 1 Sam. 21:4–7; 1 Kings 7:48; 1 Chron. 9:32; 23:29; 28:16; 2 Chron. 2:4; 4:1 9; 13:11; 29:18; Neh. 10:33; Ezek. 41:21–22; 1 Macc. 1:22; 4:49; 2 Macc. 10:3

Cereal Offerings: Lev. 2:1–16; 6:14–18; 7:9–10; Neh. 13:9; Jer. 17:26; 41:5; Isa. 43:23; 66:3

Other: Mal. 1:11

NT Background: Matt. 12:4; Mark 2:26; Luke 6:4; Heb. 9:2

Catechism Background: 1178; 1181; 1183; 1330; 1374; 1378–1381; 1418; 2581; 2715

Type: LH, ET.1.Sa, 2R: St. Cyril of Jerusalem, Jerusalem Catecheses, 22, Mystagogica 4, 1.3–6.9: PG 33, 1098–1106; LH, Corpus Christi, MP, Ant2

Related: EUCHARIST: *Symbols:* Altar / Table; Bread and Wine / Nourishment

• The bread of the Presence of the Old Covenant has come to an end. Now in the New Covenant there is the bread from heaven and the cup of salvation, which are the Body and Blood of Christ (LH, ET.1.Sa, 2R: St. Cyril of Jerusalem, Jerusalem Catecheses, 22, Mystagogica 4, 1.3–6.9: PG 33, 1098–1106).

• On the feast of Corpus Christi, the 2nd Antiphon of Morning Prayer of the Liturgy of the Hours implicitly associates the Old Covenant offering of bread and incense with the Eucharist: "Holy priests will offer incense and bread to God, alleluia." In the Old Covenant, the offering of bread and incense took place with the Bread of the Presence (*cf.* Lev. 24:5–7; Exod. 25:29–30; 37:16; Num. 4:7; *cf. also* 2 Chron. 2:4; 13:11; 1 Macc. 4:49; 2 Macc. 10:3) and with some cereal offerings (*cf.* Lev. 2:1–2, 15–16; 6:14–18;

Neh. 13:9; Jer. 17:26; 41:5; Isa. 43:23; 66:3) (LH, Corpus Christi, MP, Ant2).

BREAD FOR THE JOURNEY OF ELIJAH

OT Background: Gen. 28:20; 1 Kings 17:4–6, 9; 19:4–8; Ps. 23:5; 81:16; 111:5; Prov. 30:8

NT Background: Luke 1:53; John 6; Rev. 12:6, 14

Catechism Background: 163; 1090; 1275; 1392; 1394; 1419; 1436; 1524; 2583–2584

Type: Lectionary 116; 976; RM, Masses and Prayers for Various Needs and Occasions, For Holy Church, For Religious, A, Communion Antiphon (1 Kings 19:7)

Related: EUCHARIST: *Symbols*: Bread for the Journey / Daily Bread / Viaticum

- In Votive Masses of the Most Holy Eucharist, the first reading may be 1 Kings 19:4–8, where an angel gives Elijah bread and "in the strength of that food" (1 Kings 19:8) he walks forty days and forty nights to mount Horeb (Lectionary 976).
- On the Nineteenth Sunday in Ordinary Time the first reading is 1 Kings 19:4–8 and the Gospel is John 6:41–51 (Lectionary 116).
- The Communion Antiphon of the Mass for Religious is 1 Kings 19:7, where the angel tells Elijah to rise and eat, lest the journey be too much for him (RM, Masses and Prayers for Various Needs and Occasions, For Holy Church, For Religious, A, Communion Antiphon [1 Kings 19:7]).

HOLOCAUST OF ELIJAH

OT Background: Lev. 19:24; Judg. 6:21; 1 Kings 18:20–40; 1 Chron. 21:26; 2 Chron. 7:1; Sir. 48:1, 3

NT Background: Luke 12:49; John 11:42; Acts 2:3–4

Catechism Background: 696; 1105–1107; 1109; **1127**; **1353**; 2581; **2582**; **2583**; 2584

Type: CCC 2583

Related: BAPTISM: *Symbols*: Baptism of Fire; CONFIRMATION: *Symbols*: Fire

- As the fire from heaven came down to consume the sacrifice of Elijah on Mount Carmel (*cf.* 1 Kings 18:38), so the fire of the Holy Spirit transforms whatever he touches (CCC 696).
- As Elijah prayed, "Answer me, O LORD, answer me," and the Lord's fire consumed the holocaust, so the Easter liturgies lift up this same prayer in the Eucharistic epiclesis over the bread and wine that the fire of the Holy Spirit may transform them into the Body and Blood of Christ (CCC 2583; *cf.* CCC 1127; 1353; *cf. also* RM, Eucharistic Prayer I, 94).
- If the words of Elijah were powerful enough to call down fire from heaven to consume the sacrifice, will not the words of Christ spoken in the words of consecration have the power to transform bread and wine into the Body and Blood of Christ? (LH, OT.15.Sa, 2R: St. Ambrose, On the Mysteries, 52–54.58: SC 25 bis, 186–188.190; *cf. also* LH, OT.15.We, 2R: St. Ambrose, On the Mysteries, 19–21.24.26–38: SC 25 bis, 164–170)

WISDOM'S BANQUET

OT Background: Ps. 4:7; 34:8; Prov. 9:1–6; Eccles. 9:7–8; Song 5:1; Sir. 15:3; Isa. 25:6; 55:1–3

NT Background: Matt. 14:13–21; Luke 14:16–24; 15:1–2, 22–32; 24:30–32; John 21:12

Catechism Background: 1166

Type: Lectionary 119; 976; LH, OT.7.Fr, 2R: St. Gregory of Agrigentum, Commentary on Ecclesiastes, Lib. 8, 6: PG 98, 1071–1074; LH, OT.6.We, 2R: Procopius of Gaza, Commentary on the Book of Proverbs, Ch. 9: PG 87–1, 1299–1303; LH, OT.6.We, 2R, Resp [Prov. 9:1–2; John 6:57]

Related: BAPTISM: *Types*: Fruit of the Tree of Life; EUCHARIST: *Types*: Fruit of the Tree of Life; Passover / Passover Lamb; Water to Wine; *Symbols*: Altar / Table; Banquet

- The banquet which Wisdom provides for her followers, in its spiritual meaning, refers to the Eucharist (LH, OT.7.Fr, 2R: St. Gregory of Agrigentum, Commentary on Ecclesiastes, Lib. 8, 6: PG 98, 1071–1074):
  - The literal sense of Eccles. 9:7 is that one should live simply, with genuine faith, so as to be able to eat and drink with a glad heart.

- The spiritual meaning refers to the Eucharist: an invitation to eat the bread which has come down from heaven and brings life to the world, and to drink with a cheerful heart the spiritual wine which flowed from the side of the true vine on the cross.

- Whoever receives the Eucharist enjoys true happiness and exclaims with the psalmist, "You have put more joy in my heart" (*cf.* Ps. 4:7).

- Similarly, Wisdom speaks of this same bread and wine in Prov. 9:5, which refers to the mystical sharing in the Word, a sharing which clothes in light and anoints with the oil of the Spirit of truth (*cf.* Eccles. 9:8).

- Procopius of Gaza provides a spiritual interpretation of Prov. 9:1–6 (LH, OT.6.We, 2R: Procopius of Gaza, Commentary on the Book of Proverbs, Ch. 9: PG 87–1, 1299–1303):

  - *Wisdom built herself a house*: God created the universe, and man in his image.

  - *And has set up seven pillars*: Wisdom gave the seven gifts of the Holy Spirit.

  - *She mingled her wine in a bowl and spread her table*: Christ, the bread from heaven, both nourishes and quenches man's thirst, gladdening him with his teachings.

  - *She invites all to come and drink the wine she has mixed*: She sends forth the apostles to preach Christ, in whom the divine and human natures have been mixed while remaining distinct.

  - *She invites to eat and drink*: Christ invites to eat the bread which is his Body and drink the wine which is his Blood.

- The Church exhorts her children to come to the Eucharist, saying, "Neighbors, come and eat; brethren drink and be filled" (*cf.* Song 5:1). Similarly, the Holy Spirit invites the faithful to receive the Eucharist, saying, "Taste and see that the Lord is good" (*cf.* Ps. 34:8) (LH, OT.15.Sa, 2R: St. Ambrose, On the Mysteries, 52–54.58: SC 25 bis, 186–188.190).

- The table which Wisdom has prepared and the wine which she has mixed is the Eucharist (LH, OT.6.We, 2R, Resp [Prov. 9:1–2; John 6:57]; LH, Corpus Christ, MD, Reading; *cf. also* LH, Lent.1[=3, 5].Sa, MP, 1st intercession).

- The bread which Wisdom offers and the wine which she has mixed is the Eucharist (LH, OT.18.Sa, 2R, Resp [Luke 22:19–20; Prov. 9:5]; RM, Ritual Masses, I, 3, B, Prayer over the Offerings).
- The Church prays that from the banquet of the Eucharist the faithful may draw the hidden wisdom of the eternal Word (RM, St. John [Dec 27], Prayer over the Offerings).
- The Eucharist is the sacrament of God's wisdom (RM, Commons, Common of Holy Men and Women, II, B, Prayer after Communion).
- In Votive Masses of the Most Holy Eucharist, the first reading may be Prov. 9:1–6, in which Wisdom prepares a banquet and sends out an invitation to eat of her bread and drink of the wine that she has mixed (Lectionary 976).
- On the Twentieth Sunday in Ordinary Time, Year B, the first reading is Prov. 9:1–6, in which Wisdom prepares a banquet and sends out an invitation to eat of her bread and drink of the wine that she has mixed, and the Gospel is John 6:51–58, in which Christ invites his disciples to eat his Body and drink his Blood (Lectionary 119).
- On the Eighteenth Sunday in Ordinary Time, Year A, the first reading is Isa. 55:1–3, in which God invites his people to come and buy without price food and drink that satisfies, and the Gospel is Matt. 14:13–21, the multiplication of the loaves (Lectionary 112; *cf.* EUCHARIST: *Types*: Multiplication of the Loaves).

WATER FROM THE ROCK

OT Background: Exod. 17:2–7; Num. 20:8–13; Deut. 8:15; Neh. 9:15; Ps. 78:15–20; Ps. 81:16 (=Ps. 81:17 NAB); 105:41; 114:5–8; Wisd. 11:4–8; Isa. 48:21; 49:10; Jer. 2:13

NT Background: John 4:14; 6:35, 53–56; 7:37–39; 1 Cor. 10:1–6; Rev. 7:17; 22:1

Catechism Background: 129; 694; 1094

Type: LH, OT.15.Fr, 2R: St. Ambrose, On the Mysteries, 43.47–49: SC 25 bis, 178–180.182

Related: BAPTISM: *Types*: Water from the Side of Christ; *Symbols*: Fountain of Water; EUCHARIST: *Types*: Blood from the Side of Christ

Prefigured the Spiritual Gifts of Christ / Holy Spirit

- The Israelites drank supernatural drink from the supernatural Rock that followed them in the desert, and this rock was Christ (*cf. for example* 1 Cor. 10:4; LH, Lent.2.We, 2R: St. Irenaeus, Against Heresies, Book 4, 14, 2–3; 15, 1: SC 100, 542.548; LH, OT.12.Mo, 2R: St. Gregory of Nyssa, On Christian Perfection: PG 46, 254–255).

- The water from the rock (Exod. 17:2–7) is a figure of the spiritual gifts of Christ (CCC 1094; 1 Cor. 10:1–4) and of the living water from Christ crucified welling up in us to eternal life (CCC 694, footnote 29).

- As the Israelites received so many gifts from God, including the water from the rock, and still were ungrateful, the Christian is likewise in danger of being ungrateful and forgetting the far greater wonders God has worked for him (1 Cor. 10:1–6; LH, OT.3.Fr, 2R: St. John Fisher, Ps. 101: Opera Omnia, ed. 1597, pp. 1588–1589).

- The Liturgy of the Hours correlates the water from the rock (Exod. 17:2–7), the promise of drawing water from the springs of salvation (Isa. 12:3–4), and the water that Christ promises the Samaritan woman (John 4:14). The implication seems to be that the water from the rock prefigures the gift of the Holy Spirit in believers, which was prophesied by Isaiah (LH, Lent.2.We, 1R, Resp [Isa. 12:3–4; John 4:14], following the reading of Exod. 17:1–16).

- The water from the rock prefigures the gift of the Holy Spirit (LH, ET.2[=4, 6].Th, MP, 5th intercession [Latin]).

- As God is capable of bringing forth a fountain of living water from a rock for his thirsty people, so he is also capable of bringing forth tears of sorrow for sin from the hardness of our heart (RM, Masses and Prayers for Various Needs and Occasions, III, 38, B, Collect).

Prefigured the Eucharist

- In the desert, water flowed from the rock; for the baptized, blood flows from the side of Christ, and is given in the Eucharist to drink. While that water only quenched thirst for a time, this blood cleanses forever (LH, OT.15.Fr, 2R: St. Ambrose, On the Mysteries, 43.47–49: SC 25 bis, 178–180.182).

The Liturgy of the Hours

For our fathers, water flowed from the rock; for you, blood flows from Christ. Water satisfied their thirst for a time; blood cleanses you for ever. The Jew drinks and still thirsts, but when you drink you will be incapable of thirst. What happened in symbol is now fulfilled in reality.

If what you marvel at is a shadow, how great is the reality whose very shadow you marvel at. Listen to this, which shows that what happened in the time of our fathers was but a shadow. "They drank," it is written, "from the rock that followed them, and the rock was Christ. All this took place as a symbol for us." You know now what is more excellent: light is preferable to its shadow, reality to its symbol, the body of the Giver to the manna he gave from heaven.

LH, OT.15.Fr, 2R: St. Ambrose, On the Mysteries, 43.47–49: SC 25 bis, 178–180.182

• In the Old Covenant, God promised the gift of finest wheat and honey from the rock (Ps. 81:16 [=Ps. 81:17 NAB]). In the New Covenant, he gave us his Body and Blood in the Eucharist (*cf.* RM, Corpus Christi, Entrance Antiphon [Ps. 81:16 [=Ps. 81:17 NAB]]; RM, Ritual Masses, For the Administering of Viaticum, Entrance Antiphon [Ps. 81:16 [=Ps. 81:17 NAB]]. Meaning implied in light of the Eucharistic theme of the celebrations of Corpus Christi and Viaticum).

• The faithful refresh their souls on the Blood of Christ in the Eucharist as from a fountain (LH, Lent.4.Fr, 2R: St. Athanasius, Easter Letter 5, 1–2: PG 26, 1379–1380; *cf. also* LH, Lent.2.Mo, 2R: St. John Chrysostom, Cat. 3, 24–27: SC 50, 165–167; *cf.* RM, Ritual Masses, X, For the Dedication of an Altar, Preface).

• As Moses struck the rock and brought forth water, Christ strikes the table [of the Last Supper] and from it the Spirit flows forth like a fountain to refresh the flock (LH, Lent.2.Mo, 2R: St. John Chrysostom, Cat. 3, 24–27: SC 50, 165–167; *cf.* RM, Ritual Masses, X, For the Dedication of an Altar, Preface).

· At the Eucharistic Celebration, through the bread and wine transformed into the Body and Blood of Christ the wellspring of all blessing is laid open before the faithful (RM, OT.26.Su, Prayer over the Offerings; *cf. also* RM, Commons, Common of Holy Men and Women, II, C, Prayer after Communion; RM, Votive Masses, The Mercy of God, Prayer after Communion).

WATER TO WINE

OT Background: Exod. 7:20; Ps. 23:5; Song 3:11; Isa. 25:6; Jer. 31:12–14; Ezek. 16:8; Hos. 14:7; Joel 3:18; Amos 9:13–14

NT Background: Matt. 9:14–15; Mark 2:19; Luke 5:33–35; John 2:1–12; 3:34; 6:13; Rev. 8:8–9; 19:7, 9

Catechism Background: 528; **1335**; 1613; **2618**

Type: CCC 2618; LH, CT.AE.Mo, 2R: St. Peter Chrysologus, Sermo 160: PL 52, 620–622; LH, ET.5.Th, 2R: St. Gaudentius of Brescia, Tract. 2: CSEL 68, 26.29–30

Related: BAPTISM: *Symbols*: White Garment / Wedding Garment; EUCHARIST: *Types*: Multiplication of Loaves; *Symbols*: Banquet; Bread and Wine / Nourishment

· The transformation of water to wine at Cana (John 2:1–12) points to "the wedding of the Lamb, where [Jesus] gives his body and blood at the request of the Church, his Bride" (CCC 2618).

· At Cana, Christ transformed water into wine. But it still must be transformed "into the sacrament of his blood, so that Christ may offer spiritual drink from the chalice of his body" (LH, CT.AE.Mo, 2R: St. Peter Chrysologus, Sermo 160: PL 52, 620–622, citing Ps. 23:5).

· Jesus Christ is Creator and Lord of all things. As he had changed water into wine, so he changed wine into his own blood (LH, ET.5.Th, 2R: St. Gaudentius of Brescia, Tract. 2: CSEL 68, 26.29–30).

· The transforming of water into wine at Cana "makes manifest the fulfillment of the wedding feast in the Father's kingdom, where the faithful will drink the new wine that has become the Blood of Christ(cf. John 2:11; Mark 14:25)" (CCC 1335; *cf. also* Matt. 26:29; Luke 22:18).

· In the Eucharistic Celebration, the mixing of wine with a little bit of water is called a "mystery," which symbolizes the recipient of the Eucharist's coming "to share in the divinity of Christ who humbled himself to share in our humanity" (RM, Order of Mass, Liturgy of the Eucharist, 24).

MULTIPLICATION OF LOAVES

OT Background: 1 Kings 17:9–16; 2 Kings 4:1–7, 42–44; Ps. 132:15
NT Background: Matt. 14:13–21; 15:32–39; 16:9–10; Mark 6:32–44; 8:2–9; Luke 9:10–17; John 6:1–13
Catechism Background: 549; 1329; 1335
Type: CCC 1335
Related: EUCHARIST: *Types*: Wisdom's Banquet; Water to Wine; *Symbols*: Bread for the Journey / Daily Bread / Viaticum; Breaking of Bread

- The multiplication of the loaves by Jesus Christ prefigures the superabundance of the bread of the Eucharist (CCC 1335, citing Matt. 14:13–21; 15:32–39).
- On the Seventeenth Sunday in Ordinary Time, Year B, the Gospel is John 6:1–15. The first reading is 2 Kings 4:42–44, the multiplication of loaves by Elisha. The following Sunday Gospels continue the reading of John 6, with first readings and psalms that are often related to the Eucharist (*cf.* APPENDICES: *Readings from the Liturgy*: Eucharist) (Lectionary 110).

BLOOD FROM THE SIDE OF CHRIST

OT Background: Zech. 12:10–13:1
NT Background: John 19:34–37; 1 John 5:6–8
Catechism Background: 478; 766; 1225
Type:[5] CCC 1225
Related: BAPTISM: *Types*: Water from the Side of Christ; EUCHARIST: *Types:* Water from the Rock

- The piercing of Christ's side fulfilled the prophecy of Zechariah that "They shall look on him whom they have pierced" (John 19:37 in reference to Zech. 12:10). The text continues shortly thereafter stating: "On that day there shall be a fountain opened for the house of David and the inhabitants

---

5 Paragraph 1225 of the Catechism is relevant to the question of whether types are limited to the Old Testament, or whether there are types in the New Testament as well. Here is the pertinent phrase in the Latin text: "Sanguis et aqua quae de aperto Iesu crucifixi exiverunt latere, typi sunt Baptismi et Eucharistiae, vitae novae sacramentorum" (CCC 1225; *cf. also* CCC 1335).

of Jerusalem to cleanse them from sin and uncleanness" (Zech. 13:1). The liturgy relates this prophecy of Zechariah to the water and the blood flowing from the side of Christ (LH, OT.33.Sa, 1R, Resp which explicitly correlates Zech. 13:1 and Zech. 14:8 with John 19:34). The importance given to the water and the blood flowing from the side of Christ (*cf.* John 19:35) may be at least in part related to this prophecy of Zechariah (*cf. also* 1 John 5:6–8 and Baptism: *Types:* Water from the Side of Christ).

• The pierced side of Christ and his Sacred Heart are the wellspring of the Church's sacraments (RM, Sacred Heart of Jesus, Preface in reference to John 19:34 and Isa. 12:3; LH, Sacred Heart, 2R: St. Bonaventure, On the Tree of Life, 29–30.47: Opera Omnia 8, 79; *cf. also* LH, Common of the Dedication of a Church, EP [=EP2], 3rd intercession).

• The water and blood flowing from Christ's side on the cross (John 19:34–35) point to the life-giving Sacraments of Baptism (*cf.* John 3:5) and the Eucharist (*cf.* John 6:53–54) (CCC 1225), which continually give new life to the Church and thus symbolize her birth (CCC 766; RB 54, B; LH, Lent.HW.Fr, 2R: St. John Chrysostom, Catecheses 3, 13–19: SC 50, 174–177; *cf. also* LH, OT.23.Fr, 2R: Bl. Isaac of Stella, Sermo 11: PL 194, 1728–1729; LH, Baptism of the Lord, EP2, Resp, which may be a reference to Baptism and the Eucharist as symbolized by the blood and water).

• While from Adam's side was born a woman who, having been deceived, was to become the death-bearer, from Christ's side came forth a fountain of life that regenerates the world in Baptism and feeds the reborn in the Eucharist (LH, OT.19.Mo, 2R: Theodoret of Cyr, On the Incarnation, 26–27: PG 75, 1466–1467).

• From Christ's side flowed the true wine, which Christ spoke of when he said "This is my blood of the new covenant, which is poured out for many for the forgiveness of sins" (Matt. 26:28). Whoever drinks this mystical wine enjoys true happiness, and exclaims with joy, "You have put more joy in my heart" (Ps. 4:7) (LH, OT.7.Fr, 2R: St. Gregory of Agrigentum, Commentary on Ecclesiastes, Lib. 8, 6: PG 98, 1071–1074).

• In the Eucharistic chalice is found the Blood of Christ which flowed from his side and was the price he paid for us (LH, Corpus Christi, 2R, Resp).

The Liturgy of the Hours

Know that in this bread is the body of Christ
which hung on the cross,
and in this cup, the blood of Christ
which flowed from his side.
Take, therefore, and eat his body;
take and drink his blood,
—and you will become members of his body.

Eat this sacred food,
so that your bond of unity with Christ may never be broken.
Drink this sacred blood, the price he paid for you,
so that you may never lose heart because of your sinfulness.
—And you will become members of his body.

LH, Corpus Christi, 2R, Resp

• From the pierced side of Christ flowed forth a stream of immortality, blood and water for the world's cleansing (LH, Triumph of the Cross [Sep 14], 2R: St. Andrew of Crete, Oratio 10 in Exaltatione sanctae crucis: PG 97, 1018–1019.1022–1023).

SYMBOLS

Altar / Table

OT Background:[6]

Altar: Gen. 8:20–21; 12:8; 22:9; 26:25; 35:1; Exod. 20:24–26; 24:4–8; 27:1–8; 40:10; Lev. 8:11; Num. 7:10–11, 84, 88; Josh. 22:16, 19, 23, 26–29; 1 Chron. 22:1; Ezra 3:2; Ps. 43:4; 51:19; 84:3; Sir. 47:9; Isa. 19:19; 56:7; Ezek. 43:13–27; Joel 1:13; 1 Macc. 4:56

Altar called a Table: Ezek. 40:39–43; 41:22; 44:16; Mal. 1:7, 12

Table: Exod. 25:23–30; 2 Sam. 9:7, 10–11, 13; 19:28; 1 Kings 2:7; Job 36:16; Ps. 23:5; 78:19; 128:3

---

6 Only a small sampling of texts regarding the altar and table are included here.

NT Background: Matt. 5:23–24; 23:18–20; 26:20, 26–28; Mark 14:18, 22–24; Luke 12:37; 14:10; 22:14, 19–20, 27–30; John 6:51; 1 Cor. 10:15–21; 11:23–29; Heb. 7:13; 9:2; 13:10; Rev. 6:9; 8:5; 11:1; 16:7
Catechism Background: 103; 545; 551; 1181; 1182; 1183; 1244; 1346; 1347; 1350; 1364; 1368; 1383; 1402; 1689
Related: EUCHARIST: *Types*: Passover / Passover Lamb; Animal Sacrifices; *Symbols*: Banquet

The Altar in General

• The altar around which the Christian community gathers to celebrate the Eucharist represents (CCC 1383):
  ▪ the altar of sacrifice (*cf.* EUCHARIST: *Types*: Animal Sacrifices; Passover / Passover Lamb);
  ▪ the table of the Lord (*cf.* EUCHARIST: *Types*: Passover / Passover Lamb; *Symbols*: Banquet; Bread and Wine / Nourishment);
  ▪ Christ himself, insofar as the altar is an image of the Body of Christ, the "altar" upon which Christ offered himself up to the Father on the cross (CCC 1383, citing RM, Eucharistic Prayer I, 94 and St. Ambrose, De Sacr. 4, 2, 7 and 5, 2, 7: PL 16, 437D.447C).

Catechism of the Catholic Church

The *altar*, around which the Church is gathered in the celebration of the Eucharist, represents the two aspects of the same mystery: the altar of the sacrifice and the table of the Lord. This is all the more so since the Christian altar is the symbol of Christ himself, present in the midst of the assembly of his faithful, both as the victim offered for our reconciliation and as food from heaven who is giving himself to us. "For what is the altar of Christ if not the image of the Body of Christ?" asks St. Ambrose. He says elsewhere, "The altar represents the body [of Christ] and the Body of Christ is on the altar" (St. Ambrose, De Sacr. 4, 2, 7 and 5, 2, 7: PL 16, 437D and 447C). The liturgy expresses this unity of sacrifice and communion in many prayers. Thus the Roman Church prays in its anaphora (*cf.* RM, Eucharistic Prayer I, 94):

> We entreat you, almighty God,
> that by the hands of your holy Angel
> this offering may be borne to your altar in heaven
> in the sight of your divine majesty,
> so that as we receive in communion at this altar
> the most holy Body and Blood of your Son,
> we may be filled with every heavenly blessing and grace.
>
> *CCC 1383*

- The altar symbolizes the tomb of Christ, who truly died and is truly risen (CCC 1182).
- The Eucharist is "the Blessed Sacrament of the altar" (*cf. for example* CCC 1183; LH, St. Cajetan [Aug 7], 2R: St. Cajetan, Epist. ad Elisabeth Porto: Studi e Testi 177, Città del Vaticano 1954, p. 50–51) or "the sacrament of the altar" (*cf. for example* CCC 1418; LH, OT.28.Fr, 2R: St. Augustine, City of God, Book 10, 6: CCL 47, 278–279; LH, St. Margaret Mary Alacoque [Oct 16], 2R: St. Margaret Mary Alacoque, Letter, Vie et Oeuvres 2, Paris 1915, 321.336.493.554).

Where the Memorial of Christ is Made Present

- The altar of the New Covenant is the cross, from which the sacraments flow (CCC 1182, citing Heb. 13:10; *cf.* CCC 1366–1367).
- The one sacrifice of Christ is made present on the altar of the church (CCC 1182; *cf.* CCC 1181; 1364; 1367).
- In the Eucharistic Celebration, the memorial of Christ's sacrifice is celebrated, which he offered to God "on the altar of the Cross" (RM, Ritual Masses, For the Dedication of a Church and an Altar, 2, Preface; *cf. also* RM, Votive Masses, The Mystery of the Holy Cross, Prayer over the Offerings; LH, Corpus Christi, MP, 2nd intercession [Latin]).
- On the altar, "the Sacrifice of Christ is ever offered in mystery," "perfect praise is rendered to [God] and redemption flows forth for us" (RM, Ritual Masses, For the Dedication of a Church and an Altar, 2, Preface).
- During the Eucharistic Celebration, at God's altar "the Sacrament of sacrifice is celebrated" (RM, Ritual Masses, For the Dedication of a Church and an Altar, 2, Prayer after Communion).

- The oblation of the Eucharist "on the altar of the Cross canceled the offense of the whole world" (RM, The Exaltation of the Holy Cross [Sep 14], Prayer over the Offerings).
- God renews the new and eternal covenant with his people in the sacrament of the altar (LH, Lent, Ash Wednesday, EP2, 1st intercession [=LH, Lent.2[=4].We, EP, 1st intercession]).
- In the Eucharistic Celebration the members of the Body of Christ unite themselves to the one offering of Christ, present on the altar (CCC 1368; 1372, quoting St. Augustine, De civ. Dei, 10, 6: PL 41, 283 and citing Rom. 12:5; LH, OT.28.Fr, 2R: St. Augustine, City of God, Book 10, 6: CCL 47, 278–279).
- In the Eucharistic Celebration, the spiritual sacrifice is placed on God's altar with loving devotion (RM, Votive Masses, 9, B, Prayer over the Offerings).

Gifts Are Offered and Received

- When the altar is dedicated, the Church prays that the Holy Spirit will come down upon the altar to sanctify the gifts of God's people and cleanse the hearts of all who receive them (RM, Ritual Masses, For the Dedication of a Church and an Altar, 2, Prayer over the Offerings).
- The liturgy prays that the Holy Spirit will sanctify the gifts laid on the altar as he once sanctified the womb of the Blessed Virgin Mary (RM, Adv.4.Su, Prayer over the Offerings).
- In the Eucharistic Celebration, the faithful bring the offerings to God's altar (RM, Dec 22, Prayer over the Offerings; *cf.* RM, Lent.AAW.Th, Prayer over the Offerings; RM, OT.9.Su, Prayer over the Offerings; *cf. also* RM, OT.4.Su, Prayer over the Offerings; RM, Votive Masses, 15, Prayer over the Offerings; RM, St. Elizabeth Ann Seton [Jan 4], Prayer over the Offerings; RM, St. John Neumann [Jan 5], Prayer over the Offerings; RM, St. Anthony [Jan 17], Prayer over the Offerings; RM, The Nativity of St. John the Baptist [June 24], At the Mass During the Day, Prayer over the Offerings; RM, St. Peter and St. Paul [June 29], At the Vigil Mass, Prayer over the Offerings; RM, St. Charles Borromeo [Nov 4], Prayer over the Offerings; RM, Commons, Common of Martyrs, III, B, Prayer over the Offerings; RM, Commons, Common of Pastors, II, 1, Prayer over the Offerings; RM, Commons, Common of Pastors, III, B, 1, Prayer over the

Offerings; RM, Commons, Common of Holy Men and Women, II, D, 2, Prayer over the Offerings).

- In the Eucharistic Celebration, the faithful receive gifts from God's altar (RM, ET.6.Ascension, At the Vigil Mass, Prayer after Communion; *cf. also* RM, St. Mark [Apr 25], Prayer after Communion; RM, St. Luke [Oct 18], Prayer after Communion; RM, Commons, Common of Holy Men and Women, I, A, 3, Prayer over the Offerings [Latin]; RM, Commons, Common of Holy Men and Women, I, A, 4, Prayer over the Offerings).

- The Church prays that God's angel may take the Eucharistic "gifts" to God's altar on high, so that, through participation at the altar the faithful may be filled "with every grace and heavenly blessing" (RM, Eucharistic Prayer I, 94; *cf.* CCC 1402).

Source of Nourishment, Salvation, and Unity

- At the altar of the Eucharistic Celebration, the faithful drink "from the streams that flow from Christ, the spiritual rock, through whom they, too, become a holy oblation, a living altar" (RM, Ritual Masses, For the Dedication of a Church and an Altar, 2, Preface).

- God nourishes his family with food from the altar (RM, St. Joseph [Mar 19], Prayer after Communion).

- Unless one is united to the altar (*"nisi quis intra altare sit"*), he is deprived of the bread of God (LH, OT.2.Su, 2R [Latin]: St. Ignatius of Antioch, Letter to the Ephesians, 2, 2–5, 2: Funk 1, 175–177).

- In the Eucharistic Celebration, the faithful welcome God's salvation from the altar (RM, Commons, Common of Pastors, IV, B, Prayer after Communion [Latin]).

- The faithful should be careful to stay united to their bishop and to the Church, avoiding schismatics. There is only one Eucharist, one flesh of Jesus Christ and one cup that unites us with his blood, one altar, and one bishop with his presbyters and deacons (LH, OT.27.Th, 2R: St. Ignatius of Antioch, Letter to the Philadelphians 1, 1–2, 1; 3, 2–5, 1: Funk 1, 226–229; *cf. also* LH, OT.16.Mo, 2R: St. Ignatius of Antioch, Letter to the Magnesians, 6, 1–9, 2: Funk 1, 195–199).

- At marriages held during the Eucharistic Celebration, the Church prays that the newlyweds, coming together before God's altar, may be confirmed in their love for one another (RM, Ritual Masses, For the Celebration of

Marriage, B, Collect; RM, Ritual Masses, For the Celebration of Marriage, B, Nuptial Blessing).

- Shortly before dying, St. Monica asked her sons only that after her death they would remember her at the altar of the Lord (LH, St. Monica [Aug 27], 2R: St. Augustine, Confessions, Book 9, 10–11: CSEL 33, 215–219; *cf.* CCC 1371, quoting Conf. 9, 11, 27: PL 32, 775).

Can Be Approached after Baptism

- Having received Baptism, the faithful can come before the altar and look upon the mystery of the Savior (LH, OT.13.Th, 2R: St. Jerome, Sermon on Ps. 41 addressed to newly baptized: CCL 78, 542–544).
- The recently baptized hasten to the altar of Christ, like the psalmist in Ps. 43:4 (LH, OT.15.Fr, 2R: St. Ambrose, On the Mysteries, 43.47–49: SC 25 bis, 178–180.182).
- In the Latin Church, the newly baptized baby is brought to the altar for the praying of the Our Father in order to express the orientation of Baptism to the Eucharist (CCC 1244).

Ministering at the Altar

- The Church prays that she may be worthy to minister with a pure heart at the altar, just as St. Joseph served God's Son with loving care (RM, St. Joseph [Mar 19], Prayer over the Offerings; *cf. also* RM, St. Charles Lwanga and Companions [June 3], Prayer over the Offerings; RM, Commons, Common of Holy Men and Women, I, A, 1, Prayer over the Offerings; RM, Commons, Common of Holy Men and Women, II, A, Prayer over the Offerings).
- God has willed that priests should minister at his holy altar (RM, Ritual Masses, For the Conferral of Holy Orders, 2, A [=B], Prayer over the Offerings; RM, Masses and Prayers for Various Needs and Occasions, I, 6, Prayer over the Offerings).
- The liturgy prays that deacons may be worthy ministers at God's altar (RM, Ritual Masses, For the Conferral of Holy Orders, 4, Collect).
- God entrusted deacons with "preaching the Gospel and serving both altar and people" (RM, Ritual Masses, For the Conferral of Holy Orders, 4, Solemn Blessing).

- The liturgy applies Ps. 47:8–10 to St. Ephrem, a fourth century deacon who wrote many liturgical hymns (LH, St. Ephrem [June 9], 2R, Resp [Sir. 47:8–10]).

Table of the Sacrifice of the Lord

- Jesus celebrated the Last Supper "at table" with his apostles (*cf.* Matt. 26:20; Mark 14:18; Luke 22:14).
- At the Last Supper, at table with his apostles, Jesus offered his body and his blood for the salvation of many (Matt. 26:26–28; Mark 14:22–24; Luke 22:19–20; 1 Cor. 11:23–26).
- When Christians celebrate the Last Supper, they "proclaim the Lord's death until he comes" (1 Cor. 11:26).
- St. Paul compares and contrasts the sacrifices and sacred meals of Jews, pagans, and Christians (1 Cor. 10:14–21). Implicit in the comparison is that the "table of the Lord" (1 Cor. 10:21) through which Christians participate in the body and blood of Christ (1 Cor. 10:16) is also an altar, as is the case for the table / altar of the Israelites (1 Cor. 10:18; *cf. also* Ezek. 40:39–43; 41:22; 44:16; Mal. 1:7, 12) and of the pagans (1 Cor. 10:20–21) (*cf. also* Matt. 26:26–28; Mark 14:22–24; Luke 22:19–20; John 6:51; 1 Cor. 11:23–29; Heb. 13:10).
- Those who minister at the table of the Lord must live a holy life (LH, St. John of Capistrano [Oct 23], 2R: St. John of Capistrano, Mirror of the Clergy, Pars 1, Venetiae 1580, 2).

Table of the Word of God and the Body of Christ

- The Eucharistic table is both the table of the Word of God and the table of the Body of Christ (CCC 103; 1346; RM, Votive Masses, 10, C, Prayer after Communion; LH, Lent.AAW[=2, 4].Th, EP, 3rd intercession; *cf.* CCC 1347, citing Luke 24:13–35; LH, Psalter.3.We, MP, 5th intercession [Latin]).
- The faithful receive life-giving nourishment at the table of the Body and Blood of Christ, handed down from the apostles; they receive light and joy at the table of God's Word, prepared by the apostles (LH, Conversion of St. Paul [Jan 25], MP, 2nd and 3rd intercession [=LH, Chair of Peter [Feb 22], MP, 2nd and 3rd intercession; LH, St. Philip and St. James [May 3],

MP, 2nd and 3rd intercession; LH, St. Andrew [Nov 30], MP, 2nd and 3rd intercession; LH, Common of Apostles, MP, 2nd and 3rd intercession]).

Table as Fountain

- From Christ's side flowed forth two streams of life, one to renew us in the baptismal font, the other to feed us at the divine table, as babies are nourished on milk (LH, OT.19.Mo, 2R [Latin]: Theodoret of Cyr, On the Incarnation, 26–27: PG 75, 1466–1467).
- Jesus strikes the spiritual rock, his table, and brings forth the living water of the Spirit like a fountain to which the faithful can approach and refresh themselves (LH, Lent.2.Mo, 2R: St. John Chrysostom, Cat. 3, 24–27: SC 50, 165–167; cf. EUCHARIST: Types: Water from the Rock).

Table That Nourishes and Refreshes

- The Christian community is a family, united by the Eucharist. Jesus is the father who prepares the table for his family. At this holy table all the children receive the same food, Jesus Christ (LH, St. Peter Julian Eymard [Aug 2], 2R: St. Peter Julian Eymard, La Présence réelle, vol. 1, Paris, 1950, pp. 270–271 and 307–308; cf. also 1 Cor. 10:17).
- Wisdom has set the Eucharistic table and invited the faithful to eat and drink (LH, OT.6.We, 2R: Procopius of Gaza, Commentary on the Book of Proverbs, Ch. 9: PG 87–1, 1299–1303; cf. EUCHARIST: Types: Wisdom's Banquet).
- God plentifully nourishes the faithful at the altar (RM, Ritual Masses, For the Dedication of a Church and an Altar, 2, Collect; cf. LH, OT.19.Mo, 2R: Theodoret of Cyr, On the Incarnation, 26–27: PG 75, 1466–1467).

Roman Missal

O God, who willed to draw all things
to your Son, lifted high on the altar of the Cross,
fill your Church, we pray, with heavenly grace
as she dedicates to you this altar,
the table at which you will plentifully nourish
the faithful you gather as one
and will shape day by day,

through the outpouring of the Spirit,

a people consecrated to yourself.

Through our Lord Jesus Christ, your Son,

who lives and reigns with you in the unity of the Holy Spirit,

    one God, for ever and ever.

RM, Ritual Masses, For the Dedication of a Church and an Altar,
2, Collect

- In the Eucharistic Celebration, the faithful taste the delights of God's table (RM, Masses and Prayers for Various Needs and Occasions, I, 11, C, Prayer after Communion).
- The Eucharist is "the refreshment" of the sacred table (RM, Lent.2.Tu, Prayer after Communion).
- The treasure hidden within the faithful since Baptism grows ever richer at the Lord's sacramental table, where the faithful daily embrace and receive the Lord into their bodies. At the Lord's spiritual table they receive his memorial (LH, St. Ephrem [June 9], 2R: St. Ephrem, Sermo 3, de fine et admonitione, 2.4–5: ed. Lamy, 3, 216–222).

The Liturgy of the Hours

In your sacrament we daily embrace you and receive you into our bodies; make us worthy to experience the resurrection for which we hope. We have had your treasure hidden within us ever since we received baptismal grace; it grows ever richer at your sacramental table. Teach us to find our joy in your favor! Lord, we have within us your memorial, received at your spiritual table; let us possess it in its full reality when all things shall be made new.

LH, St. Ephrem (June 9), 2R: St. Ephrem, Sermo 3, de fine et
admonitione, 2.4–5: ed. Lamy, 3, 216–222

The Faithful Gather at the Table

- The People of God are invited to the table of the Lord (CCC 1182; 1383; *cf.* CCC 1396; RM, Appendix to the Order of the Mass, Eucharistic Prayer for Use in Masses for Various Needs, II, 7; *cf. also* RM, St. Augustine [Aug 28], Prayer after Communion).

- In the Eucharistic Celebration, the Father gathers the faithful at the table of his Son (RM, Appendix to the Order of Mass, Eucharistic Prayer for Reconciliation II, 7; *cf. also* RM, Ritual Masses, For the Dedication of a Church and an Altar, 2, Solemn Blessing).

- The newly baptized hasten to the altar, and seeing the altar prepared exclaim: "You prepare a table before me" (Ps. 23:5) (LH, OT.15.Fr, 2R: St. Ambrose, On the Mysteries, 43.47–49: SC 25 bis, 178–180.182).

- At the Eucharistic Celebration, the faithful "approach the table of this wondrous Sacrament" (RM, The Order of the Mass, The Liturgy of the Eucharist, Preface II of the Most Holy Eucharist).

- Having done penance, the faithful can approach the holy table with confidence (LH, OT.21.Tu, 2R: St. John Chrysostom, Homily De diabolo tentatore 2, 6: PG 49, 263–264).

- In the Eucharistic Celebration, the faithful participate at God's table (RM, Masses and Prayers for Various Needs and Occasions, I, 18, B, Prayer after Communion).

Table That Unites and Sanctifies

- In the Eucharistic Celebration, the faithful partake of the table of unity and charity (RM, Masses and Prayers for Various Needs and Occasions, II, 26, A, Prayer after Communion).

- St. Lawrence (who ministered the sacred Blood of Christ as deacon of the Church of Rome) partook of a gift of self at the table of the Lord. Understanding this gift, he put it in practice in his martyrdom (LH, St. Lawrence [Aug 10], 2R: St. Augustine, Sermo 304, 1–4: PL 38, 1395–1397).

- In the Eucharistic Celebration is prepared the table of the Lord, where God's children, "fed by the Body of Christ, are gathered into the one, the holy Church" (RM, Ritual Masses, For the Dedication of a Church and an Altar, 2, Preface).

Roman Missal

It is truly right and just, our duty and our salvation,
always and everywhere to give you thanks,

Lord, holy Father, almighty and eternal God,
through Christ our Lord.

Having become both the true Priest and the true oblation,
he has taught us to celebrate for ever
the memorial of the Sacrifice
that he himself offered to you on the altar of the Cross.

Therefore, Lord, your people have raised this altar,
which we dedicate to you with joyful praise.

Truly this is an exalted place,
where the Sacrifice of Christ is ever offered in mystery,
where perfect praise is rendered to you
and redemption flows forth for us.

Here is prepared the table of the Lord,
where your children, fed by the Body of Christ,
are gathered into the one, the holy Church.

Here the faithful drink of your Spirit
from the streams that flow from Christ, the spiritual rock,
through whom they, too, become a holy oblation, a living
altar.

RM, Ritual Masses, For the Dedication of a Church and an Altar,
2, Preface

- The faithful dishonor the table of the Lord when they do not judge those in need worthy of sharing their food, for God has judged the poor worthy to share in the Eucharist (CCC 1397, quoting St. John Chrysostom, Homily in 1 Cor. 27, 4: PG 61, 229–230 and citing Matt. 25:40).
- The faithful should approach the table of the Eucharist with humility, partake of the meal of Christ who laid down his life for them, meditate devoutly on the gift they receive there, and then go out and share that meal

with others, laying down their life for others as did the martyrs (LH, Lent. HW.We, 2R: St. Augustine, Treatise on John, Tract. 84, 1–2: CCL 36, 536–538).

- Christ should be honored first of all by serving him in the poor, the Body of Christ. Only after this can Christ be also honored by adorning his table with golden cups and cloths (LH, OT.21.Sa, 2R: St. John Chrysostom, Homily on Matthew, 50, 3–4: PG 58, 508–509).

- Divisions in the Church which prevent the common participation of the faithful at the table of the Lord invite the faithful to work toward the full unity of Christians (CCC 1398).

- In the Eucharistic Celebration, God welcomes married couples to the table of his family (RM, Masses and Prayers for Various Needs and Occasions, For Holy Church, On the Anniversaries of Marriage, B, Prayer after Communion).

- When marriage is held during the Eucharistic Celebration, the Church prays that:

  ▪ Desiring to approach God's table as a couple joined in marriage in God's presence, the newlyweds may one day partake of the heavenly banquet (RM, Ritual Masses, For the Celebration of Marriage, B, Nuptial Blessing).

  ▪ Having been made partakers of God's table, the newlyweds may hold fast to God and proclaim his name to the world (RM, Ritual Masses, For the Celebration of Marriage, B, Prayer after Communion).

Participation in the Heavenly Table

- In the Eucharistic Celebration, the faithful come to the table of God's eternal banquet (RM, Masses for the Dead, IV, 1, C, Prayer after Communion).

- At the Eucharistic Celebration, the faithful are renewed by bread from the heavenly table (RM, OT.22.Su, Prayer after Communion; RM, Masses and Prayers for Various Needs and Occasions, I, 9, Prayer after Communion; RM, Masses for the Dead, IV, 3, B, Prayer after Communion).

- In the Eucharistic Celebration, the faithful partake "at the heavenly table" (RM, St. Basil the Great and St. Gregory of Nazianzus [Jan 2], Prayer after Communion; RM, St. Catherine of Siena [Apr 29], Prayer after Communion; RM, The Assumption of the Blessed Virgin Mary [Aug 15], At the Vigil Mass, Prayer after Communion; RM, Commons, Common of Pastors, III, B, 1, Prayer after Communion; RM, Masses and Prayers for Various Needs and Occasions, I, 1, A, Prayer after Communion; RM, Masses and Prayers for Various Needs and Occasions, I, 2, Prayer after Communion; RM, Votive Masses, The Most Holy Eucharist, Prayer after Communion; *cf. also* RM, St. Elizabeth Ann Seton [Jan 4], Prayer after Communion; RM, St. Pius X [Aug 21], Prayer after Communion; RM, St. Josaphat [Nov 12], Prayer after Communion).

- The liturgy prays that the faithful may pass from the pilgrim table of the Eucharist to the banquet of the heavenly homeland (RM, All Saints [Nov 1], Prayer after Communion; *cf. also* RM, Masses for the Dead, I, A, Prayer after Communion).

Other

- Jesus offered himself up on the altar of the cross (*cf. for example* RM, The Solemnities of the Lord during Ordinary Time, Our Lord Jesus Christ, King of the Universe, Preface; RM, Ritual Masses, For the Dedication of a Church and an Altar, 2, Collect; RM, Votive Masses, 10, C, Collect)
- Jesus invites sinners to the table of the Kingdom (*cf. for example* CCC 545, citing Matt. 2:17; 1 Tim. 1:15; CCC 589, citing Luke 15:1–2, 22–32; CCC 1443).
- Jesus conferred on his apostles a kingdom, so that they might eat and drink with him at his table (*cf.* Luke 22:29–30; CCC 551, citing Luke 22:29–30).
- Christians exercise the common priesthood when they "offer the spotless offerings of devotion on the altar of the heart" (CCC 786, quoting St. Leo the Great, Sermo 4, 1: PL 54, 149; LH, Leo the Great [Nov 10], 2R: Leo the Great, Sermo 4, 1–2: PL 54, 148–149; *cf. also for example* CCC 2655).
- Christians are living stones, forming a spiritual building. Jesus forms the altar from those stones who day and night make offerings of prayers and supplications to God (*cf. for example* LH, Common of the Dedication of a Church, 2R: Origen, Homily on Joshua 9, 1–2: SC 71, 244–246).
- At the funeral for a baptized child, the liturgy prays that as God has given that child a place at the table in his heavenly Kingdom, so the faithful present may too find a place there (RM, Masses for the Dead, I, E, 2, Prayer after Communion).
- In the heavenly banquet, "all the elect will be seated at the table of the kingdom" (CCC 1344; *cf. also for example* CCC 1689).

BANQUET

OT Background: Exod. 24:11; 1 Kings 3:15; Song 2:4; Isa. 25:6; 55:1–3

NT Background: Matt. 8:11–12; 22:4; 25:10; 26:26–29; Mark 14:22–25; Luke 13:29; 14:15–24; 15:1–2, 21–24, 22:19–20, 28–30; 24:30–31, 35; John 2:1–12; 21:12; 1 Cor. 10:16; 11:20–34; Rev. 3:20; 19:9

Catechism Background: 589; **1166**; **1323**; 1328–1329; 1344; 1346; 1347; **1382**; 1388–1390; **1391**; **1402**; **1408**; 1417; 1439; **1617**; 2770

Related: BAPTISM: *Types*: Fruit of the Tree of Life; EUCHARIST: *Types*: Fruit of the Tree of Life; Passover / Passover Lamb; Wisdom's Banquet; Water to Wine; *Symbols*: Altar / Table

- Sunday is the day of the Lord, and the Lord's Supper is at its center, "for there the whole community of the faithful encounters the Risen Lord who invites them to his banquet(cf. John 21:12; Luke 24:30)" (CCC 1166).
- The Eucharistic Celebration is:
  - a banquet (RM, ET.7.Fr, Prayer after Communion; RM, Masses and Prayers for Various Needs and Occasions, For Holy Church, For the Laity, Prayer after Communion; LH, Lent.1[=3, 5].TuMP, 2nd intercession);
  - a banquet which offers the hidden wisdom of the eternal Word (RM, St. John [Dec 27], Prayer over the Offerings);
  - a banquet which nourished the martyrs (LH, Lent.HW.We, 2R: St. Augustine, Treatise on John, Tract. 84, 1–2: CCL 36, 536–538);
  - a paschal banquet, in which Christ is consumed (CCC 1323; 1402);
  - the banquet of Christ's love (RM, Holy Thursday, Collect);
  - a saving banquet (RM, Eucharistic Prayer for Reconciliation II, 7; RM, Votive Masses, 16, Prayer after Communion);
  - a holy banquet that nourishes the faithful (RM, The Exaltation of the Holy Cross [Sep 14], Prayer after Communion; RM, Votive Masses, The Mystery of the Holy Cross, Prayer after Communion);
  - a holy banquet that can inflame the hearts of the faithful with charity (RM, St. Maximilian Kolbe [Aug 14], Prayer after Communion);
  - the banquet which Wisdom prepared (*cf.* EUCHARIST: *Types*: Wisdom's Banquet);
  - a divine banquet (RM, Commons, Common of Martyrs, II, A, 1, Prayer after Communion);

- a divine banquet that proclaims the death of God's Son (RM, Commons, Common of Martyrs, II, B, Prayer after Communion);
- a divine banquet that offers delights to the faithful (RM, St. Peter Julian Eymard [Aug 2], Collect);
- a divine banquet that nourishes and fortifies (RM, Masses and Prayers for Various Needs and Occasions, III, 48, B, Prayer after Communion);
- a heavenly banquet (RM, Commons, Common of Martyrs, III, B, Prayer after Communion);
- a sacred banquet of communion which is "wholly directed toward the intimate union of the faithful with Christ through communion" (CCC 1382).
- a sacred banquet, in which Christ is our food, his Passion is recalled, grace fills our hearts, and we receive a pledge of the glory to come (LH, Corpus Christi, EP2, Magn).
- a precious and wonderful banquet, that brings salvation and contains all sweetness (LH, Corpus Christi, 2R: St. Thomas Aquinas, Opusculum 57, in festo Corporis Christi, lect. 1–3).

The Liturgy of the Hours

O precious and wonderful banquet that brings us salvation and contains all sweetness! Could anything be of more intrinsic value? Under the old law it was the flesh of calves and goats that was offered, but here Christ himself, the true God, is set before us as our food. What could be more wonderful than this? No other sacrament has greater healing power; through it sins are purged away, virtues are increased, and the soul is enriched with an abundance of every spiritual gift. It is offered in the Church for the living and the dead, so that what was instituted for the salvation of all may be for the benefit of all. Yet, in the end, no one can fully express the sweetness of this sacrament, in which spiritual delight is tasted at its very source, and in which we renew the memory of that surpassing love for us which Christ revealed in his passion.

LH, Corpus Christi, 2R: St. Thomas Aquinas, Opusculum 57, in festo Corporis Christi, lect. 1–3

- Life in Christ is founded in the Eucharistic banquet, for "he who eats me will live because of me' (John 6:57)" (CCC 1391).
- In the Eucharist, priests set before God's children the paschal banquet (RM, Chrism Mass, Preface [=RM, Ritual Masses, IV, 1, A, Preface; RM, Ritual Masses, IV, 2, A [=B], Preface]).
- Jesus Christ is the invisible guest/host [Latin: *hospes*] of the Eucharistic banquet, who stands at the door and knocks, to come and eat with us, and us with him (LH, Corpus Christi, MP, 6th intercession; *cf.* Rev. 3:20).
- In the Eucharistic Celebration, Jesus Christ is the one who invites; he is also the one who gives himself as food and drink. The martyrs understood this, and gave to Christ the same gift they had received (LH, St. Cosmas and St. Damian [Sep 26], 2R: St. Augustine, Sermo 329, 1–2: PL 38, 1454–1455; LH, Common of One Martyr, 2R: St. Augustine, Sermo 329, 1–2: PL 38, 1454–1456; compare 1 John 3:16).
- By receiving the Lord's Body and Blood in the Eucharist, the faithful participate in the liturgical banquet and join themselves more perfectly to the one act of worship that is the Eucharistic Celebration (CCC 1408; 1388; *cf.* CCC 1389–1390; 1417).
- The Eucharist is the wedding feast of Christ and the Church (CCC 1617; *cf. also* LH, Corpus Christi, OR, Ant1).
- Sacramental communion anticipates the banquet of the kingdom in heaven (CCC 2770; RM Lent.3.We, Prayer after Communion; *cf. also* RM, St. Cyril and St. Methodius [Feb 14], Prayer after Communion; RM, All Saints [Nov 1], Prayer after Communion; RM, Masses for the Dead, IV, 1, C, Prayer after Communion; LH, Common of Holy Men, EP [=EP2], 5th intercession).

The Liturgy of the Hours

In the glorious deeds of the holy martyrs who everywhere adorn the Church, we verify the truth of what we have been singing: "Precious in the sight of the Lord is the death of his saints" (Ps. 116:15). . . . Elsewhere we read: "You have taken your seat at the great table; consider carefully what is set before you, for you must prepare the same in return" (*cf.* Sir. 31:12; Prov. 23:1). The great table is the one at which the Lord of the banquet is himself the food. No one feeds the guests with his very self, yet that is what Christ the Lord does. He invites and he is the food and drink. The martyrs took careful note of what they ate and drank, so that they might return the same.

LH, St. Cosmas and St. Damian (Sep 26), 2R: St. Augustine,
Sermo 329, 1–2: PL 38, 1454–1455

- In the Eucharist, the faithful feast at the banquet of the heavenly Lamb (RM, The Nativity of St. John the Baptist [June 24], At the Mass during the Day, Prayer after Communion; *cf.* Rev. 19:9).
- The Eucharistic banquet anticipates the wedding feast of the Lamb in the heavenly Jerusalem (CCC 1329, citing 1 Cor. 11:20; Rev. 19:9; *cf.* CCC 1135; 1344; EUCHARIST: *Types:* Water to Wine).
- As God has gathered the faithful around the table of his Son, the Eucharist, so the Church prays that he will allow them to share in "the unending banquet of unity in a new heaven and a new earth" (RM, Eucharistic Prayer for Reconciliation II, 7).

BREAD AND WINE / NOURISHMENT

OT Background: Gen. 27:28; 49:11; Exod. 16:15; Job 36:31; Ps. 4:7; 78:20; 81:16; 104:13–15; 147:14; Prov. 9:5; Eccles. 9:7–8; Wisd. 16:20–21, 25–26; Isa. 25:6; 30:23; 55:2; Hos. 2:8; Joel 2:19; 3:18; Amos 9:13

NT Background: Matt. 24:45; 26:29; Mark 14:25; Luke 12:42; 22:18; John 2:9–10; 4:32, 34; 6:27, 31–35, 51, 54–58; 12:24; 15:1, 4–5; Acts 2:42, 46; 1 Cor. 10:3–4, 16–17; Col. 2:19; 2 Tim. 4:6; Heb. 6:4–5; 13:9; Rev. 12:6, 14

Catechism Background: 141; 728; 777; 1003; 1148; 1333–1335; 1345; 1350; 1355; **1392; 1394;** 1402; 1405; 1419; 1426; 1436; 2031; 2040; 2041; 2047–2048; 2624; 2837; 2861

Related: EUCHARIST: *Types:* Wisdom's Banquet; Water to Wine; *Symbols:* Altar / Table; Banquet; Bread for the Journey / Daily Bread / Viaticum; Gift of Finest Wheat

Overview

- St. Irenaeus reflects at length about the meaning of the bread and wine which become the Body and Blood of Christ (LH, ET.3.Th, 2R: St. Irenaeus, Against Heresies, Book 5, 2, 2–3: SC 153, 30–38):

  - The Word of God nourishes us through creation, which is his gift to all.

  - The Lord declared that his chalice, which comes to us from creation, is his Blood, which nourishes our blood.

  - The Lord declared that the bread, which comes from his creation, is his Body, and he made it nourishment for our body.

  - We mix the chalice, and we bake the bread. When the chalice and the bread receive the Word of God they become the Body and Blood of Christ, by which our bodies live and grow and are seen to be capable of receiving God's gift of eternal life.

  - When Paul says that we are members of Christ's body (in Eph. 5:30) he "is not speaking of some spiritual and incorporeal kind of man, 'for spirits do not have flesh and bones'" (Luke 24:39). Rather it is a real human body, of flesh and bones, "nourished by the chalice of Christ's blood and receiving growth from the bread which is his body."

  - The slip of vine planted in the ground bears fruit at the proper time; the grain of wheat falls in the ground and decays, but is raised up by the Spirit of God; these things are placed by the Wisdom of God at the service of man; when they receive God's Word they become the Eucharist, which is the Body and Blood of Christ.

  - It is similar with bodies nourished by the Eucharist. They will be placed in the ground and decay, but the Word of God will raise them up again at the appointed time to the glory of God the Father.

Fruit of the Earth and Work of Human Hands

- The signs of bread and wine signify "the goodness of creation" (CCC 1333).
- The daily bread in Israel, fruit of the promised land, was a reminder that God is faithful to his promises (CCC 1334).
- In the Old Covenant, the first fruits of the earth, including bread and wine, were offered in sacrifice "as a sign of grateful acknowledgment to the Creator" (CCC 1334; *cf. also* CCC 1148; LH, OT.18.Sa, 2R: St. Irenaeus,

Against Heresies, Book 4, 17, 4–6: SC 100, 590–594; EUCHARIST: *Types*: Offering of the First Fruits).

- In the Offertory, the Church gives thanks to the Creator for the gifts of bread and wine, which are the fruit of God's creation and the work of human hands (RM, The Order of Mass, 23; 25; CCC 1333, citing Ps. 104:13–15; *cf.* CCC 1350; 1357).

- God brought forth "bread from the earth to sustain our lives and wine to gladden the heart." In the Eucharist, they become "the Sacrament of our salvation" (RM, Masses and Prayers for Various Needs and Occasions, III, 48/1, B, Prayer over the Offerings).

- Just as the bread, which is from the earth, becomes the Eucharist, made up of two elements, one earthly and one heavenly, so also our bodies, in receiving the Eucharist, are no longer corruptible, for they have the hope of resurrection (LH, OT.2.Sa, 2R: St. Irenaeus, Against Heresies, Book 4, 18, 1–2.4.5: SC 100, 596–598.606.610–612).

Wheat and Grapes

- It is fitting that the faithful receive the Body of Christ in the form of bread (LH, ET.2.Th, 2R: St. Gaudentius of Brescia, Tract. 2: CSEL 68, 30–32):
  - as there are many grains of wheat in the flour which become one bread, so many members make up the one Body of Christ (*cf. also* 1 Cor. 10:17);
  - as the flour is mixed with water when making bread, so Jesus received the Holy Spirit by descending into the Jordan River at his baptism, sanctifying the waters of Baptism;
  - as the flour mixed with water is baked into bread with fire, so the Body of Christ is brought to maturity by the fire of the Holy Spirit.
- It is fitting that the faithful should receive the Blood of Christ in the form of wine (LH, ET.2.Th, 2R: St. Gaudentius of Brescia, Tract. 2: CSEL 68, 30–32):
  - the faithful are like grapes of the vineyard, planted by Christ;
  - the grape juice is extracted from the faithful in the winepress of the cross;
  - when the faithful receive the grape juice of the cross in their lives with believing hearts, which are ample wineskins, it ferments within them, becoming the wine of Christ's Blood.

The Liturgy of the Hours

It is appropriate that we should receive the body of Christ in the form of bread, because, as there are many grains of wheat in the flour from which bread is made by mixing it with water and baking it with fire, so also we know that many members make up the one body of Christ which is brought to maturity by the fire of the Holy Spirit. Christ was born of the Holy Spirit, and since it was fitting that he should fulfill all justice, he entered into the waters of baptism to sanctify them. When he left the Jordan he was filled with the Holy Spirit who had descended upon him in the form of a dove. As the evangelist tells us: Jesus, full of the Holy Spirit, returned from the Jordan.

Similarly, the wine of Christ's blood, drawn from the many grapes of the vineyard that he had planted, is extracted in the winepress of the cross. When men receive it with believing hearts, like capacious wineskins, it ferments within them by its own power.

LH, ET.2.Th, 2R: St. Gaudentius of Brescia, Tract. 2: CSEL 68,
30–32

• In the Eucharistic Celebration, the faithful bring many grains of wheat made into bread to be changed into the Body of God's Son (RM, Masses and Prayers for Various Needs and Occasions, II, 27, B, Prayer over the Offerings).

Wine

• It is fitting that wine becomes the Blood of Christ, for Christ said, "I am the true vine" (*cf.* John 15:1). In this way Christ declared clearly enough that wine offered as a figure of his Passion is his Blood. This also explains Jacob's prophecy that the Christ would "wash his tunic in wine and his cloak in the blood of the grape" (*cf.* Gen. 49:11). The tunic, in fact, is our body, Christ's garment which he washed clean in his own blood (LH, ET.5.Th, 2R [Latin]: St. Gaudentius of Brescia, Tract. 2: CSEL 68, 26.29–30).

- The mixing of a small amount of water with the wine symbolizes our share "in the divinity of Christ, who humbled himself to share in our humanity" (RM, The Order of the Mass, 24; *cf. also* CCC 1345).
- The Blood of Christ inebriates the faithful (LH, ET.2.We, 2R: St. Leo the Great, Sermo 12 de Passione, 3, 6–7: PL 54, 355–357; LH, OT.15.Sa, 2R: St. Ambrose, On the Mysteries, 52–54.58: SC 25 bis, 186–188.190; *cf.* LH, OT.6.We, 2R: Procopius of Gaza, Commentary on the Book of Proverbs, Ch. 9: PG 87–1, 1299–1303).
- The faithful who love God and their neighbor become inebriated by drinking the cup of the Lord's love, the Eucharist, putting to death whatever in their nature is rooted in earth and being clothed with the Lord Jesus Christ (LH, OT.28.Mo, 2R [Latin]: St. Fulgentius, Against Fabianus, Ch. 28, 16–19: CCL 91A, 813–814).
- The transforming of water into wine at Cana "makes manifest the fulfillment of the wedding feast in the Father's kingdom, where the faithful will drink the new wine that has become the Blood of Christ(cf. John 2:11; Mark 14:25)" (CCC 1335; *cf. also* Matt. 26:29; Luke 22:18; EUCHARIST: *Types*: Water to Wine; for some examples of biblical background of wine as a sign of eschatological blessing *cf.* Isa. 25:6; Amos 9:13; Joel 3:18).

Food

- The Eucharist is Christ's flesh and blood, offered as food for the life of the world (John 6:51, 54–58).
- As material food is to our bodily life, so the Eucharist is to our spiritual life. The Eucharist nourishes the faithful, preserving, increasing, and renewing the life of grace received at Baptism (CCC 1392).
- The Eucharist is not ordinary food and drink, for just as Jesus Christ became a man of flesh and blood by the power of the Word of God, so also the food that we eat, by the power of the words of Jesus contained in the prayer of thanksgiving, becomes the Flesh and Blood of the Incarnate Jesus (LH, ET.3.Su, 2R: St. Justin Martyr, First Apology, 66–67: PG 6, 427–431).
- God gave men food and drink to enjoy that they might praise his name. Now, in the Eucharist, through Jesus Christ he has given the faithful spiritual food and spiritual drink, together with eternal life (LH, OT.14.We, 2R: Didache 9, 1–10, 6; 14, 1–3: Funk 2, 19–22.26).

- While in the Old Covenant the flesh of calves and goats were offered, here it is Christ himself who is set before the faithful as their food. Through it sins are purged, "virtues are increased, and the soul is enriched with an abundance of every spiritual gift." In this sacrament, spiritual delight is tasted at its very source (LH, Corpus Christi, 2R: St. Thomas Aquinas, Opusculum 57, in festo Corporis Christi, lect. 1–3; *cf. also* EUCHARIST: *Types:* Animal Sacrifices).

- The Eucharist is food (*cf. for example* John 6:55; CCC 1355, quoting St. Justin, Apol. 1, 66, 1–2: PG 6, 428; CCC 1392; 1402; 1405; 1426; 2837; RM, The Order of the Mass, The Communion Rite, 137; RM, St. Joachim and St. Anne [July 26], Prayer after Communion; RM, St. Bernard [Aug 20], Prayer after Communion; RM, St. Matthew [Sep 21], Prayer after Communion; RM, St. Teresa of Jesus [Oct 15], Prayer after Communion; RM, Commons, Common of Martyrs, I, A, 5, Prayer after Communion; RM, Commons, Common of Pastors, IV, A, Collect; RM, Commons, Common of Holy Men and Women, III, Prayer after Communion; RM, Ritual Masses, X, 2, Preface; RM, Masses and Prayers for Various Needs and Occasions, III, 39, Prayer after Communion; RM, Masses for the Dead, II, D, Prayer after Communion; LH, Lent.4.Fr, 2R: St. Athanasius, Easter Letter 5, 1–2: PG 26, 1379–1380; LH, ET.3.Su, 2R, Resp; LH, OT.25.Sa, 2R: St. Hilary, Discourse on Psalm 64, 14–15: CSEL 22, 245–246; LH, St. Peter Julian Eymard [Aug 2], 2R: St. Peter Julian Eymard, La Présence réelle, vol. 1, Paris, 1950, pp. 270–271 and 307–308; LH, St. Cosmas and St. Damian [Sep 26], 2R: St. Augustine, Sermo 329, 1–2: PL 38, 1454–1455; LH, St. Albert the Great [Nov 15], 2R: St. Albert the Great, Commentary on Luke 22, 19: Opera Omnia, Paris 1890–1899, 23, 672–674; LH, Common of One Martyr, 2R: St. Augustine, Sermo 329, 1–2: PL 38, 1454–1456).

- When the faithful receive the Eucharist, they feed upon heavenly delights / food (RM, OT.6.Su, Prayer after Communion; RM Lent.3.We, Prayer after Communion; RM, St. Catherine of Siena [Apr 29], Prayer after Communion; RM, St. Joseph [May 1], Prayer after Communion; RM, St. Philip Neri [May 26], Prayer after Communion; RM, St. Justin Martyr [June 1], Prayer after Communion; RM, St. Aloysius Gonzaga [June 21], Prayer after Communion; RM, St. Peter Julian Eymard [Aug 2], Collect; RM, Commons, Common of the Blessed Virgin Mary, I, 3,

Prayer after Communion; RM, Commons, Common of the Blessed Virgin Mary, I, 6, Prayer after Communion; RM, Commons, Common of Martyrs, III, A, Prayer after Communion; RM, Commons, Common of Pastors, V, 3, Prayer over the Offerings; RM, Commons, Common of Doctors of the Church, 2, Prayer after Communion; RM, Ritual Masses, III, Prayer after Communion; RM, Ritual Masses, IV, 3, A [=B], Prayer after Communion; RM, Ritual Masses, IV, 4, Prayer after Communion; RM, Masses and Prayers for Various Needs and Occasions, I, 8, Prayer after Communion; RM, Masses and Prayers for Various Needs and Occasions, I, 11, A, Prayer after Communion; RM, Masses and Prayers for Various Needs and Occasions, I, 13, B, Prayer after Communion; RM, Votive Masses, 7, Prayer after Communion, 2nd option; RM, Votive Masses, 9, B, Prayer after Communion; RM, Masses for the Dead, IV, 3, B, Prayer after Communion; LH, ET.5.Mo, 2R: St. Gregory of Nyssa, Oratio 1 in Christi resurrectionem: PG 46, 603–606.626–627; LH, OT.11.Th, 2R: St. Cyprian, Treatise on the Lord's Prayer, 18.22: CSEL 3, 280–281.283–284; LH, OT.15.Fr, 2R: St. Ambrose, On the Mysteries, 43.47–49: SC 25 bis, 178–180.182; LH, Corpus Christi, EP2, Magn; *cf. also* LH, Corpus Christi, EP, Ant1; LH, Corpus Christi, MD, Verse; LH, Psalter.3.We, 5th intercession [Latin]; EUCHARIST: *Symbols*: Bread from Heaven / Bread of Life / Bread of Angels).

- The Eucharist is saving food that strengthens / refreshes (RM, ET.2[=4, 6].Th, Prayer after Communion [=RM, ET.3[=5].Mo, Prayer after Communion; RM, ET.6.Su, Prayer after Communion]; RM, Votive Masses, 7, Prayer after Communion).

- The Eucharist is spiritual food (RM, ET, Pentecost, At the Mass during the Day, Prayer after Communion; RM, Masses and Prayers for Various Needs and Occasions, I, 14, Prayer after Communion; RM, Masses and Prayers for Various Needs and Occasions, III, 49, B, Prayer after Communion; LH, OT.15.Sa, 2R: St. Ambrose, On the Mysteries, 52–54.58: SC 25 bis, 186–188.190; LH, OT.21.Mo, 2R: St. Thomas Aquinas, Exposition on John, Ch. 10, 3; *cf. also* 1 Cor. 10:3–4, 16–17).

- The Eucharist is the food of the valiant (RM, St. Andrew Kim Tae-gŏn and St. Paul Chŏng Ha-sang and Companion Martyrs, Prayer after Communion).

- The Eucharist is the food of charity (RM, OT.22.Su, Prayer after Communion).
- The Eucharist is the food of immortality (RM, Our Lord Jesus Christ, King of the Universe, Prayer after Communion; *cf. also* EUCHARIST: *Symbols:* Medicine of Immortality).
- The Eucharist is food for the journey (RM, Masses for the Dead, I, A, Prayer after Communion; *cf. also* EUCHARIST: *Symbols:* Bread for the Journey / Daily Bread / Viaticum).
- Moses raised his hands to heaven and brought down manna; the new Moses raises his hands to heaven and gives the food of eternal life *(*LH, Lent.2.Mo, 2R: St. John Chrysostom, Cat. 3, 24–27: SC 50, 165–167; *cf. also* LH, Lent.2.Tu, 1R, Resp [Wisd. 16:20; John 6:32]; LH, Corpus Christi, MP, Ant1; EUCHARIST: *Types*: Manna).

Nourishment

- The Eucharist is food that nourishes (CCC 1392; RM, St. Joseph [Mar 19], Prayer after Communion; RM, St. Andrew Kim Tae-gŏn and St. Paul Chŏng Ha-sang and Companion Martyrs, Prayer after Communion; RM, Commons, Common of the Blessed Virgin Mary, I, 6, Prayer after Communion; RM, Masses and Prayers for Various Needs and Occasions, II, 26, A, Prayer over the Offerings; RM, Votive Masses, 9, B, Prayer after Communion; LH, Corpus Christi, MP, 5th intercession).
- As a woman nourishes her child with her own blood and milk, so Christ nourishes with his own Blood [in context referring to the Eucharist] those to whom he has given life [in context refering to Baptism] (LH, Lent. HW.Fr, 2R: St. John Chrysostom, Catecheses 3, 13–19: SC 50, 174–177; *cf. also* LH, OT.19.Mo, 2R: Theodoret of Cyr, On the Incarnation, 26–27: PG 75, 1466–1467).
- The Eucharist is food of spiritual nourishment (RM, Adv.1[=3].Tu[=Fr], Prayer after Communion [=RM, Adv.2.Su[=Tu, Fr], Prayer after Communion]; *cf. also* RM, Commons, Common of the Blessed Virgin Mary, I, 7, Prayer after Communion).
- The Eucharist nourishes (CCC 777; 1003; 1392; 1394; 1436; 2040; 2624; 2861; LH, ET.2.Th, 2R: St. Gaudentius of Brescia, Tract. 2: CSEL 68, 30–32; RM, Lent.1.We, Prayer after Communion; RM, Lent.3.Sa, Prayer after Communion; RM, St. Timothy and St. Titus [Jan 26], Prayer

after Communion; RM, The Holy Guardian Angels [Oct 2], Prayer after Communion; RM, Commons, Common of Pastors, V, 2, Prayer after Communion; RM, Ritual Masses, X, 2, Collect; LH, Adv.2.Tu, 2R: Vatican II, Lumen Gentium 48; *cf. also* LH, St. John Damascene [Dec 4], 2R: St. John Damascene, Statement of Faith, Ch. 1: PG 95, 417–419; LH, ET.1[=3, 5].Fr, EP, 2nd intercession; LH, OT.6.We, 2R: Procopius of Gaza, Commentary on the Book of Proverbs, Ch. 9: PG 87–1, 1299–1303; LH, St. Peter Julian Eymard [Aug 2], 2R, Resp [1 Cor. 10:17; John 6:58a]; LH, St. Martin de Porres [Nov 3], 2R [Latin]: St. John XXIII, Homily at the Canonization of St. Martin de Porres, May 6, 1962: AAS 54 [1962], 306–309).

- "'The Church has always venerated the divine Scriptures as she has the Body of the Lord: (Dei Verbum 21)' both nourish and govern the whole Christian life" (CCC 141; *cf.* CCC 2040; *cf. also* CCC 2665; 2698; RM, OT.23.Su, Prayer after Communion; LH, ET.2[=4, 6].Sa, MP, 2nd intercession).
- Nourished with the Body of Christ in the Eucharist, the faithful belong to the Body of Christ (CCC 1003; *cf.* 1 Cor. 10:16–17; CCC 777; *cf. also* John 6:56; CCC 787).
- The moral life, which is a spiritual worship, is nourished in the liturgy and the sacraments (CCC 2047; *cf.* CCC 2041; 2048; *cf. also* CCC 2031).
- As bodily nourishment strengthens and restores, so the Eucharist strengthens charity and wipes away venial sins (CCC 1394).
- St. Cyril of Jerusalem explains the symbolism of bread and wine in the Eucharist (LH, ET.1.Sa, 2R: St. Cyril of Jerusalem, Jerusalem Catecheses, 22, Mystagogica 4, 1.3–6.9: PG 33, 1098–1106):
  - Jesus Christ gave the faithful his body and blood under the symbols of bread and wine. These sanctify both body and soul, the bread being adapted to the sanctification of the body, the Word to the sanctification of the soul (*cf. also* RM, OT.11.Su, Prayer over the Offerings).
  - David referred to the Eucharist long ago when he spoke of bread that strengthens "man's heart and makes his face shine with the oil of gladness" (*cf.* Ps. 104:15). By receiving the Eucharist as spiritual bread, the faithful strengthen their heart and bring joy to the face of their souls.
- The faithful receive life-giving nourishment at the table of the Body and Blood of Christ, handed down from the apostles; they receive light and joy at the table of God's Word, prepared by the apostles (LH, Conversion of

St. Paul [Jan 25], MP, 2nd and 3rd intercession [=LH, Chair of Peter [Feb 22], MP, 2nd and 3rd intercession; LH, St. Philip and St. James [May 3], MP, 2nd and 3rd intercession; LH, St. Andrew [Nov 30], MP, 2nd and 3rd intercession; LH, Common of Apostles, MP, 2nd and 3rd intercession]; *cf.* EUCHARIST: *Symbols*: Altar / Table).

- From Christ's side flowed forth two streams of life, one to renew us in the baptismal font, the other to feed us at the divine table, as babies are nourished on milk (LH, OT.19.Mo, 2R [Latin]: Theodoret of Cyr, On the Incarnation, 26–27: PG 75, 1466–1467; *cf.* EUCHARIST: *Symbols*: Altar / Table).

- God plentifully nourishes the faithful at the altar (RM, Ritual Masses, For the Dedication of a Church and an Altar, 2, Collect; *cf.* EUCHARIST: *Symbols*: Altar / Table).

- God nourishes his family with food from the altar (RM, St. Joseph [Mar 19], Prayer after Communion; *cf.* EUCHARIST: *Symbols*: Altar / Table).

- The Eucharistic Celebration is a banquet which nourished the martyrs (LH, Lent.HW.We, 2R: St. Augustine, Treatise on John, Tract. 84, 1–2: CCL 36, 536–538; *cf.* EUCHARIST: *Symbols*: Banquet).

- The Eucharistic Celebration is a holy banquet that nourishes the faithful (RM, The Exaltation of the Holy Cross [Sep 14], Prayer after Communion; RM, Votive Masses, The Mystery of the Holy Cross, Prayer after Communion; *cf.* EUCHARIST: *Symbols*: Banquet).

- The Eucharistic Celebration is a divine banquet that nourishes and fortifies (RM, Masses and Prayers for Various Needs and Occasions, III, 48, B, Prayer after Communion; *cf.* EUCHARIST: *Symbols*: Banquet).

- The Eucharist acts as bread for the pilgrimage, nourishing and strengthening the Christian in his journey through life (CCC 1392; 1419; *cf.* RM, Masses for the Dead, I, A, Prayer after Communion; EUCHARIST: *Symbols: Bread for the Journey / Daily Bread / Viaticum*).

- The Eucharist is viaticum, i.e. "nourishment for the journey" to eternal life (CCC 1020; *cf. also* CCC 1392; EUCHARIST: *Symbols:* Bread for the Journey / Daily Bread / Viaticum).

- The petition for "daily bread" in the Our Father refers (among other things) to the Body of Christ, "the indispensable, (super-) essential nourishment of the feast of the coming Kingdom anticipated in the Eucharist" (CCC 2861; *cf.* EUCHARIST: *Symbols*: Bread for the Journey / Daily Bread / Viaticum).

- Daily conversion and penance find nourishment in the Eucharist (CCC 1436).
- The bread of heaven, the Eucharist, nourishes the faithful (RM, Advent, Dec 17, Prayer over the Offerings; RM, OT.2.Su, Prayer after Communion; RM, St. Michael, St. Gabriel, and St. Raphael [Sep 29], Prayer after Communion; RM, The Dedication of the Basilicas of St. Peter and St. Paul [Nov 18], Prayer after Communion; RM, Commons, Common of Martyrs, I, A, 2, Prayer after Communion; RM, Ritual Masses, I, 4, C, Prayer after Communion; LH, ET.5.Mo, 2R: St. Gregory of Nyssa, Oratio 1 in Christi resurrectionem: PG 46, 603–606.626–627; *cf. also* RM, Masses and Prayers for Various Needs and Occasions, I, 7, B, Prayer after Communion).
- The Church prays that the living Bread of the Eucharist which came down from heaven may give those who receive it strength to relieve their brothers and sisters in need (RM, Masses and Prayers for Various Needs and Occasions, For Civil Needs, 33, A, Prayer after Communion; RM, OT.22. Su, Prayer after Communion; RM, Masses and Prayers for Various Needs and Occasions, For Civil Needs, 33, B, Prayer after Communion).
- The heavenly bread of the Eucharist nourishes faith, increases hope, and strengthens charity (RM, Lent.1.Su, Prayer after Communion).

BREAD FOR THE
JOURNEY / DAILY BREAD / VIATICUM

OT Background: Gen. 28:20–21; Exod. 16:4; 1 Kings 19:4–8; Ps. 111:5; Prov. 30:8–9; Wisd. 16:20–21

NT Background: Matt. 6:11; 15:32, 35–39; Mark 8:2–3, 6–9; Luke 11:3; John 6:34, 49–58; James 2:15–17; Rev. 12:6, 14

Catechism Background: 163; 311; 972; **1020**; **1090**; 1111; 1186; 1198; **1331–1332**; **1334**; 1344; **1389**; **1392**; 1394; **1419**; **1436**; **1517**; **1524–1525**; 1533; 1683; 2583; **2835**; **2837**; 2861

Related: EUCHARIST: *Types*: Manna; Bread for the Journey of Elijah; Multiplication of Loaves

Bread for the Journey

- The earthly liturgy is a foretaste of the heavenly liturgy, "which is celebrated in the Holy City of Jerusalem toward which we journey as pilgrims"

(CCC 1090; *cf.* CCC 1111; LH, OT.3.Su, 2R: Vatican II, Sacrosanctum Concilium 7–8.106; *cf. also* CCC 1344).

- The Church, as Mother, bears the Christian sacramentally in her womb during his earthly pilgrimage (CCC 1683).

- The Eucharist acts as bread for the pilgrimage, nourishing and strengthening the Christian in his journey through life (CCC 1392; 1419; *cf.* RM, Masses for the Dead, I, A, Prayer after Communion).

- The Eucharistic sacrifice is sustenance for the journey, by which the Christian is nourished and supported along the road of life (LH, ET.2.Th, 2R: St. Gaudentius of Brescia, Tract. 2: CSEL 68, 30–32).

- In the Eucharistic Celebration, the Church prays that "we may pass from this pilgrim table to the banquet of our heavenly homeland" (RM, All Saints [Nov 1], Prayer after Communion; *cf. also* RM, Masses for the Dead, I, A, Prayer after Communion).

The Roman Missal

As we adore you, O God, who alone are holy
and wonderful in all your Saints,
we implore your grace,
so that, coming to perfect holiness in the fullness of your love,
we may pass from this pilgrim table
to the banquet of our heavenly homeland.
Through Christ our Lord.

RM, All Saints (Nov 1), Prayer after Communion

- Participation in the Holy Sacrifice sustains the strength of the faithful along the pilgrimage of this life (CCC 1419).

- The Sacraments of Baptism, Confirmation, and Eucharist "confer the graces needed for the life according to the Spirit during this life as pilgrims on the march towards the homeland" (CCC 1533).

- In the Eucharistic Celebration of the twenty-fifth anniversary of religious profession, the Church prays that the religious, having been refreshed with the heavenly food and drink, may proceed happily on the journey toward God which they have already begun (RM, Masses and Prayers for Various Needs and Occasions, I, 13, B, Prayer after Communion).

- The Eucharistic Celebration is called "Mass" ("Missa") because it "concludes with the sending forth (*missio*) of the faithful, so that they may fulfill God's will in their daily lives" (CCC 1332).

Daily Bread

- The daily bread in Israel, fruit of the promised land, was a reminder that God is faithful to his promises (CCC 1334).
- By praying for daily bread in the Our Father (*cf.* Matt. 6:11; Luke 11:3), Christians pray for everything they need, including the Eucharist, which is necessary to gain everlasting happiness (LH, OT.29.Tu, 2R: St. Augustine, Letter to Proba, 130, 11, 21–12, 22: CSEL 44, 63–64).
- By praying for daily bread in the Our Father, Christians ask God to give not only physical bread but also "the Bread of Life: The Word of God accepted in faith, the Body of Christ received in the Eucharist (Cf. John 6:26–58)" (CCC 2835; *cf.* CCC 2861).
- Both the Eucharist and the Word of God are our daily bread, and are necessities for our pilgrimage (CCC 2837, quoting St. Augustine, Sermo 57, 7: PL 38, 389).
- The spiritual meaning of the petition in the Our Father for "our daily bread" is the Eucharist. Christians pray that they might receive Eucharistic communion daily, and that they do not have to abstain from receiving communion on account of some serious sin which separates them from the Body of Christ (LH, OT.11.Th, 2R: St. Cyprian, Treatise on the Lord's Prayer, 18.22: CSEL 3, 280–281.283–284).
- "Daily" in the Our Father is *epiousios* (*cf.* Matt. 6:11), the literal etymological meaning of which is "super-essential." As such, it refers to the Bread of Life, the Eucharist, "without which we have no life within us" (CCC 2837, citing St. Ignatius of Antioch, Ad Eph. 20, 2: PG 5, 661 and John 6:53–56; *cf.* CCC 2861).
- In the liturgy, the Church asks the heavenly Father, who feeds the birds of the sky and clothes the grass of the field (*cf.* Matt. 6:26, 28–30), that he will give to all people the daily and super-essential bread ("cotidianum et supersubstantialem panem") (LH, St. Joseph, Husband of Mary [Mar 19], EP [=EP2], 3rd intercession [Latin]; LH, St. Joseph the Worker [May 1], EP, 3rd intercession).

- Daily the faithful receive the Lord in the Eucharist (LH, St. Ephrem [June 9], 2R: St. Ephrem, Sermo 3, de fine et admonitione, 2.4–5: ed. Lamy, 3, 216–222).
- The Church strongly encourages the faithful to receive the Eucharist on Sundays and feast days, and even daily (CCC 1389).
- "Daily conversion and penance find their source and nourishment in the Eucharist" (CCC 1436).
- The living charity of the Eucharist wipes away daily faults against charity, forgiving venial sins (CCC 1394; 1436).

Viaticum

- The Eucharist is viaticum, i.e. "nourishment for the journey" to eternal life (CCC 1020; *cf. also* CCC 1331; 1392).
- The Eucharist, sacrament of Christ's Passover (i.e. his death and Resurrection) has particular importance and meaning at the time of death, the moment of the soul's "passing over" (i.e. "Passover") to the Father. The Eucharist is "the seed of eternal life and the power of resurrection, according to the words of the Lord: 'He who eats my flesh and drinks my blood has eternal life, and I will raise him up on the last day' (John 6:54)" (CCC 1524; *cf.* John 13:1; CCC 1517; EUCHARIST: *Types:* Passover).
- "The Eucharist should always be the last sacrament of the earthly journey, the 'viaticum' for 'passing over' to eternal life" (CCC 1517).
- The Church prays that those who receive viaticum may be strengthened by the Eucharist and may journey in peace to God's Kingdom (RM, Ritual Masses, For the Administering of Viaticum, Collect).
- Together with Penance and Anointing of the Sick, the Eucharist as viaticum prepares the person for their heavenly homeland and completes the earthly pilgrimage (CCC 1525).

BREAD FROM HEAVEN / BREAD OF LIFE / BREAD OF ANGELS

OT Background: Exod. 16:4, 8, 12–15, 19–21; 31–35; Num. 11:6–9; 21:5; Deut. 8:3, 16; Josh. 5:11–12; 1 Kings 19:4–8; Neh. 9:15, 20; Ps. 78:24–25; 105:40; Wisd. 16:20

NT Background: Matt. 4:4; Luke 4:4; John 6:31–35, 41, 48–51, 58; Heb. 9:4; Rev. 2:17

Catechism Background: 103; 1094; 1212; 1331; 1334; **1338; 1355; 1392; 1406**; 1413; 1509; **1524; 2835; 2837**; 2861

Related: EUCHARIST: *Types:* Fruit of the Tree of Life; Manna; Bread for the Journey of Elijah; Wisdom's Banquet; *Symbols*: Medicine of Immortality

Note: Manna / bread from heaven is presented as both a type and a symbol. For texts whose meaning is primarily typological, cf. EUCHARIST: *Types:* Manna.

Bread from Heaven

- The Eucharist is the bread from heaven (John 6:50–51, 58; CCC 1331; RM, St. Teresa of Jesus [Oct 15], Prayer after Communion; RM, St. Ignatius of Antioch [Oct 17], Prayer after Communion; RM, Commons, Common of Virgins, II, 3, Prayer after Communion; RM, Masses and Prayers for Various Needs and Occasions, II, 33, A, Prayer after Communion; RM, Votive Masses, 11, Prayer after Communion; LH, ET.1.Sa, 2R: St. Cyril of Jerusalem, Jerusalem Catecheses, 22, Mystagogica 4, 1.3–6.9: PG 33, 1098–1106; LH, ET.3.Th, EP, Magn; LH, ET.5.Th, 2R: St. Gaudentius of Brescia, Tract. 2: CSEL 68, 26.29–30; LH, Corpus Christi, EP, Ant3; LH, Corpus Christi, EP [=EP2], Resp; LH, Corpus Christi, EP, Magn; LH, Corpus Christi, EP [=EP2], 1st intercession; LH, St. Peter Julian Eymard [Aug 2], 2R, Resp [1 Cor. 10:17; John 6:58a]; LH, Common of Holy Men, EP [=EP2], 5th intercession).
- The Eucharist is the bread come down from heaven that gives life (*cf. for example* John 6:50–51, 58; LH, ET.2.Th, 2R, Resp [Luke 22:19; John 6:58]; LH, OT.29.Mo, 2R, Resp [Luke 22:19; John 6:58]; LH, Corpus Christi, 1R, Resp [John 6:48–52]; *cf. also* LH, ET.3.Tu, EP, Magn).
- The Eucharist is bread from the heavenly table (RM, OT.22.Su, Prayer after Communion; RM, Masses and Prayers for Various Needs and Occasions, I, 9, Prayer after Communion).
- The Eucharist is the one bread of heaven (RM, Masses and Prayers for Various Needs and Occasions, III, 40, Prayer after Communion).
- Jesus Christ is the bread of heaven, who, "sown in the Virgin, raised up in the flesh, kneaded in the Passion, baked in the oven of the tomb, reserved in

churches, brought to altars, furnishes the faithful each day with food from heaven" (CCC 2837, quoting St. Peter Chrysologus, Sermo 67: PL 52, 392 and citing John 6:51).

- The Eucharist is not common bread, but it is made up of two elements, one earthly and one heavenly. So also our bodies after receiving the Eucharist are no longer corruptible, but have the hope of resurrection (LH, OT.2.Sa, 2R: St. Irenaeus, Against Heresies, Book 4, 18, 1–2.4.5: SC 100, 596–598.606.610–612).

- The bread of heaven, the Eucharist, nourishes the faithful (RM, Advent, Dec 17, Prayer over the Offerings; RM, OT.2.Su, Prayer after Communion; RM, St. Michael, St. Gabriel, and St. Raphael [Sep 29], Prayer after Communion; RM, The Dedication of the Basilicas of St. Peter and St. Paul [Nov 18], Prayer after Communion; RM, Commons, Common of Martyrs, I, A, 2, Prayer after Communion; RM, Ritual Masses, I, 4, C, Prayer after Communion; LH, ET.5.Mo, 2R: St. Gregory of Nyssa, Oratio 1 in Christi resurrectionem: PG 46, 603–606.626–627; *cf. also* RM, Masses and Prayers for Various Needs and Occasions, I, 7, B, Prayer after Communion).

- The bread of heaven, the Eucharist, contains all delights (LH, Corpus Christi, MD, Verse).

- The Church prays that the living Bread of the Eucharist which came down from heaven may give those who receive it strength to relieve their brothers and sisters in need (RM, Masses and Prayers for Various Needs and Occasions, For Civil Needs, 33, A, Prayer after Communion; RM, OT.22. Su, Prayer after Communion; RM, Masses and Prayers for Various Needs and Occasions, For Civil Needs, 33, B, Prayer after Communion).

- The heavenly bread of the Eucharist nourishes faith, increases hope, and strengthens charity (RM, Lent.1.Su, Prayer after Communion).

- In Eucharistic communion, the faithful receive the bread from heaven, the Body and Blood of Christ offered for the life of the world (CCC 1355; *cf.* John 6:51).

- The Father gave the living bread, which came down from heaven, and which should always be eaten worthily (LH, Office for the Dead, MP, 3rd intercession).

- Christ gave himself to us as bread from heaven (LH, Lent.1[=3, 5].Tu, MP, 1st intercession).

Bread of Life

- Jesus Christ is the Bread of Life (*cf. for example* John 6:32–35; LH, OT.21. We, 2R: St. Columban, Instr. 13, De Christo fonte vitae, 1–2: Opera, Dublin 1957, 116–118).

- Jesus Christ is the Bread of Life that came down from heaven (*cf. for example* John 6:32–35, 48, 51; CCC 1338; 1406; LH, OT.6.We, 2R: Procopius of Gaza, Commentary on the Book of Proverbs, Ch. 9: PG 87–1, 1299–1303).

- The Eucharist is the bread of life that came down from heaven (John 6:51, 58; LH, ET.3.Th, EP, Magn; LH, ET.5.Th, 2R: St. Gaudentius of Brescia, Tract. 2: CSEL 68, 26.29–30; LH, OT.15.Fr, 2R: St. Ambrose, On the Mysteries, 43.47–49: SC 25 bis, 178–180.182; LH, Corpus Christi, 1R, Resp [John 6:48–52]; LH, Corpus Christi, MP, CantZech; LH, ET.3.Th, 2R, Resp [John 6:48–52]).

- The Eucharist is the Bread of Life (RM, Thursday of the Lord's Supper, 26; RM, The Order of Mass, The Liturgy of the Eucharist, 23; RM, Eucharistic Prayer I, 92; RM, Eucharistic Prayer II, 105; RM, Appendix to the Order of the Mass, Eucharistic Prayer for Use in Masses for Various Needs, I, 7; RM, Appendix to the Order of the Mass, Eucharistic Prayer for Use in Masses for Various Needs, II, 7; RM, Appendix to the Order of the Mass, Eucharistic Prayer for Use in Masses for Various Needs, III, 7; RM, Appendix to the Order of the Mass, Eucharistic Prayer for Use in Masses for Various Needs, IV, 7; RM, Masses for the Dead, III, A, 5, Prayer over the Offerings; LH, Lent.2[=4].Su, EP, 3rd intercession; LH, ET.1[=3, 5].Fr, EP, 2nd intercession).

- Jesus says, "He who eats my flesh and drinks my blood has eternal life, and I will raise him up at the last day" (John 6:54; *cf.* John 6:56; *cf. also* CCC 1212; 1524; 1406).

- As the sun gives life to the earth so the Eucharist gives life to the soul and to societies (LH, St. Peter Julian Eymard [Aug 2], 2R: St. Peter Julian Eymard, La Présence réelle, vol. 1, Paris, 1950, pp. 270–271 and 307–308).

The Liturgy of the Hours

The Eucharist is the life of all nations. It affords the very principle of life. If there is no impediment, whether due to one's nation or one's language, all can come to the feasts of the Church. The Eucharist brings to them the law of charity and this sacrament is its source. For this very reason, it forms among them a common bond, that of Christian relationship. All eat of the same bread, all are Jesus Christ's guests, and he supernaturally forms among them a certain harmony of brotherly customs. The Acts of the Apostles affirm that the primitive throng of Christians, both of converted Jews and baptized pagans, formed a single heart and soul even though coming from different regions. Why? Because they were assiduous in listening to the doctrine of the Apostles and persevering in the breaking of the bread.

The Eucharist is therefore the life of the soul as well as the life of human society, just as the sun is the life of the body as well as that of the earth. Without it the earth is sterile. The sun gladdens, adorns and fills it with good things; it gives effectiveness, strength and beauty to the body. Before the marvels of the world we ought not to do as the pagans do, which is to worship the sun as if it were a god of the world. The daystar itself obeys the uppermost Star, the divine Word, Jesus Christ. He illuminates all those who come to this world, and acts himself through the Eucharist, sacrament of life, in their innermost being and by that he forms families and nations. Happy is the soul that finds this hidden treasure, and that drinks from the source of life by often eating the Bread of Life.

LH, St. Peter Julian Eymard (Aug 2), 2R:
St. Peter Julian Eymard, La Présence réelle, vol. 1,
Paris, 1950, pp. 270–271 and 307–308

- Jesus Christ became the living bread of eternal life for our sake (LH, CT.AE. We, MP, 5th intercession).
- Christ is present, living and glorious, in the Eucharist under the appearance of bread and wine (CCC 1413).

- Man lives not by bread alone, but by the Word of God, present in the Scriptures and in the Eucharist (CCC 2835, citing Deut. 8:3, Matt. 4:4, and John 6:26–58; *cf. also* CCC 1334).
- The Church offers the faithful the Bread of Life in the Scriptures and in the Eucharist (CCC 103; *cf. also* RM, Ritual Masses, IV, 2, A [=B], Solemn Blessing; LH, Psalter.3.We, MP, 5th intercession).
- On the last day, Jesus Christ, bread of life, will resurrect those who shared at the table of his Word and of his Body (LH, ET.1[=3, 5].Sa, MP, 1st intercession).
- The Church prays that the faithful "learn to hunger for Christ, the true and living Bread, and strive to live by every word that proceeds from [God's] mouth" (RM, Lent.1.Su, Prayer after Communion; *cf. also* RM, St. Gregory the Great [Sep 3], Prayer after Communion; RM, Commons, Common of Doctors of the Church, 1, Prayer after Communion).

The Roman Missal

Renewed now with heavenly bread,
by which faith is nourished, hope increased,
and charity strengthened,
we pray, O Lord,
that we may learn to hunger for Christ,
the true and living Bread,
and strive to live by every word
which proceeds from your mouth.
Through Christ our Lord.

RM, Lent.1.Su, Prayer after Communion

- As material bread nourishes our bodily life, so the Eucharist nourishes our spiritual life (CCC 1392; LH, ET.1.Sa, 2R: St. Cyril of Jerusalem, Jerusalem Catecheses, 22, Mystagogica 4, 1.3–6.9: PG 33, 1098–1106; *cf.* EUCHARIST: *Symbols*: Bread and Wine / Nourishment).
- The liturgy prays that those who eat here below of the bread of life might be allowed to eat as victors from the tree of life in paradise (RM, Commons, Common of Martyrs, II, A, 1, Prayer after Communion; *cf.* EUCHARIST: *Types*: Fruit of the Tree of Life).

- The Eucharist is the seed of eternal life and the power of resurrection (CCC 1524, citing John 6:54).
- The bread of life frees those who receive it from the bond of sin and restores strength (RM, Masses and Prayers for Various Needs and Occasions, III, 49, A, Prayer after Communion).
- The "daily bread" in the Our Father refers, among other things, "to the Bread of Life, the Body of Christ, the 'medicine of immortality,' without which we have no life within us (St. Ignatius of Antioch, Ad Eph. 20, 2: PG 5, 661; John 6:53–56)" (CCC 2837; cf. also CCC 2861; LH, OT.29.Tu, 2R: St. Augustine, Letter to Proba, 130, 11, 21–12, 22: CSEL 44, 63–64).
- Jesus Christ is the bread of life, whom we receive in the Eucharist. He who shares in Eucharistic communion will live forever. The petition, "Give us this day our daily bread," is a prayer that no one will have to abstain from Eucharistic communion due to some serious sin, lest he be separated from the Body of Christ and from salvation (LH, OT.11.Th, 2R: St. Cyprian, Treatise on the Lord's Prayer, 18.22: CSEL 3, 280–281.283–284).

The Liturgy of the Hours

Now, we who live in Christ and receive his Eucharist, the food of salvation, ask for this bread to be given us every day. Otherwise we may be forced to abstain from this communion because of some serious sin. In this way we shall be separated from the Body of Christ, as he taught us in the words: "I am the bread of life which has come down from heaven. Anyone who eats my bread will live for ever and the bread that I will give is my flesh for the life of the world." Christ is saying, then, that anyone who eats his bread will live for ever. Clearly they possess life who approach his body and share in the Eucharistic communion. For this reason we should be apprehensive and pray that no one has to abstain from this communion, lest he be separated from the body of Christ and be far from salvation. Christ has warned of this: "If you do not eat the flesh of the Son of man and drink his blood you will have no life in you." We pray for our daily bread, Christ, to be given to us.

With this help, we who live and abide in him will never be
separated from his body and his grace.

LH, OT.11.Th, 2R: St. Cyprian, Treatise on the Lord's Prayer,
18.22: CSEL 3, 280–281.283–284

- St. Paul suggests that "the Eucharist, the bread that gives eternal life . . . is
  connected with bodily health (cf. John 6:54, 58; 1 Cor. 11:30)." "The life-
  giving presence of Christ" is particularly present in the Eucharist (CCC
  1509).

Bread of Angels

- The Eucharist is the bread of angels (CCC 1331).
- In the Eucharist, man eats the bread of angels (LH, Corpus Christi, EP
  [=EP2], Resp; *cf. also* LH, OT.22.Tu, 2R: Thomas à Kempis, The Imitation
  of Christ, Book 3, 14).
- *Cf.* EUCHARIST: *Types:* Manna.

BREAKING OF BREAD

OT Background: Lev. 2:6; Isa. 58:7 (Hebrew); Jer. 16:7; Lam. 4:4 (Hebrew)

NT Background: Matt. 14:19; 15:36; 26:26; Mark 6:41; 8:6, 19; 14:20,
22; Luke 9:16; 22:19; 24:30, 35; John 6:51; Acts 2:42, 46; 20:7, 11;
27:35; 1 Cor. 10:16–17; 11:24

Catechism Background: 84; 949; 1148; 1189; **1329**; 1342–1343; 1347;
1355; **1377**; **1396**; 1405; 2624

Related: EUCHARIST: *Types*: Passover / Passover Lamb

The Eucharistic Assembly

- The Eucharist is called the "breaking of bread" because Jesus used this rite,
  "part of a Jewish meal, when as master of the table he blessed and distrib-
  uted the bread (Cf. Matt. 14:19; 15:36; Mark 8:6, 19), above all at the Last
  Supper (Cf. Matt. 26:26; 1 Cor. 11:24)" (CCC 1329; *cf.* CCC 1355; *cf. also*
  RM, Eucharistic Prayer I, 89 and parallels; EUCHARIST: *Types*: Passover /
  Passover Lamb).
- By the action of the breaking of the bread, the disciples recognized Jesus af-
  ter the Resurrection (Luke 24:30, 35; CCC 1329, citing Luke 24:13–35; *cf.*

CCC 1347; LH, ET.6.We, 2R: St. Leo the Great, Sermo 1 de Ascensione, 2–4: PL 54, 395–396).

- The first Christians used the term "breaking of bread" to designate the Eucharistic assembly (Acts 2:42, 46; 20:7, 11; CCC 1329, citing Acts 2:42, 46; 20:7, 11; *cf.* CCC 1342, quoting Acts 2:42, 46; CCC 1343, quoting Acts 20:7; *cf. also* 1 Cor. 10:16–17; CCC 2624; LH, OT.14.We, 2R: Didache 9, 1–10, 6; 14, 1–3: Funk 2, 19–22.26).

- Following the tradition of the first Christians, the term "breaking of bread" is oftentimes used to refer to the Eucharistic assembly (*cf. for example* CCC 84; 949).

- Now for Christians at the Eucharistic Celebration, Jesus once again opens the Scriptures and breaks the bread (RM, Eucharistic Prayers for Use in Masses for Various Needs, I [=II, III, IV], 2; *cf. also* LH, Psalter.4.Mo, EP, Prayer).

- Today Jesus is recognized in the breaking of the bread of the Eucharistic Celebration (RM, The Presentation of the Lord [Feb 2], 4; *cf. also* LH, Corpus Christi, MA, Ant).

One Bread, One Body

- By using the term "breaking of bread" for the Eucharist, Christians signify that Christ is the "one broken bread," and by sharing in that one bread they enter into communion with him and form one body (1 Cor. 10:16–17; CCC 1329, citing 1 Cor. 10:16–17; *cf. also* CCC 1331; 1353; LH, OT.14. We, 2R, Resp [1 Cor. 10:16–17]).

- Receiving the "bread which we break" of the Eucharist fulfills the call of Baptism to form one body. The Eucharist makes the Church, the Body of Christ (CCC 1396, quoting 1 Cor. 10:16–17; *cf. also* LH, ET.2.Tu, 2R: St. Fulgentius of Ruspe, Book addressed to Monimus, 2, 11–12: CCL 91, 46–48; LH, ET.3.Th, 2R: St. Irenaeus, Against Heresies, Book 5, 2, 2–3: SC 153, 30–38).

- The first Christians were one in heart and soul (*cf.* Acts 4:32) because they devoted themselves to listening to the teachings of the Apostles and to the breaking of bread (*cf.* Acts 2:42) (LH, St. Peter Julian Eymard (Aug 2), 2R: St. Peter Julian Eymard, La Présence réelle, vol. 1, Paris, 1950, pp. 270–271 and 307–308).

- At the Eucharistic Celebrations of the first Christians, the priest would pray over the broken bread asking that, "As this broken bread scattered on the mountains was gathered and became one, so too, may your Church be gathered together from the ends of the earth into your kingdom" (LH, OT.14. We, 2R: Didache 9, 1–10, 6; 14, 1–3: Funk 2, 19–22.26).
- In the Eucharistic Celebration, shortly before communion, the breaking of the bread takes place (RM, The Communion Rite, 129; *cf.* CCC 1355).
- The breaking of the bread does not divide Christ, who is wholly present in each of the species of bread (CCC 1377; *cf. also* CCC 1405).
- The Church prays that the faithful, by "persevering in the breaking of the bread and in the teaching of the Apostles," may be one in heart and soul and may be made steadfast in God's love (RM, St. Peter and St. Paul [June 29], Prayer after Communion; *cf. also* RM, Votive Masses, 14, Prayer after Communion).
- The faithful should be careful to stay united to their bishop and to the Church, avoiding schismatics. There is only one Eucharist, one flesh of Jesus Christ and one cup that unites us with his blood, one altar one bishop with his presbyters and deacons (LH, OT.27.Th, 2R: St. Ignatius of Antioch, Letter to the Philadelphians 1, 1–2, 1; 3, 2–5, 1: Funk 1, 226–229).

Other

- Breaking bread can refer to sharing food with those in need (*cf. for example* Isa. 58:7 [Hebrew]; Lam. 4:4 [Hebrew]).
- Breaking bread can refer to the sharing of a meal as part of a mourning ritual for the death of someone beloved (Jer. 16:7).
- Breaking bread is a symbol taken from the social life of man. It can express "the sanctifying presence of God and man's gratitude toward his Creator" (CCC 1148; *cf. also* CCC 1189).
- The cereal offering of unleavened bread baked on a griddle was broken into pieces (Lev. 2:5–6).

CUP OF SALVATION

OT Background:

Cup of God's Wrath: Ps. 11:6; 75:8; Isa. 51:17, 22; Jer. 25:15, 17, 27–28; 49:12; Ezek. 23:31–33; Hab. 2:15–16

Cup of Salvation: Ps. 116:13

Cup of Consolation: Jer. 16:7

Other: Ps. 16:5; 23:5

NT Background: Matt. 20:22–23; 26:27–28, 39, 42; Mark 10:38–39; 14:23–25, 36; Luke 22:17, 20, 42; John 18:11; 1 Cor. 10:16–17, 21; 11:25–30; Rev. 14:10; 16:19; 18:6

Catechism Background: 607; **612**; 1148; **1334**; **1355**; 1365; 1385; **1396**

Related: EUCHARIST: *Types*: Passover / Passover Lamb; *Symbols*: Bread from Heaven / Bread of Life / Bread of Angels

Cup of the New Covenant

- The cup of the Last Supper and Gethsemani may be understood as Jesus' drinking of the cup of God's wrath (*cf.* Ps. 11:6; 75:8; Isa. 51:17, 22; Jer. 25:15, 17, 27–28; 49:12; Ezek. 23:31–33; Hab. 2:15–16; Rev. 14:10; 16:19; 18:6), which he transforms into the cup of blessing and salvation (*cf.* 1 Cor. 10:16–17; Ps. 116:13) through the self-offering of his blood on the cross (*cf.* Matt. 20:22–23; 26:27–28, 39, 42; Mark 10:38–39; 14:23–25, 36; Luke 22:17, 20, 42; John 18:11; 1 Cor. 10:16, 25–30; 11:25–30; CCC 612).

- At the Last Supper, Jesus offered himself in the cup of the New Covenant. In the garden of Gethsemane, Jesus accepted this cup back from his Father when he accepted that his Father's will be done (CCC 612, citing Matt. 26:42; Luke 22:20; *cf. also* CCC 607; 1365).

- The consecrated wine, the Blood of Christ, is the chalice of the New Covenant (RM, Masses and Prayers for Various Needs and Occasions, I, 7, B, Prayer after Communion).

Cup of Blessing

- The "cup of blessing" at the end of the Passover meal (*cf.* 1 Cor. 10:16) "adds to the festive joy of wine an eschatological dimension: the messianic expectation of the rebuilding of Jerusalem. When Jesus instituted the Eucharist, he gave a new and definitive meaning to the blessing of the bread and the cup" (CCC 1334).

- The "cup of blessing" is a participation in the Blood of Christ (1 Cor. 10:16–17; *cf.* CCC 1396).

- The consecrated wine, the Blood of Christ, is the "cup of the Lord" (1 Cor. 11:27–29; *cf.* CCC 1385).

Cup of Salvation

- The cup of salvation (*cf.* Ps. 116:13) is the Eucharist (CCC 1355; *cf.* Ps. 116:13; LH, Corpus Christi, EP2, Ant2; LH, ET.1.Sa, 2R: St. Cyril of Jerusalem, Jerusalem Catecheses, 22, Mystagogica 4, 1.3–6.9: PG 33, 1098–1106).
- The chalice used at the Eucharistic Celebration is the chalice of salvation (RM, Appendix IV: Rite of Blessing of a Chalice and Paten Within Mass, 6 and 8; *cf.* Ps. 116:13).

Chalice of Christ

- Martyrdom is referred to as a sharing in the chalice of Christ or the chalice of his sufferings (*cf. for example* Matt. 20:22–23; Mark 10:38–39; RM, St. Polycarp [Feb 23], Collect; RM, St. Peter and St. Paul [June 29], Entrance Antiphon; RM, St. James [July 25], Prayer over the Offerings; RM, St. James [July 25], Communion Antiphon; LH, St. Raymond of Penyafort [Jan 7], 2R: St. Raymond of Penyafort, Letter, Monumenta Ord. Praed. Hist. 6, 2, Romae 1901, pp. 84–85; LH, St. Polycarp [Feb 23], 2R: Letter on the Martyrdom of St. Polycarp by the Church of Smyrna, Ch. 13, 2–15, 2: Funk 1, 297–299; LH, St. Polycarp [Feb 23], EP, Magn; LH, St. Cosmas and St. Damian [Sep 26], 2R: St. Augustine, Sermo 329, 1–2: PL 38, 1454–1455; LH, St. Isaac Jogues and St. John de Brébeuf [Oct 19], 2R: St. John de Brébeuf, Spiritual Diary: The Jesuit Relations and Allied Documents, The Burrow Brothers Co, Cleveland 1898, 164.166; LH, Common of One Martyr, 2R: St. Augustine, Sermo 329, 1–2: PL 38, 1454–1456).
- Those who do not drink the cup of Christ's bodily sufferings may still drink the cup of Christ's love. The gift of love enables the faithful to become in reality what they celebrate as mystery in the sacrifice [of the Eucharist] (LH, OT.28.Mo, 2R: St. Fulgentius, Against Fabianus, Ch. 28, 16–19: CCL 91A, 813–814).

Chalice of the Body of Christ

- In the Eucharist, Christ offers spiritual drink from the chalice of his body to fulfill the prophecy of Ps. 23:5 (LH, CT.AE.Mo, 2R: St. Peter Chrysologus, Sermo 160: PL 52, 620–622).

GIFT OF FINEST WHEAT

OT Background:

Finest Wheat: Deut. 32:14; Ps. 78:24; 81:16; 147:14

Fine Flour (Literal): Gen. 18:6; Exod. 29:2, 40; Lev. 2:1–7; 5:11; 6:15, 20; 7:12; 14:10, 21; 23:13, 17; 24:5; Num. 6:15; 7:13, 19, 25, 37, 43, 49, 55, 61, 67, 73, 79; 8:8; 15:4, 6, 9; 28:5, 9, 12–13, 20, 28; 29:3, 9, 14

Fine Flour (Symbolic): Sir. 35:2 (RSV = Sir. 35:3 NAB, NRSV); 38:11; Ezek. 16:19

Other: Deut. 8:8

NT Background: Matt. 3:12; 13:25, 29–30; Luke 3:17; John 12:24; 1 Cor. 15:36–37

Catechism Background: 681; 827; **1412**; 2713

Related: EUCHARIST: *Types*: Bread of the Presence / Cereal Offerings; *Symbols*: Bread and Wine / Nourishment

- The manna in the desert is called "bread of heaven" (Ps. 78:24).
- The finest of wheat can refer to the abundance of God's blessings, which nourish and sustain (*cf.* Ps. 81:16; *cf. also* Ps. 147:14; Deut. 32:14; Ezek. 16:19).
- Cereal offerings, the Bread of the Presence, as well as other offerings involving bread, were to be made from the finest flour (Exod. 29:2, 40; Lev. 2:1–7; 6:15, 20; 7:12; 14:10, 21; 23:13, 17; 24:5; Num. 6:15; 7:13, 19, 25, 37, 43, 49, 55, 61, 67, 73, 79; 8:8; 15:4, 6, 9; 28:5, 9, 12–13, 20, 28; 29:3, 9, 14).
- One who returns a kindness makes on offering of the finest wheat (Sir. 35:3).
- The Eucharist is implicitly called "finest wheat" (RM, OT.19.Su, Communion Antiphon [Ps. 147:12, 14]; RM, Corpus Christi, Entrance Antiphon [Ps. 81:16]; RM, Ritual Masses, For the Administering of Viaticum, Entrance Antiphon [Ps. 81:16]; LH, Holy Thursday, MP, Ant3; LH, Corpus Christi, EP, Ant2; LH, Corpus Christi, OR, Ant3).

- In the Eucharistic Celebration, the Church offers up "grains of wheat made into bread" so that they may be changed into the Body of Christ (RM, Masses and Prayers for Various Needs and Occasions, II, 27, B, Prayer over the Offerings).
- The bread for celebrating the Eucharist must be made from wheat (CCC 1412).
- One loaf of bread is formed from many grains of wheat mixed with water and baked in fire. It is thus fitting that bread should be used for the Eucharist, in which many people become the one Body of Christ, which is brought to maturity by the fire of the Holy Spirit (LH, ET.2.Th, 2R: St. Gaudentius of Brescia, Tract. 2: CSEL 68, 30–32).
- The Church prays that God will accept the bread and wine of the Eucharist as he once accepted the offering of St. Ignatius of Antioch, the "wheat of Christ," who was made "pure bread through his martyrdom and passion" (RM, St. Ignatius of Antioch [Oct 17], Prayer over the Offerings; *cf. also* John 12:24; 1 Cor. 15:36–37; LH, OT.10.Mo, 2R: St. Ignatius of Antioch, Letter to the Romans, 3, 1–5, 3: Funk 1, 215–219; LH, St. Ignatius of Antioch [Oct 17], 2R: St. Ignatius of Antioch, Letter to the Romans, Ch. 4, 1–2; 6, 1–8, 3: Funk 1, 217–223).

MEAL

Cf. EUCHARIST: *Symbols:* Altar / Table; Banquet; Bread and Wine / Nourishment; *cf. also* EUCHARIST: *Types:* Passover / Passover Lamb

MEDICINE OF IMMORTALITY

OT Background: Gen. 2:9; 3:22; Isa. 53:5; Ezek. 47:12; Mal. 4:2

NT Background: John 6:50–51, 53–54, 57–58; 1 Cor. 11:27–32; 1 Pet. 2:24; Rev. 2:7; 22:2, 14

Catechism Background: 1331; 1405; 2837

Related: EUCHARIST: *Types*: Fruit of the Tree of Life; EUCHARIST: *Symbols*: Bread from Heaven / Bread of Life / Bread of Angels; Cup of Salvation; HOLY ORDERS: *Symbols*: Physician

- The Eucharist is "'the medicine of immortality, the antidote for death, and the food that makes us live forever in Jesus Christ' (St. Ignatius of Antioch, Ad Eph. 20, 2: SCh 10, 76)" (CCC 1405; 1331; *cf. also* John 6:50–51,

53–54, 57–58; EUCHARIST: *Symbols:* Bread from Heaven / Bread of Life / Bread of Angels).

- The Church prays that the reception of the Eucharist may act as heavenly medicine, to "purge all evil from our heart and strengthen us with eternal protection" (RM, Lent.5.We, Prayer after Communion; *cf. also* RM, OT.10. Su, Prayer after Communion [Latin]).

- The petition for "our daily bread" in the Our Father (*cf.* Matt. 6:11; Luke 11:3) refers, among other things, "to the Bread of Life, the Body of Christ, the 'medicine of immortality,' without which we have no life within us (St. Ignatius of Antioch, Ad Eph. 20, 2: PG 5, 661; John 6:53–56)" (CCC 2837).

- St. Frances of Rome cared for the poor and the sick, seeking to provide doctors to cure their bodies and priests who could administer the necessary medicine for their souls ("necessariam animabus medicinam") in the Sacraments of Penance and the Eucharist (LH, St. Frances of Rome [Mar 9], 2R: Mary Magdalene Anguillaria, Life of St. Frances of Rome, Ch. 6–7: Acta Sanctorum Martii 2, *185–*187).

SACRIFICE

Cf. EUCHARIST: *Types:* Passover / Passover Lamb; Animal Sacrifice; *cf. also* EUCHARIST: *Types:* Gifts of Abel; Offering of Melchizedek; Sacrifice of Abraham; Offering of the First Fruits; Blood of the Covenant; Bread of the Presence / Cereal Offerings; Holocaust of Elijah; Blood from the Side of Christ; *Symbols:* Altar / Table; Breaking of Bread.

PENANCE

Definition: The liturgical celebration of God's forgiveness of the sins of the penitent, who is thus reconciled with God and with the Church. The acts of the penitent—contrition, the confession of sins, and satisfaction or reparation—together with the prayer of absolution by the priest, constitute the essential elements of the Sacrament of Penance (Glossary of the Catechism of the Catholic Church for Penance, Sacrament of; *cf. also* Confession; Reconciliation; Remission of Sins).

TYPES

FORGIVENESS OF DAVID BY NATHAN

OT Background: Exod. 22:1; Lev. 20:10; 24:17; Deut. 22:22; 2 Sam. 12:13; Ps. 32:5; 51; Prov. 28:13; Sir. 47:11

NT Background: Matt. 16:19; 18:18; Luke 18:31; John 20:22–23; 2 Cor. 5:18

Catechism Background: 1481

Type: CCC 1481

Related: PENANCE: *Symbols*: Publican; Second Plank of Salvation; Tears of Repentance

- As God, through the prophet Nathan forgave David when he confessed his sins (2 Sam. 12:13), so the priest in Penance, though a sinner, forgives the penitent both in this life and the next (CCC 1481, quoting the Byzantine Liturgy; *cf. also* RP 109).

Catechism of the Catholic Church

The Byzantine Liturgy recognizes several formulas of absolution, in the form of invocation, which admirably express the mystery of forgiveness: "May the same God, who through the Prophet Nathan forgave David when he confessed his sins, who forgave Peter when he wept bitterly, the prostitute when she washed his feet with her tears, the publican, and the prodigal son, through me, a sinner, forgive you both in this life and in the next and enable you to appear before his awe-inspiring tribunal without condemnation, he who is blessed for ever and ever. Amen."

CCC 1481, quoting the Byzantine Liturgy

LEPERS SENT TO THE PRIESTS

OT Background: Lev. 13:2, 6, 13, 17, 23, 28, 34, 37, 49; 14:2–4; Deut. 24:8; 2 Kings 5:14

NT Background: Matt. 8:4; 16:19; 18:18; Luke 5:14; 17:14; 18:31; John 20:22–23; 2 Cor. 5:18; Eph. 5:32; James 5:14–15

Catechism Background: 772–776; 796; 1545

Type: LH, OT.23.Fr, 2R: Bl. Isaac of Stella, Sermo 11: PL 194, 1728–1729

Related: PENANCE: *Symbols*: Second Plank of Salvation; Washing

- In the Old Covenant, cleansed lepers were examined by the priest and, once pronounced clean by them, were reintegrated into the community of Israel (*cf.* Lev. 13:2, 6, 13, 17, 23, 28, 34, 37, 49; 14:2–4; Deut. 24:8).
- Through the Mystical Body, Christ has married the Church, and all that is his is hers and all that is hers is his. As the lepers were sent by Christ to the priests, so in the Sacrament of Penance the sinner is sent by him to the priests, to whom he has entrusted the power to forgive sins (LH, OT.23.Fr, 2R: Bl. Isaac of Stella, Sermo 11: PL 194, 1728–1729 in reference to Matt. 8:4, Luke 5:14 and Eph. 5:31–32).[1]

---

1 Some of the Church Fathers see in the sending of lepers to the priests a type of the Sacrament of Penance. For example, St. John Chrysostom writes: "The Jewish priests had authority to release the body from leprosy, or, rather, not to release it but only to examine those who were already released, and you know how much the office of priest was contended for at that time. But our priests have received authority to deal, not with bodily leprosy, but spiritual uncleanness—not to pronounce it removed after examination, but actually and absolutely to take it away" (On the Priesthood, 3:6). Although Blessed Isaac of Stella does not explicitly develop this typological relationship, he seems to presuppose it, while also emphasizing the relationship of the Sacrament of Penance to the unity of the Body of Christ, which is Christ and the Church together, who, he states, share all things.

The Liturgy of the Hours

The prerogative of receiving the confession of sin and the power to forgive sin are two things that belong properly to God alone. We must confess our sins to him and look to him for forgiveness. Since only he has the power to forgive sins, it is to him that we must make our confession. But when the Almighty, the Most High, wedded a bride who was weak and of low estate, he made that maid-servant a queen. He took her from her place behind him, at his feet, and enthroned her at his side. She had been born from his side, and therefore he betrothed her to himself. And as all that belongs to the Father belongs also to the Son because by nature they are one, so also the bridegroom gave all he had to the bride and he shared in all that was hers. He made her one both with himself and with the Father. Praying for his bride, the Son said to the Father: "I want them to be one with us, even as you and I are one" (*cf.* John 17:21).

And so the bridegroom is one with the Father and one with the bride. Whatever he found in his bride alien to her own nature he took from her and nailed to his cross when he bore her sins and destroyed them on the tree. He received from her and clothed himself in what was hers by nature and gave her what belonged to him as God. He destroyed what was diabolical, took to himself what was human, and conferred on her what was divine. So all that belonged to the bride was shared in by the bridegroom, and he who had done no wrong and on whose lips was found no deceit could say: "Have pity on me, Lord, for I am weak" (*cf.* Ps. 6:2). Thus, sharing as he did in the bride's weakness, the bridegroom made his own her cries of distress, and gave his bride all that was his. Therefore, she too has the prerogative of receiving the confession of sin and the power to forgive sin, which is the reason for the command: "Go, show yourself to the priest" (*cf.* Matt. 8:4, Luke 5:14).

The Church is incapable of forgiving any sin without Christ, and Christ is unwilling to forgive any sin without the Church. The Church cannot forgive the sin of one who has not repented, who has not been touched by Christ; Christ will not forgive the sin of one who despises the Church. "What God has joined together, man must not separate. This is a great mystery, but I understand it as referring to Christ and the Church" (*cf.* Eph. 5:31–32).

Do not destroy the whole Christ by separating head from body, for Christ is not complete without the Church, nor is the Church complete without Christ. The whole and complete Christ is head and body. This is why he said: "No one has ever ascended into heaven except the Son of Man whose home is in heaven" (*cf.* John 3:13). He is the only man who can forgive sin.

LH, OT.23.Fr, 2R: Bl. Isaac of Stella, Sermon 11: PL 194,
1728–1729

SYMBOLS

COMING TO THE LIGHT

OT Background:

God is light / dwells in light: 2 Sam. 22:13; Ps. 27:1; 50:2; 94:1; 104:2; Wisd. 7:26–29; Isa. 51:4; Ezek. 1:4, 27–28; 8:2; 10:4; Dan. 2:22; Hos. 6:5; Hab. 3:4

God gives light: Num. 6:25; 2 Sam. 22:29; Job 22:28; 29:3; Ps. 4:6; 18:28; 19:8; 27:1; 31:16; 36:9; 43:3; 67:1; 80:3, 7, 19; 94:1; 118:27; 119:105, 130, 135; Prov. 6:23; Wisd. 18:1–4; Sir. 34:17; Isa. 42:16; 60:1, 19–20; Bar. 1:12; Ezek. 43:2; Dan. 9:17; Mic. 7:8–9; Mal. 4:2

Living / walking in the light: Job 18:5–6; Ps. 89:15; 90:8; Wisd. 5:6; Sir. 50:29; Isa. 2:5; 9:2; Bar. 3:14; 4:2; 5:9

Light of God's People: Exod. 34:29–30, 35; 2 Sam. 23:4; Job 11:17; Ps. 34:5; 37:6; 97:11; 112:4; Prov. 4:18; 13:9; Eccles. 8:1; Sir. 32:16; Isa. 42:6; 49:6; 58:8–10; 60:1–5; Dan. 12:3

Light of things: Gen. 1:2–5; 23:4; Esther 10:6; 11:11; Job 24:13–16; Prov. 15:30; Wisd. 7:10; Sir. 42:16; Bar. 3:20, 33

Other: 2 Sam. 21:17; 1 Kings 11:36; 15:4; 2 Kings 8:19; 2 Chron. 21:7; Tob. 14:10; Job 21:17; Ps. 132:17; Prov. 20:27; 21:4; 24:20; Dan. 10:6

NT Background:

Light of Christ / God: Matt. 17:2–5; Luke 2:32; John 1:4–9; 3:19; 8:12; 9:5; 12:35–36, 46; Eph. 5:14; 1 Tim. 6:16; James 1:17; 1 John 1:5; Rev. 21:23; 22:5

Light of God's People: Matt. 5:14–16; 13:43; 25:1; Luke 12:35; 16:8; John 5:35; 12:36; Acts 13:47; Rom. 2:19; Eph. 5:8; Phil. 2:15; 1 Thess. 5:5

Living / walking in the light: Matt. 4:16; 6:22; Luke 1:78–79; 11:34–36; John 3:19–21; 8:12; 9:5; 11:9–10; 12:35–36, 46; Acts 26:18, 23; 2 Cor. 3:7–8; Eph. 5:9; Col. 1:12–13; Heb. 6:4; 10:32; 1 Pet. 2:9; 1 John 1:7–10; 2:8–11; Rev. 21:24; 22:5

Light of the Gospel: 2 Cor. 4:4–6; Eph. 1:17–18; 2 Pet. 1:19

Light of angels: Matt. 28:3; Luke 2:9; Rev. 18:1

Public knowledge: Matt. 10:27; Mark 4:21–22; Luke 8:16–17; 12:3; Eph. 5:11–13

Catechism: 736; 1147; **1165–1168**; 1216; 1236; 1243; 1268; **1454**; **1458**; **1480**

Related: BAPTISM: *Types:* Pillar of Cloud and Fire; *Symbols:* White Garment / Wedding Garment; PENANCE: *Symbols:* Liberation; Wedding Garment

- Whoever confesses his sins does the truth and comes to the light (CCC 1458, quoting St. Augustine, Tractates on John 12, 13: PL 35, 1491; *cf.* 1 John 1:7–10; *cf. also* RP 204.1, 10th intercession).
- Through the Sacrament of Penance, God calls the sinner out of darkness into the splendor of his light (RP 62).
- Contrition for sins, "the most important act of the penitent" in the Sacrament of Penance, implies considering, judging, and arranging one's life "according to the holiness and love of God," revealed in Christ. This leads to "a progressively deeper enlightenment and an ever-closer likeness to Christ" (RP 6a).

- Through the reading of the Word of God, "Christians receive light to recognize their sins and are called to conversion and to confidence in God" (RP 17; *cf. also* RP 24; CCC 1216; 1236; 1454; 1480).
- Some of the passages from the Word of God that can shed the most light for an examination of conscience are "the Ten Commandments, the moral catechesis of the Gospels and the apostolic Letters, such as the Sermon on the Mount and the apostolic teachings (Cf. Matt. 5–7; Rom. 12–15; 1 Cor. 12–13; Gal. 5; Eph. 4–6; etc.)" (CCC 1454; *cf. also* RP 24).
- The Sacrament of Penance opens with a prayer ("in these or similar words") that God, "who has enlightened every heart," will help the penitent to know his or her sins and trust in God's mercy (RP 42).

FINDING THE LOST SHEEP

OT Background: Gen. 49:24; 1 Sam. 9:3; Ps. 23; 28:9; 77:20; 119:176; Isa. 40:11; Jer. 3:15; 23:4; 31:10; Ezek. 34:11–16, 22–24; Mic. 5:2–4

NT Background: Matt. 15:24; 18:10–14; Luke 15:3–7; 19:10; John 10:1–18; 21:15–17; Acts 20:28; Eph. 4:11; Heb. 13:20; 1 Pet. 2:25; 5:2; Rev. 7:17

Catechism Background: 553; **605**; 635; **753–754**; 857; 861–862; 896; **1465**; 1548; 1586; 2179

Related: PENANCE: *Symbols*: Jesus Eating with Sinners; Prodigal Son's Homecoming; Second Plank of Salvation

- In the Sacrament of Penance, "the priest is fulfilling the ministry of the Good Shepherd who seeks the lost sheep," acting as a "sign and the instrument of God's merciful love for the sinner" (CCC 1465; *cf. also* RP 10c; 57).
- In the Sacrament of Penance, "Christ places the lost sheep on his shoulders and brings them back to the sheepfold" (RP 6d; *cf. also* RP 54, 2nd Example, 5th intercession; 202.5; 203.3; 205.2, 6th intercession).

The Rite of Penance

Through the sign of absolution God grants pardon to sinners who in sacramental confession manifest their change of heart to the Church's minister; this completes the sacrament of penance. For in God's design the humanity and loving kindness of our Savior have visibly appeared to us (*cf.* Titus 3:4–5) and so God uses visible signs to give salvation and to renew the broken covenant.

In the sacrament of penance the Father receives the repentant children who come back to him, Christ places the lost sheep on his shoulders and brings them back to the sheepfold, and the Holy Spirit resanctifies those who are the temple of God or dwells more fully in them. The expression of all this is the sharing in the Lord's table, begun again or made more ardent; such a return of children from afar brings great rejoicing at the banquet of God's Church (*cf.* Luke 15:7, 10, 32).

RP 6d

JESUS EATING WITH SINNERS

OT Background: Exod. 24:9–11; 2 Sam. 3:20; Ps. 25:8–9; Song 2:4; Hos. 6:6

NT Background: Matt. 9:9–13; 11:19; Mark 2:14–17; Luke 5:29–32; 7:34, 48–50; 19:5–10

Catechism Background: 1443–1444; *cf. also* 545; 574

Related: PENANCE: *Symbols*: Finding the Lost Sheep; Medicine for the Soul; Prodigal Son's Homecoming

- Jesus chose to be called the friend of sinners (RP 90; 54, 2nd Example, 4th intercession; *cf.* Matt. 9:9–13; 11:19; Mark 2:14–17; Luke 5:29–32; 7:34, 48–50; 19:5–10).
- Jesus welcomed sinners, and reconciled them with the Father (RP 1).
- By eating with sinners, Jesus expressed both God's forgiveness as well as the reintegration of forgiven sinners "into the community of the People of God from which sin had alienated or even excluded them" (CCC 1443).
- Similarly, through the Sacrament of Penance, Jesus has given his apostles his own power to forgive sins and the authority to reconcile sinners with the Church (CCC 1444).
- Through the Sacrament of Penance, the forgiven sinner is able to share once again (or more ardently) in the Lord's Table (RP 6d).

LIBERATION

OT Background:

From slavery in Egypt: Exod. 4:23; 5:1; 6:6, 11; 7:2, 16; 8:1, 20; 9:1, 13, 28; 10:3; 14:21–15:21; 18:10; Lev. 26:13; Deut. 5:6; Jer. 2:20

From exile: Ps. 126:1; Isa. 45:13; 49:9; 52:2; 61:1; Jer. 28:2–4; 30:8; 2 Macc. 1:27

God freeing captives: Job 12:18; Ps. 68:6; 102:20; 107:14; 116:16; 142:7; 146:7; Isa. 42:7; 61:1; Jer. 30:8; Ezek. 34:27; Nah. 1:13; Zech. 9:11

Through wisdom: Wisd. 1:6; 6:15; 12:2; 16:14; Sir. 6:18–31

Through death: Tob. 3:6, 13

Other: Ezek. 13:20; 30:18; Dan. 3:25; Hos. 11:4

NT Background:

Through Christ: Luke 4:18; 13:12–16; John 8:32–36; 11:44

Through faith: Acts 13:39

From sin / death / the Mosaic law: Acts 2:24; Rom. 6:3–7, 18–22; 7:6; 8:2, 21; Gal. 3:27–4:7; 5:1; Rev. 1:5

Power to loose: Matt. 16:19; 18:18; John 20:21–23

Other: Acts 7:34; 12:6–10, 17; 13:39

Catechism: 553; 979; 1282; 1444–1445; 1455

Related: BAPTISM: *Symbols:* Liberation; PENANCE: *Symbols:* Second Plank of Salvation

- "The Son of God made man lived among us in order to free us from the slavery of sin" and lead us to his light (RP 1, citing John 8:34–36 and 1 Pet. 2:9).

- The forgiveness of sins allows the Christian to serve God in true freedom (RP 97; *cf. also* RP 204.1, 4th intercession).

- The confession or disclosure of sin frees the sinner, and facilitates reconciliation, even from a purely human point of view (CCC 1455; *cf. also* RP 54, 1st example, 1st intercession).

The Catechism of the Catholic Church

The confession (or disclosure) of sins, even from a simply human point of view, frees us and facilitates our reconciliation with others. Through such an admission man looks squarely at the sins he is guilty of, takes responsibility for them, and thereby opens himself again to God and to the communion of the Church in order to make a new future possible.

CCC 1455

- Through the keys of the kingdom (*cf.* Matt. 16:19; 19:19; John 20:21–23), the Church has received from Christ the power to loosen the bondage of sin. This power applies not only to sins committed prior to Baptism but to all sins, up to the last moment before death, through the Sacrament of Penance (CCC 979–980; *cf. also* 553; 1221; 1237; 1282; 1446; RP 6b).
- In the sacraments, God frees the Christian from slavery to sin (RP 57; *cf. also* RP 204.1, 4th intercession).
- Through the Sacrament of Penance, God frees the sinner from his or her sins (*cf.* RP 59; 93; *cf. also* RP 90; RP 204.11, 11th, 12th, and 14th intercession).
- Through the Sacrament of Penance, the sinner is released from the debt of sin (RP 54, 1st example, 2nd intercession).

Medicine for the Soul

OT Background: Ps. 41:3–4; 103:3; Isa. 33:24; 53:5; Jer. 30:12–17; 33:1–9; Ezek. 47:12

NT Background: Matt. 9:1–8, 12; Mark 2:1–12, 17; Luke 5:17–26, 31; 10:33–34; John 5:14; James 5:14–16; 1 Pet. 2:24; Rev. 22:2

Catechism Background: 1421; 1456; 1458–1459; 1465; 1484

Related: Eucharist: *Symbols:* Medicine of Immortality; Holy Orders: *Symbols:* Physician

- Jesus Christ is the physician of our souls and bodies (*cf. for example* Matt. 9:18; Mark 2:1–12; Luke 5:17–26; John 5:14). He has willed that his work of healing be continued in the Sacraments of Penance and the Anointing of the Sick (CCC 1421; *cf.* John 20:21–23; James 5:14–16).
- Through the Sacrament of Penance, Jesus Christ personally forgives sins and acts as a physician, "tending each one of the sick who need him to cure them (cf. Mark 2:17)" (CCC 1484; *cf. also* RP 99; 205.2, 1st intercession).
- In the Sacrament of Penance, the priest fulfills the ministry of the Good Samaritan who binds up wounds, and is "the sign and the instrument of

God's merciful love for the sinner" (CCC 1465; *cf.* Luke 10:29–37; RP 54, 1st Example, 1st Intercession).

- St. Frances of Rome cared for the poor and the sick, seeking to provide doctors to cure their bodies and priests who could administer the necessary medicine for their souls (Latin: "necessariam animabus medicinam") in the Sacraments of Penance and the Eucharist (LH, St. Frances of Rome [Mar 9], 2R: Mary Magdalene Anguillaria, Life of St. Frances of Rome, Ch. 6–7: Acta Sanctorum Martii 2, *185–*187).

- The confession of sins[2] is medicine which heals the wounds of sin (LH, OT.21.Tu, 2R: St. John Chrysostom, Homily De diabolo tentatore 2, 6: PG 49, 263–264).

- All mortal sins of which the penitent is conscious must be recounted for the confession to be valid, "for if the sick person is too ashamed to show his wound to the doctor, the medicine cannot heal what it does not know" (CCC 1456, quoting Council of Trent: DS 1680, and citing St. Jerome, In Eccl. 10, 11: PL 23:1096).

- Confession of venial sins, although not strictly necessary, is recommended as a way to "be healed by Christ and progress in the life of the Spirit" (CCC 1458).

- While the Sacrament of Penance forgives sins, it does not remedy all the disorders caused by sin. Doing penance for one's sins helps the sinner recover "full spiritual health" (CCC 1459; *cf. also* CCC 1460; 1472; RP 6c; 18).

SEAL

OT Background:

Used literally: Gen. 38:18, 25; 41:42; Exod. 28:11, 21, 36; 39:6, 14, 30; 1 Kings 21:8; Neh. 9:38; 10:1; Tob. 7:14 (RSV = Tob. 7:13 NAB, NRSV); 9:5; Esther 3:10, 12; 8:2, 8, 10; Sir. 38:27; 42:6; Jer. 32:10–11, 14, 44; Dan. 6:17; 14:11, 14, 17; 2 Macc. 2:5

---

2 This text is ambiguous as to whether it refers to the sacramental confession of sins to a priest, or to the confession of sins in general. Other texts of St. John Chrysostom, such as On the Priesthood 3:5, clearly refer to the power of priests to forgive sins committed after Baptism. In light of this and similar texts, either or both possibilities may be in mind.

Used symbolically: Gen. 4:15; Deut. 32:34; Job 9:7; 14:17; 37:7; 38:14; 41:15; Song 4:12; 8:6; Wisd. 2:5; Sir. 22:27; 32:5–6; Isa. 8:16; 29:11–12; Jer. 22:24; Ezek. 9:4–6; Dan. 8:26; 9:24; 12:4, 9; Hag. 2:23

NT Background: Matt. 27:66; John 3:33; 6:27; Acts 2:1–4, 38; Rom. 4:11; 8:29; 1 Cor. 9:2; 2 Cor. 1:21–22; Eph. 1:13–14; 4:30; 2 Tim. 2:19; Rev. 5:1–10; 6:1–12; 7:2–8; 8:1; 9:4; 10:4; 13:16–17; 14:9, 11; 16:2; 19:20; 20:3–4; 22:10

Catechism Background: 1295; 1467; 2490; 2511

Related: CONFIRMATION: *Symbols:* Seal; HOLY ORDERS: *Symbols:* Seal; MATRIMONY: *Symbols:* Seal

Note: For the topic of "Seal" in general, cf. CONFIRMATION: *Symbols:* Seal.

• The Sacrament of Penance permanently "seals" the sins, which can never be revealed by the priest. This "sacramental seal" can never be broken and admits of no exceptions (CCC 1467; *cf.* CCC 2490).

• The priest comes to know the secrets of another's conscience only because he is a minister of God; as such he is absolutely obliged to preserve the seal unbroken (RP 10d).

PRODIGAL SON'S HOMECOMING

OT Background:

Legal background: Lev. 11:7; Deut. 14:8; 21:15–17, 18–21

As regards the Father: Gen. 18:7; 25:5–6; 29:13; 33:4; 41:42; 43:16; 45:14–15; 46:29; 1 Sam. 28:24; Tob. 8:21; 11:9; Esther 3:10; 6:11; 8:2; Ps. 103:13; Sir. 33:20–24; Zech. 3:3–5; 1 Macc. 6:15

As regards the prodigal son: Exod. 10:16; 1 Sam. 15:24; Ps. 51:4; Prov. 29:3; Isa. 65:4

Israel and the prodigal son: Jer. 3:6, 12; 31:18–20; Ezek. 16:10; 37:21–23; Hos. 4:15

NT Background: Luke 15:1–2, 3–10, 11–32; 16:1; John 1:12; 5:24; 8:35; Acts 20:37; Rom. 6:13; Eph. 2:1–5, 13, 17; Col. 2:13; 1 Tim. 5:6

Catechism Background: 1423; 1439; **1465**; **1481**; 1700; **2839**

Related: BAPTISM: *Symbols:* White Garment / Wedding Garment; PENANCE: *Symbols:* Finding the Lost Sheep; Second Plank of Salvation; Wedding Garment

- This sacrament is called the "sacrament of conversion" because "it makes sacramentally present Jesus' call to conversion, the first step in returning to the Father (cf. Mark 1:15;Luke 15:18) from whom one has strayed by sin" (CCC 1423).
- The robe, ring, and festive banquet symbolize the new life "of anyone who returns to God and to the bosom of his family, which is the Church" (CCC 1439; cf. Luke 15:22–23).

The Catechism of the Catholic Church

The process of conversion and repentance was described by Jesus in the parable of the prodigal son, the center of which is the merciful father [Cf. Luke 15:11–24]: the fascination of illusory freedom, the abandonment of the father's house; the extreme misery in which the son finds himself after squandering his fortune; his deep humiliation at finding himself obliged to feed swine, and still worse, at wanting to feed on the husks the pigs ate; his reflection on all he has lost; his repentance and decision to declare himself guilty before his father; the journey back; the father's generous welcome; the father's joy – all these are characteristic of the process of conversion. The beautiful robe, the ring, and the festive banquet are symbols of that new life – pure, worthy, and joyful – of anyone who returns to God and to the bosom of his family, which is the Church. Only the heart Of Christ Who knows the depths of his Father's love could reveal to us the abyss of his mercy in so simple and beautiful a way.

CCC 1439

- In the Sacrament of Penance, "the Father receives the repentant children who come back to him" (cf. Luke 15:20–24) (RP 6d; cf. RP 202.4).
- In the Sacrament of Penance, the repentant sinner returns to the Father like the prodigal son, admitting his sin (cf. Luke 15:18, 21) (RP 88; cf. RP 202.4).

The Rite of Penance

Father of mercy,
like the prodigal son
I return to you and say:
"I have sinned against you
and am no longer worthy to be called your son."

Christ Jesus, Savior of the world,
I pray with the repentant thief
to whom you promised paradise:
"Lord, remember me in your kingdom."

Holy Spirit, fountain of love,
I call on you with trust:
"Purify my heart,
and help me to walk as a child of the light."

RP 88

- When a Christian sins and repents, he or she returns like the prodigal son to the Father, and receives "the efficacious and undoubted sign of his forgiveness in the sacraments of his Church (cf. Matt. 26:28; John 20:23)" (CCC 2839, citing Luke 15:11–32).

- In the Sacrament of Penance, the priest fulfills the ministry of the Father who awaits the return of his son and welcomes him back (CCC 1465; 1481; *cf.* Luke 15:20–24).

PUBLICAN

OT Background: Ezra 9:6; Job 22:29; Ps. 51:1, 3; Ezek. 21:26; 33:13

NT Background: Matt. 18:4; 23:12; Luke 1:52; 14:11; 18:9–14; 1 Tim. 1:15; James 4:6; 1 Pet. 5:5

Catechism Background: 588; **1481**; 2559; 2613; 2631; 2667; **2839**

Related: PENANCE: *Symbols*: Jesus Eating with Sinners; Prodigal Son's Homecoming; Second Plank of Salvation

- In the Sacrament of Penance, the same God who forgave the publican (*cf.* Luke 18:9–14) now forgives the sinner through the ministry of the priest (CCC 1481).

- The repentant sinner, like the publican (*cf.* Luke 18:9–14), recognizes his sin and asks for forgiveness, confessing his own wretchedness and God's mercy. The repentant sinner finds the "efficacious and undoubted sign of his forgiveness in the sacraments of the Church (cf. Matt 26:28; John 20:23)" (CCC 2839, citing Luke 18:13).

- Before receiving absolution, the penitent expresses sorrow for his or her sins. One formula proposed by the liturgy to express this sorrow is an adapted version of the words of the publican, "Lord Jesus, Son of God, have mercy on me, a sinner" (RP 45; 92; *cf.* Luke 18:13; *cf. also* RP 87; CCC 2667).

Repentant Thief

OT Background: Judg. 16:28; 1 Sam. 1:11, 19; 25:31; Neh. 5:19; Job 14:13; Ps. 106:4; Isa. 51:3

NT Background: Luke 23:39–43

Catechism Background: 1021; 1386; 2605; 2616

Related: Penance: *Symbols*: Jesus Eating with Sinners; Publican

- As Christ was merciful to the repentant thief, so he is merciful to the repentant sinner (RP 54, 2nd example, 8th intercession; 205.2, 7th intercession).

- In the Sacrament of Penance, the penitent is identified with the repentant thief, and prays: "Lord, remember me in your kingdom" (RP 88).

- As Jesus Christ brought the repentant thief from suffering to joy, so the liturgy prays that he may bring us, who confess our sins, to him through the gates of heaven (LH, Psalter.1[=2, 3, 4].Fr, MA, Prayer).

Second Plank of Salvation

OT Background: Num. 5:6–7; 2 Sam. 14:14; 2 Chron. 7:14; Isa. 1:18; 43:25; 55:6–7; Jer. 3:22; 18:7–10; Ezek. 3:20–21; 18:23–32; 33:11–20; 37:11–14; Hos. 14:1, 4

NT Background: Luke 15:11–32; 22:61–62; John 5:24; 21:15–17; 1 Cor. 5:11; 2 Pet. 3:9; Rev. 2:5, 16

Catechism Background: 979; 1428–1429; 1446; 1468; 1470; 1856

Related: PENANCE: *Symbols*: Finding the Lost Sheep; Prodigal Son's Homecoming; Tears of Repentance

- The Fathers of the Church compare the loss of grace due to mortal sin committed after Baptism to a shipwreck, and the Sacrament of Penance to a second plank of salvation (CCC 1446, citing Tertullian, De Pænit. 4, 2: PL 1, 1343; *cf. also* CCC 979–980; 1429).
- When a child of God abandons the Father's Home through serious sin (*cf.* Luke 15:11–32), the Sacrament of Penance brings about a true "spiritual resurrection," that is, the "restoration of the dignity and blessings of the life of the children of God, of which the most precious is friendship with God (cf. Luke 15:32)" (CCC 1468; *cf. also* RP 44 and 46 for Penance as "spiritual resurrection").
- The liturgy prays that as Jesus raised Lazarus from the dead, so through faith and penance, sinners may come back to life (LH, Lent.1.Su, EP1, 4th intercession).

TEARS OF REPENTANCE

OT Background: Esther 4:3; Joel 2:12–13; Zech. 12:10
NT Background: Matt. 26:75; Mark 14:72; Luke 7:37–38, 44–48; 22:61–62; John 21:15–17; 1 Pet. 4:8
Catechism Background: 1428; **1429**; 1431–1432; **1434**; **1481**
Related: PENANCE: *Symbols*: Finding the Lost Sheep; Prodigal Son's Homecoming; Tears of Repentance

- Scripture and the Fathers of the Church "cite as means of obtaining forgiveness of sins: efforts at reconciliation with one's neighbor, tears of repentance, concern for the salvation of one's neighbor . . . the intercession of the saints, and the practice of charity 'which covers a multitude of sins' (1 Pet. 4:8; *cf.* James 5:20)" (CCC 1434).
- The Rite of Penance sees in the Sacraments of Baptism and of Penance two waters that both purify from sin and restore to grace: the waters of Baptism and the tears of repentance (RP 2; *cf. also* CCC 1429).
- St. Peter's tears of repentance and subsequent forgiveness (*cf.* Matt. 26:75; Mark 14:72; Luke 7:37–38; John 21:15–17) are implicitly compared to

the tears of repentance and forgiveness in the Sacrament of Penance (CCC 1429; *cf. also* RP 2).

• As Jesus Christ forgave the prostitute who washed his feet with her tears, so he forgives the repentant sinner in the Sacrament of Penance through the ministry of the priest (CCC 1481; *cf.* Luke 7:37–38, 44–48).

WASHING

OT Background:[3] Exod. 30:20–21; 40:32; Lev. 8:5–6; 14:8–9; 15:1–33; 16:3–4; Ps. 51:1–2, 7–10; Isa. 1:16–20; 4:3–4; Ezek. 16:3–9; 36:24–29; Zech. 13:1 (*cf.* 12:10)

NT Background: John 13:3–11; Eph. 5:25–27; Heb. 10:22; Rev. 7:14; 22:14

Catechism: 1148; 1189; 1337; 1425

Related: BAPTISM: *Symbols:* Washing; PENANCE: *Symbols*: Coming to the Light; Medicine for the Soul; Second Plank of Salvation; Tears of Repentance

• The rite of Penance remembers how Jesus Christ washed away our sin in his blood (RP 49).

• The Church is at the same time holy and in need of cleansing, "and so is unceasingly intent on repentance and reform" (RP 3, citing Lumen Gentium 8).

• Through the bath of Baptism and Penance sin is washed clean (LH, Conversion of St. Paul [Jan 25], MP, 5th intercession [Latin]; LH, Chair of Peter [Feb 22], MP, 5th intercession [Latin]; LH, St. Philip and St. James [May 3], MP, 5th intercession [Latin]; LH, St. Andrew [Nov 30], MP, 5th intercession [Latin]).

• In the Sacrament of Penance, the Holy Spirit cleanses "in the waters of repentance" (RP 50).

• When the sinner acknowledges his guilt, God cleanses the heart (RP 54).

• The penitent may pray, "Create in me a clean heart" (*cf.* Ps. 51:10), or may ask God, "cleanse me from every stain of sin in the blood you shed for me," as an act of contrition before receiving absolution (RP 91–92; *cf. also* RP 54, 2nd Example, 1st intercession).

---

3 This topic is too broad to include a wide selection of references to background texts. A sampling of some of the more significant references to the topic of washing is included.

- Before giving general absolution, the priest prays that God "cleanse your hearts and clothe you in his glory" (RP 62).

WEDDING GARMENT

OT Background:[4]

God's garments: Ps. 93:1; 104:1–2; Dan. 7:9

God clothes: Gen. 3:21; Ezek. 16:8–10

Liturgical garments: Exod. 28:42–43; 39:27–29; Lev. 16:3–4, 32; 2 Sam. 6:14; 1 Chron. 15:27; 2 Chron. 6:41; Ps. 132:9

Righteousness / wisdom as a garment: 2 Chron. 6:41; Job 29:14; Ps. 51:7; 132:9; Sir. 6:29–31; Isa. 1:18; 59:17; 61:3, 10

Other: Exod. 24:8; Eccles. 9:8; Song 1:5, 15; 8:5 (LXX); Isa. 52:1; Zech. 3:3–5; 1 Macc. 2:10–11

NT Background:

Jesus' garments: Matt. 17:2; Mark 9:3; Luke 9:29

Garments of the righteous: Matt. 13:43; 22:11–13; Rom. 13:12, 14; 1 Cor. 15:53; Gal. 3:27; Eph. 4:22–24; Col. 3:9–10; Rev. 3:4–5, 18; 4:4; 6:11; 19:8, 14; 21:2; 22:14

Angels' garments: Matt. 28:3; Mark 16:5; Luke 24:4; Acts 10:30; Rev. 7:9–14; 15:6

Catechism: 1243; 1244; 1395; 1446; 1682; 1856; 1861; 1874; 2839

Related: BAPTISM: *Symbols:* White Garment / Wedding Garment; PENANCE: *Symbols:* Second Plank of Salvation

- In the context of a liturgy to prepare for the Sacrament of Penance, a prayer is raised up that the penitent may be clothed in the wedding garment of grace and welcomed to God's table (RP 204.1, 8th intercession; *cf.* CCC 1244; 1682; 1856).

- Before giving general absolution, the priest prays that God "cleanse your hearts and clothe you in his glory" (RP 62).

---

4 Clothing imagery abounds throughout Scripture, to indicate both holiness and sinfulness. A sampling of some of the more significant references to the topic of white garments or garments related to salvation is included here.

ANOINTING OF THE SICK

Definition: One of the seven sacraments, also known as the "sacrament of the dying," administered by a priest to a baptized person who begins to be in danger of death because of illness or old age through prayer and the anointing of the body with the oil of the sick. The proper effects of the sacrament include a special grace of healing and comfort to the Christian who is suffering the infirmities of serious illness or old age, and the forgiving of the person's sins (Glossary of the Catechism of the Catholic Church).

TYPES

Note: The Catechism of the Catholic Church and the liturgy present the Sacrament of the Anointing of the Sick as having foundations in the divine economy of salvation in the way that illness and suffering were lived and experienced by people in the Old Testament (cf. CCC 1502). In the New Testament, Christ's healing ministry signified the presence of God and of his Kingdom, often accompanied by physical signs or symbolic gestures (cf. CCC 1151, which cites John 9:6; Mark 7:33–35; 8:22–26; CCC 1503–1504). With his death and Resurrection he gave a new meaning to suffering, allowing it to become a means of configuring ourselves to him and uniting ourselves to his redemptive Passion (cf. CCC 1505). Jesus gave the Church the charge to continue his ministry of compassion and healing, particularly through the sacraments and in a special way through the Sacrament of the Anointing of the Sick (cf. CCC 1506–1510). While the Sacrament of the Anointing of the Sick has its foundations in the Old Testament, and is inaugurated and described in the New Testament (cf. James 5:14–15; CCC 1510), the Bible, the Catechism, and the Liturgy do not present the Sacrament of the Anointing of the Sick as being prefigured by types. The Summa Theologiæ gives the following reason for the lack of types for the Sacrament of Anointing of the Sick: "This sacrament prepares man for glory immediately, since it is given to those who are departing from this life. And as, under the Old Law, it was not yet time to enter into glory, because 'the Law brought nobody to perfection' (Heb. 7:19), so this sacrament had not to be fore-shadowed therein by some corresponding sacrament, as by a figure of the same kind. Nevertheless it was somewhat foreshadowed remotely by all the healings related in the Old Testament" (Supplementum, Q. 29, a. 1, ad 2).

SYMBOLS

ANOINTING

OT Background: Lev. 14:15–18, 26–29; 2 Chron. 28:15; Tob. 6:8 (RSV = Tob. 6:9 NAB, NRSV); 11:8; Jth. 10:3; 16:8 (RSV = Jth. 16:7 NAB, NRSV); Isa. 1:6; 61:3; Ezek. 16:9

NT Background: Mark 6:13; 14:8; 16:1; Luke 7:38, 46; 10:34; John 9:6, 11; 11:2; 12:3; 2 Cor. 2:14–16; James 5:14–15; Rev. 3:18

Catechism Background: 695; 739; **1020**; 1148; 1151–1152; 1189; **1294**; 1499; 1504–1505; **1510**; **1511–1513**; **1519–1523**; 1525–1526; 1531–1532; 1682–1683

Related: CONFIRMATION: *Symbols:* Anointing; ANOINTING OF THE SICK: *Symbols:* Laying on of Hands

Note: *For the topic of anointing in general cf.* CONFIRMATION: *Symbols:* Anointing; BAPTISM: *Types:* Anointing of Priests, Prophets, and Kings.

• The anointing (together with the laying on of hands, *cf.* ANOINTING OF THE SICK: *Symbols:* Laying on of Hands) signifies and gives a particular gift of the Holy Spirit which (CCC 1520 in light of CCC 1519; *cf. also* James 5:14–15; CCC 695; PCS 6; 25; 107 [USCCB]; 121 [=OUI 70]; 123 [=OUI 75]; 124 [=OUI 76]; 125A [=OUI 77; 90]; 125D [=OUI 243]):

  ▪ strengthens (*cf. also* James 5:14–15; CCC 1020, which quotes PCS 220A [=OUI 146]; CCC 1511; RBOC 2; PCS 5; 240C [=OUI 119]; 250A [=OUI 244]);

  ▪ gives comfort and courage to overcome the difficulties or afflictions that accompany illness or old age (*cf. also* CCC 1294 and PCS 123 [=OUI 75]; 125 [=OUI 77; 90]; 140 [=OUI 75; 75B; 82B]; 140B [=OUI 242]; 248 [=OUI 126]; 268 [=OUI 135]; 270A [=OUI 246]); 270B [=OUI 245];

- renews trust and faith in God;
- strengthens against temptations of the devil, especially those of discouragement or anguish in the face of death (*cf. also* RBOC 2);
- gives healing of soul (*cf. also* Mark 6:13; James 5:14–15; CCC 1294; PCS 25; 123 [=OUI 75]; RBOC 20) and spirit (PCS 123 [=OUI 75]; 125C [=OUI 77]);
- and if God wishes, of the body (*cf. also* Mark 6:13; James 5:14–15; CCC 1294; 1512; 1532; PCS 123 [=OUI 25]; 125 [=OUI 77; 243]; RBOC 20) and mind (RBOC 2; 20; PCS 125B [=OUI 77]);
- and the forgiveness of sins (*cf. also* James 5:15; PCS 25; RBOC 2; CCC 1532).

The Catechism of the Catholic Church

The Christian who unites his own death to that of Jesus views it as a step towards him and an entrance into everlasting life. When the Church for the last time speaks Christ's words of pardon and absolution over the dying Christian, seals him for the last time with a strengthening anointing, and gives him Christ in viaticum as nourishment for the journey, she speaks with gentle assurance:

Go forth, Christian soul, from this world
in the name of God the almighty Father,
who created you,
in the name of Jesus Christ, the Son of the living God,
who suffered for you,
in the name of the Holy Spirit,
who was poured out upon you.
Go forth, faithful Christian!

May you live in peace this day,
may your home be with God in Zion,
with Mary, the virgin Mother of God,
with Joseph, and all the angels and saints. . . .

> May you return to [your Creator]
> who formed you from the dust of the earth.
> May holy Mary, the angels, and all the saints
> come to meet you as you go forth from this life. . . .
> May you see your Redeemer face to face. . . .
>
> *CCC 1020, quoting PCS 220A (=OUI 146)*

- The anointing unites the sick person to Christ in his Passion, consecrating them to bear fruits by participating in the saving work of the Lord (CCC 1521 in light of CCC 1519; CCC 1532; *cf. also* CCC 1499; PCS 3; 125C [=OUI 77]; 250 [=OUI 244]).
- The anointing signifies the prayers of the Church for the sick person, and the consecration of the sick person to offer up their sufferings in intercession for the Church (CCC 1522 in light of CCC 1519; *cf. also* James 5:14–15; CCC 1499; 1532; 695; PCS 90 [Latin]; 125A [=OUI 77; 90]; 250 [=OUI 244]; 270A [=OUI 246]).
- The anointing of the sick, when given to those preparing for death (CCC 1523 in light of CCC 1519; *cf. also* CCC 1020; 1525; 1532; 1683; PCS 124 [=OUI 76]; 125C [=OUI 77]; 125D [=OUI 243]; 220A [=OUI 146]; 270A [=OUI 246]):
  - signifies and completes ("perficit") their conformity to Christ in his death and Resurrection begun in Baptism and strengthened in Confirmation;
  - fortifies them, like a solid rampart, for the final struggles (*cf. also* LH, St. Fidelis of Sigmaringen [Apr 24], 2R: From a eulogy for St. Fidelis of Sigmaringen).

LAYING ON OF HANDS

OT Background:
Filling with the spirit of wisdom: Deut. 34:9
Blessing: Gen. 48:13–18; Ps. 139:5; Sir. 50:20–21
NT Background:
Blessing: Matt. 19:13–15; Mark 10:13, 16; Rev. 1:17
Giving the Holy Spirit: Acts 8:14–19; 9:17; 19:5–6; Heb. 6:2 (*cf.* CCC 1288)
Healing: Matt. 9:18; Mark 5:23; 6:5; 7:32; 8:23–25; 16:17–18; Luke 4:40; 13:13; Acts 5:12; 9:12, 17; 14:3; 28:8; James 5:14–15

Catechism Background: 699; 1150–1151; 1507; **1510**; **1519**; 1520–1523; 1526

Related: CONFIRMATION: *Symbols:* Laying on of Hands; HOLY ORDERS: *Symbols:* Laying on of Hands; ANOINTING OF THE SICK: *Symbols:* Anointing

- The laying on of hands is the "biblical gesture of healing and indeed Jesus' own usual manner of healing" (PCS 106 [USCCB]; *cf.* CCC 699; 1151; 1520; Matt. 9:18; Mark 5:23; 6:5; 7:32; 8:23–25; 16:18; Luke 4:40; 13:13; Acts 5:12; 9:12, 17; 14:3; 28:8; James 5:14–15).

- The sick are invited to call "the elders [*presbyters*] of the Church and let them pray over him, anointing him with oil in the name of the Lord; and the prayer of faith will save the sick man, and the Lord will raise him up; and if he has committed sins, he will be forgiven" (James 5:14–15 as quoted in CCC 1510; *cf. also* CCC 1519; 1526).

- The laying on of hands signifies blessing (*cf.* CCC 699).

- The laying on of hands signifies the invocation of the Holy Spirit (*cf.* CCC 699; 1520 in light of CCC 1519).

- The laying on of hands signifies prayer for healing and strengthening (*cf.* CCC 1520 in light of CCC 1519; PCS 121 [=OUI 70; 73; 90]; 138 [=OUI 73; 82B; 241]; James 5:14–15).

- The laying on of hands unites the sick person to Christ in his Passion, consecrating them to bear fruits by participating in the saving work of the Lord (CCC 1521 in light of CCC 1519).

- The laying on of hands indicates that this person is the object of the prayer of faith of the Church (*cf.* CCC 1522 in light of CCC 1519; James 5:14–15).

- The laying on of hands accompanies the final anointing, and strengthens the dying for the end of human life (CCC 1523 in light of CCC 1519).

HOLY ORDERS

Definition: The Sacrament of Apostolic Ministry by which the mission entrusted by Christ to his Apostles continues to be exercised in the Church through the laying on of hands. This sacrament has three distinct degrees or "orders": deacon, priest, and bishop. All three confer a permanent, sacramental character (Glossary of the Catechism of the Catholic Church).

TYPES

Note: The Bible, the Catechism, and the Liturgy present multiple prefigurations of the one priesthood of Jesus Christ. As the Catechism states, "Everything that the priesthood of the Old Covenant prefigured finds its fulfillment in Christ Jesus, the 'one mediator between God and men' (1 Tim. 2:5)" (CCC 1544).

Both the common priesthood of the baptized and the ministerial priesthood of the ordained share, each in their own way, in the one priesthood of Christ through participation, "without diminishing the uniqueness of Christ's priesthood" (CCC 1545; cf. CCC 1546–1547).

Symbols and types of the priesthood, as a general rule, thus primarily refer to the priesthood of Jesus Christ, and secondarily to that one priesthood as it is shared in by both the common priesthood of the baptized and the ministerial priesthood. As Lumen Gentium explains, though "they differ from one another in essence and not only in degree, the common priesthood of the faithful and the ministerial or hierarchical priesthood are nonetheless interrelated: each of them in its own special way is a participation in the one priesthood of Christ" (Lumen Gentium 10).

In accord with the specific topic of this book, while samplings of text which refer primarily to the priesthood of Jesus Christ are at times included at the beginning of the topic, the primary focus is on texts which emphasize prefigurations of the priesthood of Jesus Christ as participated in through the ministerial priesthood or diaconate.

MELCHIZEDEK

OT Background: Gen. 14:17–20; Ps. 110:4

NT Background: Heb. 5:1–10; 6:13–7:22

Catechism Background: 58; **1333**; **1350**; **1544**; 1545

Type: CCC 1333; 1350; 1544 (in light of CCC 1545); RO 162 (=ROP 25)

Related: EUCHARIST: *Types*: Offering of Melchizedek; HOLY ORDERS: *Types*: High Priest; *Symbols*: Presentation of the Paten and Chalice

- Melchizedek prefigures the priesthood of Christ (Heb. 5:1–10; 6:13–7:22; CCC 1544, citing Heb. 5:10; 6:19–20; Gen. 14:18; *cf. also* LH, Lent.4.Mo, 2R, Resp [Heb. 6:20; 7:2, 3]; LH, Lent.5.Su, 2R, Resp [Heb. 6:20; John 1:29]; LH, Lent.5.We, 1R, Resp [Heb. 6:19–20; 7:24–25]; LH, Lent.5.Th, 1R, Resp [Gen. 14:18; Heb. 7:3, 16; Ps. 110:5]; LH, Lent.5.Fr, 1R, Resp [Heb. 5:5, 6; 7:20, 21]; LH, OT.12.Su, 2R: Faustus Luciferanus, Treatise on the Trinity, 39–40: CCL 69, 340–341; LH, OT.12.Su, 2R, Resp; LH, Corpus Christi, EP2, Ant1; Psalter.2.Su, EP2, Ant1).

- The priesthood of Christ, prefigured by Melchizedek (CCC 1544), is made present in the Church through the ministerial priesthood (CCC 1545) by means of a special participation in the one priesthood of Christ (CCC 1546–1547).

- In the Rite of Ordination of Priests, immediately after the laying on of hands and the prayer of ordination (*cf.* RO 158–159 [=ROP 20–22), the faithful sing Ps. 110 while the newly ordained are vested with stole and chasuble and have their hands anointed (RO 162 [=ROP 25]). Ps. 110:4 states, "You are a priest for ever according to the order of Melchizedek."

- The offering by the king-priest Melchizedek of bread and wine (*cf.* Gen. 14:17–20) prefigures the offering up of bread and wine which become the Body and Blood of Jesus Christ (CCC 1333; 1350; RM, Eucharistic Prayer I, 93; *cf.* RO 162 [=ROP 25]; EUCHARIST: *Types:* Offering of Melchizedek). In this offering participate both the common as well as the ministerial priesthood (CCC 1350–1351; RM, Eucharistic Prayer I, 92–94; *cf. also* CCC 901) in different but complementary ways (CCC 1546–1547).

- At the ordination of priests or bishops, the first reading may be Heb. 5:1–10, which speaks about how Melchizedek prefigured the priesthood of Jesus Christ (Lectionary 771; RO 348).

• At the ordination of priests and deacons, the responsorial psalm may be Ps. 110:1, 2, 3, 4, with the antiphon "Christ the Lord, a priest for ever in the line of Melchizedek, offered bread and wine" or the antiphon "You are a priest for ever, in the line of Melchizedek" (Lectionary 772; RO 349).

HIGH PRIEST

OT Background: Exod. 28; 30:7–10; 40:13; Lev. 4:3–21; 16:1–34; 21:10–15; Num. 18:1; 35:25; 2 Chron. 19:11; Jth. 4:6–8, 14; 15:8; Sir. 45:24; 50:19; Hag. 1:1, 12, 14; 2:2, 4; Zech. 3:1, 8; 6:11; 2 Macc. 15:12

NT Background: Matt. 26:62–64; John 1:29; 11:49–52; 17:1–26; Heb. 2:17; 3:1; 4:14–15; 5:1–10; 6:20; 7:24–27; 8:1–6; 9:7, 11–28; 10:19–21; 13:11; Rev. 5:6

Catechism Background: 433; 540; 662; 784; **893**; 1137; **1348**; 1372; 1410; **1542**; 1544–1545; 1546; **1548**; 1549; **1557**; **1586**; 2474; 2604; 2746–2751

Type: RO 47 (=ROB 26); CCC 1542; LH, OT.15.Su, 2R: St. Ambrose, On the Mysteries, 1–7: SC 25 bis, 156–158; RM, Commons, Common of Pastors, For a Pope or for a Bishop, 1, Entrance Antiphon (Sir. 50:1; 44:16, 22)

Related: HOLY ORDERS: *Types*: Anointing of Priests, Prophets, and Kings; Melchizedek; Priesthood

Jesus Christ is High Priest

• God established Jesus Christ as the eternal high priest (*cf. for example* Heb. 2:17; 3:1; 4:14–15; 5:1–10; 6:20; 7:24–27; 8:1, 3–6; 9:11–28; 10:19–21; RM, Votive Masses, Our Lord Jesus Christ, the Eternal High Priest, Collect; *cf. also* RO 151 [=ROP 14]; RO 152 [=ROP 15]; RM, Chrism Mass, 9; RM, Chrism Mass, Preface [=RM, Ritual Masses, For the Conferral of Holy Orders, For the Ordination of a Bishop, A [=B], Preface; RM, Ritual Masses, For the Conferral of Holy Orders, For the Ordination of Priests, A [=B], Preface; RM, Ritual Masses, For the Conferral of Holy Orders, For the Ordination of Deacons, A [=B], Preface]; RM, Masses and Prayers for Various Needs and Occasions, For Holy Church, For Priests, Collect; LH, Lent.5.Su, 2R: St. Athanasius, Easter Letter 14, 1–2: PG 26, 1419–1420; LH, St. Thomas Becket [Dec 29], 2R: St. Thomas Becket, Letter 74:

PL 190, 533–536; LH, Common of Pastors, 2R, For a priest: Vatican II, Presbyterorum ordinis Ch. 3, 12).

- Jesus Christ the high priest offered himself to the Father as a sacrifice (*cf. for example* Heb. 7:24–27; 9:11–28; RO 152 [=ROP 15]; LH, Lent.4.Mo, 1R, Resp [Heb. 9:11, 12, 24]; LH, Lent.4.Mo, 2R: Origen, Homily on Leviticus, 9, 5.10: PG 12, 515.523; LH, Lent.4.Mo, 2R, Resp [Heb. 6:20; 7:2, 3]; LH, Lent.5.Mo, 2R: St. John Fisher, Commentary on the Psalms 129: Opera omnia, edit. 1579, p. 1610).

- Before his crucifixion at the Last Supper, Jesus prayed as high priest to the Father (John 17; *cf.* CCC 2746–2751).

- As high priest, Jesus Christ intercedes eternally for us (*cf. for example* Heb. 7:24–27; 9:11–28; Rev. 5:6; CCC 1069; 1137; 1187; 2604; RM, Ascension, Vigil Mass, Prayer over the Offerings; *cf. also* RM, ET.2.Th, Collect; LH, Lent.5.Mo, 1R, Resp [Heb. 2:11, 17; Bar. 3:37]; LH, Lent.5.We, 1R, Resp [Heb. 6:19b–20; 7:24b–25]; LH, Lent.5.Sa, 1R, Resp [Heb. 8:1–2; 9:24]; LH, ET.6.Th, 2R, Resp [Heb. 8:1; 10:22–23]).

- When we offer up prayers and sacrifices through Jesus Christ, the high priest, they are acceptable because they are united to his offering (*cf. for example* CCC 2749; LH, OT.2.Th, 2R: St. Fulgentius of Ruspe, Epist. 14, 36–37: CCL 91, 429–431; *cf. also* LH, St. Clement I [Nov 23], 2R: St. Clement, Letter to the Corinthians, Ch. 35, 1–5; 36, 1–2; 37, 1.4–5; 38, 1–2.4).

- The wise men offered three gifts to the Lord: gold, which signified the power of a king; frankincense, which signified the office of high priest; and myrrh, which signified the Lord's burial (LH, CT.AE.Mo, 2R, Resp).

Prefigured in the Old Covenant

- Jesus Christ as high priest was prefigured by the high priest Melchizedek (*cf. for example* Heb. 5:1–10; 6:13–7:22; CCC 1544; RM, Eucharistic Prayer I, 93; LH, Lent.4.Mo, 1R, Resp [Heb. 9:11, 12, 24]; LH, Lent.4.Mo, 2R, Resp [Heb. 6:20; 7:2–3]; LH, Lent.5.Su, 2R, Resp [Heb. 6:20; John 1:29]; LH, Lent.5.We, 1R, Resp [Heb. 6:19b–20; 7:24b–25]; LH, Lent.5.Fr, 1R, Resp [Heb. 5:5–6; 7:20–21]; LH, OT.12.Su, 2R, Resp; *cf. also* HOLY ORDERS: *Types:* Melchizedek).

- Jesus Christ as high priest was foreshadowed by the high priest of the Old Covenant, who went in to the Holy of Holies every year to offer up the blood of bulls and goats (LH, Lent.5.Fr, 2R: St. Fulgentius of Ruspe, Treatise on Faith Addressed to Peter, Ch. 22, 62: CCL 91 A, 726.750–751; *cf. also for example* CCC 433).

- It is fitting that the Lord commanded Moses to "assemble" all the people for the appointing of Aaron as high priest, as a foreshadowing of the high priest, Jesus Christ, who would "assemble" the Jews and Gentiles in the Catholic "Church" (= "assembly" in Greek) (LH, OT.17.We, 2R: St. Cyril of Jerusalem, Catechetical Instruction 18, 23–25: PG 33, 1043–1047).

- "Christ is the source of all priesthood: the priest of the old law was a figure of Christ, and the priest of the new law acts in the person of Christ" (CCC 1548, quoting St. Thomas Aquinas, Summa Theologiæ III, 22, 4c).

Bishops Share in the High Priesthood of Jesus Christ

- God the Father made his only begotten Son the high priest of the new and eternal covenant, and decreed that "his one priesthood should continue in the Church" through the common priesthood and through the ministerial priesthood (RM, Chrism Mass, Preface [=RM, Ritual Masses, For the Conferral of Holy Orders, For the Ordination of a Bishop, A [=B], Preface; RM, Ritual Masses, For the Conferral of Holy Orders, For the Ordination of Priests, A [=B], Preface; RM, Ritual Masses, For the Conferral of Holy Orders, For the Ordination of Deacons, A [=B], Preface]; *cf. also* CCC 784; 1545–1548).

- In the ecclesial service of bishops and priests, Jesus Christ the high priest is present to his Church. By means of the priestly consecration, the bishop and priest are truly made like to Christ the high priest and possess the authority to act in persona Christi Capitis (CCC 1548; *cf.* RO 39 [=ROB 18]).

- The bishop has been raised up by God to be high priest (CCC 1557; RBOC 1; RM, Ritual Masses, For the Conferral of Holy Orders, For the Ordination of a Bishop, A [=B], Solemn Blessing; *cf. also* RM, Ritual Masses, For the Conferral of Holy Orders, For the Ordination of a Bishop, A [=B], Prayer over the Offerings; RM, Ritual Masses, For the Conferral of Holy Orders, For the Ordination of a Bishop, B, Collect; RM, Masses and Prayers for Various Needs and Occasions, For the Bishop, Prayer over the Offerings).

- The fullness of the Sacrament of Holy Orders is conferred by episcopal ordination. This fullness has been traditionally referred to by the Church Fathers and by the liturgical tradition of the Church as the "high priesthood" (CCC 1557).

- The bishop is "the steward of the grace of the supreme priesthood (Lumen Gentium 26)," especially in the Eucharist (CCC 893; *cf. also* CCC 1069; 1137; 1187; 1348; 1372; 1410).

- The consecrating bishop prays that the newly ordained bishop may "fulfill before you [God the Father] without reproach the ministry of high priest," and that "by the power of the Spirit of the high priesthood" God may grant him "the power to forgive sins according to your command, distribute offices according to your decree, and loosen every bond in accord with the power you gave the Apostles" (RO 47 [=ROB 26]; CCC 1586; *cf.* Matt. 16:19; 18:18; John 20:22–23; Acts 14:23; 1 Tim. 3:1–7; 4:14; Titus 1:5–9).

- While anointing the head of the newly ordained bishop with chrism, the ordaining bishop prays "May God, who has made you a sharer in the High Priesthood of Christ, pour upon you the oil of mystical anointing and make you fruitful with an abundance of spiritual blessings" (RO 49 [=ROB 28]).

- God placed the pope as high priest over his flock (RM, Masses for the Dead, Various Prayers for the Dead, For a Pope, B, Prayer over the Offerings; *cf. also* RM, St. Clement [Nov 23], Collect; LH, St. Thomas Becket [Dec 29], 2R: St. Thomas Becket, Letter 74: PL 190, 533–536).

Prefigured in the Old Covenant

- As in the Old Covenant the priests and Levites assisted Moses and Aaron, so in the New Covenant the priests and deacons assist the bishop (RO 159 [=ROP 22]; CCC 1542).

- As the Lord chose Simon son of Onias to be high priest, so he has chosen holy bishops and popes as high priests of Jesus Christ (RM, Commons, Common of Pastors, For a Pope or for a Bishop, 1, Entrance Antiphon [Sir. 50:1; 44:16, 22]).

- St. Ambrose, in his mystagogical instructions after Baptism, reminds the newly baptized how "the holy of holies was opened up" for them when they approached the baptismal font, and how there they saw "the Levite," "the priest," and "the high priest" (i.e. the deacon, the priest, and the bishop)

(LH, OT.15.Su, 2R: St. Ambrose, On the Mysteries, 1–7: SC 25 bis, 156–158).

Priests and the High Priesthood

• Jesus Christ the great priest "chose some of his disciples to carry out publicly in the Church a priestly office in his name" (RO 151 [=ROP 14]).

• Priests are ministers of Christ, the high priest (RM, Chrism Mass, 9; RM, Masses and Prayers for Various Needs and Occasions, For Holy Church, For Priests, Collect; LH, Common of Pastors, 2R, For a priest: Vatican II, Presbyterorum ordinis Ch. 3, 12).

• In the ecclesial service of bishops and priests, Jesus Christ the high priest is present to his Church. By means of the priestly consecration, the bishop and priest are truly made like to Christ the high priest and possess the authority to act *in persona Christi Capitis* (CCC 1548).

PRIESTHOOD

OT Background: Exod. 19:22; 28:1–3, 41–43; 29:1–9, 44; 30:30–38; 40:12–16; Lev. 13:9; 14:2; 21:1–24; Num. 3:3; 4:16; 10:8; 16:40; 18:1–20; 25:10–13; 27:21; Deut. 20:2–4; 1 Sam. 2:28; 1 Chron. 6:49; 2 Chron. 13:10; 15:3; 26:18; Neh. 3:22, 28; Ps. 115:10, 12; 118:3; 135:19; Sir. 7:29, 31; 45:15–24; Jer. 18:18; Bar. 1:15–18; Joel 2:17; Mal. 2:7; 2 Macc. 14:31–36

NT Background:

In relation to the Old Covenant: Matt. 8:4; 12:4–5; Mark 1:44; 2:26; Luke 1:5, 8; 5:14; 6:4; 10:31; 17:14; John 1:19; Acts 6:7; Heb. 7:12; 8:4–5; 9:6–14; 10:11–14

In relation to the New Covenant: Luke 10:1–2; Acts 14:23; 15:2, 4, 6, 22–23; 16:4; 20:17; 21:18; Rom. 15:16; 1 Thess. 5:12; 1 Tim. 4:14; 5:17, 19–20; Titus 1:5; James 5:14; 1 Pet. 5:1, 5; 2 John 1; 3 John 1; Rev. 4:4, 10; 5:5–6, 8, 11, 14; 7:11, 13; 11:16; 14:3; 19:4

Catechism Background: 436; 611; **1150**; 1539–1540; **1541**; **1542**; 1544–1545; 1547; **1548**

Type: CCC 1150; 1541; 1542; RO 159 (=ROP 22); LH, Lent.5.Tu, 2R: St. Leo the Great, Sermo 8 de passione Domini, 6–8: PL 54, 340–342; LH, OT.15.Su, 2R: St. Ambrose, On the Mysteries, 1–7: SC 25 bis,

156–158; LH, OT.23.Fr, 2R: Bl. Isaac of Stella, Sermo 11: PL 194, 1728–1729

Related: HOLY ORDERS: *Types*: Seventy Elders of Moses; Anointing of Priests, Prophets, and Kings; High Priest; Laying on of Hands; Melchizedek; *Symbols*: Anointing; Laying on of Hands; Presentation of the Paten and Chalice; Seal

- All that was prefigured by the priesthood of the Old Covenant "finds its fulfillment in Christ Jesus" (CCC 1544; *cf. also for example* Heb. 9:6–14; 10:11–14; CCC 436; RM, The Order of the Mass, Preface V of Easter; LH, Lent.4.Su, 1R, Resp [Heb. 7:23, 24; Sir. 45:7, 8]; LH, Lent.4.Mo, 1R, Resp [Heb. 9:11, 12, 24]; LH, Lent.5.Fr, 2R: St. Fulgentius of Ruspe, Treatise on Faith Addressed to Peter, Ch. 22, 62: CCL 91 A, 726.750–751; LH, OT.5.Tu, 2R: Origen, Homily on Genesis 8, 6.8.9: PG 12, 206–209).

- The anointing of Aaron as priest prefigured the anointing of Jesus Christ as priest (LH, OT.4.Mo, 2R: St. Hilary of Poitiers, Commentary on the Psalms, Ps. 132 [Ps. 133]: PLS 1, 244–245).

- Through the ministerial priesthood, the one priesthood of Jesus Christ is made present, without diminishing its uniqueness (CCC 1555; *cf. also* CCC 1546–1547). In this way, the priest acts *in persona Christi Capitis*. "Christ is the source of all priesthood: the priest of the old law was a figure of Christ, and the priest of the new law acts in the person of Christ" (CCC 1548, quoting St. Thomas Aquinas, Summa Theologiæ, III, 22, 4c).

- Through the death and Resurrection of Christ, there is "a more distinguished order of Levites, a greater dignity for the rank of elders, a more sacred anointing for the priesthood" (LH, Lent.5.Tu, 2R: St. Leo the Great, Sermo 8 de passione Domini, 6–8: PL 54, 340–342).

- The priesthood of Aaron in the Old Covenant prefigured the ordained ministry of the New Covenant (CCC 1541; *cf. also* CCC 1150).

- The priests of the Old Covenant, the sons of Aaron, accompanied and assisted Moses and Aaron and offered sacrifices in the tabernacle. They prefigured the priests of the New Covenant, who assist the bishop as co-workers and are stewards of God's mysteries (RO 159 [=ROP 22]; CCC 1541; 1542, which cites ROP 22 [=RO 159]).

- The sacrifices of the sons of Aaron in the tabernacle where "a shadow of the good things to come" (RO 159 [=ROP 22]).

- If being chosen as a priest in the Old Covenant was a great benefit, how much more in the New Covenant when the figures have given way to truth, and night to day? The priest of Jesus Christ is like the Virgin Mary, who brings Christ to the world in the Eucharist. He is called to great holiness (LH, St. John of Avila [May 10], 2R: St. John of Avila, Talk sent to Fr. Francisco Gómez, SJ: BAC 304, Obras completas del santo maestro Juan de Ávila, 3, p. 364–365.370.373).

- St. Ambrose, in his mystagogical instructions after Baptism, reminds the newly baptized how "the holy of holies was opened up" for them when they approached the baptismal font, and how there they saw "the Levite," "the priest," and "the high priest" (i.e. the deacon, the priest, and the bishop) (LH, OT.15.Su, 2R: St. Ambrose, On the Mysteries, 1–7: SC 25 bis, 156–158).

- As the Levites and priests carried the ark of the covenant across the Jordan River, with the water standing like a wall to let them pass (cf. Josh. 3:1–5:1), so the neophyte, through the ministry of Levites and priests, crosses the Jordan and enters into the promised land through the Sacrament of Baptism (LH, OT.10.We, 2R: Origen, Homily on Joshua, 4, 1: PG 12, 842–843).

- Through the Mystical Body, Christ has married the Church, and all that is Christ's is the Church's and all that is Church's is Christ's. As the lepers were sent by Christ to the priests, so in the Sacrament of Penance the sinner is sent by him to the priests, to whom he has entrusted the power to forgive sins (LH, OT.23.Fr, 2R: Bl. Isaac of Stella, Sermo 11: PL 194, 1728–1729).

- As the priests of the Old Covenant offered to God incense and bread, so the priests of the New Covenant offer up the Body and Blood of Jesus Christ (*implied* by LH, Corpus Christi, MP, Ant2).

- The liturgy applies 1 Sam. 2:28 and Sir. 45:16–17 (originally applied to priests of the Old Covenant) to St. Clement I, pope and martyr, stating that he was chosen by God to be his priest, and that as a priest he was pleasing to God (LH, St. Clement I [Nov 23], 2R, Resp [Matt. 7:24; 1 Pet. 2:22; 1 Sam. 2:28]).

Anointing of Priests, Prophets, and Kings

Definition: A symbol of the Holy Spirit, whose "anointing" of Jesus as Messiah fulfilled the prophecies of the Old Testament. Christ (in Hebrew *Messiah*) means the one "anointed" by the Holy Spirit. Anointing is the sacramental sign of Confirmation, called Chrismation in the Churches of the East. Anointings form part of the liturgical rites of the catechumenate, and of the Sacraments of Baptism and Holy Orders (Glossary of the Catechism of the Catholic Church).

OT Background:

Temple and related: Gen. 28:18–22; 31:13; 35:14; Exod. 29:21, 36; 30:22–33; 40:9–11; Lev. 7:10–11; 8:10–11, 30; Num. 7:1, 10, 84, 88; Sir. 35:6; Dan. 9:24

Priest: Exod. 28:41; 29:7, 21, 29; 30:30–33; 40:12–15; Lev. 4:3, 5, 16; 6:20, 22; 7:12, 36; 8:12, 30; 10:7; 16:32; 21:10, 12; Num. 3:3; 35:25; 1 Chron. 29:22; Ps. 133:2; Sir. 45:15; Zech. 4:14; 2 Macc. 1:10

King: Judg. 9:8, 15; 1 Sam. 2:10, 35; 9:16; 10:1; 12:3, 5; 15:1, 17; 16:1–13; 24:6, 10; 26:9, 11, 16, 23; 2 Sam. 1:14, 16; 2:4, 7; 3:39; 5:3, 17; 12:7; 19:10, 21; 22:51; 23:1; 1 Kings 1:34, 39, 45; 5:1; 19:15–16; 2 Kings 9:1–13; 11:12; 23:30; 1 Chron. 11:3; 14:8; 29:22; 2 Chron. 6:42; 22:7; 23:11; Ps. 2:2; 18:50; 20:6; 28:8; 45:7–8; 84:9; 89:20, 38, 51; 132:10, 17; Sir. 46:13, 19; 48:8; Isa. 11:2; 45:1; Lam. 4:20; Dan. 9:25–26; Hos. 8:10; Hab. 3:13; Zech. 4:14

Prophet: 1 Kings 19:16; 1 Chron. 16:22; Ps. 105:15; Isa. 61:1

Suffering Servant: Isa. 42:1

Other: Ps. 23:5; 133:2; Isa. 61:1, 3

NT Background:

Jesus Christ: Luke 4:16–21; John 1:41; 4:25; Acts 4:26–27; 10:38; Heb. 1:9

Believers / Other: John 9:6, 11; 2 Cor. 1:21–22; 2:14–16; Eph. 1:13–14; 1 Pet. 2:5, 9; 1 John 2:20, 27; Rev. 1:6; 3:18; 5:10; 20:6

Catechism Background: **436**; 453; 486; 690; 695; 698; 713–714; 727; 739; 745; 782; 783–786; 901; 1141; 1148; **1150–1151**; 1183; 1189; 1216; 1237; 1241; 1293–1296; 1297; **1544–1545**; 1558; 1563; 1574; 1581–1584; 1597; 2579; 2672; 2769; 2782

Type: CCC 1150; RBOC 25; LH, Lent.5.Tu, 2R: St. Leo the Great, Sermo 8 de passione Domini, 6–8: PL 54, 340–342; LH, OT, St. Cyril

and Methodius [Feb 14], 2R, Resp [Ps. 89:20, 21–22; Jer. 3:15];
Lectionary 770; RM, Ritual Masses, For the Ordination of a Bishop,
A [=B], Entrance Antiphon [Luke 4:18]

Related: BAPTISM: *Types*: Anointing of Priests, Prophets, and Kings;
CONFIRMATION: *Symbols:* Anointing

*Note: Anointing is presented as both a type and a symbol. CCC 1150 speaks of
"signs" which "prefigure" the sacraments, mentioning among them "anointing
and consecration of kings and priests." It is not easy, and sometimes probably
impossible, to distinguish too sharply between symbolism and typology in this
and similar cases. Presented here are texts which speak primarily of anointing as
a type, or texts which are closely related to the types of anointing, even if they also
speak of symbolism. Cf. HOLY ORDERS: Symbols: Anointing for texts which
primarily speak of anointing as a symbol of the anointing of Holy Orders, and
CONFIRMATION: Symbols: Anointing for a broader vision of the symbolism
of anointing.*

- The anointing of prophets, priests, and kings (*cf. OT Background* above) pre-
  figured the anointing of Christ as prophet, priest, and king (Luke 4:16–21;
  RBOC 2; 25; *cf. also*; CCC 436; 1544; 2579; LH, OT.12.Su, 2R: Faustus
  Luciferanus, Treatise on the Trinity, 39–40: CCL 69, 340–341).
- The anointing of Aaron as priest prefigured the anointing of Jesus Christ
  as priest (LH, OT.4.Mo, 2R: St. Hilary of Poitiers, Commentary on the
  Psalms, Ps. 132 [Ps. 133]: PLS 1, 244–245).
- By the anointing of the Holy Spirit, God made Jesus Christ high priest of
  the new and eternal covenant, a priesthood which by God's design continues
  in the Church (RM, Chrism Mass, Preface [=RM, Ritual Masses, For the
  Conferral of Holy Orders, For the Ordination of a Bishop, A [=B], Preface;
  RM, Ritual Masses, For the Conferral of Holy Orders, For the Ordination
  of Priests, A [=B], Preface; RM, Ritual Masses, For the Conferral of Holy
  Orders, For the Ordination of Deacons, A [=B], Preface]).
- The anointing of Aaron as priest by Moses (*cf.* Exod. 40:12–15) fore-
  shadowed a greater reality to come (RBOC 25; for a summary of all the
  types mentioned in RBOC 25, *cf.* BAPTISM: *Types*: Anointing of Priests,
  Prophets, and Kings).

- The anointing of priests and kings in the Old Covenant prefigures the sacramental anointing of the New Covenant (CCC 1150–1151; RBOC 25; *cf. also* CCC 1151–1152; 1544).
- Through the death and Resurrection of Christ, there is "a more distinguished order of Levites, a greater dignity for the rank of elders, a more sacred anointing for the priesthood" (LH, Lent.5.Tu, 2R: St. Leo the Great, Sermo 8 de passione Domini, 6–8: PL 54, 340–342).
- The liturgy interprets the lives of St. Cyril, a priest, and St. Methodius, a bishop, in light of God's anointing of David (in Ps. 89:20) and God's promise to give shepherds after his own heart (in Jer. 3:15) (LH, OT, St. Cyril and Methodius [Feb 14], 2R, Resp [Ps. 89:20, 21–22; Jer. 3:15]).
- The first reading for the ordination of priests or bishops is optionally Isa. 61:1–3abcd: "The spirit of the Lord God is upon me, because the Lord has anointed me . . ." (Lectionary 770; RO 347).
- The Entrance Antiphon in the ordination of bishops is "The Spirit of the Lord is upon me, for he has anointed me and sent me to preach the good news to the poor, to heal the broken hearted" (RM, Ritual Masses, For the Ordination of a Bishop, A [=B], Entrance Antiphon [Luke 4:18]).

LEVITES

OT Background: Lev. 25:32–33; Num. 1:47–53; 3:5–51; 7:5–6; 8:5–26; 18:2–6, 21–28; Deut. 10:8–9; 12:12; 18:1–2, 6–8; 27:14; Josh. 13:14, 33; 14:3; 18:7; 1 Sam. 6:15; 1 Chron. 6:48; 15:2; 16:4–6; 2 Chron. 5:4; 19:8; Ezra 3:8; Neh. 8:7; Ezek. 40:46; 44:10–14

NT Background: Acts 6:1–7; Heb. 7:5, 9–11

Catechism Background: 1539; **1541**; **1543**; 1544–1545; 1569–1571

Type: CCC 1541; 1543; RO 235 (=ROD 21); RM, Easter Vigil, 19; LH, Lent.5.Tu, 2R: St. Leo the Great, Sermo 8 de passione Domini, 6–8: PL 54, 340–342; Lectionary 770; LH, OT.15.Su, 2R: St. Ambrose, On the Mysteries, 1–7: SC 25 bis, 156–158; LH, OT.10.We, 2R: Origen, Homily on Joshua, 4, 1: PG 12, 842–843

Related: HOLY ORDERS: *Types*: Laying on of Hands; Priesthood; High Priest

- God gave the Levites (and other aspects of the law of the Old Covenant) as a prefiguration of what was to come in Christ (LH, Lent.2.We, 2R: St. Irenaeus, Against Heresies, Book 4, 14, 2–3; 15, 1: SC 100, 542.548).

- The Levites, whom God chose to minister in the tabernacle, prefigured the order of deacons, who minister at the holy altar of God and assist the Apostles in the daily ministry of serving at table (RO 235 [=ROD 21]; CCC 1541; 1543).

- When a deacon sings the Easter Proclamation (*Exsultet)* at the Easter Vigil, he invites all present to invoke "the mercy of God almighty, that he, who has been pleased to number me, though unworthy, among the Levites, may pour into me his light unshadowed, that I may sing [the paschal candle's] perfect praises" (RM, Easter Vigil, 19).

- Through the death and Resurrection of Christ, there is "a more distinguished order of Levites, a greater dignity for the rank of elders, a more sacred anointing for the priesthood" *(*LH, Lent.5.Tu, 2R: St. Leo the Great, Sermo 8 de passione Domini, 6–8: PL 54, 340–342).

- St. Ambrose, in his mystagogical instructions after Baptism, reminds the newly baptized how "the holy of holies was opened up" for them when they approached the baptismal font, and how there they saw "the Levite," "the priest," and "the high priest" (i.e. the deacon, the priest, and the bishop) (LH, OT.15.Su, 2R: St. Ambrose, On the Mysteries, 1–7: SC 25 bis, 156–158).

- As the Levites and priests carried the ark of the covenant across the Jordan River, with the water standing like a wall to let them pass (*cf.* Josh. 3:1–5:1), so the neophyte, through the ministry of Levites and priests, crosses the Jordan and enters into the promised land through the Sacrament of Baptism *(*LH, OT.10.We, 2R: Origen, Homily on Joshua, 4, 1: PG 12, 842–843).

- In the Rite of Ordination of Deacons, immediately after the laying on of hands and the prayer of ordination (*cf.* RO 234–235 [=ROD 20–21]), the faithful sing Ps. 84 while the newly ordained deacons are vested with stole and dalmatic (RO 237 [=ROD 23]). Ps. 84:4 states, "Blessed are those who dwell in your house, ever singing your praise," referring to the priests and Levites who dwelt in the Temple (*cf. for example* Num. 1:53; 3:15–51; Deut. 18:6–8).

• In the Rite of Ordination of a Deacon, the first reading is Num. 3:5–9, in which the Lord commands Moses to entrust the Levites to Aaron the priest and to his sons, that they might assist them (Lectionary 770; RO 347).

LAYING ON OF HANDS

OT Background:
Appointing for ministry: Num. 8:5–16; 27:18–23; Deut. 34:9
Filling with the spirit of wisdom: Deut. 34:9
Blessing: Gen. 48:13–18; Ps. 139:5; Sir. 50:20–21
NT Background:
Blessing: Matt. 19:13–15; Mark 10:13, 16; Rev. 1:17
Giving the Holy Spirit: Acts 8:14–19; 9:17; 19:5–6; Heb. 6:2 (*cf.* CCC 1288)
Healing: Matt. 9:18; Mark 5:23; 6:5; 7:32; 8:23–25; 16:18; Luke 4:40; 13:13; Acts 5:12; 9:12, 17; 14:3; 28:8; James 5:14–15
Ordaining for ministry: Acts 6:1–6; 13:2–3; 14:23; 1 Tim. 3:1; 4:14; 5:22; 2 Tim. 1:6; Titus 1:5
Catechism Background: 699; **1150**; **1538**; **1556**; **1558**; 1568; **1569**; **1571**; **1573**; 1587; **1590**; **1597**
Type: CCC 1150
Related: HOLY ORDERS: *Types*: Anointing of Priests, Prophets, and Kings

In General

• In the Old Covenant, the Levites were appointed for ministry through the laying on of hands (Num. 8:5, 10, 14). Similarly, Joshua was appointed by Moses and entrusted with some of his authority through the laying on of hands (Num. 27:18–23; Deut. 34:9). In the New Covenant, the apostles ordain men for ministry through the laying on of hands, entrusting communities to them (*cf.* Acts 6:6; 13:2–3; 14:23; 1 Tim. 3:1; 4:14; 5:22; 2 Tim. 1:6; Titus 1:5). The Church sees in the liturgical sign of the laying on of hands in the Old Covenant a prefiguration of the sacraments of the New Covenant (CCC 1150).

• The laying on of hands is the visible sign of "the sacramental act which integrates a man into the order of bishops, presbyters, or deacons," and "confers a gift of the Holy Spirit that permits the exercise of a 'sacred power' (*sacra potestas*) [Cf. Lumen Gentium 10] which can come only from Christ himself through his Church" (CCC 1538; *cf.* CCC 1573; 1597). It is a consecration which sets the recipient apart for Christ and the Church.

- Jesus Christ chooses men "to become sharers in his sacred ministry through the laying on of hands" (RM, Chrism Mass, Preface [=RM, Ritual Masses, For the Conferral of Holy Orders, For the Ordination of a Bishop, A [=B], Preface; RM, Ritual Masses, For the Conferral of Holy Orders, For the Ordination of Priests, A [=B], Preface; RM, Ritual Masses, For the Conferral of Holy Orders, For the Ordination of Deacons, A [=B], Preface]).

- The Church prays that bishops, priests, and deacons may be more closely united to Christ through the mystery of the Eucharist, so that the grace received through the imposition of hands may be ever renewed (LH, Lent. AAW[=2, 4].Th, EP, 2nd intercession [Latin]).

Bishops

- The apostles selected others to help them, and by laying hands on them conferred the Sacrament of Holy Orders in its fullness, and handed on the gift of the Holy Spirit which they themselves had received from Christ, so that the work of Jesus Christ might continue and grow even to our times (RO 39 [=ROB 18]; *cf.* Acts 13:2–3; 14:23; 1 Tim. 4:14; 5:22; 2 Tim. 1:6; Titus 1:5; RO 40 [=ROB 19]; CCC 1556; *cf. also* RO 45 [=ROB 24]).

- Through the laying on of hands and the words of consecration, "the grace of the Holy Spirit is given, and a sacred character is impressed in such wise that bishops, in an eminent and visible manner, take the place of Christ himself, teacher, shepherd, and priest, and act as his representative' (Lumen Gentium 21)" (CCC 1558).

- For the ordination of bishops, the first reading may be 2 Tim. 1:6–14, in which St. Paul invites St. Timothy to stir into flame the gift of God he has received through the laying on of hands (Lectionary 771; RO 348).

- For the ordination of bishops or priests, the first reading may be 1 Tim. 4:12–16, in which St. Paul invites St. Timothy to not neglect the gift he has received through the laying on of hands (Lectionary 771; RO 348).

- The bishop is admitted into the college of bishops by the laying on of hands (RO 39 [=ROB 18]; *cf.* CCC 1559; 877; RO 45 [=ROB 24]).

Priests

- The priest is consecrated by the laying on of hands (*cf.* RO 158 [=ROP 20]).
- For the ordination of bishops or priests, the first reading may be 1 Tim. 4:12–16, in which St. Paul invites St. Timothy to not neglect the gift he has received through the imposition of hands (Lectionary 771; RO 348).
- Priests who concelebrate at a priestly ordination lay hands on the newly ordained priest(s) as a sign of their incorporation into the presbyterate (RO 112; CCC 1568; *cf.* RO 158 [=ROP 21]).

Deacons

- The deacon is consecrated by the laying on of hands which has come down from the apostles (RO 227 [=ROD 14]; CCC 1571; *cf.* Acts 6:1–6; RO 234 [=ROD 20]).
- The deacon is ordained by the laying on of hands "'not unto the priesthood, but unto the ministry' (Lumen Gentium 29; *cf.* CD 15)" (CCC 1569; *cf.* Acts 6:1–6; RO 235 [=ROD 21]; *cf. also* RO 228 [=ROD 15]).
- In the Rite of Ordination of Deacons, only the bishop lays hands on the candidate, "thus signifying the deacon's special attachment to the bishop in the tasks of his 'diakonia'" (CCC 1569, referring to St. Hippolytus, Trad. ap. 8: SCh 11, 58–62; *cf. also* RO 234 [=ROD 20]).
- The grace of the diaconate given through the laying on of hands strengthens those who serve in the liturgical and pastoral life of the Church, binds them more closely to the altar, and makes their ministry more fruitful (CCC 1571, which quotes Ad Gentes 16 § 6).

SEVENTY ELDERS OF MOSES

OT Background: Num. 11:11–17, 24–30 (*cf. also* Exod. 24:1–2, 9–11)

NT Background: Acts 14:23; 15:2, 4, 6, 22–23; 16:4; 20:17; 21:18; 1 Thess. 5:12; 1 Tim. 4:14; 5:17, 19–20; Titus 1:5; James 5:14; 1 Pet. 5:1, 5; 2 John 1; 3 John 1; Rev. 4:4, 10; 5:6, 8; 7:13; 11:16; 14:3

Catechism Background: 1542; 1562–1568

Type: CCC 1542; RO 159 (=ROP 22)

Related: HOLY ORDERS: *Types*: Priesthood

- As God extended the spirit of Moses to the seventy elders "and with their help he ruled your people with greater ease," so God grants the dignity of the priesthood of Jesus Christ to men called to be "a worthy co-worker with our Order, so that by his preaching and through the grace of the Holy Spirit the words of the Gospel may bear fruit in human hearts and reach even to the ends of the earth. . . . Thus may the full number of the nations, gathered together in Christ, be transformed into your one people" (RO 159 [=ROP 22]; CCC 1542, which cites ROP 22 [=RO 159]; *cf. also* CCC 1562; 1565; 1567).

• Through the death and Resurrection of Christ, there is "a more distinguished order of Levites, a greater dignity for the rank of elders, a more sacred anointing for the priesthood" *(LH, Lent.5.Tu, 2R:* St. Leo the Great, Sermo 8 de passione Domini, 6–8: PL 54, 340–342).

• At the ordination of priests, the first reading is optionally Numbers 11:11b– 12, 14–17, 24–25 (Lectionary 770; RO 347), which presents the command of God to Moses to call seventy elders to assist him.

SYMBOLS

Note: To better organize the symbols related to Holy Orders, they have been divided according to whether they are symbols related to some aspect of the celebration of Holy Orders or symbols or metaphors regarding the ordained minister. This division rather loosely corresponds to the classical distinction in theology between the sacramentum in fieri (the sacrament in the act of being constituted) and the sacramentum in facto esse (the sacrament in the act of being lived out). Of course, more than one of these symbols apply in one way or another to both the sacrament in the act of being constituted and the sacrament as it is lived out.

SYMBOLS FROM THE
CELEBRATION OF HOLY ORDERS

Anointing

Definition: A symbol of the Holy Spirit, whose "anointing" of Jesus as Messiah fulfilled the prophecies of the Old Testament. Christ (in Hebrew *Messiah*) means the one "anointed" by the Holy Spirit. Anointing is the sacramental sign of Confirmation, called Chrismation in the Churches of the East. Anointings form part of the liturgical rites of the catechumenate, and of the Sacraments of Baptism and Holy Orders (Glossary of the Catechism of the Catholic Church).

OT Background:

Temple and related: Gen. 28:18–22; 31:13; 35:14; Exod. 29:21, 36; 30:22–33; 40:9–11; Lev. 7:10–11; 8:10–11, 30; Num. 7:1, 10, 84, 88; Sir. 35:6; Dan. 9:24

Priest: Exod. 28:41; 29:7, 21, 29; 30:30–33; 40:12–15; Lev. 4:3, 5, 16; 6:20, 22; 7:12, 36; 8:12, 30; 10:7; 16:32; 21:10, 12; Num. 3:3; 35:25; 1 Chron. 29:22; Ps. 133:2; Sir. 45:15; Zech. 4:14; 2 Macc. 1:10

King: Judg. 9:8, 15; 1 Sam. 2:10, 35; 9:16; 10:1; 12:3, 5; 15:1, 17; 16:1–13; 24:6, 10; 26:9, 11, 16, 23; 2 Sam. 1:14, 16; 2:4, 7; 3:39; 5:3, 17; 12:7; 19:10, 21; 22:51; 23:1; 1 Kings 1:34, 39, 45; 5:1; 19:15–16; 2 Kings 9:1–13; 11:12; 23:30; 1 Chron. 11:3; 14:8; 29:22; 2 Chron. 6:42; 22:7; 23:11; Ps. 2:2; 18:50; 20:6; 28:8; 45:7–8; 84:9; 89:20, 38, 51; 132:10, 17; Sir. 46:13, 19; 48:8; Isa. 11:2; 45:1; Lam. 4:20; Dan. 9:25–26; Hos. 8:10; Hab. 3:13; Zech. 4:14

Prophet: 1 Kings 19:16; 1 Chron. 16:22; Ps. 105:15; Isa. 61:1

Suffering Servant: Isa. 42:1

Other: Exod. 19:6; Lev. 14:15–18, 26–29; Deut. 11:13–14; 32:13; Judg. 9:9; 2 Sam. 12:20; 2 Chron. 28:15; Ruth 3:3; Tob. 6:8 (RSV = Tob. 6:9 NAB, NRSV); 11:8; Jth. 10:3; 16:8 (RSV = Jth. 16:7 NAB, NRSV); Job 29:6; Ps. 23:5; 92:10; 104:15; 133:2; Prov. 27:9; Eccles. 9:8; Song 1:3–4; 4:10; Isa. 1:6; 61:3, 6; Ezek. 16:9; 28:14; 36:25–26; Dan. 13:17; Joel 2:24; Amos 6:6

NT Background:

Jesus Christ: Mark 14:8; 16:1; Luke 4:16–21; 7:38, 46; John 1:41; 4:25; 11:2; 12:3; Acts 4:26–27; 10:38; Heb. 1:9

Believers / Other: Matt. 6:17; Mark 6:13; Luke 10:34; John 9:6, 11; Rom. 15:16; 2 Cor. 1:21–22; 2:14–16; Eph. 1:13–14; James 5:14–15; 1 Pet. 2:5, 9; 1 John 2:20, 27; Rev. 1:6; 3:18; 5:10; 20:6

Catechism Background: 436; 438; 453; 486; 690; 695; **698**; **713–714**; 727; 739; 745; 782; 783–786; 901; 1141; 1148; **1150**; 1151; 1183; 1189; 1241; **1293–1294**; 1295–1296; 1297; **1558**; **1563**; **1574**; **1581–1584**; **1597**; 2579; 2672; 2769; 2782

Related: BAPTISM: *Types:* Anointing of Priests, Prophets, and Kings; CONFIRMATION: *Symbols:* Anointing; HOLY ORDERS: *Types:* Anointing of Priests, Prophets, and Kings

Note: Anointing is presented as both a type and a symbol. CCC 1150 speaks of "signs" which "prefigure" the sacraments, mentioning among them "anointing and consecration of kings and priests." It is not easy, and sometimes probably impossible, to distinguish too sharply between symbolism and typology in this and similar cases. Presented here are texts which speak primarily of anointing as a symbol of the anointing of the Sacrament of Holy Orders. For other symbolic meanings of anointing cf. CONFIRMATION: Symbols: Anointing. For texts which speak primarily of anointing as a type cf. HOLY ORDERS: Types: Anointing of Priests, Prophets, and Kings and BAPTISM: Types: Anointing of Priests, Prophets, and Kings.

- In the Old Covenant, anointing symbolized the priest, prophet, or king's consecration to God for a mission (*cf. for example* CCC 436; Exod. 28:41; 1 Sam. 15:1; 1Kings 19:16; and *OT Background* above). Jesus Christ is God's anointed *par excellence* (*cf. for example* Luke 4:16–21; John 1:41; Acts 4:26–27; 10:38; Heb. 1:9; CCC 436; 438; 453; 486; 690; 695; 727; 745; 782; 783).

- The anointing of the priest and bishop symbolizes his being made a sharer in the consecration of Jesus Christ, who was anointed by the Holy Spirit (RM, Chrism Mass, 7–8; RM, Chrism Mass, Preface [=RM, Ritual Masses, For the Conferral of Holy Orders, For the Ordination of a Bishop, A [=B], Preface; RM, Ritual Masses, For the Conferral of Holy Orders, For the Ordination of Priests, A [=B], Preface; RM, Ritual Masses, For the Conferral of Holy Orders, For the Ordination of Deacons, A [=B], Preface]; *cf.* CCC 1294; *cf. also* CCC 739; 782–786; 1141; 1241).

- By the anointing of the Holy Spirit in the Sacrament of Holy Orders, the priest is signed with a special character that configures him to Christ in such a way that he is able to act in the person of Christ the head (CCC 1563; *cf.* CCC 1558; 1581; HOLY ORDERS: *Symbols*: Head of the Body). This indelible character is oftentimes symbolized by "the seal," a symbol similar to that of anointing (CCC 698; 1293–1296; 1581–1584; 1597 *cf.* HOLY ORDERS: *Symbols*: Seal).

- The anointing of the hands of the priest symbolizes his "distinctive participation in Christ's priesthood" (RO 113).
- The chrism which consecrates the baptized with the generous and rich grace of the common priesthood "has richer effects" in the Sacrament of Holy Orders (LH, Leo the Great [Nov 10], 2R: Leo the Great, Sermo 4, 1–2: PL 54, 148–149; cf. also CCC 901).
- As Christ was consecrated by the Father and sent into the world, giving himself to redeem mankind, so priests are consecrated by the anointing of the Holy Spirit and sent by Christ into the world, so that, putting an end to sin in their selfish nature they may give themselves wholly to the service of mankind and grow in holiness (LH, Common of Pastors, 2R, For a priest: Vatican II, Presbyterorum ordinis Ch. 3, 12).
- The anointing with chrism in the Sacrament of Holy Orders symbolizes the Holy Spirit (CCC 695), and is "a sign of the special anointing of the Holy Spirit who makes their ministry fruitful" (CCC 1574).
- While anointing the hands of the newly ordained priest, the bishop says, "The Lord Jesus Christ, whom the Father anointed with the Holy Spirit and power, guard and preserve you, that you may sanctify the Christian people and offer sacrifice to God" (RO 161 [=ROP 24]). While this is taking place, the faithful sing Psalm 110 (ROP 25 [=RO 162]).
- Before the laying on of hands and prayer of ordination of a new bishop, the ordaining bishop prays, "pour out upon this your servant the power of your blessing flowing from the horn of priestly grace" (RO 43 [=ROB 22]).
- While the ordaining bishop anoints the head of the newly ordained bishop, he prays, "May God, who has made you a sharer in the High Priesthood of Christ, pour upon you the oil of mystical anointing and make you fruitful with an abundance of spiritual blessings" (RO 49 [=ROB 28]).
- The liturgy interprets the lives of St. Cyril, a priest, and St. Methodius, a bishop, in light of God's anointing of David, where his anointing is associated with God's protecting strength accompanying him (LH, OT, St. Cyril and Methodius [Feb 14], 2R, Resp [Ps. 89:20–22; Jer. 3:15]; cf. also CCC 2579).
- The first reading for the ordination of priests or bishops is optionally Isa. 61:1–3abcd: "The spirit of the Lord God is upon me, because the Lord has anointed me . . ." (Lectionary 770; RO 347).

• The Entrance Antiphon in the ordination of bishops is "The Spirit of the Lord is upon me, for he has anointed me and sent me to preach the good news to the poor, to heal the broken hearted" (RM, Ritual Masses, For the Ordination of a Bishop, A [=B], Entrance Antiphon [Luke 4:18]; *cf. also* RM, St. Vincent de Paul [Sep 27], Entrance Antiphon [Luke 4:18]; RM, Commons, Common of Pastors, For Pastors, B, 2, Entrance Antiphon [Luke 4:18]; RM, Masses and Prayers for Various Needs and Occasions, For Holy Church, For Priests, Entrance Antiphon [Luke 4:18]; *cf. also* CCC 713–714).

BOOK OF THE GOSPELS

OT Background: Exod. 3:10–15; Judg. 6:14; 2 Sam. 12:1, 25; Ps. 105:26; Isa. 6:8; Jer. 1:7; 26:12, 15; Ezek. 2:3

NT Background: Matt. 4:4; Luke 8:21; John 1:1; 3:34; 8:47; 10:35; Acts 6:2; 13:5, 26, 46; 15:7; 17:13; 18:11; 20:32; Rom. 3:4; 2 Cor. 2:17; 4:2; Eph. 6:17; Col. 1:25; 3:16; 4:3; 1 Thess. 2:13; 2 Tim. 2:9, 15; Titus 1:3; Heb. 4:12; 13:7; 1 Pet. 1:23; 4:10–11; 2 Pet. 1:20; 1 John 2:5; Rev. 1:1–2, 9; 6:9; 20:4; 22:18–19

Catechism Background: 1574

Related: HOLY ORDERS: *Types*: Levites; High Priest; *Symbols*: Servant; Steward

Deacons

• The giving of the Book of the Gospels to the newly ordained deacon symbolizes the mission he has just received to proclaim the Gospel of Christ (CCC 1574).

• The giving of the Book of the Gospels "signifies the deacon's office of proclaiming the Gospel in liturgical celebrations and of preaching the faith of the Church in word and in deed (RO 188).

• The newly ordained deacon receives the Book of the Gospels from the hands of the bishop, who says, "Receive the Gospel of Christ, whose herald you have become: believe what you read, teach what you believe, and practice what you teach" (RO 238 [=ROD 24]).

Bishops

- Immediately before the prayer of ordination, the ordaining bishop "receives the Book of Gospels from one of the deacons and places it open upon the head of the Bishop-elect; two deacons, standing on the right and on the left of the Bishop-elect, hold the Book of Gospels above his head until the end of the Prayer of Ordination" (RO 46 [=ROB 25]; the Prayer of Ordination is in RO 47 [=ROB 26]).

- Immediately after the prayer of ordination, the deacons remove the Book of the Gospels from above the head of the newly ordained bishop (RO 48 [=ROB 27]). After the bishop's head is anointed with chrism (RO 49 [=ROB 28]), the celebrating bishop hands the Book of the Gospels to the newly ordained bishop, saying, "Receive the Gospel and preach the word of God with all patience and sound teaching" (RO 50 [=ROB 29]). The giving of the Book of the Gospels to the newly ordained bishop symbolizes "his apostolic mission to proclaim the Word of God" (CCC 1574).

- Both the ordination of the bishop with the open Book of the Gospels above his head as well as the giving of the Book of the Gospels "illustrate that the faithful preaching of the word of God is the pre-eminent obligation of the office of Bishop" (RO 26).

- The ordination of the bishop under the open Book of the Gospels could also be understood as a visible reminder that the bishop is "under" the Gospel that Christ entrusted to the Church. The bishop-elect, in fact, just publically promised to "preach the Gospel of Christ with constancy and fidelity," to "guard the deposit of faith," and to remain one with the Church "under the authority of the successor of Saint Peter" (RO 40 [=ROB 19]; cf. 2 Cor. 2:17; 4:2; 2 Tim. 2:15; Titus 1:3; 1 Pet. 4:10–11; 2 Pet. 1:20).

INVESTITURE WITH RING, MITER, AND PASTORAL STAFF

OT Background:
Ring: Gen. 41:42; Esther 3:10, 12; 8:2, 8, 10; Isa. 3:21; Jer. 22:24; Hag. 2:23
Miter: Exod. 28:4, 36–39; 29:6; 39:27–31, 31; Lev. 8:9; 16:4; Job 29:14; Ezek. 21:26; Zech. 3:5

Pastoral Staff: Exod. 4:2–5, 20–21; 7:9–10, 17; 8:5, 16–17; 9:23; 10:13; 14:16; 17:5–6, 9; Lev. 27:32; Num. 17:8–10; 20:8–11; 1 Sam. 17:39–40; Ps. 2:9; 23:4; 89:32; Isa. 10:24; 11:4; Ezek. 20:37; 34:23–24

NT Background:

Ring: Matt. 10:40; Luke 10:16; 15:22; John 13:20; 1 Tim. 4:14

Pastoral Staff: Mark 6:8; 1 Cor. 4:21; Heb. 1:8; 9:4; 11:21; Rev. 2:27; 12:5; 19:15

Catechism Background: 1558; 1574

Related: HOLY ORDERS: *Types:* Priesthood; High Priest; *Symbols:* Head of the Body; Seal; Shepherd

In General

• The ring, the miter, and the pastoral staff symbolize the pastoral office (Rite of Blessing of the Pontifical Insignia).

Ring

• In the Old Covenant, apart from their use as jewelry, rings symbolized authority and often were used as seals (*cf.* Gen. 41:42; Esther 3:10, 12; 8:2, 8, 10; Isa. 3:21; Jer. 22:24; Hag. 2:23).

• The giving of the ring "symbolizes the Bishop's fidelity to the Bride of God, the Church" (RO 26).

• The episcopal ring is given to the bishop as a "seal of fidelity" to the bride of Christ, the holy Church. (RO 51 [=ROB 30]; *cf.* CCC 1574; *cf. also* MATRIMONY: *Symbols:* Wedding Ring).

• The wearing of the episcopal ring symbolizes being "adorned with undefiled faith," with which the newly ordained bishop is called to "preserve unblemished the bride of God, the holy Church" (RO 51 [=ROB 30]).

Pallium

• The pallium, which is "brought from the tomb of St. Peter," signifies the archbishop's "authority as metropolitan." It is a "symbol of unity, a sign of communion with the Apostolic See, a bond of charity, and a spur to courage" (RO 52).

Miter

- In the Old Covenant, the high priest wore a miter with the text "Holy to the Lord" (*cf.* Exod. 28:4, 36–39; 29:6; 39:27–31; Lev. 8:9; 16:4; Zech. 3:5). The miter also was worn by the king Zedekiah (Ezek. 21:26). Job uses the miter as a symbol of righteousness (Job 29:14).
- The miter, together with the pastoral staff, symbolizes the bishop's "office as shepherd of the Lord's flock" (CCC 1574).
- The giving of the miter symbolizes the bishop's resolve to pursue holiness (RO 26).
- The consecrating bishop places the miter on the head of the newly ordained bishop, saying, "Receive the miter, and may the splendor of holiness shine forth in you, so that when the chief shepherd appears you may deserve to receive from him an unfading crown of glory" (RO 53).

Pastoral Staff

- In the Old Covenant, the staff of shepherds symbolized the care and protection that the shepherd gave the sheep (*cf.* Ps. 23:4). The staffs of Moses and Aaron were used by God to work miracles (*cf.* Exod. 4:2–5, 20–21; 7:9–10, 17; 8:5, 16–17; 9:23; 10:13; 14:16; 17:5–6, 9; Num. 20:8–11). Later, the staff of Aaron budded, as a sign from God of the authenticity of his priesthood (*cf.* Num. 17:8–10; Heb. 9:4). David, a shepherd, defeated Goliath with only a staff, five stones, and a sling (1 Sam. 17:39–40). The staff also indicates God's authority and punishment for sin (*cf.* Ps. 2:9; 89:32; Isa. 11:4).
- In the New Covenant, the staff indicates God's authority (*cf.* Heb. 1:8; Rev. 2:27; 12:5; 19:15). This authority is shared in by St. Paul, who hopes to continue to use it gently (1 Cor. 4:21).
- The handing on of the pastoral staff "signifies the office of guiding and governing the Church" entrusted to the bishop (RO 26).
- The miter, together with the pastoral staff, symbolizes the bishop's "office as shepherd of the Lord's flock" (CCC 1574; *cf.* RO 54 [=ROB 32]).

JOINED HANDS BETWEEN THOSE OF THE BISHOP

Catechism Background: 1567

Related: HOLY ORDERS: *Types*: High Priest; Levites; Priesthood

- The priest and deacon promise respect and obedience to the bishop and to his successors. While doing so, and symbolizing this promise, the priest and deacon place their joined hands between those of the bishop (RO 153 [=ROP 16]; RO 229 [=ROD 16]).
- The promise of obedience to the bishop and the subsequent kiss of peace from the bishop "mean that the bishop considers them his co-workers, his sons, his brothers and his friends, and that they in return owe him love and obedience" (CCC 1567).

PRESENTATION OF THE PATEN AND CHALICE

OT Background:

Paten: Gen. 14:18; Exod. 12:8, 15–20; 13:6–7; 16:3–4, 8, 12, 15, 21–23, 31–35; 23:15, 18; 40:22–23; Num. 4:7; 9:11; 11:6–9; 28:17; Deut. 8:3, 9, 16; 16:3; Josh. 5:12; 1 Sam. 21:5, 7; 2 Sam. 6:19; Neh. 9:20; Ps. 78:24; 105:40; Wisd. 16:20; Isa. 30:20; 55:2, 10–11;

Chalice: Ps. 16:5; 23:5; 75:9; 116:13; Sir. 50:15; Isa. 51:17, 22; Jer. 25:15, 17, 28; 49:12; Hab. 2:16

NT Background:

Paten: Matt. 6:11; 26:17, 26; Mark 8:12, 22; Luke 11:3; 22:7, 19; 24:30, 35; John 6:31–71; Acts 2:42, 46; 20:7, 11; 1 Cor. 10:16–17; 11:23–24, 26–28

Chalice: Matt. 20:22–23; 26:27–29, 39, 42; Mark 10:38–39; 14:23–25, 36; Luke 22:17–18, 20, 42; John 18:11; 1 Cor. 10:16, 21; 11:25–28; Rev. 14:10; 16:19; 18:6

Catechism Background: 607; 612; 1148; 1334; 1339; **1350**; 1365–1367; **1574**

Related: HOLY ORDERS: *Types*: Melchizedek; Priesthood; *Symbols*: Head of the Body

- The presentation of the paten and the chalice signifies the priest's "office of presiding at the celebration of the Eucharist and of following Christ crucified" (RO 113).
- The bishop presents the newly ordained a "paten holding the bread and a chalice containing the wine mixed with water," which have been brought up by the faithful, saying "Receive the offering of the holy people to be rendered to God" (RO 163 [=ROP 26]; *cf.* CCC 1574).

• The paten and the chalice also point to the mystery that is celebrated in the Mass, and that the priest is called to conform his own life to: the death and Resurrection of Jesus Christ. The bishop tells the newly ordained priest when he hands him the paten and the chalice: "Understand what you do, imitate what you celebrate, and conform your life to the mystery of the Lord's cross" (RO 163 [=ROP 26]).

SEAL

OT Background:

Used literally: Gen. 38:18, 25; 41:42; Exod. 28:11, 21, 36; 39:6, 14, 30; 1 Kings 21:8; Neh. 9:38; 10:1; Tob. 7:14 (RSV = Tob. 7:13 NAB, NRSV); 9:5; Esther 3:10, 12; 8:2, 8, 10; Sir. 38:27; 42:6; Jer. 32:10–11, 14, 44; Dan. 6:17; 14:11, 14, 17; 2 Macc. 2:5

Used symbolically: Gen. 4:15; Deut. 32:34; Job 9:7; 14:17; 37:7; 38:14; 41:15; Song 4:12; 8:6; Wisd. 2:5; Sir. 22:27; 32:5–6; Isa. 8:16; 29:11–12; Jer. 22:24; Ezek. 9:4–6; Dan. 8:26; 9:24; 12:4, 9; Hag. 2:23

NT Background: Matt. 27:66; John 3:33; 6:27; Acts 2:1–4, 38; 6:6; 13:3; Rom. 4:11; 8:29; 1 Cor. 9:2; 2 Cor. 1:21–22; Eph. 1:13–14; 4:30; 1 Tim. 4:14; 2 Tim. 1:6–7; 2:19; Rev. 5:1–10; 6:1–12; 7:2–8; 8:1; 9:4; 10:4; 13:16–17; 14:9, 11; 16:2; 19:20; 20:3–4; 22:10

Catechism Background: 698; 1121; 1183; 1558; 1559; 1563; 1568; 1574; 1582–1583; 1597; 1955

Related: BAPTISM: *Types:* Circumcision; Anointing of Priests, Prophets, and Kings; *Symbols:* Seal; CONFIRMATION: *Symbols:* Anointing; Seal; Sign of the Cross; PENANCE: *Symbols:* Seal; HOLY ORDERS: *Types:* Anointing of Priests, Prophets, and Kings; *Symbols:* Anointing; Investiture with Ring, Miter, and Pastoral Staff; MATRIMONY: *Symbols:* Seal

Note: *For the topic of "Seal" in general, cf.* CONFIRMATION: *Symbols:* Seal.

• The Sacrament of Holy Orders imprints an indelible character or "seal" which configures the ordained to Christ and to the Church (CCC 1121; *cf.* CCC 698; 1582–1583; 1597; *cf. also* CCC 1183; HOLY ORDERS: *Symbols:* Anointing).

- Episcopal ordination impresses character "'in such wise that bishops, in an eminent and visible manner, take the place of Christ himself, teacher, shepherd, and priest, and act as his representative (in Eius persona agant)' (Lumen Gentium 21)" (CCC 1558).
- Priestly ordination impresses character which configures "'to Christ the priest in such a way that they [the priests] are able to act in the person of Christ the head' (PO 2)" (CCC 1563).
- Priests in virtue of the priestly character are bound together by an intimate sacramental brotherhood, forming "'one priestly body in the diocese to which they are attached under their own bishop' (PO 8)" (CCC 1568). Similarly, bishops are joined in the episcopal college (CCC 1559).
- For the episcopal ring as a seal, *cf.* HOLY ORDERS: *Symbols*: Investiture with Ring, Miter, and Pastoral Staff.

SYMBOLS OF THE ORDAINED MINISTER

FATHER

OT Background:

God as father: Deut. 1:31; 8:5; 10:18; 32:6; Ps. 68:5; 103:13; Prov. 3:12; Isa. 63:16; 64:8; Mal. 2:10

Messiah as father: Isa. 9:6 [Isa. 9:5 NAB]

Human fatherhood: Gen. 45:8; Deut. 6:7; 32:7; Josh. 24:15; 2 Kings 2:12; 6:21; Prov. 1:8; 4:1; 6:20; 13:1; 15:5; Job 1:5; 29:16; Ps. 44:1; 78:3; 127:4–5; Isa. 22:20–22

NT Background: Matt. 16:19 (in light of Isa. 22:21–22); 23:9; Luke 15:11– 32; John 6:32; 14:9; 1 Cor. 4:14–15, 17; 8:6; 2 Cor. 12:14; Gal. 4:19; Eph. 3:14–15; 4:6; Phil. 2:22; Col. 1:15; 1 Thess. 2:11; 1 Tim. 1:2, 18; 2 Tim. 1:2; 2:1; Titus 1:4; Philem. 10; 1 Pet. 5:13; 1 John 2:1; 3 John 4

Catechism Background: 239; 270; **896**; 1186; **1458**; **1465**; **1549**; **1554**; **1586**; 2214; 2367

Related: HOLY ORDERS: *Symbol*: Head of the Body; Shepherd

Spiritual Fatherhood in General

- God is the source and origin of all fatherhood (*cf. for example* Matt. 23:9; 1 Cor. 8:6; Eph. 3:14–15; 4:6; CCC 239; 270; 2214; 2367; RM, St. Andrew

Dũng-Lac and Companion Martyrs [Nov 24], Collect [=LH, St. Andrew Dũng-Lac and Companion Martyrs [Nov 24], OR, Prayer]; RM, Ritual Masses, For the Blessing of an Abbot or an Abbess, 1, Solemn Blessing; LH, Lent.2.Tu, EP, Magn).

- Joseph says that he is a "father" to Pharaoh (Gen. 45:8).
- Job calls himself a "father" to the poor (Job 29:16).
- Abraham is:
  - the "father of all who believe" (*cf. for example* Rom. 4:11; CCC 146; LH, Adv.2.Th, 2R: St. Peter Chrysologus, Sermo 147: PL 52, 594–595; LH, CT.Epiphany, 2R: St. Leo the Great, Sermo 3 in Epiphania Domini, 1–3.5: PL 54, 240–244);
  - "father in faith" (*cf. for example* RM, Eucharistic Prayer I, 93; RM, Appendix I, The Nativity of Our Lord Jesus Christ from the Roman Martyrology; LH, ET.2.We, 2R: St. Leo the Great, Sermo 12 de Passione, 3, 6–7: PL 54, 355–357);
  - also the father of Christians (*cf. for example* Acts 7:2; Rom. 4:16; James 2:21; CCC 2569).
  - He is the "father of many nations" (*cf. for example* Gen. 17:5; Sir. 44:19; Rom. 4:18; RM, Easter Vigil, 25; CCC 59; 1819; LH, CT.Epiphany, 2R: St. Leo the Great, Sermo 3 in Epiphania Domini, 1–3.5: PL 54, 240–244; LH, ET.2.We, 2R: St. Leo the Great, Sermo 12 de Passione, 3, 6–7: PL 54, 355–357; LH, Lent.1.We, 2R: Aphrahat, Dem. 11, On Circumcision, 11–12: PS 1, 498–503).
  - Having Abraham as father, in fact, is different from and greater than biological descent from him (*cf. for example* Luke 3:8; John 8:39).
- Isaac is the father of Christians (Rom. 9:10).
- King David is "father" of the Israelites (*cf. for example* Mark 11:10) and of Christians (*cf. for example* Acts 4:25; LH, ET.Psalter.3.Fr, EP, Ant2).
- Elisha calls Elijah his "father" (2 Kings 2:12).
- The King of Israel calls Elisha "father" (2 Kings 6:21).
- God calls Eliakim a "father" to the inhabitants of Jerusalem and of Judah (Isa. 22:20–21).
- The visible Church "is a symbol of the Father's house," open and welcoming, the house of all God's children (*cf. for example* CCC 1186).

Spiritual Fatherhood of Jesus Christ

• Jesus Christ is father (*cf. for example* Isa. 9:6 [Isa. 9:5 NAB]; LH, Jan 3, MP, 3rd intercession; LH, Jan 3, MP, 5th intercession; LH, ET.2.Mo, 2R: Pseudo-Chrysostom, Ancient Easter Homily: PG 59, 723–724; LH, ET.4.Tu, 2R: St. Peter Chrysologus, Sermo 108: PL 52, 499–500).

• Jesus Christ is father of Christians through his life-giving marriage with the Church (*cf. for example* LH, OT.19.Fr, 2R: St. Pacian, Sermon on Baptism, 5–6: PL 13, 1092–1093).

Spiritual Fatherhood of the Apostles

• St. Peter (and his successors) is the father of all Christians (LH, St. Gregory VII [May 25], 2R: St. Gregory VII, Letter 64 extra Registrum: PL 148, 709–710; *cf. also* LH, St. Louis [Aug 25], 2R: St. Louis, From a spiritual testament to his son: Acta Sanctorum Augusti 5 [1868], 546; *cf. also* Matt. 16:19 in light of Isa. 22:21–22 where Eliakim is called "father" to Jerusalem and Judah).

• St. Paul often refers to himself as a spiritual father:
  ▪ He became the father of the Corinthians through the Gospel (1 Cor. 4:14–15; *cf.* 2 Cor. 12:14).
  ▪ He is a spiritual parent to the Galatians (Gal. 4:19; *cf.* LH, OT.5.Fr, 2R: St. Augustine, On Galatians, 37–38: PL 35, 2131–2132).
  ▪ St. Paul, St. Timothy, and St. Silvanus are spiritual fathers to the Church in Thessalonica (1 Thess. 2:11; *cf.* 1 Thess. 1:1).
  ▪ He is the spiritual father of St. Timothy (1 Cor. 4:17; Phil. 2:22; 1 Tim. 1:2, 18; 2 Tim. 1:2; 2:1).
  ▪ He is the spiritual father of St. Titus (Titus 1:4).
  ▪ He is the spiritual father of Onesimus (Philem. 10).
  ▪ He is a father to Christians today (LH, St. Anthony Zaccaria [Jul 5], 2R: St. Anthony Zaccaria, Sermon to fellow members of his society, J.A. Gabutio, Historia Congregationis Clericorum Regularium S. Pauli, 1, 8).

• St. Peter is the spiritual father of St. Mark (1 Pet. 5:13).

• St. John is the spiritual father of the recipients of his letter (1 John 2:1; 3 John 4).

Spiritual Fatherhood of Bishops

- The bishop is a living image ("typos") of God the Father (LH, OT.27.Tu, 2R: St. Ignatius of Antioch, Letter to the Trallians, 1, 1–3, 2; 4, 1–2; 6, 1; 7, 1–8, 1: Funk 1, 203–209; RO 39 [=ROB 18]; CCC 1549, citing St. Ignatius of Antioch, Letter to the Trallians 3, 1: SCh 10, 96 and Ad Magn. 6, 1: SCh 10, 82–84; *cf.* CCC 1554; compare with Col. 1:15 and John 14:9).

- When the faithful and priests defer to the bishop, it is "not to him but to the Father of Jesus Christ, the bishop of all" that they defer. If a man tries to deceive the bishop he can see, it is as if he were trying to deceive the bishop he cannot see. He will have to reckon with God who knows the secrets of the heart (LH, OT.16.Su, 2R: St. Ignatius of Antioch, Letter to the Magnesians 1, 1–5, 2: Funk 1, 191–195).

- The bishop has been chosen by the Father to rule over God's family, whom he should love as a father and a brother (RO 39 [=ROB 18]; *cf. also* RO 40, 6th question [=ROB 19, 6th question]).

- Episcopal ordination gives the grace of "the governing Spirit" (RO 47 [=ROB 26]), i.e. the grace "to guide and defend his Church with strength and prudence as a father and pastor" (CCC 1586; *cf. also* RO 39 [=ROB 18]).

- Bishops should be true fathers of their flock, uniting and molding the entire family (LH, St. Turibius de Mongrovejo [Mar 23], 2R: Vatican II, Christus Dominus 12–13.16).

- The bishop should promote the welfare of his subjects as his very own children. The faithful should be attached to the bishop as Christ was to the Father (CCC 896).

Spiritual Fatherhood of Priests

- In the Sacrament of Baptism, through the ministry of priests the soul is reborn as a child of God (LH, ET.6.Mo, 2R: Didymus of Alexandria, On the Trinity, 2, 12: PG 39, 667–674), in such a way that the priest, like St. Paul, can say "In Christ I have begotten you" (1 Cor. 4:15) (LH, OT.19.Fr, 2R: St. Pacian, Sermon on Baptism, 5–6: PL 13, 1092–1093).

- In the Sacrament of Penance, the priest fulfills the ministry of the Father, who awaits his prodigal son and welcomes him home on his return (CCC

1465; 1458; *cf.* Luke 15:11–32; *cf. also* LH, Lent.4.We, 2R: St. Maximus the Confessor, Letter 11: PG 91, 454–455).

- As Jesus did nothing apart from his Father to whom he was united, so the faithful should do nothing apart from their bishop and priests (LH, OT.16. Mo, 2R: St. Ignatius of Antioch, Letter to the Magnesians, 6, 1–9, 2: Funk 1, 195–199).

- The preaching of a priest should be that of a compassionate and loving father, not dry and abstract (LH, St. Vincent Ferrer [Apr 5], 2R: St. Vincent Ferrer, Treatise on the Spiritual Life, Ch. 13: ed. Garganta-Forcada, p. 513–514).

- St. John Bosco, St. Vincent de Paul, St. Martin of Tours, St. Ignatius of Loyola, St. Francis Xavier, and other bishops or priests in the liturgy are referred to as "father" (*cf. for example* RM, St. John Bosco [Jan 31], Collect; LH, St. John Bosco [Jan 31], OR, Prayer; LH, St. Isaac Jogues and St. John de Brébeuf [Oct 19], 2R: St. John de Brébeuf, Spiritual Diary: The Jesuit Relations and Allied Documents, The Burrow Brothers Co, Cleveland 1898, 164.166; LH, St. Martin of Tours [Nov 11], 2R: Sulpicius Severus, Letter 3, 6.9–10.11.14–17.21: SC 133, 336–344; LH, St. Vincent de Paul [Sep 27], 2R, Resp [1 Cor. 9:19, 22; Job 29:15–16]).

- St. John Bosco exhorts priests who are in charge of orphanages to regard the boys in their care as sons, as true fathers, as the Lord did with his apostles (LH, St. John Bosco [Jan 31]: St. John Bosco, Letter, Turin 1959, 4, 201–203).

HEAD OF THE BODY

OT Background: Gen. 2:23–24; Deut. 28:13; 2 Sam. 22:44; Ps. 18:43; Isa. 9:14–16; 29:10

NT Background: Rom. 12:4–5; 1 Cor. 11:3–16; 12:12–31; Eph. 1:22–23; 4:15–16; 5:23–33; Col. 1:18–20; 2:9–10, 18–19

Catechism Background: 504; 568; 616; 661; 666; 669; 686; **739**; 747; 753; 774; 782; 789; 792–795; **796**; 797; 807; 830–831; 846; **875**; 877; 879–886; 935; 947; 957; 963; 973; 1039; 1043; 1070; **1119**; 1140; **1142**; **1188**; 1348; 1368; 1369; 1372; **1462**; **1548**; **1549**; **1552**; 1553; 1559; **1561**; **1563**; 1566; **1581**; **1591**; 1691; 1698; 1997; 2045; 2616; 2637; 2782

Related: HOLY ORDERS: *Types:* High Priest; Anointing of Priests, Prophets, and Kings; *Symbols:* Father; Investiture with Ring, Miter, and Pastoral Staff; Shepherd; MATRIMONY: *Symbols:* One Flesh

Jesus Christ is Head of the Body, the Church

• Jesus Christ is the head of the body, the Church (*cf. for example* 1 Cor. 11:3; Eph. 1:22–23; 4:15–16; 5:22–23; Col. 1:18–20; 2:9–10, 18–19; CCC 504; 568; 616; 661; 666; 669; 586; 739; 747; 753; 774; 782; 789; 792–797; 807; 830–831; 846; 947; 957; 963; 973; 1039; 1043; 1070; 1119; 1140; 1348; 1368; 1372; 1561; 1563; 1566; 1581; 1691; 1698; 1997; 2045; 2616; 2637; 2782; LH, OT.3.Su, 2R: Vatican II, Sacrosanctum Concilium 7–8.106; LH, Adv.2.Sa, 2R: Bl. Isaac of Stella, Sermo 51: PL 194, 1862–1863, 1865; LH, Dec31, 2R: St. Leo the Great, Sermo 6 in Nativitate Domini, 2–3, 5: PL 54, 213–216; *cf. also* LH, OT.7.Mo, 2R: St. Gregory of Nyssa, Homily on Ecclesiastes, 5: PG 44, 683–686; LH, St. Nereus and St. Achilleus [May 12], 2R: St. Augustine, Commentary on the Psalms, 61, 4: CCL 39, 773–775; LH, St. John Eudes [Aug 19], 2R: St. John Eudes, On the Admirable Heart of Jesus, Book 1, 5: Opera Omnia 6, 107.113–115; LH, All Saints [Nov 1], 2R: St. Bernard, Sermo 2: Opera Omnia, Edit. Cisterc. 5 [1968], 364–368; *cf. also* Rom. 12:4–5; 1 Cor. 12:12–13).

• When the Church celebrates the liturgy, it is the Mystical Body in its fullness that prays, that is, Jesus Christ as head together with his body, the Church (CCC 1070; 1119; 1140; 1187; 1368; 1372; 1552–1553; LH, OT.3.Su, 2R: Vatican II, Sacrosanctum Concilium 7–8.106; *cf.* LH, ET.6.Fr, MP, After the Ascension, 4th intercession; *cf. also* CCC 2616; 2637; LH, OT.23.Fr, 2R: Bl. Isaac of Stella, Sermo 11: PL 194, 1728–1729; LH, Lent.5.We, 2R: St. Augustine, Commentary on the Psalms, 85, 1: CCL 39, 1176–1177; LH, ET.5.Fr, 2R: Blessed Isaac of Stella, Sermo 42: PL 194, 1831–1832; LH, OT.3.Su, 2R, Resp).

Bishops and Priests Act in the Person of Christ the Head

• The priest shares "in the office of Christ, Head and Shepherd" (RO 151 [=ROP 14]; LH, Lent.2.Su, EP2, 2nd intercession [=LH, Lent.4.Su, EP2, 2nd intercession]; *cf. also* CCC 1119–1121; LH, Common of Pastors, 2R, For a priest: Vatican II, Presbyterorum ordinis Ch. 3, 12).

- The Sacrament of Holy Orders allows the ordained "to represent Christ as head of the Body" (CCC 1188; cf. 1552; 1581). The ordained priests and bishops receive from Christ the mission and faculty to act *in persona Christi Capitis* (in the person of Christ the Head) (CCC 875; 1142; 1348; 1563; 1591; cf. also CCC 935).
- Through the Sacrament of Holy Orders the ordained minister is enabled to represent "Christ, Head of the Church, in his triple office of priest, prophet, and king" (CCC 1581; cf. also CCC 1548).
- *In persona Christi Capitis* means that in "the ecclesial service of the ordained minister, it is Christ himself who is present to his Church as Head of his Body, Shepherd of his flock, high priest of the redemptive sacrifice, Teacher of Truth" (CCC 1548).
- In the sacrifice of the Mass, Jesus Christ is present in the person of the minister (LH, OT.3.Su, 2R: Vatican II, Sacrosanctum Concilium 7–8.106). The ordained minister is, as it were, an "icon" of Christ the priest (CCC 1142; LH, Common of Pastors, 2R, For a priest: Vatican II, Presbyterorum ordinis Ch. 3, 12).

Bishops and Priests as Visible Head

- Christ's presence as head of the Church is made visible through the ministry of bishops and priests (CCC 1549).
- The bishop is the visible head of a particular church (CCC 1462; 1594; cf. CCC 886).
- The Eucharist celebrated by the bishop is particularly significant as an expression of the Church praying together with "the one who represents Christ, the Good Shepherd and Head of his Church, presiding (Cf. SC 41; Lumen Gentium 26)" (CCC 1561; cf. also CCC 1369).
- As such, the bishop is "the moderator of the penitential discipline (Cf. Lumen Gentium 26 § 3)." Priests receive the commission to celebrate the sacrament of Penance from the bishop (CCC 1462).
- The reform of the Church begins with the reform of the bishops and priests, lest the Church seem to demand of the body what is not found in the head (LH, St. John Leonardi [Oct 9], 2R: St. John Leonardi, Letter to Pope Paul V: in archivo Ordinis Clericorum Regularium Matris Dei).
- The bishop of Rome is the common head of the Christian faithful (CCC 899; cf. CCC 885), and the head of the college of bishops (CCC 877;

879–885; 891; 936; 1559; *cf. also* LH, St. Thomas Becket [Dec 29], 2R: St. Thomas Becket, Letter 74: PL 190, 533–536).

• Christ entrusted the unity of his flock to St. Peter, choosing to make St. Peter one with himself, like bridegroom and bride, and like head and body (LH, OT.25.Fr, 2R: St. Augustine, Sermon On Pastors 46, 29–30: CCL 41, 555–557).

• The martyrs are precious in the eyes of the Lord. Two of them, St. Peter and St. Paul, have been raised by the grace of God to be like two eyes (as models and support for our faith) that bring light to the body whose head is Christ (LH, Dedication of the Churches of Peter and Paul [Nov 18], 2R: St. Leo the Great, Sermo 82, in natali apostolorum Petri et Pauli 1, 6–7: PL 54, 426–428).

Judge

OT Background:[1]
God as Judge: Gen. 18:25; Judg. 11:27; Job 23:7; Ps. 7:11; 50:6; 68:5; 94:2; Isa. 33:22
Human judges: Exod. 18:13, 22; 22:9; 28:30; Deut. 1:16; 16:18; 19:17; Judg. 2:16; 1 Sam. 8:20; 2 Sam. 15:4; 1 Chron. 23:4; 2 Chron. 19:5–7, 8–11; Ezra 7:25; Isa. 1:26; Ezek. 44:24; Hag. 2:11

NT Background:
God / Jesus as Judge: Matt. 25:31–46; Luke 12:14; John 5:22, 30; 8:15–16; 9:39; 12:47; 16:11; Acts 10:42; 17:31; 2 Tim. 4:1, 8; Heb. 12:23; 13:4; James 4:12; 5:9; Rev. 18:20; 20:12
Human judges: Matt. 16:19; 18:18; 19:28; Luke 22:29–30; John 20:22–23; 1 Cor. 5:12; 6:2–6; Rev. 20:4

Catechism Background: 1465; 1470
Related: HOLY ORDERS: *Symbol*: Father; Head of the Body; Physician; Sea Captain; Steward

• In the Sacrament of Penance, the priest fulfills the ministry of the "just and impartial judge whose judgment is both just and merciful. The priest is the sign and the instrument of God's merciful love for the sinner" (CCC 1465; *cf. also* John 20:22–23; CCC 1470).

---

1 This topic is extremely common in the Bible. A sampling of Old Testament and New Testament background texts is presented here.

- In order that the priest may act as a wise judge, he must "acquire the needed knowledge and prudence by constant study under the guidance of the Church's magisterium and especially by praying fervently to God. For the discernment of spirits is indeed a deep knowledge of God's working in the human heart, a gift of the Spirit, and an effect of charity" (RP 10a).

LABORER OF THE HARVEST

OT Background: Lev. 6:16, 26; 7:6, 31–32; Num. 5:9–10; 18:8–31; 19:16; Deut. 18:1–5; 24:14–15; 25:4 (*cf.* 1 Cor. 9:8–12); Prov. 27:18; Song 1:6; 8:12

NT Background: Matt. 9:37–38; 10:10; 20:1–16; Luke 10:2, 7; John 4:35–37; 1 Cor. 9:4–18; 1 Tim. 5:17–18

Catechism Background: 543; 765; 2122; 2611

Related: HOLY ORDERS: *Types*: Levites; Priesthood; *Symbols*: Servant; Steward

- Jesus Christ tells his disciples to pray to the Lord of the harvest that he send laborers for the harvest, for "The harvest is plentiful, but the laborers are few; pray therefore the Lord of the harvest to send out laborers into his harvest" (Matt. 9:37–38; Luke 10:2).
- Jesus Christ tells his disciples that the laborer deserves his food (Matt. 10:10; Luke 10:7; *cf.* John 4:35–37; 1 Cor. 9:4–18; 1 Tim. 5:17–18).
- Regarding the priests and bishops as laborers of the harvest (LH, OT.27. Sa, 2R: St. Gregory the Great, Homily on the Gospels, 17, 3, 14: PL 76, 1139–1140.1146, making reference to Matt. 9:37–38, Luke 10:2, and Song 1:6; similar is LH, St. Luke [Oct 18], 2R: St. Gregory the Great, Homily on the Gospels, 17, 1–3: PL 76, 1139):
  - It is important to pray to the Lord of the harvest to send out laborers for the harvest (*cf.* Matt. 9:37–38; Luke 10:2).
  - The harvest in fact is great but the laborers are few.
  - There are so many priests, but so few are true laborers of the harvest; many do not fulfill the demands of their office.
  - Pray therefore that those who already are priests or bishops preach the Word of God without fear, correcting and guiding the flock, and do not become absorbed by external affairs.

- Regarding laborers for the harvest (LH, St. Thomas Becket [Dec 29], 2R: St. Thomas Becket, Letter 74: PL 190, 533–536):
  - The faith has spread so far, and there are so many people! Many are needed to plant, and many to water; many are needed to reap and gather into the granary of the Lord.
  - Regardless of who plants and waters, "God gives no harvest unless what he plants is the faith of Peter, and unless he himself assents to Peter's teaching."
  - The faithful are God's garden, and should thus welcome the laborer "who does the visible work of planting and watering the seed, even though the growth comes from one who works invisibly" (LH, St. Januarius [Sep 19], 2R: St. Augustine, Sermo 340, 1: PL 38, 1483–1484; *cf. also* CCC 543).
  - The laborer deserves his wages (Matt. 10:10; Luke 10:7; 1 Cor. 9:4–18; 1 Tim. 5:17–18; CCC 2122).
- The Church prays that the Lord will send workers to the harvest (Matt. 9:37–38; Luke 10:2; LH, CT.AE.Fr, EP, 5th intercession; LH, Holy Trinity, EP1, 3rd intercession [=LH, Holy Trinity, EP2, 3rd intercession]; LH, Psalter.1.Th, EP, 5th intercession; LH, OT.27.Sa, 2R, Resp [Luke 10:2; Ps. 62:9]; LH, St. Peter Chanel [Apr 28], 2R, Resp [Luke 10:2; Acts 1:8]; LH, St. Peter and St. Paul [June 29], EP, 2nd intercession [=LH, St. Peter and St. Paul [June 29], EP2, 2nd intercession]; LH, St. Francis Xavier [Dec 3], 2R, Resp [Luke 10:2; Acts 1:8]; RM, Masses and Prayers for Various Needs and Occasions, 9, Entrance Antiphon; RM, Masses and Prayers for Various Needs and Occasions, 18, A, Collect).
- The liturgy asks the Lord of the Harvest that he will help his workers to support the day's burden and never complain about the Lord's wishes (*cf.* Matt. 20:1–16) (LH, Psalter.1, MD, Prayer [Latin] [=LH, Psalter.2.Mo, MD, Prayer [Latin]; LH, Psalter.3.Mo, MD, Prayer [Latin]; LH, Psalter.4.Mo, MD, Prayer [Latin]]).
- The liturgy prays that the labors of priests may please God and that the Church may bear fruit which lasts for ever (RM, Ritual Masses, For the Conferral of Holy Orders, For the Ordination of Priests, A [=B], Prayer over the Offerings; RM, Masses and Prayers for Various Needs and Occasions, For Holy Church, For Priests, Prayer over the Offerings).

Physician

OT Background:

God heals: Job 5:18; Ps. 30:3; 103:3; 147:3; Wisd. 16:10–12; Sir. 38:9, 12, 14–15; Isa. 19:22; 30:26; 38:5; 57:18–19; 58:8; Jer. 3:22; 17:14; 30:17; 33:6; Ezek. 34:16; Hos. 6:1; 7:1; 14:5

Other: Prov. 12:18; Sir. 3:28; 38:9, 12, 14–15; Isa. 53:5; 61:1; Jer. 51:8–9; Ezek. 34:4; 47:12; Zech. 11:16

NT Background:

Jesus heals: cf. for example Matt. 4:23; 9:1–8, 12, 35; Mark 2:1–12, 17; Luke 4:23; 5:17–26, 31; 1 Pet. 2:24

Other: Matt. 10:1, 8; Mark 6:13; Luke 10:8–9, 33–34; Acts 4:10, 14, 22, 30; 5:16; 8:7; 9:34; 14:9–10; 28:8–9; 1 Cor. 12:9, 28, 30; Heb. 12:13; James 5:16; Rev. 22:2

Catechism Background: 1421; 1456; 1484; 1503; **1504;** 1505–1508; **1509; 1510;** 1848

Related: EUCHARIST: *Symbols*: Medicine of Immortality; PENANCE: *Symbols*: Medicine for the Soul

* Jesus Christ had compassion toward the sick, and healed many in soul and body as "a resplendent sign that . . . the Kingdom of God is close at hand" (CCC 1503; *cf. also for example* Matt. 4:23; 9:1–8, 12, 35; Mark 2:1–12, 17; Luke 4:23; 5:17–26, 31; 1 Pet. 2:24; CCC 1503; 1505–1508; RM, Adv.2.We, Collect).

* Jesus Christ sent out his disciples to heal in his name (*cf.* Matt. 10:1, 8; Mark 6:13; Luke 10:8–9). This healing ministry continued after the Resurrection of Christ (*cf.* Acts 4:10, 14, 22, 30; 5:16; 8:7; 9:34; 14:9–10; 28:8–9; 1 Cor. 12:9, 28, 30; Heb. 12:13; James 5:16).

* In the power of the Holy Spirit, the healing work of Jesus Christ, physician of souls and bodies, is continued in the sacraments of the Church (CCC 1421), where Jesus Christ continues to touch the faithful in order to heal them (CCC 1504; *cf. also* CCC 1509; 1510; EUCHARIST: *Symbols*: Medicine of Immortality; PENANCE: *Symbols*: Medicine for the Soul).

* The priest is compared to a doctor of the soul, who provides the remedies of the Sacraments of Penance and of the Eucharist (LH, St. Frances of Rome [Mar 9], 2R: Mary Magdalene Anguillaria, Life of St. Frances of Rome, Ch. 6–7: Acta Sanctorum Martii 2, *185–*187; *cf. also* CCC 1421; 1509;

EUCHARIST: *Symbols*: Medicine of Immortality; PENANCE: *Symbols*: Medicine for the Soul).

• Through the Sacrament of Penance, Jesus Christ personally forgives sins and acts as a physician, "tending each one of the sick who need him to cure them (cf. Mark 2:17)" (CCC 1484; *cf. also* RP 99; 205.2, 1st intercession).

• In the Sacrament of Penance, the priest fulfills the ministry of the Good Samaritan who binds up wounds, and is "the sign and the instrument of God's merciful love for the sinner" (CCC 1465; *cf.* Luke 10:29–37; RP 54, 1st Example, 1st Intercession).

• In the Sacrament of Penance, confession to a priest of all known mortal sins is essential, for "if the sick person is too ashamed to show his wound to the doctor, the medicine cannot heal what it does not know" (CCC 1456, quoting St. Jerome, In Eccl. comm. 10, 11: PL 23:1096).

• In the Sacrament of the Eucharist, the priest offers the faithful the medicine of immortality *(cf.* EUCHARIST: *Symbols:* Medicine of Immortality).

• The priest acts as a physician who offers the bandage of consolation, binds up the broken one, and strengthens the one who is weak *(*LH, OT.24.Sa, 2R: St. Augustine, Sermon on Pastors 46, 11–12: CCL 41, 538–539; *cf. also* HOLY ORDERS: *Symbols*: Shepherd).

• The priest is called by God to strengthen the weak and to heal those who are ill due to sin and evil desires. Those who fail to do this are negligent and wicked (LH, OT.25.Su, 2R: St. Augustine, Sermon on Pastors 46, 13: CCL 41, 539–540, citing Ezek. 34:4, 16; *cf. also* HOLY ORDERS: *Symbols*: Shepherd).

SEA CAPTAIN

OT Background: Gen. 6:5–9:17; Job 38:8–11; Ps. 18:16; 65:7; 69:1–2; 89:8–9; 104:6–7; 107:23–32; 124:2–5; Prov. 1:5 (LXX); 11:14 (LXX); Wisd. 10:4; Isa. 43:2

NT Background: Matt. 8:23–27; 10:40; 14:23–33; 16:18–19; 18:18; Mark 4:36–41; Luke 5:3–10; 6:46–49; 8:23–25; 10:16; John 6:16–21; 13:20; 20:22–23; 21:15–17; 1 Cor. 12:28; Gal. 4:14; 1 Pet. 3:20–21

Catechism Background: 845

Related: BAPTISM: *Types*: Flood; HOLY ORDERS: *Symbols*: Father; Head of the Body; Investiture with Ring, Miter, and Pastoral Staff; Shepherd

Jesus Christ as Sea Captain

- The Church is that ship which, prefigured by Noah's ark, alone saves from the flood, and navigates in this world "in the full sail of the Lord's cross, by the breath of the Holy Spirit" (CCC 845, quoting St. Ambrose, De virg. 18, 118: PL 16, 297B; *cf. also* BAPTISM: *Types:* Flood).
- The ship of Peter has weathered so many storms because it has Christ on board (LH, St. Thomas Becket [Dec 29], 2R: St. Thomas Becket, Letter 74: PL 190, 533–536).
- Christ is the true sea captain, and the soul that is without him "drifts in darkness, buffeted by the waves of passion, storm-tossed at the mercy of evil spirits, its end is destruction" (LH, OT.34.We, 2R: St. Macarius [attributed], Homily 28: PG 34, 710–711).

The Bishop as Sea Captain

- The bishop sits at the helm of the Church and pilots the ship against the waves and storms of the world with the rudder of faith (LH, St. Ambrose [Dec 7], 2R: St. Ambrose, Letter 2, 1–2.4–5.7: PL [edit. 1845] 879, 881).
- The bishops steer the great ship of the Church, the bride of Jesus Christ, "by teaching and defending her, by their labors and sufferings, even to the shedding of blood" (LH, St. Boniface [June 5], 2R: St. Boniface, Letter 78: MGH, Epistolae, 3, 352.354).

The Liturgy of the Hours

In her voyage across the ocean of this world, the Church is like a great ship being pounded by the waves of life's different stresses. Our duty is not to abandon ship but to keep her on her course.

The ancient fathers showed us how we should carry out this duty: Clement, Cornelius and many others in the city of Rome, Cyprian at Carthage, Athanasius at Alexandria. They all lived under emperors who were pagans; they all steered Christ's ship—or rather his most dear spouse, the Church. This they did by teaching and defending her, by their labors and sufferings, even to the shedding of blood.

I am terrified when I think of all this. Fear and trembling came upon me and the darkness of my sins almost covered me. I would gladly give up the task of guiding the Church which I have accepted if I could find such an action warranted by the example of the fathers or by holy Scripture.

Since this is the case, and since the truth can be assaulted but never defeated or falsified, with our tired mind let us turn to the words of Solomon: "Trust in the Lord with all your heart and do not rely on your own prudence. Think on him in all your ways, and he will guide your steps" (Prov. 3:5–6)....

Let us trust in him who has placed this burden upon us. What we ourselves cannot bear let us bear with the help of Christ. For he is all-powerful and he tells us: "My yoke is easy and my burden is light" (Matt. 11:30).

Let us continue the fight on the day of the Lord. The days of anguish and of tribulation have overtaken us; if God so wills, let us die for the holy laws of our fathers, so that we may deserve to obtain an eternal inheritance with them.

LH, St. Boniface (June 5),
2R: St. Boniface, Letter 78: MGH, Epistolae, 3, 352.354

- The bishop must adapt to the circumstances, like a ship pilot who adapts to the winds, and like a sailor in a storm who keeps his eye on the harbor (LH, OT.17.Fr, 2R: St. Ignatius of Antioch, Letter to Polycarp 1, 1–4, 3: Funk 1, 247–249).
- The successor of Peter, the pope, has not abandoned the helm of the Church which was entrusted to him by Jesus Christ (LH, Common of Pastors, 2R, For a pope: St. Leo the Great, Sermo 3 de natali ipsius, 2–3: PL 54, 145–146; *cf. also* LH, St. Peter and St. Paul, EP [=EP2], 3rd intercession).

SERVANT

- **OT Background**: Isa. 42:1–4; 49:1–6; 50:4–9; 52:13–53:12
- **NT Background**:
- *Jesus Christ as servant*: Matt. 12:17–18, 20:28; Mark 10:43–45; Luke 22:27; John 1:29, 36; 13:4, 13–15; Acts 4:27–28; 8:32–35; Phil. 2:7

- *Ministers of the Gospel as servants*: Acts 6:1–7; 26:16; Rom. 1:1; 15:16; 1 Cor. 3:5; 4:1; 9:19; 12:5; 2 Cor. 4:5; 6:4; 11:23; Gal. 1:10; Eph. 3:7; Phil. 1:1; Col. 1:7, 23, 25; 1 Tim. 3:10, 13; 4:6; 2 Tim. 1:3; 2:24; James 1:1; 1 Pet. 5:3; 2 Pet. 1:1; Jude 1; Rev. 1:1
- *Other*: Matt. 18:23–35; 20:26–27; 23:11; 24:42–51; 25:14–30; Mark 9:35; 10:43; 13:34–37; Luke 12:35–48; 15:19, 22–24; 17:7–10; 22:26; John 15:15; 2 Cor. 11:15; Gal. 4:7; 1 Pet. 2:16; Rev. 7:3
- **Catechism Background**: 440; 461; 536; 539; 555; 565; 580; 600–601; 608; 615; 623; 713; 786; **859; 876; 983**; 1120; **1142; 1543; 1547; 1551; 1554**; 1567; **1570; 1579; 1588; 1591; 1592**; 2235; 2749

Related: HOLY ORDERS: *Types*: Levites; Priesthood; *Symbols*: Laborer of the Harvest; Steward

Jesus Christ as Servant

- In his Incarnation, the Son of God took the form of a servant (*cf. for example* Phil. 2:7; CCC 461).
- Jesus Christ came not to be served, but to serve and give his life as a ransom for many (*cf. for example* Matt. 20:28; Mark 10:45).
- Jesus Christ fulfilled the redemptive mission of the Suffering Servant (*cf.* Isa. 42:1–4; 49:1–6; 50:4–9; 52:13–53:12; Matt. 12:17–18; 20:28; Mark 10:45; Acts 4:27–28; *cf. also for example* CCC 440; 536; 539; 555; 565; 580; 600–601; 608; 615; 623; 713; 2749).
- Jesus Christ, King and Lord of the universe, became the servant of all. For Christians, to reign is to serve Christ, especially in the poor and the suffering (*cf. for example* CCC 786, citing Matt. 20:28 and Lumen Gentium 8).

The Ordained Minister as Servant

- Christ sent forth his apostles as servants of the divine will to proclaim the Gospel and invite all to come and eat and drink at Wisdom's Banquet (LH, OT.6.We, 2R: Procopius of Gaza, Commentary on the Book of Proverbs, Ch. 9: PG 87-1, 1299–1303; *cf.* EUCHARIST: *Types*: Wisdom's Banquet).
- Christ's apostles were conscious of being "servants of God" and "servants of Christ and stewards of the mysteries of God (2 Cor. 6:4; 1 Cor. 4:1)" (CCC 859; *cf. also* Acts 6:1–7; 26:16; Rom. 1:1; 15:16; 1 Cor. 3:5; 9:19; 12:5; 2

Cor. 4:5; 11:23; Gal. 1:10; Eph. 3:7; Phil. 1:1; Col. 1:7, 23, 25; 1 Tim. 3:10, 13; 4:6; 2 Tim. 1:3; 2:24; James 1:1; 1 Pet. 5:3; 2 Pet. 1:1; Jude 1; Rev. 1:1).

- The ordained minister is truly a slave of Christ, who freely became a slave for us. He is called to freely become the slave of all (CCC 876, citing Rom. 1:1, Phil. 2:7, and 1 Cor. 9:19; *cf.* CCC 1142; *cf. also* CCC 2235).
- The ordained minister has the task of serving the community in the name of Christ (CCC 1591).
- In the Latin Church, all ordained ministers, with the exception of permanent deacons, are taken from men who have freely chosen to remain celibate "for the sake of the kingdom of heaven" (Matt. 19:12). Celibacy is a sign of the consecration of the minister to the service of Christ and the Church (CCC 1579).
- At the ordination Mass of bishops, priests, or deacons, the Gospel is optionally Luke 12:35–44, where Jesus says "Blessed are those servants whom the master finds awake on his arrival" (Lectionary 774; RO 351; *cf. also* RM, Commons, Common of Pastors, For a Bishop, 1, Communion Antiphon [Luke 12:36–37]).
- God established three ranks of ministers to serve his name (RO 235 [=ROD 21]; CCC 1543).

Bishop as Servant

- The bishop or priest is a servant of God (RO 154 [=ROP 17]; RO 156 [=ROP 19]; RO 159 [=ROP 22]; RO 43 [=ROB 22]; RO 47 [=ROB 26]; CCC 1586; RM, Ritual Masses, For the Conferral of Holy Orders, For the Ordination of a Bishop, A [=B], 1st Collect; RM, Ritual Masses, For the Conferral of Holy Orders, For the Ordination of a Bishop, A [=B], 2nd Collect; RM, Ritual Masses, For the Conferral of Holy Orders, For the Ordination of a Bishop, A [=B], Prayer over the Offerings; RM, Ritual Masses, For the Conferral of Holy Orders, For the Ordination of a Bishop, A [=B], Hanc igitur; RM, Ritual Masses, For the Conferral of Holy Orders, For the Ordination of a Bishop, A [=B], Prayer after Communion; RM, Ritual Masses, For the Ordination of Priests, A [=B], Prayer after Communion; RM, Masses and Prayers for Various Needs and Occasions, For the Bishop, Collect; RM, Masses and Prayers for Various Needs and Occasions, For the Bishop, Prayer over the Offerings; RM, Masses and Prayers for Various Needs and Occasions, For the Bishop, Prayer after

Communion; RM, Masses and Prayers for Various Needs and Occasions, For Holy Church, For the Priest Himself, B, Prayer after Communion; RM, Masses and Prayers for Various Needs and Occasions, For Holy Church, For the Priest Himself, C, Prayer over the Offerings; RM, Masses and Prayers for Various Needs and Occasions, For Holy Church, For Vocations to Holy Orders, Prayer after Communion; RM, Masses for the Dead, IV, 2, A; RM, Masses for the Dead, IV, 2, B; RM, Masses for the Dead, IV, 3, A; RM, Masses for the Dead, IV, 3, B; RM, Masses for the Dead, IV, 4; LH, OT.24. Th, 2R: St. Augustine, Sermon On Pastors 46, 9: CCL 41, 535–536; LH, St. Blase [Feb 3], 2R: St. Augustine, Sermo Guelferbytanus 32, De ordinatione episcopi: PLS 2, 639–640).

- The bishop is a servant of Christ, who has been placed as a steward over his household. He must not be a lazy servant, but must hand out to the flock "their portion of food at the proper time" (Luke 12:42), that is, the mystery of faith which the bishop hands out to his flock according "to the measure of faith which God has assigned him" (Rom. 12:3) (LH, Common of Pastors, 2R, For a bishop: St. Fulgentius of Ruspe, Sermo 1, 2–3: CCL 91A, 889–890).

- The bishop should be among his people as one who serves (LH, St. Turibius de Mongrovejo [Mar 23], 2R: Vatican II, Christus Dominus 12–13.16).

- The Mass offered for the bishop recalls how Jesus Christ came not to be served but to serve (RM, Masses and Prayers for Various Needs and Occasions, For the Bishop, Communion Antiphon [Matt. 20:28]).

- The bishop is the "servant of the unity, catholicity and apostolicity of his Church, and hence the connection with the apostolic origins of Christ's Church" (CCC 1292). The pope is the "servant of the unity of the universal Church" (CCC 1369; cf. also RM, Eucharistic Prayer I, 84; RM, Eucharistic Prayer III, 113; RM, Eucharistic Prayer IV, 122; RM, Masses and Prayers for Various Needs and Occasions, For the Pope, 2nd and 3rd Collect; RM, Masses for the Dead, IV, 1, A; RM, Masses for the Dead, IV, 1, B; RM, Masses for the Dead, IV, 1, C).

- By finding joy chiefly in the redemption of his own soul, and not so much in the position of honor which he holds, the bishop becomes a better servant of his flock and shows himself grateful to God for having made him his servant (LH, St. Januarius [Sep 19], 2R: St. Augustine, Sermo 340, 1: PL 38, 1483–1484).

Priest as Servant

- Priests serve God's people (RM, Ritual Masses, For the Ordination of Priests, A [=B], Prayer over the Offerings; RM, Ritual Masses, For the Ordination of Priests, A [=B], Hanc igitur; *cf. also* RM, Ritual Masses, For the Ordination of Priests, A [=B], Solemn Blessing; RM, Masses and Prayers for Various Needs and Occasions, For Holy Church, For the Priest Himself, B, Collect).

- The priesthood is ministerial, entirely dependent on Christ and entirely at the service of men. The use of its authority is to be measured against the example of Christ, who made himself the servant of all out of love (CCC 1551, citing Mark 10:43–45 and 1 Pet. 5:3; *cf. also* CCC 1547; 1567; LH, Common of Pastors, 2R, For a priest: Vatican II, Presbyterorum ordinis Ch. 3, 12).

- The ministerial priesthood is at the service of the baptismal priesthood, by guaranteeing that "it really is Christ who acts in the sacraments through the Holy Spirit for the Church" (CCC 1120).

- In the Sacrament of Baptism, the priest performs a humble service but God works with mighty power, sending forth the spirit of adoption (RM, Easter Vigil, 43).

- The power to forgive sins reflects the will of Christ "that his lowly servants accomplish in his name all that he did when he was on earth" (CCC 983, quoting St. Ambrose, De poenit. I, 15: PL 16, 490).

- The priest is the servant of God's forgiveness, not its master. As such, he "should unite himself to the intention and charity of Christ (Cf. PO 13)" (CCC 1466).

- Jesus' words, "No longer do I call you servants, but my friends," are applied by the liturgy to the newly ordained priest (RO 165 [=ROP 28], paraphrasing John 15:15).

- The liturgy refers to many canonized priests and bishops as servants (*cf. for example* LH, St. Cyril and Methodius [Feb 14], 2R: From an Old Slavonic Life of Constantine, Ch. 18: Denkschriften der kaiserl. Akademie der Wissenschaften, 19 [Wien 1870], p. 246; RM, St. Norbert [June 6], Collect; RM, Blessed Miguel Agustín Pro [Nov 23], Collect).

Deacon as Servant

- The apostles chose seven men to serve tables and to help in the daily distribution so that they could dedicate themselves to the ministry of the Word (Acts 6:1–7).
- The deacon is not a mere servant with food and drink. He is an emissary of God's Church and minister of the mysteries of Jesus (LH, OT.27.Tu, 2R: St. Ignatius of Antioch, Letter to the Trallians, 1, 1–3, 2; 4, 1–2; 6, 1; 7, 1–8, 1: Funk 1, 203–209).
- Strengthened by the grace of ordination, the deacon dedicates himself to "'the service (*diakonia*) of the liturgy, of the Gospel, and of works of charity' (Lumen Gentium 29)" (CCC 1588).
- The diaconate is at the service of the ministerial priesthood, i.e. of the bishops and priests (CCC 1554; *cf.* Acts 6:1–7; RM, Ritual Masses, For the Ordination of Deacons, A [=B], Hanc igitur).
- The Sacrament of Holy Orders configures the deacon to Christ, who made himself servant of all (CCC 1570, citing Mark 10:45; Luke 22:27; St. Polycarp, Ad Phil. 5, 2: SCh 10, 182; *cf.* RM, Ritual Masses, For the Ordination of Deacons, A [=B], Communion antiphon [Matt. 20:28]).
- The deacon is a servant to all (RO 227 [=ROD 14]; *cf. also* RM, Ritual Masses, For the Ordination of Deacons, A [=B], Hanc igitur; RM, Ritual Masses, For the Ordination of Deacons, A [=B], Solemn Blessing).
- The deacon is servant of God (RO 230 [=ROD 17]; RO 235 [=ROD 21]; RM, Ritual Masses, For the Ordination of Deacons, A [=B], Entrance Antiphon [John 12:26]; RM, Ritual Masses, For the Ordination of Deacons, A [=B], Collect; RM, Ritual Masses, For the Ordination of Deacons, A [=B], Prayer after Communion).
- Faithful deacons will be received by the Lord on the last day, who will tell them, "Well done, good and faithful servant, enter into the joy of your Lord" (RO 227 [=ROD 14], paraphrasing Matt. 25:21, 23).

SHEPHERD

OT Background:

God as shepherd: Gen. 48:15; 49:24; Ps. 23; 28:9; 74:1; 77:20; 78:52; 79:13; 80:1; 95:7; 100:3; Sir. 18:13; Isa. 40:11; Jer. 23:3–4; 31:10; 50:19; Ezek. 20:37; 34:11–31; Mic. 2:12–13; 7:14; Zech. 9:16; 10:3

Messianic shepherd: Ezek. 34:22–24; 37:24; Mic. 5:2–4; Zech. 11:4–14; 13:7
Faithful human shepherds: Gen. 4:2–4; 31:38–40; Exod. 2:16–17; 3:1; Num.
 27:15–18; 1 Sam. 16:11; 17:34–35; 2 Sam. 5:2; 7:7; 1 Chron. 11:2;
 Ps. 77:20; 78:70–72; Isa. 44:28; Jer. 3:15; 23:4
Lost sheep: 1 Sam. 9:3; Ps. 119:176; Isa. 53:6; Jer. 50:6; Ezek. 34:11–16
False shepherds: 1 Kings 22:17–18; Isa. 56:11; Jer. 2:8; 10:21; 12:10; 23:1–2;
 25:34–36; 50:6; Ezek. 34:1–10; Zech. 10:2–3; 11:5, 15–17
NT Background:
Jesus Christ as shepherd: Matt. 2:6; 9:36; 15:24; 25:31–33; 26:31–32; Mark
 6:34; 14:27; Luke 19:10; John 10:1–18, 26–27; Heb. 13:20; 1 Pet.
 2:25; 5:4; Rev. 7:17
Apostles and bishops as shepherds: Matt. 10:6; John 21:15–17; Acts 20:28; 1
 Cor. 9:7; Eph. 4:11; 1 Pet. 5:1–4
False shepherds: Matt. 7:15; John 10:8, 12–13; Acts 20:29
Other: Matt. 10:16; 12:11–12; 18:12–14; Luke 12:32; 15:3–7
Catechism Background: 553; 605; 635; **753–754**; 764; 801; 816; **857**;
 861; **862**; **874**; 879; **881**; 882; 886; **890–892**; **893**; **896**; 936; 939;
 1038; **1465**; **1548**; **1551**; **1558**; **1560–1561**; **1564**; 1574; **1575**;
 1585–1586; **1592**; 1595–1596; 1676; 2033; 2041; **2179**; 2442;
 2578–2579; 2594; 2665; **2686**
Related: PENANCE: *Symbols*: Finding the Lost Sheep; HOLY ORDERS:
 Types: Investiture with Ring, Miter, and Pastoral Staff; *Symbols*:
 Father; Head of the Body

Jesus as Good Shepherd

• Jesus is the Good Shepherd (John 10:11; *cf. also for example* Matt. 2:6; 9:36;
 15:24; 25:32; 26:31–32; Mark 6:34; 14:27; Luke 19:10; John 10:1–18,
 26–27; Heb. 13:20; 1 Pet. 2:25; 5:4; Rev. 7:17; CCC 553; 754; 764; 896;
 2665; RM, ET.4.Su; LH, Adv.1.Tu, 2R: St. Gregory of Nazianzus, Oratio
 45, 9, 22.26.28: PG 36, 634–635.654.658–659.662; LH, Lent.4.We, 2R:
 St. Maximus the Confessor, Letter 11: PG 91, 454–455; LH, Lent.5.Su,
 2R: St. Athanasius, Easter Letter 14, 1–2: PG 26, 1419–1420; LH,
 ET.2.We, 2R, Resp [John 10:14; Ezek. 34:11, 13]; LH, ET.3.Sa, 2R, Resp
 [John 10:10, 14–15]; LH, ET.4.Su, 2R: St. Gregory the Great, Homily on
 the Gospels 14, 3–6: PL 76, 1129–1130; LH, ET.4.Su, 2R, Resp [John

10:14–15; 1 Cor. 5:7]; LH, OT.13.Mo, 2R: St. Augustine, Sermo 47, 1.2.3.6, De ovibus: CCL 41, 572–573.575–576; LH, OT.13.Mo, 2R, Resp [John 10:27–28; Ezek. 34:15]; LH, OT.13.Tu, 2R: St. Augustine, Sermo 47, 12–14, De ovibus: CCL 41, 582–584; LH, OT.19.Tu, 2R: Theodoret of Cyr, On the Incarnation, 28: PG 75, 1467–1470; LH, OT.21.Mo, 2R: St. Thomas Aquinas, Exposition on John, Ch. 10, 3; LH, OT.25.Th, 1R, Resp [Ezek. 37:21–22; John 10:11, 16]; LH, OT.25.Th, 2R, Resp [John 10:14; Ezek. 34:11, 13]; LH, OT.25.Fr, 2R, Resp; LH, OT.33.Tu, 2R, Resp [John 10:15, 18; Jer. 12:7]; LH, OT.33.Th, 2R: St. Gregory of Nyssa, Commentary on the Song of Songs, Ch. 2: PG 44, 802; LH, OT.33.Fr, 1R, Resp [Matt. 26:31; Zech. 13:7]; LH, OT.34.Th, 2R: St. John Chrysostom, Homily 33, 1.2: PG 57, 389–390; LH, Common of Pastors, EP, Ant3; LH, Common of Pastors, MP, 1st intercession).

• Jesus Christ is the gateway to the sheepfold, which is the Church (John 10:1–10; CCC 754; *cf. also for example* LH, OT.21.Mo, 2R: St. Thomas Aquinas, Exposition on John, Ch. 10, 3).

• Jesus Christ seeks out the lost sheep (*cf.* Matt. 18:12–14; Luke 15:3–7; CCC 605; 635; LH, Lent.1.Th, 2R: St. Asterius of Amasea, Homily 13: PG 40, 355–358.362; LH, Lent.HW.Sa, 2R: From an ancient homily on Holy Saturday: PG 43, 439.451.462–463; LH, OT.24.Mo, 2R, Resp [Ezek. 34:15–16]; *cf. also for example* Ezek. 34:11–31; LH, Common of Pastors, EP, Ant2).

• At the Last Judgment, Jesus Christ will separate those who have done good from those who have done evil, like a shepherd separates the sheep from the goats (*cf. for example* Matt. 25:31–46; CCC 1038; LH, OT.13.Mo, 2R: St. Augustine, Sermo 47, 1.2.3.6, De ovibus: CCL 41, 572–573.575–576).

Ordained Ministers as Shepherds

• Jesus Christ watches over and protects his flock through bishops and priests (RM, Preface I of Apostles; CCC 857; *cf. also* CCC 874; 881; 1548; 1575; RO 151 [=ROP 14]; RM, Ritual Masses, For the Conferral of Holy Orders, For the Ordination of a Bishop, A [=B], 2nd Collect; LH, Lent.2[=4]. Su, EP2, 2nd intercession; LH, ET.2[=4, 6].We, EP, 3rd intercession; LH, ET.7.Su, EP2, 2nd intercession; LH, Common of Pastors, EP, Ant1).

• Although Christ has delegated the care of his sheep to many shepherds, he still continues to personally watch over his beloved flock (LH, Common of

Pastors, 2R, For a pope: St. Leo the Great, Sermo 3 de natali ipsius, 2–3: PL 54, 145–146; CCC 754; *cf. also* RM, St. Leo the Great [Nov 10], Prayer over the Offerings; LH, OT.10.Tu, 2R: St. Ignatius of Antioch, Letter to the Romans, 6, 1–9, 3: Funk 1, 219–223; LH, OT.13.Tu, 2R: St. Augustine, Sermo 47, 12–14, De ovibus: CCL 41, 582–584; LH, Common of Pastors, MP, 2nd and 3rd intercession).

• The grace proper to the Sacrament of Holy Orders is "configuration to Christ as Priest, Teacher, and Pastor" (CCC 1585; *cf. also* RO 151 [=ROP 14]). This service is exercised by divine worship (*munus liturgicum*), teaching (*munus docendi*), and pastoral governance (*munus regendi*) (CCC 1592).

• Jesus Christ entrusted St. Peter and his successors with the mission of shepherding his flock (*cf.* John 21:15–17; CCC 553; 816; 857; 881–882; 936; *cf. also* RM, The Chair of St. Peter the Apostle [Feb 22], Prayer over the Offerings; RM, Masses and Prayers for Various Needs and Occasions, For Holy Church, For the Pope; RM, Masses and Prayers for Various Needs and Occasions, For Holy Church, For the Election of a Pope or a Bishop; RM, Masses for the Dead, IV, 1, A, Collect; RM, Masses for the Dead, IV, 1, C, Collect; LH, ET.2[=4, 6].Tu, EP, 3rd intercession; LH, ET.2.We, 2R: St. Leo the Great, Sermo 12 de Passione, 3, 6–7: PL 54, 355–357; LH, Common of Pastors, 2R, For a missionary: Vatican II, Ad gentes 4–5; LH, OT.21.Mo, 2R: St. Thomas Aquinas, Exposition on John, Ch. 10, 3; LH, Chair of Peter [Feb 22], 2R: St. Leo the Great, Sermo 4 de natali ipsius, 2–3: PL 54, 149–151; LH, Chair of Peter [Feb 22], EP, Magn; LH, St. Martin I [Apr 13], 2R: St. Martin I, Letter 17: PL 87, 203–204; LH, St. Gregory VII [May 25], 2R: St. Gregory VII, Letter 64 extra Registrum: PL 148, 709–710; LH, St. Peter and St. Paul [June 29], EP [=EP2], 4th intercession; LH, St. Peter and St. Paul [June 29], 2R: St. Augustine, Sermo 295, 1–2.4.7–8: PL 38, 1348–1352; LH, St. Peter and St. Paul [June 29], EP2, Ant3; LH, St. Gregory the Great [Sep 3], MP, CantZech).

• The apostles, who received the office of shepherding the Church, by divine institution handed this office on to other men (bishops) to take their place, urging them to shepherd the whole flock (CCC 861–862, citing Acts 20:28, St. Clement of Rome, Ad Cor. 42, 44: PG 1, 291–300 and Lumen Gentium 20; *cf. also* 1 Pet. 5:1–4; RO 39 [=ROB 18]; LH, OT.27.Tu, 1R, Resp [Acts 20:28; 1 Cor. 4:2]).

- In order to preserve God's people from deviations and allow them to profess the true faith, Jesus Christ "endowed the Church's shepherds with the charism of infallibility in matters of faith and morals" (CCC 890; *cf.* CCC 891–892; *cf. also* CCC 2033).

- The shepherds of the Church have the charism of the discernment of charisms (CCC 801, citing 1 Cor. 12:7 and 1 Thess. 5:12; *cf.* CCC 1676).

- Some priests and bishops neglect speaking difficult truths or reproaching their flock for fear of losing their favor. They are not shepherds, but mercenaries, who flee when the wolf comes (*cf.* John 10:12–13) (LH, OT.27.Su, 2R: St. Gregory the Great, Pastoral Guide, Book 2, 4: PL 77, 30–31; LH, OT.27.Sa, 2R: St. Gregory the Great, Homily on the Gospels, 17, 3, 14: PL 76, 1139–1140.1146).

- The reform of the Church begins with the reform of bishops and priests, that they might be men "to whom guidance of the Lord's flock can be safely entrusted" (LH, St. John Leonardi [Oct 9], 2R: St. John Leonardi, Letter to Pope Paul V: in archivo Ordinis Clericorum Regularium Matris Dei).

- The Church prays for vocations to Holy Orders, reminding God that he willed to provide shepherds for his people (RM, Masses and Prayers for Various Needs and Occasions, For Holy Church, 9, Collect).

- The Church prays that God will help the shepherds of his pilgrim people so that they might zealously feed the flock (LH, Adv.1[=3].Fr, EP, 3rd intercession).

- Shepherds must tend the sheep even to the point of martyrdom, remembering that they are Christ's sheep, not their own, (LH, St. Nicholas [Dec 6], 2R: St. Augustine, Treatise on John 123, 5: CCL 36, 678–680).

- The newly ordained bishop prays that as shepherd he may not be without the obedience of his flock, nor his flock be without the care of its shepherds (RO 63, 3rd Blessing [=ROB 39, 3rd Blessing]; compare RM, St. Adalbert [Apr 23], Collect; RM, Ritual Masses, For the Conferral of Holy Orders, For the Ordination of a Bishop, A [=B], Solemn Blessing, 1st Option; RM, Masses and Prayers for Various Needs and Occasions, For Holy Church, 1, D, Collect; RM, Masses and Prayers for Various Needs and Occasions, For Holy Church, 7, A, Prayer over the Offerings; LH, Lent.1[=3, 5].We, EP, 2nd intercession).

- The shepherds of Christ's Church prevent the flock from being snatched from his hand. Through them, Christ gives eternal life to his flock (LH, Common of Pastors, EP [=EP2], 6th intercession).
- Christ himself is the inheritance of the Church's holy shepherds (LH, Common of Pastors, EP [=EP2], 5th intercession [Latin]).
- Ordained ministers, as servants of the Good Shepherd, "are ordained to lead the People of God to the living waters of prayer: the Word of God, the liturgy, the theologal life (the life of faith, hope, and charity), and the Today of God in concrete situations (Cf. PO 4–6)" (CCC 2686).

Homily of St. Augustine on Shepherds

St. Augustine's homily on Shepherds is presented in thirteen consecutive readings in the Liturgy of the Hours. Presented here is a summary of these thirteen readings.

- As members of the flock, the shepherds of the Church will give an account for their own life; but they also have the responsibility as shepherds to shepherd their sheep, and they will have to give an account to God of this stewardship (LH, OT.24.Su, 2R: St. Augustine, Sermon on Pastors 46, 1–2: CCL 41, 529–530; *cf. also* LH, OT.13.Mo, 2R: St. Augustine, Sermo 47, 1.2.3.6, De ovibus: CCL 41, 572–573.575–576).
- Some shepherds feed themselves instead of the flock. Shepherds deserve a wage from the people for their work. St. Paul, while recognizing this right, rejected the wages offered him because he did not need them. This is praiseworthy, but not required (LH, OT.24.Mo, 2R: St. Augustine, Sermon on Pastors 46, 3–4: CCL 41, 530–531).
- St. Paul gives good example by always seeking only the advantage of his flock, even when they did give him gifts. If a shepherd receives wages from his flock, let it be only what is truly necessary; God himself will repay him for his stewardship (LH, OT.24.Tu, 2R: St. Augustine, Sermon on Pastors 46, 4–5: CCL 41, 531–533).
- Shepherds who take advantage of their flock seek milk (sustenance) and wool (honors) and then neglect the sheep. St. Paul tended the sheep, and had God for his sustenance and honor. He received sustenance and honor from his flock, but he did not seek these things, but the things of Christ (LH, OT.24.We, 2R: St. Augustine, Sermon on Pastors 46, 6–7: CCL 41, 533–534).

- Wicked shepherds kill the sheep through their bad example and their wicked lives. A wicked shepherd is a murderer, just as he who lusts after a woman in his heart is an adulterer (LH, OT.24.Th, 2R: St. Augustine, Sermon on Pastors 46, 9: CCL 41, 535–536).

- The wicked shepherd neglects to strengthen the weak by not preparing them for temptations and the cross for fear of giving offense. Some wicked shepherds even promise worldly prosperity. This is building on sand, and will lead to ruin. To build on rock is to build on Christ, which means persecution and suffering (LH, OT.24.Fr, 2R: St. Augustine, Sermon on Pastors 46, 10–11: CCL 41, 536–538).

- God chastised his only Son; since we are adopted sons, he will chastise us as well. A shepherd who strengthens the weak does so by preparing them for suffering and temptations and trials by speaking of God's fidelity and love; he binds up the broken by promising him God's mercy when he is held back by fear (LH, OT.24.Sa, 2R: St. Augustine, Sermon on Pastors 46, 11–12: CCL 41, 538–539).

- The weak sheep must be strengthened so as to not break under temptation and so as to be able to endure suffering. They can still do good works. The ill sheep, however, have already given in to evil desires, and have no strength to even do good works, like the paralytic. The shepherd is called to open the roof and lower him down to Christ (LH, OT.25.Su, 2R: St. Augustine, Sermon on Pastors 46, 13: CCL 41, 539–540).

- Oftentimes sheep who are lost do not want to be found. The shepherd must seek them out anyway for God does not want them to be lost (LH, OT.25. Mo, 2R: St. Augustine, Sermon on Pastors 46, 14–15: CCL 41, 541–542).

- The Catholic Church is shepherd of the sheep. She is a vine. Some sheep stray, and some branches fall off, or are cut off to prune the vine. But the Church, especially through her shepherds, who are not and will never be lacking, seeks out the lost sheep, and knows that God can graft back on the separated branches (LH, OT.25.Tu, 2R: St. Augustine, Sermon on Pastors 46, 18–19: CCL 41, 544–546).

- Shepherds have the duty to warn the sheep about sin. In the case of unfaithful shepherds, Christ will still shepherd the sheep as long as they do what the shepherds say and not what they do (LH, OT.25.We, 2R: St. Augustine, Sermon on Pastors 46, 20–21: CCL 41, 546–548).

- Christ shepherds the sheep through the Scriptures, which are healthy and green pastures, and he judges rightly what each sheep needs (LH, OT.25.Th, 2R: St. Augustine, Sermon on Pastors 46, 24–25.27: CCL 41, 551–553).
- All good shepherds are united in Christ, the Good Shepherd, who shepherds the flock through them. Jesus entrusted the unity of the flock to St. Peter in a special way, and Christ is especially united to him, like a bridegroom with his bride and like a head with its body (LH, OT.25.Fr, 2R: St. Augustine, Sermon on Pastors 46, 29–30: CCL 41, 555–557).

Apostles and Bishops as Shepherds

- The apostles were shepherds (*cf. for example* Matt. 10:6; John 21:15–17; Acts 20:28; 1 Pet. 5:1–4; *cf. also for example* 1 Cor. 9:7; Eph. 4:11).
- Bishops are shepherds (CCC 939; RO 47 [=ROB 26]; RM, Chrism Mass, 9; RM, Ritual Masses, For the Conferral of Holy Orders, For the Ordination of a Bishop, A [=B], Hanc igitur; RM, Masses and Prayers for Various Needs and Occasions, For Holy Church, For the Bishop; RM, Masses and Prayers for Various Needs and Occasions, For Holy Church, For the Election of a Pope or a Bishop; LH, St. Boniface [June 5], 2R: St. Boniface, Letter 78: MGH, Epistolae, 3, 352.354; LH, St. Thomas Becket [Dec 29], 2R: St. Thomas Becket, Letter 74: PL 190, 533–536; LH, Psalter.2.Tu, EP, 2nd intercession).
- The bishop, like St. Peter, is asked by Christ, "Do you love me? Feed my sheep." He shows his love for Christ by feeding his sheep and by suffering for them (LH, St. Blase [Feb 3], 2R: St. Augustine, Sermo Guelferbytanus 32, De ordinatione episcopi: PLS 2, 639–640; *cf. also* CCC 1551, citing John 21:15–17 and St. John Chrysostom, De sac. 2, 4: PG 48, 636).

The Liturgy of the Hours

After his resurrection our Lord asked: "Peter, do you love me?" and Peter replied: "I do love you." The question and the answer were repeated three times. And each time the Lord added: "Feed my sheep." In other words, if you want to show that you love me, then "feed my sheep." What will you give me if you love me, since you look for everything to come from me? Now you know what you are to do if you love me: "Feed my sheep." Thus we have the same question and answer once, twice, three times. "Do you love me? I do love you. Feed my sheep." Three times Peter had denied in fear; three times he confessed out of love. By his replies and his profession of love, Peter condemned and wiped out his former fear. And so the Lord, after entrusting his sheep to him for the third time, immediately added: "When you were a young man, you would gird yourself and go wherever you wished. But when you are old, another will gird you and take you where you do not wish to go. This he spoke signifying by what death he was about to glorify God." Thus he foretold Peter's own sufferings and crucifixion. By this the Lord suggested that "feed my sheep" meant suffer for my sheep.

LH, St. Blase (Feb 3), 2R: St. Augustine, Sermo Guelferbytanus 32, De ordinatione episcopi: PLS 2, 639–640

- The bishop is the shepherd of his particular church (*cf.* CCC 879; 886; 1560; LH, OT.17.Fr, 2R: St. Ignatius of Antioch, Letter to Polycarp 1, 1–4, 3: Funk 1, 247–249).
- Episcopal consecration confers character in such a way that bishops, "'in an eminent and visible manner, take the place of Christ himself, teacher, shepherd, and priest, and act as his representative *(in Eius persona agant)*' (Lumen Gentium 21)" (CCC 1558; *cf.* RO 39 [=ROB 18]). The bishop represents Christ, the Good Shepherd (CCC 1561). This grace impels him to be a model for his flock, to go before it proclaiming the Gospel, and to not fear to give his life for his flock were it necessary (CCC 1586; *cf.* RO 39 [=ROB 18]).
- The giving of the pastoral staff (crosier) to the newly ordained bishop symbolizes his pastoral office and duty to "keep watch over the whole flock in which the Holy Spirit has placed you as Bishop to govern the Church of God" (RO 54 [=ROB 32]; *cf.* CCC 1574; HOLY ORDERS: *Symbols: Investiture with Ring, Miter, and Pastoral Staff*).
- The bishops and the priests sanctify the Church by being an example to their flock, seeking to attain eternal life (CCC 893, citing 1 Pet. 5:3; *cf. also* LH, OT.24.Su, 2R: St. Augustine, Sermon on Pastors 46, 1–2: CCL 41, 529–530).

- The Good Shepherd's flock is the household of the Redeemer, which the master has entrusted to the bishop as a steward, who has the duty to be faithful and care for the members of the household (LH, Common of Pastors, 2R, For a bishop: St. Fulgentius of Ruspe, Sermo 1, 2–3: CCL 91A, 889–890).
- A bishop should be a good shepherd who knows his sheep and whose sheep know him. He should unite and mold the entire family of his flock (LH, St. Turibius de Mongrovejo [Mar 23], 2R: Vatican II, Christus Dominus 12–13.16; *cf.* RO 39 [=ROB 18]; *cf. also* CCC 896).
- A bishop should have unceasing concern for the spiritual and temporal welfare of his flock (LH, OT.17.Fr, 2R: St. Ignatius of Antioch, Letter to Polycarp 1, 1–4, 3: Funk 1, 247–249).
- The bishop is called to "seek out the sheep who stray and gather them into the Lord's fold" (RO 40, 8th question [=ROB 19, 8th question]).
- By finding joy chiefly in the redemption of his own soul, and not so much in the position of honor which he holds, the bishop becomes a better servant of his flock and shows himself grateful to God for having made him his servant. Both the fact that he is a shepherd, as well as any fruits of his ministry, are a grace from God (LH, St. Januarius [Sep 19], 2R: St. Augustine, Sermo 340, 1: PL 38, 1483–1484).
- The faithful should follow their shepherd, the bishop, as his flock, "for all who belong to God and Jesus Christ are with the bishop" (LH, OT.27.Th, 2R: St. Ignatius of Antioch, Letter to the Philadelphians 1, 1–2, 1; 3, 2–5, 1: Funk 1, 226–229).
- A flock that progresses in holiness is the eternal joy of a bishop (RO 63, 1st Blessing [=ROB 39, 1st Blessing]; RM, St. Gregory the Great [Sep 3], Collect; RM, Ritual Masses, For the Conferral of Holy Orders, For the Ordination of a Bishop, A [=B], Solemn Blessing, 1st Option; LH, St. Gregory the Great [Sep 3], MP, Prayer).
- The liturgy oftentimes refers to canonized bishops as shepherds (*cf. for example* RM, St. John Neumann [Jan 5], Collect; RM, St. Norbert [June 6], Collect; RM, St. Cornelius and St. Cyprian [Sep 16], Collect; RM, Commons, Common of Pastors, For a Pope or for a Bishop, 1; RM, Commons, Common of Pastors, For a Pope or for a Bishop, 2, Collect; RM, Commons, Common of Pastors, For a Bishop, 1, Entrance Antiphon [Ezek. 34:11, 23–24]; RM, Commons, Common of Pastors, For a Bishop,

2, Collect; RM, Commons, Common of Pastors, For Pastors, A, Entrance Antiphon [Jer. 3:15]; RM, Commons, Common of Pastors, For Pastors, B, 2, Collect; LH, St. Fabian [Jan 20], 2R: St. Cyprian and the Roman Church, Letter 9, 1 and 8, 2–3: CSEL 3, 488–489.487–488; LH, St. Cyril and Methodius [Feb 14], Resp [Ps. 89:20, 21–22; Jer. 3:15]; LH, St. Norbert [June 6], 2R, Resp [2 Tim. 2:4, 5; Acts 20:28]; LH, St. Norbert [June 6], OR, Prayer; LH, St. Callistus I [Oct 14], 2R, Resp [Acts 20:28; 1 Cor. 4:2]; LH, St. Martin of Tours [Nov 11], 2R: Sulpicius Severus, Letter 3, 6.9–10.11.14–17.21: SC 133, 336–44; LH, St. Josaphat [Nov 12], 2R: Pope Pius XI, Encyclical Letter Ecclesiam Dei: AAS 15 [1923], 573–582; LH, Common of Pastors, EP [=MP, EP2], Prayer; LH, Common of Pastors, 1R, For a pope or bishop, Resp [Acts 20:28; 1 Cor. 4:2]).

Priests as Shepherds

• Priests are consecrated to shepherd the faithful after the image of Christ (CCC 1564; cf. LH, Common of Pastors, 2R, For a priest: Vatican II, Presbyterorum ordinis Ch. 3, 12).

• When a priest acts *in persona Christi Capitis* (in the person of Christ the Head), it is Christ himself who is present to his Church as Shepherd of his flock (CCC 1548).

• Within a particular church there are different parishes, each one entrusted to a pastor as its shepherd, under the authority of the bishop (CCC 2179).

• Priests (and deacons) depend on the bishop in the exercise of their pastoral functions (CCC 1595–1596).

• The liturgy applies Jer. 3:15 to priests, where God promises to appoint shepherds after his own heart, who will shepherd wisely and prudently (RM, Ritual Masses, For the Conferral of Holy Orders, For the Ordination of Priests, A [=B], Entrance Antiphon [Jer. 3:15]).

• The liturgy prays that God will make priests true shepherds, "to provide the living Bread and the word of life to the faithful, that they may continue to grow in the unity of the Body of Christ" (RM, Ritual Masses, For the Conferral of Holy Orders, For the Ordination of Priests, A [=B], Solemn Blessing).

• God has pastured good shepherds, who in turn lead their flock to graze in green pastures, and refresh them with the waters of orthodox teaching (LH,

St. John Damascene [Dec 4], 2R: St. John Damascene, Statement of Faith, Ch. 1: PG 95, 417–419).

The Liturgy of the Hours

You nursed me with the spiritual milk of your divine utterances. You kept me alive with the solid food of the body of Jesus Christ, your only-begotten Son for our redemption. And he undertook the task willingly and did not shrink from it. Indeed, he applied himself to it as though destined for sacrifice, like an innocent lamb. Although he was God, he became man, and in his human will, became obedient to you, God his Father, unto death, even death on a cross.

In this way you have humbled yourself, Christ my God, so that you might carry me, your stray sheep, on your shoulders. You let me graze in green pastures, refreshing me with the waters of orthodox teaching at the hands of your shepherds. You pastured these shepherds, and now they in turn tend your chosen and special flock. Now you have called me, Lord, by the hand of your bishop to minister to your people. I do not know why you have done so, for you alone know that. Lord, lighten the heavy burden of the sins through which I have seriously transgressed. Purify my mind and heart. Like a shining lamp, lead me along the straight path. When I open my mouth, tell me what I should say. By the fiery tongue of your Spirit make my own tongue ready. Stay with me always and keep me in your sight.

Lead me to pastures, Lord, and graze there with me. Do not let my heart lean either to the right or to the left, but let your good Spirit guide me along the straight path. Whatever I do, let it be in accordance with your will, now until the end.

LH, St. John Damascene (Dec 4), 2R: St. John Damascene,
Statement of Faith, Ch. 1: PG 95, 417–419

• In the Sacrament of Penance, the priest fulfills "the ministry of the Good Shepherd who seeks the lost sheep" (CCC 1465; cf. PENANCE: *Symbols:* Finding the Lost Sheep; cf. also RO 151 [=ROP 14]).

• In a priest or bishop, concern for their flock is proof of their love for Christ (CCC 1551, citing John 21:15–17 and St. John Chrysostom, De sac. 2, 4: PG 48, 636).

• The liturgy sometimes refers to canonized priests as shepherds (cf. for example LH, St. John Baptist de la Salle [Apr 7], MP, CantZech; LH, Common of Pastors, EP [=MP, EP2], Prayer).

STEWARD

OT Background: Gen. 37:36; 39:1; 41:39–43; 45:8–9; Num. 12:7; 2 Kings 18:18; 19:2; Esther 1:8; 3:10; 8:2, 8; Ps. 105:21; Sir. 15:10; Isa. 22:20–24; 36:3, 22; 37:2; Dan. 5:29; 6:3

NT Background: Matt. 6:24; 10:40; 16:19; 24:45–51; 25:20–30; Luke 10:16; 12:42–48; 16:1–13; 19:15–26; John 13:20; 17:18; 20:21; 21:15–17; Acts 20:28; 1 Cor. 4:1–2; 9:17; 2 Cor. 3:6; 5:20; 6:4; Gal. 1:10; 2:7; Eph. 3:2; 1 Thess. 2:4; Titus 1:7; 1 Pet. 4:10; 5:2

Catechism Background: 373; 858; 859; 893; 952; 1039; 1117; 2238; 2280; 2402; 2404; 2417; 2457

Related: HOLY ORDERS: *Symbols:* Judge; Laborer of the Harvest; Servant

The Apostles as Stewards

• Jesus Christ appoints Peter as steward over his household, his Church (cf. Matt. 16:19 in light of Isa. 22:20–24; 36:3, 22; 37:2; 2 Kings 18:18; Matt. 24:45; Luke 12:42; John 21:15–17; cf. also CCC 551–553; 880–883).

• St. Paul tells the Corinthians that they should regard him as a servant of Christ and steward of the mysteries of God, and that as a steward it is required of him that he be found trustworthy (1 Cor. 4:1–2).

• St. Paul says that he assumes that the Ephesians have heard of "the stewardship of God's grace that was given to [him] for [them]" (Eph. 3:2).

• St. Paul tells St. Titus that a bishop, as God's steward, must be blameless (Titus 1:7–9).

• The apostles ministry continues that of Jesus Christ (CCC 858, citing Matt. 10:40; Luke 10:16; John 13:20; 17:18; 20:21). The apostles were conscious of being "ministers of a new covenant," "servants of God," "ambassadors for Christ," "servants of Christ and stewards of the mysteries of God (2 Cor. 3:6; 6:4; 5:20; 1 Cor. 4:1)" (CCC 859). The bishops are the successors of the apostles (CCC 861).

Bishops as Stewards

- St. Paul tells the elders ("presbyteroi") of Ephesus to care for their flock, of which the Holy Spirit has made them overseers ("episkopoi"), "to feed the Church of the Lord which he obtained with his own blood" (Acts 20:28).
- The bishop is "'the steward of the grace of the supreme priesthood' (Lumen Gentium 26)," especially in the Eucharist, offered by him and by his co-workers, the priests (CCC 893).
- The bishop is a steward of the mysteries of God. He is steward of the mysteries of Christ in the church which is entrusted to him, where he is called to be a faithful steward, moderator, and guardian (RO 39 [=ROB 18]; cf. 1 Cor. 4:1).
- The ordaining bishop prays that by the providence and stewardship of the newly ordained bishop his people and clergy may be governed happily for many years (RO 63 [=ROB 39]; cf. also RM, Ritual Masses, For the Conferral of Holy Orders, For the Ordination of a Bishop, A [=B], Solemn Blessing, 2nd Option).
- Bishops have been placed over the People of God by Christ as steward. They have received from the Master the spiritual food, that is, the mysteries of the Christian faith, to be given to the faithful (cf. Luke 12:42). They share this food whenever they, enlightened by grace, teach in accordance with the true faith (LH, Common of Pastors, 2R, For a bishop: St. Fulgentius of Ruspe, Sermo 1, 2–3: CCL 91A, 889–890, citing Luke 12:42; cf. also LH, St. Robert Bellarmine [Sep 17], 2R, Resp [Mal. 2:7; Titus 1:7, 9]; LH, Common of Pastors, EP2, Magn).
- Bishops will have to give an account to God of their stewardship (LH, OT.24.Su, 2R: St. Augustine, Sermon on Pastors 46, 1–2: CCL 41, 529–530).
- The Mass for the Ordination of a Bishop prays that the newly ordained bishop "may receive the eternal rewards of a faithful steward" (RM, Ritual Masses, For the Conferral of Holy Orders, For the Ordination of a Bishop, A [=B], Prayer after Communion; cf. also RM, Masses and Prayers for

Various Needs and Occasions, For Holy Church, For the Bishop, Prayer after Communion; RM, Masses for the Dead, Various Prayers for the Dead, For a Pope, B, Prayer after Communion; RM, Masses for the Dead, Various Prayers for the Dead, For a Pope, C, Collect).

• St. Alphonsus Liguori is called a "faithful steward and preacher" of the "great mystery" of the Eucharist (RM, St. Alphonsus Liguori [Aug 1], Prayer after Communion).

• St. Gregory the Great and St. Turibius de Mongrovejo are called faithful and prudent stewards (RM, St. Gregory the Great [Sep 3], Communion Antiphon [Luke 12:42]; LH, St. Turibius de Mongrovejo [Mar 23], EP, Ant; *cf. also* RM, Commons, Common of Pastors, For a Bishop, 1 [=2], Entrance Antiphon [Luke 12:42]; *cf. also* LH, St. Callistus I [Oct 14], 2R, Resp [Acts 20:28; 1 Cor. 4:2]; LH, Common of Pastors, 1R, For a pope or bishop, Resp [Acts 20:28; 1 Cor. 4:2]).

Priests as Stewards

• Priests have been chosen by Jesus Christ "as ministers and stewards of [God's] mysteries" (RM, Masses and Prayers for Various Needs and Occasions, For Holy Church, For Priests, Collect; *cf. also* RM, Masses for the Dead, Various Prayers for the Dead, For a Priest, A, Prayer after Communion; LH, Psalter.4.We, EP, 3rd intercession).

• Priests promise "to be faithful stewards of the mysteries of God in the Holy Eucharist and other liturgical rites" (RM, Chrism Mass, 9; *cf.* 1 Cor. 4:1).

• The Church prays that priests be faithful stewards of God's mysteries (RM, Masses and Prayers for Various Needs and Occasions, For the Priest Himself, C, Collect).

• The Church asks God for vocations to Holy Orders, praying "that the stewards of [God's] mysteries may grow in number and persevere always in [God's] love" (RM Masses and Prayers for Various Needs and Occasions, For Vocations to Holy Orders, Prayer over the Offerings).

• St. Dominic is called a faithful and prudent steward (RM, St. Dominic [Aug 8], Communion Antiphon [Luke 12:42]; *cf. also* RM, Commons, Common of Pastors, For a Bishop, 1, Entrance Antiphon [Luke 12:42]; RM, Commons, Common of Pastors, For a Pastor, 2, Prayer after Communion; LH, Common of Pastors, EP2, Ant2; LH, Common of Pastors, EP2, Magn).

- Blessed is that steward who is found fulfilling his duty when the Master comes (*cf.* Luke 12:42–44; 1 Cor. 4:2; LH, OT.25.We, 2R, Resp [Luke 12:42, 43; 1 Cor. 4:2]; *cf. also* LH, Common of Pastors, 1R, For a priest, Resp [1 Cor. 4:1–2; Prov. 20:6]).

Deacons as Stewards

- Deacons are appointed stewards of the mysteries of God (RM, Ritual Masses, For the Ordination of Deacons, A [=B], Solemn Blessing; *cf.* 1 Cor. 4:1).

MATRIMONY

Definition: A covenant or partnership of life between a man and woman, which is ordered to the well-being of the spouses and to the procreation and upbringing of children. When validly contracted between two baptized people, marriage is a sacrament (Glossary of the Catechism of the Catholic Church).

TYPES

Note: The Bible, the Catechism, and the Liturgy do not present the Sacrament of Matrimony as being prefigured by types. Rather, the Sacrament of Matrimony itself is presented as symbolizing and foreshadowing the mystical marriage of Christ with his Church (cf. for example Eph. 5:31–32; RM, Ritual Masses, For the Celebration of Marriage, A, Nuptial Blessing; RM, Ritual Mass for the Celebration of Marriage, B, 2nd Collect; RM, Ritual Masses, For the Celebration of Marriage, B, Nuptial Blessing; cf. also CCC 1617).

Intimately related, consecrated virginity for the sake of the kingdom of heaven is also a "transcendent sign of the Church's love for Christ, and an eschatological image of this heavenly Bride of Christ and of the life to come' (Ordo Consecrationis Virginum, Praenotanda 1)" (CCC 923; cf. also for example CCC 925; 932; 1619–1620).

SYMBOLS

Note: The Bible, the Catechism, and the Liturgy abound with symbolism related to marriage. The symbolism of the union between man and woman in marriage, the nuptial bath, the wedding garment, the wedding feast, the marriage ring, etc. are all richly applied to the entire Christian life, and especially to the union between Christ and the Church (cf. CCC 1617).

Marriage symbolism, for example, is found in reference to the Sacraments of Baptism, the Eucharist, Penance, and Holy Orders (cf. BAPTISM: Symbols:

Wedding Feast; White Garment / Wedding Garment; EUCHARIST: *Types: Water to Wine; Symbols:* Banquet; PENANCE: *Symbols:* Wedding Garment; HOLY ORDERS: *Symbols:* Investiture with Ring, Miter, and Pastoral Staff; *Symbols:* Head of the Body*). As well, marriage and consecrated virginity oftentimes symbolize or point to the union between Christ and the Church (or God and his People) (regarding marriage, cf. for example CCC 1661; RMat 1; 2; 33, 2nd option; 106; 116; 120; CCC 1616–1617; RM, Masses and Prayers for Various Needs and Occasions, 11, A, Collect; cf. also CCC 219; 796; 1611; 1647; 2365; 2384; regarding consecrated virginity, cf. for example CCC 923; 1619–1620).*

As with the other sacraments, here are presented texts in which the Sacrament of Matrimony or some aspect of it are symbolized.

WEDDING RING

OT Background:[1] Gen. 2:1–3; 9:12–15, 17; 17:11; Exod. 31:16–17

NT Background: Matt. 26:26–28 (and parallels); Acts 7:8; Rom. 4:11; Col. 2:11–13

Related: BAPTISM: *Types*: Circumcision; Matrimony: *Symbols*: Seal

- The marriage rings symbolize the integral fidelity the spouses are called to have toward one another (RMat 110 [Latin]; 111 [Latin]).
- The marriage ring symbolizes the love and fidelity of the spouses (RMat 27; 28; 47; 48; 62; 63; *cf. also* CCC 1642).
- The marriage rings should remind the spouses of their love (RMat 111).
- The marriage ring is given "in the name of the Father, and of the Son, and of the Holy Spirit" (RMat 28; 48; 63).

---

1 The custom of the wedding ring is not found in the Bible. It was a Roman custom that the early Church adopted and integrated into the Rite of Matrimony. The texts in the Rite of Matrimony dealing with the wedding ring are probably best understood if the ring is considered a sign and reminder of the covenant bond formed in the Sacrament of Marriage. For example, compare RMat 110 with RMat 2, which emphasize "fidelity" in light of the ring and of the covenant respectively. Similarly, compare RMat 27, where the ring is said to symbolize the "love and fidelity" of the spouses, with CCC 1642, which says that the relationship between God and his people is that of a "covenant of love and fidelity" (*cf. also* RMat 116; CCC 1601; 1639–1640; 1642; 1647; 1662). With this in mind, the texts presented here give a context for the "signs" of the covenant between God and his people. These texts can be seen to act as background to the wedding ring, which is the sign of the marriage covenant between the spouses, and indirectly points to the covenant between God and his people.

ONE FLESH

OT Background: Gen. 2:23–24; Tob. 8:4–9; Mal. 2:15–16

NT Background: Matt. 19:3–9; Mark 10:2–12; 1 Cor. 6:16; 7:10–11; 11:3; Eph. 5:23–33

Catechism Background: 372; 796; 1605; 1610; 1614; 1616; 1621; 1627; 1642; **1643**; **1644**; 2335; 2361; 2364

Related: MATRIMONY: *Symbols*: Seal; HOLY ORDERS: *Symbols*: Head of the Body

- In marriage, man and woman become "one flesh" (Gen. 2:23–24; Matt. 19:5–6; Mark 10:8; Eph. 5:23–33; RM, Ritual Masses, For the Celebration of Marriage, A, Nuptial Blessing [=RMat 33]; CCC 372; 796; 1605; 1627; 1642; 1644; 2335; 2364; *cf. also* 1 Cor. 6:16; 11:3).
- Husband and wife are one, like the head is united to the body and like Christ is united to the Church (*cf.* 1 Cor. 11:3; Eph. 5:23–33).

The Rite of Matrimony

O God, who by your mighty power
created all things out of nothing,
and, when you had set in place
the beginnings of the universe,
formed man and woman in your own image,
making the woman an inseparable helpmate to the man,
that they might no longer be two, but one flesh,
and taught that what you were pleased to make one
must never be divided;

O God, who consecrated the bond of Marriage
by so great a mystery
that in the wedding covenant you foreshadowed
the Sacrament of Christ and his Church;

O God, by whom woman is joined to man
and the companionship they had in the beginning
is endowed with the one blessing

not forfeited by original sin
nor washed away by the flood.

Look now with favor on these your servants,
joined together in Marriage,
who ask to be strengthened by your blessing.
Send down on them the grace of the Holy Spirit
and pour your love into their hearts,
that they may remain faithful in the Marriage covenant.

RM, Ritual Masses, For the Celebration of Marriage,
A, Nuptial Blessing (=RMat 33)

- Through the Sacrament of Marriage, husband and wife become "one" (RM, Ritual Masses, For the Celebration of Marriage, A, 2nd Collect [=RMat 109]; RM, Ritual Masses, For the Celebration of Marriage, A, Prayer after Communion [=RMat 122])
- Conjugal love "'aims at a deeply personal unity, a unity that, beyond union in one flesh, leads to forming one heart and soul; it demands *indissolubility* and *faithfulness* in definitive mutual giving; and it is open to *fertility*' (Familiaris consortio 13)" (CCC 1643; *cf. also* CCC 1605; 1614; 1644).
- The Church prays that husband and wife become "one in heart and mind as witnesses to [God's] presence in their marriage" (RM, Ritual Masses, For the Celebration of Marriage, B, Nuptial Blessing [=RMat 120]; *cf. also* RM, Ritual Masses, For the Celebration of Marriage, A, Prayer after Communion [=RMat 122]).
- What God has joined (as one flesh) men must not divide (RMat 26 [=46; 61]; RM, Ritual Masses, For the Celebration of Marriage, A, Nuptial Blessing [=RMat 33]; *cf. also* CCC 1605; 1614).
- By becoming "'one flesh' (Gen. 2:24)" and transmitting human life, "spouses and parents cooperate in a unique way in the Creator's work (Cf. GS 50 § 1)" (CCC 372).
- It is fitting that the spouses receive the Eucharist at their wedding, so that, "communicating in the same Body and the same Blood of Christ, they may form but 'one body' in Christ (cf. 1 Cor. 10:17)" (CCC 1621; *cf. also* CCC 1642; 1644; RMat 6; 8).

SEAL

OT Background:

Used literally: Gen. 38:18, 25; 41:42; Exod. 28:11, 21, 36; 39:6, 14, 30; 1 Kings 21:8; Neh. 9:38; 10:1; Tob. 7:14 (RSV = Tob. 7:13 NAB, NRSV); 9:5; Esther 3:10, 12; 8:2, 8, 10; Sir. 38:27; 42:6; Jer. 32:10–11, 14, 44; Dan. 6:17; 14:11, 14, 17; 2 Macc. 2:5

Used symbolically: Gen. 4:15; Deut. 32:34; Job 9:7; 14:17; 37:7; 38:14; 41:15; Song 4:12; 8:6; Wisd. 2:5; Sir. 22:27; 32:5–6; Isa. 8:16; 29:11–12; Jer. 22:24; Ezek. 9:4–6; Dan. 8:26; 9:24; 12:4, 9; Hag. 2:23

Other: Prov. 2:17; Ezek. 16:8

NT Background: Matt. 27:66; John 3:33; 6:27; Acts 2:1–4, 38; Rom. 4:11; 8:29; 1 Cor. 9:2; 2 Cor. 1:21–22; Eph. 1:13–14; 4:30; 2 Tim. 2:19; Rev. 5:1–10; 6:1–12; 7:2–8; 8:1; 9:4; 10:4; 13:16–17; 14:9, 11; 16:2; 19:20; 20:3–4; 22:10

Catechism Background: 1601; 1611; **1621**; **1624**; 1626–1627; 1638; **1639**; **1640**; 1642; 2364

Related: BAPTISM: *Types:* Circumcision; *Symbols:* Seal; CONFIRMATION: *Symbols:* Seal; PENANCE: *Symbols:* Seal; HOLY ORDERS: *Symbols:* Seal

Note: *For the topic of "Seal" in general, cf.* CONFIRMATION: *Symbols:* Seal.

Seal Formed by Consent and Consummation

• God in the beginning created man and woman "that they might form the marriage bond" (RM, Masses and Prayers for Various Needs and Occasions, 11, A, Collect).

• The free consent of the spouses makes the marriage and binds the spouses together. This consent finds its fulfillment in their becoming "one flesh" (CCC 1626–1629).

• The spouses seal the covenant between them in the presence of God (RM, Ritual Masses, For the Celebration of Marriage, A, Adesto Propitius).

• The consent by which the spouses give themselves to one another "is sealed by God himself (cf. Mark 10:9)" (CCC 1639; *cf. also* Matt. 19:6; RM,

Masses and Prayers for Various Needs and Occasions, 11, C, Collect; *cf. also* CCC 1642).

Seal is the Holy Spirit

• The Holy Spirit is the seal of the covenant of marriage (CCC 1624).
• As the seal of the covenant of marriage, the Holy Spirit acts as a fountain of love between the spouses, and provides strength to renew their fidelity (CCC 1624; *cf. also* RMat 23 [=RMat 43; 58]; CCC 1661).

Perpetual and Irrevocable Bond

• The bond between the spouses is by its very nature perpetual and exclusive (CCC 1638). It is an irrevocable bond, which "gives rise to a covenant guaranteed by God's fidelity" (CCC 1640; *cf.* Mark 10:9; *cf. also* CCC 2364; Mal. 2:14–15; Prov. 2:17; RM, Masses and Prayers for Various Needs and Occasions, 11, B, Collect).
• The Church prays that God will join the spouses, united in the covenant of marriage, in a bond of inseparable love (RM, Ritual Masses, For the Celebration of Marriage, A, 2nd Collect [=RMat 109]).
• The covenant of marriage is forged by God "as a sweet yoke of harmony and an unbreakable bond of peace" (RM, Ritual Masses, For the Celebration of Marriage, A, Preface [=RMat 115]).

Which Points to the Union of Christ and the Church

• The covenant which arises between the spouses "is integrated into God's covenant with man" (CCC 1639; *cf. also* CCC 1642).
• God consecrated the bond of marriage "by so great a mystery that in the wedding covenant [he] foreshadowed the Sacrament of Christ and his Church" (RM, Ritual Masses, For the Celebration of Marriage, A, Nuptial Blessing [=RMat 33]; RM, Ritual Masses, For the Celebration of Marriage, B, 2nd Collect [=RMat 106]).
• In the Eucharist the sacrifice by which Christ gave himself up for his bride is made present. Thus, it is fitting that the spouses "seal their consent to give themselves to each other through the offering of their own lives by uniting it [their consent] to the offering of Christ for his Church made present in the Eucharistic sacrifice, and by receiving the Eucharist so that, communicating

in the same Body and the same Blood of Christ, they may form but 'one body' in Christ (Cf. 1 Cor. 10:17)" (CCC 1621; *cf. also* CCC 1626–1627).

Other Related Symbolism

• The woman of the Song of Songs asks her beloved to set her as a seal upon his heart and arm (Song 8:6), thus indicating her desire for permanent and close union with him.

APPENDICES

Readings from the Liturgy

BAPTISM: RITE OF BAPTISM FOR CHILDREN

Readings for the Baptism of Children (RB 186–215) and from the Rite of Bringing a Baptized Child to the Church (RB 172) are included here as they are the readings most directly related to the topic of symbols and types of Baptism. Other liturgies dealing with Baptism include the Easter Vigil, Ritual Masses for the Conferral of the Sacraments of Christian Initiation, and the Baptism of the Lord. For the sake of brevity these are not included here.

Old Testament Readings

- **Exod. 17:3–7** Water from the rock.
- **Ezek. 36:24–28** Clean water, a new heart, a renewed spirit.
- **Ezek. 47:1–9, 12** The water of salvation.

From the Rite of Bringing a Baptized Child to the Church

- **1 Kings 17:17–24** Elijah prays for a dead child, who returns to life.
- **2 Kings 4:8–37** Elisha prays for a dead child, who returns to life.

New Testament Readings

- **Rom. 6:3–5** Baptism: a sharing in Christ's death and Resurrection.
- **Rom. 8:28–32** We have become more perfectly like God's own Son.
- **1 Cor. 12:12–13** Baptized in one Spirit to form one body.
- **Gal. 3:26–28** Now that you have been baptized you have put on Christ.
- **Eph. 4:1–6** One Lord, one faith, one baptism.
- **1 Pet. 2:4–5, 9–10** A chosen race, a royal priesthood.

Responsorial Psalms

- **Ps. 23:1–3a, 3b–4, 5–6** The Lord is my Shepherd; there is nothing I shall want (1).
- **Ps. 27:1, 4, 8b–9abc, 13–14** The Lord is my light and my salvation (1a). *Or:* Wake up and rise from death: Christ will shine upon you! (Eph. 5:14).
- **Ps. 34:2–3, 6–7, 8–9, 14–15, 16–17, 18–19** Come to him and receive his light! (6a). *Or:* Taste and see the goodness of the Lord (9a).

Alleluia Verse

- **John 3:16** God loved the world so much, he gave us his only Son, that all who believe in him might have eternal life.
- **John 8:12** I am the light of the world, says the Lord; the man who follows me will have the light of life.
- **John 14:6** I am the way, the truth and the life, says the Lord; no one comes to the Father, except through me.
- **Eph. 4:5–6** One Lord, one faith, one baptism. One God, the Father of all.
- **2 Tim. 1:10b** Our Savior Jesus Christ has done away with death, and brought us life through his gospel.
- **1 Pet. 2:9** You are a chosen race, a royal priesthood, a holy people. Praise God who called you out of darkness and into his marvelous light.

Gospels

- **Matt. 22:35–40** The first and most important commandment.
- **Matt. 28:18–20** Christ sends his apostles to teach and baptize.
- **Mark 1:9–11** The baptism of Jesus.
- **Mark 10:13–16** Jesus loves children.
- **Mark 12:28b–34** (longer) *or* **Mark 12:28b–31** (shorter) Love God with all your heart.
- **John 3:1–6** The meeting with Nicodemus.
- **John 4:5–14** Jesus speaks with the Samaritan woman.
- **John 6:44–47** Eternal life through belief in Jesus.
- **John 7:37b–39a** Streams of living water.
- **John 9:1–7** Jesus heals the blind man who believes in him.
- **John 15:1–11** Union with Christ, the true vine.
- **John 19:31–35** The death of Christ, the witness of John the apostle.

Confirmation: Mass for the Celebration of Confirmation

Readings for the Celebration of Confirmation (RC 61–65) are included here as they are the most directly related to the topic of symbols and types of Confirmation. Oftentimes Confirmation is celebrated during the Easter Vigil. For the sake of brevity the readings from the Easter Vigil are not included here.

Old Testament Readings

• **Isa. 11:1–4a** On him the Spirit of the Lord rests.
• **Isa. 42:1–3** I have endowed my servant with my Spirit.
• **Isa. 61:1–3a, 6a, 8b–9** The Lord God has anointed me and has sent me to bring Good News to the poor, to give them the oil of gladness.
• **Ezek. 36:24–28** I will place a new Spirit in your midst.
• **Joel 2:23a, 26–30a** (in Hebrew Joel 2:23a; 3:1–3a) I will pour out my Spirit on all mankind.

New Testament Readings

• **Acts 1:3–8** You will receive the power of the Holy Spirit, and you will be my witnesses.
• **Acts 2:1–6, 14, 22b–23, 32–33** They were all filled with the Holy Spirit and began to speak.
• **Acts 8:1, 4, 14–17** They laid hands on them and they received the Holy Spirit.
• **Acts 10:1, 33–34a, 37–44** The Holy Spirit came down on all those listening to the word of God.
• **Acts 19:1b–6a** Did you receive the Holy Spirit when you became believers?
• **Rom. 5:1–2, 5–8** The love of God has been poured into our hearts by the Holy Spirit which has been given to us.
• **Rom. 8:14–17** The Spirit himself and our spirit bear united witness that we are children of God.
• **Rom. 8:26–27** The Spirit himself will express our plea in a way that could never be put to words.
• **1 Cor. 12:4–13** There is one and the same Spirit giving to each as he wills.

- **Gal. 5:16–17, 22–23a, 24–25** If we live in the Spirit, let us be directed by the Spirit.
- **Eph. 1:3a, 4a, 13–19a** You have been signed with the seal of the Holy Spirit of the promise.
- **Eph. 4:1–6** There is one body, one Spirit, and one baptism.

Responsorial Psalms

- **Ps. 22:23–24, 26–27, 28 and 31–32** I will proclaim your name to my brothers (23). *Or*: When the Holy Spirit comes to you, you will be my witness (John 15:26–27).
- **Ps. 23:1–3a, 3b–4, 5–6** The Lord is my shepherd; there is nothing I shall want (1).
- **Ps. 96:1–2a, 2b–3, 9–10a, 11–12** Proclaim his marvelous deeds to all the nations (3).
- **Ps. 104:1ab and 24, 27–28, 30–31, 33–34** Lord, send out your Spirit, and renew the face of the earth (30).
- **Ps. 117:1, 2** You will be my witness to all the world (Acts 1:8). *Or*: Alleluia.
- **Ps. 145:2–3, 4–5, 8–9, 10–11, 15–16, 21** I will praise your name for ever, Lord (1b).

Alleluia Verse

- **John 14:16** The Father will send you the Holy Spirit, says the Lord, to be with you for ever.
- **John 15:26b, 27a** The Spirit of truth will bear witness to me, says the Lord, and you also will be my witnesses.
- **John 16:13a; 14:26b** When the Spirit of truth comes, he will teach you all truth, and bring to your mind all I have told you.
- **Rev. 1:5a, 6** Jesus Christ, you are the faithful witness, firstborn from the dead; you have made us a kingdom of priests to serve our God and Father.
- **(non-biblical)** Come, Holy Spirit, fill the hearts of your faithful; and kindle in them the fire of your love.
- **(non-biblical)** Come, Holy Spirit; shine on us the radiance of your light.

Gospels

- **Matt. 5:1–12a** Theirs is the kingdom of heaven.
- **Matt. 16:24–27** If anyone wishes to follow me, let him deny himself.

- **Matt. 25:14–30** Because you have been faithful in small matters, come into the joy of your master.
- **Mark 1:9–11** He saw the Spirit descending and remaining on him.
- **Luke 4:16–22a** The Spirit of the Lord is upon me.
- **Luke 8:4–10a, 11b–15** Some seed fell into rich soil. These are the people who receive the word and bear fruit in patience.
- **Luke 10:21–24** I bless you, Father, for revealing these things to children.
- **John 7:37b–39** From the heart of the Lord shall flow fountains of living water.
- **John 14:15–17** The Spirit of truth will be with you for ever.
- **John 14:23–26** The Holy Spirit will teach you everything.
- **John 15:18–21, 26–27** The Spirit of truth, who issues from the Father, will be my witness.
- **John 16:5b–7, 12–13a** The Spirit of truth will lead you to the complete truth.

EUCHARIST

Votive Masses of the Most Holy Eucharist

Lectionary 987–1019

Old Testament Readings

- **Gen. 14:18–20** Melchizedek brought out bread and wine.
- **Exod. 12:21–27** Seeing the blood on the lintel and the two doorposts, the Lord will pass over that door.
- **Exod. 16:2–4, 12–15** I will now rain down bread from heaven for you.
- **Exod. 24:3–8** This is the blood of the covenant that the Lord has made with you.
- **Deut. 8:2–3, 14b–16a** He fed you with manna, a food unknown to you and your fathers.
- **1 Kings 19:4–8** Strengthened by that food, he walked to the mountain of of God.
- **Prov. 9:1–6** Come, eat of my food and drink of the wine I have mixed.

New Testament Readings (during Easter)

- **Acts 2:42–47** They devoted themselves to meeting together in the temple area and to breaking bread in their homes.
- **Acts 10:34a, 37–43** We ate and drank with him after he rose from the dead.
- **Rev. 1:5–8** To him who loves us and freed us from our sins by his Blood.
- **Rev. 7:9–14** They have washed their robes and made them white in the Blood of the Lamb.

Responsorial Psalms

- **Ps. 23:1–3, 4, 5, 6** The Lord is my shepherd; there is nothing I shall want (1).
- **Ps. 34:2–3, 4–5, 6–7, 8–9, 10–11** Taste and see the goodness of the Lord (9a).
- **Ps. 40:2 and 4ab, 7–8a, 8b–9, 10** Here I am, Lord; I come to do your will (8a and 9a).
- **Ps. 78:3 and 4a and 7ab, 23–24, 25 and 54** The Lord gave them bread from heaven (24b).
- **Ps. 110:1, 2, 3, 4** You are a priest for ever in the line of Melchizedek (4b).
- **Ps. 116:12–13, 15–16bc, 17–18** Our blessing-cup is a communion with the Blood of Christ (see 1 Corinthians 10:16).
- **Ps. 145:10–11, 15–16, 17–18** You open your hand to feed us Lord; you answer all our needs (see 16).
- **Ps. 147:12–13, 14–15, 19–20** Whoever eats this bread will live forever (John 6:58c).

Second Readings

- **1 Cor. 10:16–17** We, though many, are one bread, one Body.
- **1 Cor. 11:23–26** For as often as you eat the bread and drink the cup, you proclaim the death of the Lord.
- **Heb. 9:11–15** The Blood of Christ will cleanse our consciences.
- **Heb. 12:18–19, 22–24** You have approached the sprinkled Blood that speaks more eloquently than that of Abel.
- **1 Pet. 1:17–21** You were ransomed with the precious Blood of Christ, as of a spotless unblemished Lamb.

• **1 John 5:4–8** So there are three that testify, the Spirit, the water, and the Blood.

Alleluia Verse

• **John 6:51** I am the living bread that came down from heaven, says the Lord; whoever eats this bread will live forever.
• **John 6:56** Whoever eats my Flesh and drinks my Blood remains in me, and I in him, says the Lord.
• **John 6:57** Just as the living Father sent me and I have life because of the Father, so also the one who feeds on me will have life because of me.
• *cf.* **Rev. 1:5ab** Jesus Christ, you are the faithful witness, the firstborn of the dead, you have loved us and freed us from our sins by your Blood.
• **Rev. 5:9** Worthy are you to receive the scroll and to break open its seals, for you were slain and have redeemed us with your Blood.

Gospels

• **Mark 14:12–16, 22–26** This is my Body. This is my Blood.
• **Mark 15:16–20** They clothed him in purple and, weaving a crown of thorns, placed it on him.
• **Luke 9:11b–17** They all ate and were satisfied.
• **Luke 22:39–44** His sweat became like drops of blood, falling on the ground.
• **Luke 24:13–35** They recognized him in the breaking of bread.
• **John 6:1–15** He distributed to those who were reclining as much as they wanted.
• **John 6:24–35** Whoever comes to me will never hunger, and whoever believes in me will never thirst.
• **John 6:41–51** I am the living bread that came down from heaven.
• **John 6:51–58** My Flesh is true food and my Blood is true drink.
• **John 19:31–37** One soldier thrust his lance into his side and immediately Blood and water flowed out.
• **John 21:1–14** Jesus came over and took the bread and gave it to them.

The Solemnity of the
Most Holy Body and Blood of Christ

Lectionary 1015–1039

Year A

- **Deut. 8:2–3, 14b–16a** He gave you a food unknown to you and your fathers.
- **Ps. 147:12–13, 14–15, 19–20** Praise the Lord, Jerusalem (12).
- **1 Cor. 10:16–17** The bread is one, and we, though many, are one body.
- **John 6:51** I am the living bread that came down from heaven, says the Lord; whoever eats this bread will live forever.
- **John 6:51–58** My flesh is true food, and my blood is true drink.

Year B

- **Exod. 24:3–8** This is the blood of the covenant that the Lord has made with you.
- **Ps. 116:12–13, 15–16, 17–18** I will take the cup of salvation, and call on the name of the Lord (13).
- **Heb. 9:11–15** The blood of Christ will cleanse our consciences.
- **John 6:51** I am the living bread that came down from heaven, says the Lord; whoever eats this bread will live forever.
- **Mark 14:12–16, 22–26** This is my body. This is my blood.

Year C

- **Gen. 14:18–20** Melchizedek brought out bread and wine.
- **Ps. 110:1, 2, 3, 4** You are a priest forever, in the line of Melchizedek (4b).
- **1 Cor. 11:23–26** For as often as you eat and drink, you proclaim the death of the Lord.
- **John 6:51** I am the living bread that came down from heaven, says the Lord; whoever eats this bread will live forever.
- **Luke 9:11b–17** They all ate and were satisfied.

18th Sunday in Ordinary Time, Year A

Lectionary 740
- **Isa. 55:1–3** Hasten and eat.

- **Ps. 145:8–9, 15–16, 17–18** The hand of the Lord feeds us; he answers all our needs (16).
- **Rom. 8:35, 37–39** No creature will be able to separate us from the love of God in Christ Jesus.
- **Matt. 4:4b** One does not live on bread alone, but on every word that comes forth from the mouth of God.
- **Matt. 14:13–21** They all ate and were satisfied.

17th Sunday in Ordinary Time, Year B

Lectionary 729

- **2 Kings 4:42–44** They shall eat and there shall be some left over.
- **Ps. 145:10–11, 15–16, 17–18** The hand of the Lord feeds us; he answers all our needs (16).
- **Eph. 4:1–6** One body, one Lord, one faith, one baptism.
- **Luke 7:16** A great prophet has risen in our midst. God has visited his people.
- **John 6:1–15** He distributed as much as they wanted to those who were reclining.

18th Sunday in Ordinary Time, Year B

Lectionary 744

- **Exod. 16:2–4, 12–15** I will rain down bread from heaven for you.
- **Ps. 78:3–4, 23–24, 25, 54** The Lord gave them bread from heaven (24b).
- **Eph. 4:17, 20–24** Put on the new self that has been created in God's way.
- **Matt. 4:4b** One does not live on bread alone, but by every word that comes forth from the mouth of God.
- **John 6:24–35** Whoever comes to me will never hunger, and whoever believes in me will never thirst.

19th Sunday in Ordinary Time, Year B

Lectionary 758

- **1 Kings 19:4–8** Strengthened by that food, he walked to the mountain of God.
- **Ps. 34:2–3, 4–5, 6–7, 8–9** Taste and see the goodness of the Lord (9a).
- **Eph. 4:30–5:2** Walk in love, just like Christ.

- **John 6:51** I am the living bread that came down from heaven, says the Lord; whoever eats this bread will live forever.
- **John 6:41–51** I am the living bread that came down from heaven.

20th Sunday in Ordinary Time, Year B

Lectionary 775

- **Prov. 9:1–6** Come, eat of my food and drink of the wine I have mixed.
- **Ps. 34:2–3, 4–5, 6–7** Taste and see the goodness of the Lord (9a).
- **Eph. 5:15–20** Understand what is the will of the Lord.
- **John 6:56** Whoever eats my flesh and drinks my blood remains in me and I in him, says the Lord.
- **John 6:51–58** My flesh is true food and my blood is true drink.

PENANCE: COMMUNAL CELEBRATION OF THE RITE OF PENANCE

Readings taken from RP 101–201. Other readings not listed here may also be found in RP 67–84. The Rite of Penance states that other readings may be chosen (RP 100). For an introduction to the communal celebration of the Sacrament of Penance under ordinary circumstances, cf. RP 22–30 and CCC 1482.

Old Testament Readings

- **Gen. 3:1–19** She took the fruit of the tree and ate it.
- **Gen. 4:1–15** Cain set on his brother and killed him.
- **Gen. 18:17–33** The Lord said: I will not destroy the city for the sake of ten good men.
- **Exod. 17:1–7** They tempted the Lord saying: Is the Lord here or not?
- **Exod. 20:1–21** I am the Lord your God . . . you will not have other gods.
- **Deut. 6:3–9** Love the Lord your God with your whole heart.
- **Deut. 9:7–19** Your people quickly turned away from the wrong you had showed them.
- **Deut. 30:15–20** I set before you life and prosperity, death and evil.
- **2 Sam. 12:1–9, 13** David said to Nathan: I have sinned against the Lord God. Nathan said to David: The Lord has forgiven your sin; you will not die.

- **Neh. 9:1–20** The sons of Israel assembled for a fast; and confessed their sins.
- **Wisd. 1:1–16** Love justice, for wisdom will not enter an evil soul nor live in a body subjected to sin.
- **Wisd. 5:1–16** The hope of the wicked is like chaff borne by the wind. The just, however, live for ever.
- **Sir. 28:1–7** Forgive your neighbor when he hurts you, and then your sins will be forgiven when you pray.
- **Isa. 1:2–6, 15–18** I have nourished and educated sons; however, they have rebelled against me.
- **Isa. 5:1–7** The vineyard became my delight. He looked for grapes, but it yielded wild grapes.
- **Isa. 43:22–28** On account of me your iniquities are blotted out.
- **Isa. 53:1–12** The Lord laid upon him our guilt.
- **Isa. 55:1–11** Let the wicked man forsake his way and return to the Lord, and he will have mercy on him because he is generous in forgiving.
- **Isa. 58:1–11** When you give your soul to the hungry and fulfill the troubled soul, your light will rise like dawn from the darkness, and your darkness will be like midday.
- **Isa. 59:1–4, 9–15** Your iniquities divide you and your God.
- **Jer. 2:1–13** My people have done two evils: they have abandoned me, the fountain of living water, and have dug for themselves broken cisterns which hold no water.
- **Jer. 7:21–26** Listen to my voice, and I will be your God, and you will be my people.
- **Ezek. 11:14–21** I will take the heart of stone from their bodies, and I will give them a heart of flesh, so that they may walk according to my laws.
- **Ezek. 18:20–32** If a wicked man turns away from his sins, he shall live and not die.
- **Ezek. 36:23–28** I shall sprinkle upon you clean water, put my spirit within you, and make you walk according to my commands.
- **Hos. 2:16–25** I will make a covenant for them on that day.
- **Hos. 11:1–11** I took them in my arms, and they did not know that I cured them.
- **Hos. 14:2–9** Israel, return to the Lord your God.
- **Joel 2:12–19** Return to me with your whole heart.

- **Mic. 6:1–4, 4–6** Do right and love mercy, and walk humbly with your God.
- **Mic. 7:2–7, 18–20** The Lord will turn back and have mercy on us; he will cast all our sins into the depths of the sea.
- **Zech. 1:1–6** Return to me, and I shall return to you.

Responsorial Psalms

- **Ps. 13** All my hope, O Lord, is in your loving kindness (6a).
- **Ps. 25** Turn to me, Lord, and have mercy (16a).
- **Ps. 31:2–6** You have redeemed us, Lord, God of truth (6b).
- **Ps. 32** Lord, forgive the wrong I have done (5c).
- **Ps. 36** How precious is your unfailing love, Lord (8).
- **Ps. 50:7–8, 14–23** To the upright I will show the saving power of God (23b).
- **Ps. 51** Give back to me the joy of your salvation (14a).
- **Ps. 73** It is good for me to be with the Lord (28a).
- **Ps. 90** Fill us with your love, O Lord, and we will sing for joy! (14)
- **Ps. 95** If today you hear his voice, harden not your hearts (8a).
- **Ps. 119:1, 10–13, 15–16** Happy are they who follow the law of the Lord! (1)
- **Ps. 123** Our eyes are fixed on the Lord (2c).
- **Ps. 130** With the Lord there is mercy, and fullness of redemption (7bc).
- **Ps. 139:1–18, 23–24** You have searched me, and you know me, Lord (23a).
- **Ps. 143: 1–11** Teach me to do your will, my God (10).

New Testament Readings

- **Rom. 3:22–26** All men are justified by the gift of God through redemption in Christ Jesus.
- **Rom. 5:6–11** We give glory to God through our Lord Jesus Christ, through whom we have received reconciliation.
- **Rom. 6:2b–13** Consider yourselves dead to sin but alive to God.
- **Rom. 6:16–23** The wages of sin is death; the gift of God is eternal life in Christ Jesus our Lord.
- **Rom. 7:14–25** Unhappy man that I am! Who will free me? Thanks to God through Jesus Christ our Lord.

- **Rom. 12:1–2, 9–19** Be transformed by the renewal of your mind.
- **Rom. 13:8–14** Let us cast away the works of darkness and put on the weapons of light.
- **2 Cor. 5:17–21** God reconciled the world to himself through Christ.
- **Gal. 5:16–24** You cannot belong to Christ unless you crucify the flesh with its passions and concupiscence.
- **Eph. 2:1–10** When we were dead to sin, God, on account of his great love for us, brought us to life in Christ.
- **Eph. 4:1–3, 17–32** Renew yourself and put on the new man.
- **Eph. 5:1–14** You were once in darkness; now you are light in the Lord, so walk as children of light.
- **Eph. 6:10–18** Put God's armor on so that you will be able to stand firm against evil.
- **Col. 3:1–10, 12–17** If you were raised to life with Christ, aspire to the realm above. Put to death what remains in this earthly life.
- **Heb. 12:1–5** You have not resisted to the point of shedding your blood in your struggle against sin.
- **James 1:22–27** Be doers of the word and not merely listeners.
- **James 2:14–26** What use is it if someone says that he believes and does not manifest it in works?
- **James 3:1–12** If someone does not offend in word, he is a perfect man.
- **1 Pet. 1:13–23** You have been redeemed not by perishable goods, gold or silver, but by the precious blood of Jesus Christ.
- **2 Pet. 1:3–11** Be careful so that you may make firm your calling and election.
- **1 John 1:5–10; 2:1–2** If we confess our sins, he is faithful and just and will forgive our sins and cleanse us from all injustice.
- **1 John 2:3–11** Whoever hates his brother remains in darkness.
- **1 John 3:1–24** We know that we have crossed over from death to life because we love our brothers.
- **1 John 4:16–21** God is love, and he who lives in love, lives in God, and God in him.
- **Rev. 2:1–5** Do penance and return to your former ways.
- **Rev. 3:14–22** Because you are lukewarm, neither hot or cold, I will vomit you out of my mouth.
- **Rev. 20:11–15** All have been judged according to their works.

- **Rev. 21:1–8** Whoever conquers will inherit all this, and I will be his God, and he will be my son.

Gospels

- **Matt. 3:1–12** Repent, for the kingdom of heaven is close at hand.
- **Matt. 4:12–17** Repent, for the kingdom of heaven is close at hand.
- **Matt. 5:1–12** When he saw the crowds, he went up to the hill and taught his disciples.
- **Matt. 5:13–16** Let your light shine before men.
- **Matt. 5:17–47** But I am speaking to you.
- **Matt. 9:1–8** Have confidence, my son; your sins are forgiven.
- **Matt. 9:9–13** I did not come to call the just, but sinners.
- **Matt. 18:15–20** You have won back your brother.
- **Matt. 18:21–35** This is the way my heavenly Father will deal with you unless each one forgives his brother from his heart.
- **Matt. 25:31–46** Whatever you have done to the very least of my brothers, you have done to me.
- **Matt. 26:69–75** Peter went outside and wept bitterly.
- **Mark 12:28–34** This is the first commandment.
- **Luke 7:36–50** Her many sins must have been forgiven her, because she loved much.
- **Luke 13:1–5** Unless you repent you will all perish as they did.
- **Luke 15:1–10** Heaven is filled with joy when one sinner turns back to God.
- **Luke 15:11–32** When he was still far away, his father saw him and was moved with mercy. He ran to him and embraced and kissed him.
- **Luke 17:1–4** If your brother sins against you seven times a day and returns to you seven times a day and says I am sorry, you must forgive him.
- **Luke 18:9–14** God, be merciful to me, a sinner.
- **Luke 19:1–10** The Son of Man has come to seek out and save what was lost.
- **Luke 23:39–43** Today you will be with me in paradise.
- **John 8:1–11** Go and sin no more.
- **John 8:31–36** Everyone who commits sin is a slave of sin.
- **John 15:1–8** The Father prunes every barren branch, and every branch that bears fruit he makes it bear even more.

• **John 15:9–14** You are my friends if you do what I command you.

• **John 19:13–37** They shall look upon him whom they pierced.

• **John 20:19–23** Receive the Holy Spirit; whose sins you forgive, they are forgiven.

ANOINTING OF THE SICK:
MASS FOR THE SICK

Readings for Masses for the Sick (PCS 297 [=OUI 152–223]) are included here as they are the most directly related to the topic of symbols and types of Anointing of the Sick. Other liturgies dealing with Anointing of the Sick include the Mass for Viaticum (cf. PCS 298 [=OUI 247–258]), Christian Initiation for the Dying (cf. PCS 283 [=OUI 1287]), and the Commendation of the Dying (cf. PCS 217–218 [=OUI 143–144]). For the sake of brevity these are not included here.

Old Testament Readings

• **1 Kings 19:4–8** God strengthens and sustains his servants.

• **Job 3:3, 11–17, 20–23** Why should the sufferer be born to see the light?

• **Job 7:1–4, 6–11** Remember that our life is like the wind, and yet we are destined for eternal life with God.

• **Job 7:12–21** What are we, that you make much of us?

• **Job 19:23–27a** (for the dying) I know that my Redeemer lives.

• **Wisd. 9:1, 9–18** Who could know your counsel? We ask to share in God's wisdom.

• **Isa. 35:1–10** Strengthen the feeble hands.

• **Isa. 52:13–53:12** He bore our sufferings himself.

• **Isa. 61:1–3a** The spirit of the Lord is upon me to comfort all who mourn.

New Testament Readings
Easter Season

• **Acts 3:1–10** In the name of Jesus, stand up and walk.

• **Acts 3:11–16** Faith in Jesus has given this man perfect health.

• **Acts 4:8–12** There is no other name but the name of Jesus by which we are saved.

• **Acts 13:32–39** The one whom God raised from the dead will never see corruption of the flesh.

Other Times in the Year

• **Rom. 8:14–17** If we suffer with him, we will be glorified with him.
• **Rom. 8:18–27** We groan while we wait for the redemption of our bodies. The Spirit enables us to pray in our suffering.
• **Rom. 8:31b–35, 37–39** Nothing can come between us and the love of Christ.
• **Rom. 12:1–2** All our lives, even our suffering and pain, are caught up in the offering of Christ in obedience to the will of our Father.
• **1 Cor. 1:18–25** God's weakness is stronger than human strength.
• **1 Cor. 12:12–22, 24b–27** If one member suffers, all the members suffer.
• **1 Cor. 15:1–4** The death and Resurrection of Christ is the basis of our faith.
• **1 Cor. 15:12–20** (for the dying) Christ has been raised from the dead; through him has come the resurrection of us all.
• **2 Cor. 4:16–18** Though our body is being weakened, our spirit is renewed.
• **2 Cor. 5:1, 6–10** (for the dying) We have an everlasting home in heaven.
• **Gal. 4:12–19** My illness gave me the opportunity to bring the Gospel to you.
• **Phil. 2:25–30** He was ill and almost died but God took pity on him.
• **Col. 1:22–29** In my flesh I fill up what is lacking in the sufferings of Christ for the sake of his body.
• **Heb. 4:14–16; 5:7–9** Jesus identified himself with us totally; he suffered, and through his suffering discovered the will of the Father.
• **James 5:13–16** This prayer, made in faith, will save the sick person.
• **1 Pet. 1:3–9** You will rejoice even though for a short time you must suffer.
• **1 John 3:1–2** What we shall be has not yet been revealed.
• **Rev. 21:1–7** There will be no more death or mourning, sadness or pain.
• **Rev. 22:17, 20–21** (for the dying) Come, Lord Jesus.

Responsorial Psalms

• **Isa. 38:10–12, 16–17** You saved my life, O Lord; I shall not die (*cf.* 17b).
• **Ps. 6:2–6, 9–10** Have mercy on me, Lord; my strength is gone (3a).
• **Ps. 25:4–10, 14–16** To you, O Lord, I lift my soul (1).

- **Ps. 27:1, 4–5, 7–10** Put your hope in the Lord; take courage and be strong (14).
- **Ps. 34:2–7, 10–13, 17, 19** The Lord is near to broken hearts (19a).
- **Ps. 42:3, 5; Ps. 43:3–4** Like a deer that longs for running streams, my soul longs for you, my God (42:2).
- **Ps. 63:2, 3–4, 5–6, 8–9** My soul is thirsting for you, O Lord my God (2b).
- **Ps. 71:1–2, 5–6, 8–9, 14–15** My God, come quickly to help me (12b).
- **Ps. 86:1–6, 11–13, 15–16** Listen, Lord, and answer me (1a).
- **Ps. 90:2–6, 9–10, 12, 14, 16** In every age, O Lord, you have been our refuge (1).
- **Ps. 102:2–3, 24–28, 19–21** O Lord, hear my prayer and let my cry come to you (2).
- **Ps. 103:1–4, 11–18** O bless the Lord, my soul (1).
- **Ps. 123:1–3** Our eyes are fixed on the Lord, pleading for his mercy (2).
- **Ps. 143:1–2, 5–6, 10–11** O Lord, hear my prayer (2).

Alleluia Verse

- **Ps. 34:22** Lord, let your mercy be on us, as we place our trust in you.
- **Matt. 5:4** Happy are they who mourn; they shall be comforted.
- **Matt. 8:17** He bore our sickness, and endured our suffering.
- **Matt. 11:28** Come to me, all you who labor and are burdened, and I will give you rest, says the Lord.
- **2 Cor. 1:3b–4a** Blessed be the Father of mercies and the God of all comfort, who consoles us in all our afflictions.
- **Eph. 1:3** Blessed be God, the Father of our Lord Jesus Christ, for he has blessed us with every spiritual gift in Christ.
- **James 1:12** Blessed are they who stand firm when trials come; when they have stood the test, they will win the crown of life.

Gospels

- **Matt. 5:1–12a** Rejoice and be glad, for your reward is great in heaven.
- **Matt. 8:1–4** If you wish to do so, you can cure me.
- **Matt. 8:5–17** He bore our infirmities.
- **Matt. 11:25–30** Come to me, all you who labor.
- **Matt. 15:29–31** Jesus heals large crowds.

- **Matt. 25:31–40** As often as you did it to the least of these who belong to me, you did it to me.
- **Mark 2:1–12** Seeing their faith, Jesus said to the sick man: Your sins are forgiven.
- **Mark 4:35–41** Why are you so fearful? Why do you not have faith?
- **Mark 10:46–52** Jesus, Son of David, have mercy on me.
- **Mark 16:15–20** They will place their hands on the sick and they will recover.
- **Luke 7:19–23** Go tell John what you have seen.
- **Luke 10:5–6, 8–9** Heal the sick, Jesus commanded his followers.
- **Luke 10:25–37** Who is my neighbor?
- **Luke 11:5–13** Ask and it will be given to you.
- **Luke 12:35–44** Happy are those whom the master finds watching when he returns.
- **Luke 18:9–14** O God, be merciful to me, a sinner.
- **John 6:35–40** (for the dying) It is the will of my Father that what he has given me will not perish.
- **John 6:53–58** (for the dying) Whoever eats this bread has eternal life.
- **John 9:1–7** The blind man has not sinned; it was to let God's work show forth in him.
- **John 10:11–18** The good shepherd lays down his life for his sheep.

Holy Orders

Readings for the Ordination of Deacons, Priests, and Bishops (Lectionary 770–774; RO 346–351).

Old Testament Readings

- **Num. 3:5–9** (for deacons) Summon the tribe of Levi and present them to Aaron the priest, as his assistants.
- **Num. 11:11b–12, 14–17, 24–25** (for priests) I will take some of the Spirit that is on you and I will bestow it on them.
- **Isa. 61:1–3abcd** (For bishops and priests) The Lord has anointed me; he has sent me to bring glad tidings to the lowly and to give them the oil of gladness.
- **Jer. 1:4–9** To whomever I send you, you shall go.

New Testament Readings

- **Acts 6:1–7b** (for deacons) Select from among you seven reputable men.
- **Acts 8:26–40** (for deacons) Beginning with this Scripture passage, Philip proclaimed Jesus to him.
- **Acts 10:37–43** We are witnesses of all that he did both in the country of the Jews and in Jerusalem.
- **Acts 20:17–18a, 28–32, 36** (For bishops and priests) Keep watch over yourselves and over the whole flock of which the Holy Spirit has appointed you overseers, in which you tend the Church of God.
- **Rom. 12:4–8** We have gifts that differ according to the grace given to us.
- **2 Cor. 4:1–2, 5–7** For we do not preach ourselves but Jesus Christ as Lord, and ourselves as your slaves for the sake of Jesus.
- **2 Cor. 5:14–20** He has given us the ministry of reconciliation.
- **Eph. 4:1–7, 11–13** In the work of ministry, in building up the Body of Christ.
- **1 Tim. 3:8–10, 12–13** (for deacons) Holding fast to the mystery of the faith with a clear conscience.
- **1 Tim. 4:12–16** (for priests) Do not neglect the gift you have, which was conferred on you with the imposition of hands by the presbyterate. *Or:* **1 Tim. 4:12b–16** (for bishops).
- **2 Tim. 1:6–14** (for bishops) To stir into flame the gift of God that you have through the laying on of hands.
- **Heb. 5:1–10** Christ was acclaimed by God as high priest, in the line of Melchizedek.
- **1 Pet. 4:7b–11** As good stewards of God's varied grace.
- **1 Pet. 5:1–4** Tend the flock of God in your midst.

Responsorial Psalms

- **Ps. 23:1–3a, 3b–4, 5, 6** The Lord is my shepherd; there is nothing I shall want (1).
- **Ps. 84:3–4, 5, 11** Blessed are they who dwell in your house, O Lord (5a).
- **Ps. 89:21–22, 25 and 27** For ever I will sing the goodness of the Lord (2a).
- **Ps. 96:1–2a, 2b–3, 10** Go out to the world and teach all nations, alleluia.
- **Ps. 100:1b–2, 3, 4, 5** You are my friends, says the Lord, if you do what I command you (John 15:14).

- **Ps. 110:1, 2, 3, 4** Christ the Lord, a priest for ever in the line of Melchizedek, offered bread and wine. *Or*: You are a priest for ever, in the line of Melchizedek (4b).
- **Ps. 116:12–13, 17–18** Our blessing cup is a communion with the blood of Christ (1 Cor. 10:16). *Or*: Alleluia.
- **Ps. 117:1, 2** Go out to all the world, and tell the Good News (Mark 16:15). *Or*: Alleluia.

Alleluia Verse

- **Matt. 28:19a, 20b** Go and teach all nations, says the Lord; I am with you always, until the end of the world.
- **Luke 4:18** The Lord sent me to bring glad tidings to the poor and to proclaim liberty to captives.
- **John 10:14** I am the good shepherd, says the Lord; I know my sheep, and mine know me.
- **John 15:15b** I call you my friends, says the Lord, for I have made known to you all that the Father has told me.

Gospels

- **Matt. 5:13–16** You are the light of the world.
- **Matt. 9:35–38** Ask the master of the harvest to send out laborers for his harvest.
- **Matt. 10:1–5a** Jesus chose twelve Apostles and sent them out.
- **Matt. 20:25b–28** Whoever wishes to be first among you shall be your slave.
- **Luke 10:1–9** The harvest is abundant but the laborers are few.
- **Luke 12:35–44** Blessed are those servants whom the master finds awake on his arrival.
- **Luke 22:14–20, 24–30** Do this in memory of me. I am among you as the one who serves.
- **John 10:11–16** A good shepherd lays down his life for the sheep.
- **John 12:24–26** Whoever serves me must follow me.
- **John 15:9–17** It was not you who chose me, but I who chose you.
- **John 17:6, 14–19** I consecrate myself for them, so that they also may be consecrated in truth.

- **John 20:19–23** As the Father has sent me, so I send you. Receive the Holy Spirit.
- **John 21:15–17** Feed my lambs, feed my sheep.

Matrimony

From the "Texts for use in the Marriage Rite and in the Wedding Mass" (RMat 67–105).

Old Testament Readings

- **Gen. 1:26–28, 31a** Male and female he created them.
- **Gen. 2:18–24** And they will be two in one flesh.
- **Gen. 24:48–51, 58–67** Isaac loved Rebekah, and so he was consoled for the loss of his mother.
- **Tob. 7:9–10, 11–15** May God join you together and fill you with his blessings.
- **Tob. 8:5–10** May God bring us to old age together.
- **Song 2:8–10, 14, 16a; 8:6–7a** For love is as strong as death.
- **Eccles. 26:1–4, 16–21** (LXX: Eccles. 26:1–4, 13–16) Like the sun rising is the beauty of a good wife in a well-kept house.
- **Jer. 31:31–32a, 33–34a** I will make a new covenant with the House of Israel and Judah.

New Testament Readings

- **Rom. 8:31b–35, 37–39** Who will separate us from the love of Christ?
- **Rom. 12:1–2, 9–18** (longer) *or* **Rom. 12:1–2, 9–13** (shorter) Offer to God your bodies as a living and holy sacrifice, truly pleasing to him.
- **1 Cor. 6:13e–15a, 17–20** Your body is a temple of the Spirit.
- **1 Cor. 12:31; 13:8a** If I am without love, it will do me no good whatever.
- **Eph. 5:2a, 21–33** (longer) *or* **Eph. 5:2a, 25–32** (shorter) This mystery has many implications, and I am saying it applies to Christ and the Church.
- **Col. 3:12–17** Above all have love, which is the bond of perfection.
- **1 Pet. 3:1–9** You should agree with one another, be sympathetic and love the brothers.
- **1 John 3:18–24** Our love is to be something real and active.
- **1 John 4:7–12** God is love.

• **Rev. 19:1, 5–9a** Happy are those who are invited to the wedding feast of the Lamb.

Responsorial Psalms

• **Ps. 33:12 and 18, 20–21, 22** The earth is full of the goodness of the Lord (5b).
• **Ps. 34:2–3, 4–5, 6–7, 8–9** I will bless the Lord at all times (2a). *Or:* Taste and see the goodness of the Lord (9a).
• **Ps. 103:1–2, 8 and 13, 17–18a** The Lord is kind and merciful (8a). *Or:* The Lord's kindness is everlasting to those who fear him (17).
• **Ps. 112:1–2, 3–4, 5–7a, 7bc–8, 9** Happy are those who do what the Lord commands (1b). *Or:* Alleluia.
• **Ps. 128:1–2, 3, 4–5** Happy are those who fear the Lord (1a). *Or:* See how the Lord blesses those who fear him (4).
• **Ps. 145:8–9, 10 and 15, 17–18** The Lord is compassionate to all his creatures (9a).
• **Ps. 148:1–2, 3–4, 9–10, 11–12ab, 12c–14a** Let all praise the name of the Lord (12c). *Or:* Alleluia.

Alleluia Verse

• **1 John 4:7b** Everyone who loves is born of God and knows him.
• **1 John 4:8, 11** God is love; let us love one another as he has loved us.
• **1 John 4:12** If we love one another God will live in us in perfect love.
• **1 John 4:16** He who lives in love, lives in God, and God in him.

Gospels

• **Matt. 5:1–12** Rejoice and be glad, for your reward will be great in heaven.
• **Matt. 5:13–16** You are the light of the world.
• **Matt. 7:21, 24–29** (longer) *or* **7:21, 24–25** (shorter) He built his house on rock.
• **Matt. 19:3–6** So then, what God has united, man must not divide.
• **Matt. 22:35–40** This is the greatest and the first commandment. The second is similar to it.
• **Mark 10:6–9** They are no longer two, therefore, but one body.
• **John 2:1–11** This was the first of the signs given by Jesus; it was given at Cana in Galilee.

- **John 15:9–12** Remain in my love.
- **John 15:12–16** This is my commandment: love one another.
- **John 17:20–26** (longer) *or* **20–23** (shorter) May they be completely one.

Authors of 2nd Readings
from the Liturgy of the Hours

List of authors of the 2nd readings from the Liturgy of the Hours, organized chronologically. Only authors cited in this book are included.

1. **Pope St. Clement I** (died 99)—Bishop of Rome from 92–99. Ordained by St. Peter. Martyr.
2. **St. Ignatius of Antioch** (35–107)—Bishop of Antioch. Student of St. John the Apostle. Appointed bishop of Antioch by St. Peter. Martyr.
3. **Didache** (c. 100)—Brief early Christian treatise.
4. **St. Polycarp** (69–155)—Bishop of Smyrna. Disciple of St. John the Apostle. Martyr.
5. **St. Justin Martyr** (c. 100–165)—Martyr.
6. **St. Melito of Sardis** (died c. 180)—Bishop of Sardis.
7. **St. Irenaeus** (130–202)—Bishop of Lugdunum (now Lyons, France). Student of St. Polycarp. Martyr.
8. **Tertullian** (c. 160–220)—Priest.
9. **St. Hippolytus** (170–235)—Priest. Possibly bishop and anti-pope. Possibly martyr.
10. **Origen** (c. 185–254)—Theologian.
11. **St. Cyprian of Carthage** (c. 200–258)—Bishop of Carthage. Martyr.
12. **Aphrahat (or Aphraates)** (c. 270–345)—Monk. Possibly bishop.
13. **St. Hilary of Poitiers** (c. 300–368)—Bishop of Poitiers. Doctor of the Church.
14. **St. Ephrem the Syrian** (c. 306–373)—Deacon. Doctor of the Church.
15. **St. Athanasius of Alexandria** (c. 298–373)—Bishop of Alexandria. Doctor of the Church.
16. **St. Basil the Great** (c. 330–379)—Bishop of Caesarea Mazaca. Doctor of the Church.

17. **St. Cyril of Jerusalem** (c. 313–386)—Bishop of Jerusalem. Doctor of the Church.

18. **St. Gregory of Nazianzus** (c. 329–390)—Archbishop of Constantinople. Doctor of the Church.

19. **St. Macarius** (c. 300–391)—Monk and hermit.

20. **St. Pacian** (c. 310–391)—Bishop of Barcelona from about 365–391.

21. **St. Gregory of Nyssa** (c. 335–395)—Bishop of Nyssa.

22. **St. Ambrose** (c. 340–397)—Archbishop of Milan. Doctor of the Church.

23. **Didymus of Alexandria** (c. 313–398)—Lay teacher.

24. **Faustus Luciferanus** (fourth century)—Priest.

25. **St. John Chrystostom** (c. 347–407)—Archbishop of Constantinople. Doctor of the Church.

26. **St. Gaudentius of Brescia** (died 410)—Bishop of Brescia from 387–410.

27. **St. Asterius of Amasea** (c. 350–410)—Bishop of Amasea.

28. **St. Jerome** (c. 347–420)—Priest. Doctor of the Church.

29. **St. Maximus of Turin** (died between 408 and 423)—Bishop of Turin.

30. **Sulpicius Severus** (c. 363–425)—Christian writer. Biographer of St. Martin of Tours.

31. **St. Augustine** (354–430)—Bishop of Hippo. Doctor of the Church.

32. **St. Cyril of Alexandria** (c. 376–444)—Patriarch of Alexandria from 412–444. Doctor of the Church.

33. **St. Proclus of Constantinople** (died c. 447)—Archbishop of Constantinople.

34. **St. Peter Chrysologus** (c. 380–450)—Bishop of Ravenna from about 433–450. Doctor of the Church.

35. **Theodoret of Cyr** (393–457)—Bishop of Cyr.

36. **Pope St. Leo the Great** (c. 400–461)—Bishop of Rome from 440–461. Doctor of the Church.

37. **Faustus of Riez** (c. 410–495)—Bishop of Riez.

38. **Diadochus of Photice** (fifth century)—Bishop of Photice.

39. **St. Fulgentius of Ruspe** (462 or 467–527 or 533)—Bishop of Ruspe.

40. **Procopius of Gaza** (c. 465–528)—Rhetorician.

41. **St. Caesarius of Arles** (c. 470–542)—Bishop of Arles from 502–542.

42. **Pope St. Gregory the Great** (c. 540–604)—Bishop of Rome. Doctor of the Church.

43. **St. Columban** (543–615)—Monk and missionary.

44. **St. Maximus the Confessor** (c. 580–662)—Monk.

45. **Pseudo-Chrysostom** (sixth century).

46. **Pope St. Martin I** (died 655)—Bishop of Rome from 649–655. Martyr.

47. **St. Gregory of Agrigentum** (seventh century)—Bishop of Agrigentum.

48. **St. Andrew of Crete** (c. 650–712, 726, or 740)—Bishop of Crete.

49. **St. Boniface** (c. 675–754)—Missionary. Archbishop of Mainz. Martyr.

50. **St. Bede the Venerable** (c. 673–735)—Monk. Doctor of the Church.

51. **St. John Damascene** (c. 676–749)—Priest and monk. Doctor of the Church.

52. **Old Slavonic Life of Constantine** (c. 880)—Biography of St. Cyril (born with the name Constantine) and St. Methodius (born with the name Michael), missionaries of the Slavic peoples.

53. **St. Peter Damian** (c. 1007–1073)—Monk. Reformer. Cardinal-Bishop of Ostia. Doctor of the Church.

54. **St. Bernard of Clairvaux** (1090–1153)—Abbot. Doctor of the Church.

55. **St. Aelred** (1110–1167)—Abbot.

56. **Bl. Isaac of Stella** (c. 1100–1170)—Monk.

57. **St. Thomas Becket** (c. 1120–1170)—Archbishop of Canterbury. Martyr.

58. **Pope St. Gregory VII** (c. 1051/1028–1085)—Bishop of Rome from 1073–1085.

59. **Baldwin of Canterbury** (c. 1125–1190)—Archbishop of Canterbury from 1185–1190.

60. **St. Louis IX of France** (1214–1270)—King of France from 1226–1270.

61. **St. Bonaventure** (1221–1274)—Franciscan friar and Bishop of Albano. Doctor of the Church.

62. **St. Thomas Aquinas** (1225–1274)—Dominican friar and priest. Doctor of the Church.

63. **St. Raymond of Penyafort** (c. 1175–1275)—Dominican friar. Compiler of the Decretals of Gregory IX.

64. **St. Albert the Great** (1193/1206–1280)—Dominican friar. Bishop of Regensburg from 1260–1263, when he resigned. Teacher of St. Thomas Aquinas. Doctor of the Church.

65. **St. Bridget of Sweden** (1303–1373)—Founder of the Bridgettines.

66. **St. Catherine of Siena** (1347–1380)—Tertiary of the Dominican Order. Doctor of the Church.

67. **St. Vincent Ferrer** (1350–1419)—Dominican friar.

68. **St. John of Capistrano** (1386–1456)—Franciscan friar. Priest.

69. **Thomas à Kempis** (c. 1380–1471)—Monk.

70. **St. John Fisher** (1469–1535)—Bishop of Rochester. Martyr.

71. **St. Anthony Zaccaria** (1502–1539)—Priest.

72. **St. Cajetan** (1480–1547)—Priest. Founder of the Theatines.

73. **St. John of Avila** (1499–1569)—Priest. Doctor of the Church.

74. **St. Charles Borromeo** (1538–1584)—Cardinal Archbishop of Milan from 1564–1584.

75. **St. Peter Canisius** (1521–1597)—Jesuit priest. Doctor of the Church.

76. **St. Mary Magdalene of Pazzi** (1566–1607)—Carmelite mystic.

77. **St. John Leonardi** (1541–1609)—Priest. Founder of the Clerks Regular of the Mother of God of Lucca.

78. **St. John de Brébeuf** (1593–1649)—Jesuit priest. Apostle of the Hurons. Martyr.

79. **St. John Eudes** (1601–1680)—Priest and missionary.

80. **St. Margaret Mary Alacoque** (1647–1690)—Nun and mystic. Promoted devotion to the Sacred Heart.

81. **St. Paul of the Cross** (1694–1775)—Priest. Founder of the Passionists.

82. **St. Peter Julian Eymard** (1811–1868)—Priest and founder.

83. **St. Anthony Mary Claret** (1807–1870)—Archbishop of Santiago, Cuba. Founder of the Claretians.

84. **St. Marie Bernadette Soubirous** (1844–1879)—Received apparitions at Lourdes in 1858. Nun.

85. **Pope Pius XI** (1857–1939)—Bishop of Rome from 1922–1939.

86. **St. Pope John XXIII** (1881–1963)—Bishop of Rome from 1958–1963.

87. **Vatican II** (1962–1965)—Twenty-first Ecumenical Council of the Catholic Church.

88. **Pope Paul VI** (1897–1978)—Bishop of Rome from 1963–1978.

2nd Readings from the Liturgy of Hours

ORDINARY TIME

- LH, Corpus Christi, 2R: St. Thomas Aquinas, Opusculum 57, in festo Corporis Christi, lect. 1–3 – Jesus Christ left the Eucharist as a memorial of his death and Resurrection. In doing so he fulfilled the types and figures of the Old Covenant (EUCHARIST: *Types*: Passover / Passover Lamb; Animal Sacrifices; *Symbols*: Banquet; Bread and Wine / Nourishment).
- LH, Sacred Heart, 2R: St. Bonaventure, On the Tree of Life, 29–30.47: Opera Omnia 8, 79 – The water from the side of Christ gives birth to the Church, power to the sacraments, and is a spring of living water in the hearts of those living in Christ; invitation to draw water from this spring (BAPTISM: *Types:* Water from the Side of Christ; *Symbols*: Fountain of Water; EUCHARIST: *Types*: Blood from the Side of Christ).
- LH, OT.2.Su, 2R: St. Ignatius of Antioch, Letter to the Ephesians, 2, 2–5, 2: Funk 1, 175–177 – How the faithful should be united to the bishops and the priests, forming a harmonious choir that sings the song that is Jesus Christ (EUCHARIST: *Symbols*: Altar / Table).
- LH, OT.2.Mo, 2R: St. Ignatius of Antioch, Letter to the Ephesians, 13–18, 1: Funk 1, 183–187 – How we should live in faith and love, in fidelity to the doctrine of Christ.
- LH, OT.2.Th, 2R: St. Fulgentius of Ruspe, Epist. 14, 36–37: CCL 91, 429–431 – We finish our prayers by saying "through Jesus Christ, your Son, our Lord" because it is through our union with Christ as priest that our sacrifices and offerings are pleasing to God (HOLY ORDERS: *Types:* High Priest).
- LH, OT.2.Fr, 2R: Diadochus of Photice, Treatise on Spiritual Perfection, Ch. 12.13.14: PG 65, 1171–1172 – How we should love God and not

ourselves, and how this divine love transforms our life (CONFIRMATION: *Symbols:* Fire).

- LH, OT.2.Sa, 2R: St. Irenaeus, Against Heresies, Book 4, 18, 1–2.4.5: SC 100, 596–598.606.610–612 – The offering of the Eucharist is pleasing to God. While the offerings of the Old Covenant were offerings of slaves, this is the offering of sons (EUCHARIST: *Types:* Offering of the First Fruits; Animal Sacrifices; *Symbols:* Bread and Wine / Nourishment).

- LH, OT.3.Su, 2R: Vatican II, Sacrosanctum Concilium 7–8.106 – The liturgy is the prayer of the head, Jesus Christ, and of the body, the Church, together. It is lived especially in the Sunday Eucharistic Celebration (EUCHARIST: *Types:* Passover / Passover Lamb; *Symbols:* Bread for the Journey / Daily Bread / Viaticum; HOLY ORDERS: *Symbols:* Head of the Body).

- LH, OT.3.Fr, 2R: St. John Fisher, Ps. 101: Opera Omnia, ed. 1597, pp. 1588–1589 – God lavished his love upon the Israelites in the desert and even so they were ungrateful; he has given us even greater gifts, let us not forget them (EUCHARIST: *Types:* Water from the Rock).

- LH, OT.4.Mo, 2R: St. Hilary of Poitiers, Commentary on the Psalms, Ps. 132 (Ps. 133): PLS 1, 244–245 – Believers living in harmony and unity are like the oil which anoints the head and beard of Aaron and gives off a sweet fragrance (CONFIRMATION: *Symbols:* Anointing; HOLY ORDERS: *Types:* Priesthood; Anointing of Priests, Prophets, and Kings).

- LH, OT.5.Tu, 2R: Origen, Homily on Genesis 8, 6.8.9: PG 12, 206–209 – How Abraham's sacrifice of his son Isaac prefigured the sacrifice of Jesus on the cross (HOLY ORDERS: *Types:* Priesthood).

- LH, OT.5.Fr, 2R: St. Augustine, On Galatians, 37–38: PL 35, 2131–2132 – How St. Paul suffered like a parent until Christ was fully formed in the Christians under his care (HOLY ORDERS: *Symbols:* Father).

- LH, OT.6.Su, 2R: St. Ephrem, Commentary on the Diatessaron, 1, 18–19: SC 121, 52–53 – The Word of God is like the tree of life, the living spring, the rock struck in the desert. This spring quenches thirst and is never exhausted (BAPTISM: *Symbols:* Fountain of Water).

- LH, OT.6.We, 2R: Procopius of Gaza, Commentary on the Book of Proverbs, Ch. 9: PG 87–1, 1299–1303 – How Wisdom has prepared a banquet for the soul and, through the ministry of the apostles, invites the soul to come and eat and drink (EUCHARIST: *Types:* Wisdom's Banquet; *Symbols:*

Altar / Table; Bread and Wine / Nourishment; Bread from Heaven / Bread of Life / Bread of Angels; HOLY ORDERS: *Symbols*: Servant).

- LH, OT.6.Fr, 2R: St. Augustine, Tractates on the first letter of John, 4: PL 35, 2008–2009 – The soul is like a container that only God can fill (CONFIRMATION: *Symbols:* Anointing).
- LH, OT.7.Mo, 2R: St. Gregory of Nyssa, Homily on Ecclesiastes, 5: PG 44, 683–686 – Christ is the head of the body, and the wise man keeps his eyes on him (HOLY ORDERS: *Symbols:* Head of the Body).
- LH, OT.7.Fr, 2R: St. Gregory of Agrigentum, Commentary on Ecclesiastes, Lib. 8, 6: PG 98, 1071–1074 – First a literal and then spiritual interpretation are presented of Eccles. 9:7–8. In the spiritual interpretation this passage refers to the Eucharist, which gives a mystical sharing in the Word, clothes in light, and anoints with the Spirit of truth (EUCHARIST: *Types*: Wisdom's Banquet; Blood from the Side of Christ).
- LH, OT.8.Su, 2R: St. Gregory the Great, Moral Reflections on Job, Book 1, 2.36: PL 75, 529–530.543–544 – The Christian is called to be simple as a dove and wise as a serpent. The Holy Spirit manifested himself as a dove and as fire to teach us to be simple and full of zeal (BAPTISM: *Symbols:* Dove; CONFIRMATION: *Symbols:* Fire).
- LH, OT.10.Mo, 2R: St. Ignatius of Antioch, Letter to the Romans, 3, 1–5, 3: Funk 1, 215–219 – St. Ignatius asks the Romans to allow him to reach martyrdom and Jesus Christ (EUCHARIST: *Symbols*: Gift of Finest Wheat).
- LH, OT.10.Tu, 2R: St. Ignatius of Antioch, Letter to the Romans, 6, 1–9, 3: Funk 1, 219–223 – The desire of St. Ignatius to reach martyrdom and Jesus Christ (BAPTISM: *Symbols:* Fountain of Water; HOLY ORDERS: *Symbols*: Shepherd).
- LH, OT.10.We, 2R: Origen, Homily on Joshua, 4, 1: PG 12, 842–843 – The history of Israel (Egypt → Red Sea → Jordan → Promised Land) is a type of one who is brought from paganism through catechesis and Baptism to the promised land of the Church (BAPTISM: *Types:* Crossing of the Red Sea; Crossing of the Jordan River; HOLY ORDERS: *Types:* Levites; Priesthood).
- LH, OT.11.Mo, 2R: St. Cyprian, On the Lord's Prayer, 8–9: CSEL 3, 271–272 – The Christian does not say "My Father," but "Our Father." Through Baptism he is made part of the People of God and can call God "Father" (BAPTISM: *Symbols:* Second Birth).

- LH, OT.11.Th, 2R: St. Cyprian, Treatise on the Lord's Prayer, 18.22: CSEL 3, 280–281.283–284 – Jesus Christ is the bread of life, whom we receive in the Eucharist. We pray, "Give us this day our daily bread;" that is, may we never be unable to receive the Eucharist because of serious sin. (EUCHARIST: *Symbols:* Bread and Wine / Nourishment; Bread for the Journey / Daily Bread / Viaticum; Bread from Heaven / Bread of Life / Bread of Angels).
- LH, OT.12.Su, 2R: Faustus Luciferanus, Treatise on the Trinity, 39–40: CCL 69, 340–341 – How Jesus is eternally both priest and king, anointed by the chrism of the Holy Spirit (BAPTISM: *Types:* Anointing of Priests, Prophets, and Kings; EUCHARIST: *Types:* Offering of Melchizedek; HOLY ORDERS: *Types:* Melchizedek; Anointing of Priests, Prophets, and Kings).
- LH, OT.12.Mo, 2R: St. Gregory of Nyssa, On Christian Perfection: PG 46, 254–255 – Each title of Christ indicates a different facet of his person. Like Paul, the Christian should imitate Christ in each of these facets (EUCHARIST: *Types:* Water from the Rock).
- LH, OT.12.Tu, 2R: St. Gregory of Nyssa, On Christian Perfection: PG 46, 283–286 – The entire life of a Christian, in thoughts, words, and deeds, should be like Christ. Draw pure water from him, the source of life and harmony (BAPTISM: *Symbols:* Fountain of Water).
- LH, OT.13.Su, 2R: Pope Paul VI, Homily, November 29, 1970 – Jesus Christ is our all. All things and all history converge in Christ (BAPTISM: *Symbols:* Fountain of Water).
- LH, OT.13.Mo, 2R: St. Augustine, Sermo 47, 1.2.3.6, De ovibus: CCL 41, 572–573.575–576 – God is creator and shepherd of his sheep. His shepherds are both shepherds and sheep. He cares for his sheep, who should trust him. At the final judgment he will separate the sheep from the goats (HOLY ORDERS: *Symbols:* Shepherd).
- LH, OT.13.Tu, 2R: St. Augustine, Sermo 47, 12–14, De ovibus: CCL 41, 582–584 – Christ is the Good Shepherd. His faithful shepherds live in him. We should seek to be faithful to our conscience and give good example (HOLY ORDERS: *Symbols:* Shepherd).
- LH, OT.13.Th, 2R: St. Jerome, Sermon on Ps. 41 addressed to newly baptized: CCL 78, 542–544 – The newly baptized thirst for water from the living fountain of the Trinity (BAPTISM: *Types:* Crossing of the Red Sea;

Symbols: Fountain of Water; Second Birth; White Garment / Wedding Garment; EUCHARIST: *Symbols:* Altar / Table).

- LH, OT.13.Fr, 2R: St. Augustine, On the Predestination of the Saints, 15, 30–31: PL 44, 981–983 – Christ was predestined to unite humanity to his divinity, and human nature was predestined to be elevated by this union (BAPTISM: *Symbols:* Second Birth).

- LH, OT.13.Sa, 2R: St. Cyril of Jerusalem, Catechetical Instruction, 1, 2–3.5–6: PG 33, 371.375–378 – Through faith and Baptism, the Christian is freed from slavery to sin and reborn (BAPTISM: *Symbols:* Liberation; Second Birth; Washing; CONFIRMATION: *Symbols:* Seal).

- LH, OT.14.Su, 2R: St. Augustine, Sermo 19, 2–3: CCL 41, 252–254 – The sacrifice that is pleasing to God is a humble and contrite heart (EUCHARIST: *Types:* Animal Sacrifices).

- LH, OT.14.We, 2R: Didache 9, 1–10, 6; 14, 1–3: Funk 2, 19–22.26 – A description of the Eucharistic Celebrations of the early Church (EUCHARIST: *Types:* Animal Sacrifices; *Symbols:* Bread and Wine / Nourishment; Breaking of Bread).

- LH, OT.15.Su, 2R: St. Ambrose, On the Mysteries, 1–7: SC 25 bis, 156–158 – Catechesis on the rites preceding Baptism, such as the symbolic opening of the ears and turning toward the east (BAPTISM: *Types:* Holy of Holies; Opening of the Ears and Mouth; *Symbols:* Turning toward the East; HOLY ORDERS: *Types:* High Priesthood; Priesthood; Levites).

- LH, OT.15.Mo, 2R: St. Ambrose, On the Mysteries, 8–11: SC 25 bis, 158–160 – The creation and the flood prefigured Baptism (BAPTISM: *Types:* Waters at Creation; Flood; *Symbols:* Dove).

- LH, OT.15.Tu, 2R: St. Ambrose, On the Mysteries, 12–16.19: SC 25 bis, 162–164 – The crossing of the Red Sea, the cloud of blessing, the water of Marah, and the healing of Naaman prefigured Baptism (BAPTISM: *Types:* Crossing of the Red Sea; Pillar of Cloud and Fire; Water of Marah; Healing of Naaman; *Symbols:* Washing).

- LH, OT.15.We, 2R: St. Ambrose, On the Mysteries, 19–21.24.26–38: SC 25 bis, 164–170 – Water sanctifies through the power of the Holy Spirit, as seen in the three witnesses in Baptism: the water, the blood, and the Spirit. The healing of Naaman, the healing at the Sheep Gate pool, and the baptism of Christ (with the dove) all anticipate the sanctifying power of the waters of Baptism (BAPTISM: *Types:* Dove; Healing of Naaman; Healing at the Sheep Gate Pool; Water from the Side of Christ; *Symbols:* Baptism of Fire; Immersion; Second Birth; Eucharist: *Types:* Holocaust of Elijah).

- LH, OT.15.Th, 2R: St. Ambrose, On the Mysteries, 29–30.34–35.37.42: SC 25 bis, 172–178 – The symbols of the anointing with oil and the white garment of Baptism are explained (Baptism: *Types:* Anointing of Priests, Prophets, and Kings; *Symbols:* Second Birth; White Garment / Wedding Garment; Confirmation: *Symbols:* Anointing; Seal).

- LH, OT.15.Fr, 2R: St. Ambrose, On the Mysteries, 43.47–49: SC 25 bis, 178–180.182 – The manna from heaven and the water from the rock prefigured the Eucharist (Eucharist: *Types:* Manna; Water from the Rock; *Symbols:* Altar / Table; Bread and Wine / Nourishment; Bread from Heaven / Bread of Life / Bread of Angels).

- LH, OT.15.Sa, 2R: St. Ambrose, On the Mysteries, 52–54.58: SC 25 bis, 186–188.190 – The words of consecration in the Eucharist truly change the bread and wine into the Body and Blood of Christ (Eucharist: *Types:* Manna; Holocaust of Elijah; Wisdom's Banquet; *Symbols:* Bread and Wine / Nourishment).

- LH, OT.16.Su, 2R: St. Ignatius of Antioch, Letter to the Magnesians 1, 1–5, 2: Funk 1, 191–195 – The relationships between bishop, priest, deacon, and faithful are described. Christians should live out their faith as bearers of the image of God (Holy Orders: *Symbols:* Father).

- LH, OT.16.Mo, 2R: St. Ignatius of Antioch, Letter to the Magnesians, 6, 1–9, 2: Funk 1, 195–199 – The Magnesians should live united to their priests and bishop and remain faithful to the faith they have received (Eucharist: *Symbols:* Altar / Table; Holy Orders: *Symbols:* Father).

- LH, OT.17.We, 2R: St. Cyril of Jerusalem, Catechetical Instruction 18, 23–25: PG 33, 1043–1047 – Why the Church is rightly called "Catholic" (Holy Orders: *Types:* High Priest).

- LH, OT.17.Fr, 2R: St. Ignatius of Antioch, Letter to Polycarp 1, 1–4, 3: Funk 1, 247–249 – Qualities of a good bishop (Holy Orders: *Symbols:* Sea Captain; Shepherd).

- LH, OT.18.Th, 2R: Baldwin, bishop of Canterbury, Tract. 10: PL 204, 513–514.516 – The love of Christ is as strong as death and transforms us into Christ's likeness (Confirmation: *Symbols:* Seal).

- LH, OT.18.Sa, 2R: St. Irenaeus, Against Heresies, Book 4, 17, 4–6: SC 100, 590–594 – The Eucharist is the sacrificial offering of the first fruits to

God, fulfilling Malachi's prophecy that a pure sacrifice would be offered in every place to God's name (EUCHARIST: *Types*: Offering of the First Fruits; Animal Sacrifices; *Symbols*: Bread and Wine / Nourishment).

- LH, OT.19.Mo, 2R: Theodoret of Cyr, On the Incarnation, 26–27: PG 75, 1466–1467 – Jesus patiently and freely offered his life on the cross to save us. The blood and water from his side refer to Baptism and the Eucharist (BAPTISM: *Types:* Water from the Side of Christ; *Symbols:* Fountain of Water; Second Birth; White Garment / Wedding Garment; EUCHARIST: *Types*: Blood from the Side of Christ; *Symbols*: Altar / Table; Bread and Wine / Nourishment).

- LH, OT.19.Tu, 2R: Theodoret of Cyr, On the Incarnation, 28: PG 75, 1467–1470 – The Son took up our human nature to free us from sin, giving the gift of Baptism to allow us to share in his death and Resurrection (BAPTISM: *Symbols:* Immersion; HOLY ORDERS: *Symbols*: Shepherd).

- LH, OT.19.Fr, 2R: St. Pacian, Sermon on Baptism, 5–6: PL 13, 1092–1093 – Christ as the New Adam, his marriage to the Church, and the birth of the Christian people through Baptism (BAPTISM: *Symbols:* Second Birth; Washing; CONFIRMATION: *Symbols:* Anointing; HOLY ORDERS: *Symbols:* Father).

- LH, OT.19.Sa, 2R: St. Pacian, Sermon on Baptism, 6–7: PL 13, 1093–1094 – United to Christ through Baptism we have the gift of eternal life as long as we don't sin. Baptism frees us from the shackles of sin (BAPTISM: *Symbols:* Washing; Liberation).

- LH, OT.21.Mo, 2R: St. Thomas Aquinas, Exposition on John, Ch. 10, 3 – Jesus Christ is the Good Shepherd who nourishes the flock. He is the Gate. He has appointed other shepherds, and they are good shepherds in so far as they are united to Christ (EUCHARIST: *Symbols*: Bread and Wine / Nourishment; HOLY ORDERS: *Symbols*: Shepherd).

- LH, OT.21.Tu, 2R: St. John Chrysostom, Homily De diabolo tentatore 2, 6: PG 49, 263–264 – Five paths of repentance that lead to heaven (EUCHARIST: *Symbols*: Altar / Table; PENANCE: *Symbols*: Medicine for the Soul).

- LH, OT.21.We, 2R: St. Columban, Instr. 13, De Christo fonte vitae, 1–2: Opera, Dublin 1957, 116–118 – Jesus Christ is the fountain of water and the bread from heaven. We should eat and drink of him (BAPTISM:

Symbols: Fountain of Water; EUCHARIST: *Symbols*: Bread from Heaven / Bread of Life / Bread of Angels).

- LH, OT.21.Th, 2R: St. Columban, Instr. 13, De Christo fonte vitae, 2–3: Opera, Dublin 1957, 118–120 – Christ himself is the fountain, and he who drinks from the fountain drinks God (BAPTISM: *Symbols:* Fountain of Water).

- LH, OT.21.Sa, 2R: St. John Chrysostom, Homily on Matthew, 50, 3–4: PG 58, 508–509 – Christ should be honored first of all by serving him in the poor. Only after this should he be honored by adorning the church (EUCHARIST: *Symbols*: Altar / Table).

- LH, OT.22.Tu, 2R: Thomas à Kempis, The Imitation of Christ, Book 3, 14 – Holiness is impossible apart from the grace of God (EUCHARIST: *Symbols*: Bread from Heaven / Bread of Life / Bread of Angels).

- LH, OT.23.Fr, 2R: Bl. Isaac of Stella, Sermo 11: PL 194, 1728–1729 – Only God can forgive sins. But when the Almighty married the Church, born from his side, he shared all he is and all he had with her, and they became one, head and body. When Christ forgives sins, the Church forgives, and when the Church forgives, Christ forgives (BAPTISM: *Types:* Water from the Side of Christ; EUCHARIST: *Types*: Blood from the Side of Christ; PENANCE: *Types:* Lepers sent to the priests; HOLY ORDERS: *Types:* Priesthood; *Symbols*: Head of the Body).

- LH, OT.24.Su, 2R: St. Augustine, Sermon on Pastors 46, 1–2: CCL 41, 529–530 – As members of the flock, the shepherds of the Church will give an account for their own life; but they also have the responsibility as shepherds to shepherd their sheep, and they will have to give an account to God of this stewardship (HOLY ORDERS: *Symbols*: Shepherd; Steward).

- LH, OT.24.Mo, 2R: St. Augustine, Sermon on Pastors 46, 3–4: CCL 41, 530–531 – Some shepherds feed themselves instead of the flock. Shepherds deserve a wage from the people for their work. St. Paul, while recognizing this right, rejected the wages offered him because he did not need them. This is praiseworthy, but not required (HOLY ORDERS: *Symbols*: Shepherd).

- LH, OT.24.Tu, 2R: St. Augustine, Sermon on Pastors 46, 4–5: CCL 41, 531–533 – St. Paul gives good example by always seeking only the advantage of his flock, even when they did give him gifts. If a shepherd receives wages from his flock, let it be only what is truly necessary; God himself will repay him for his stewardship (HOLY ORDERS: *Symbols*: Shepherd).

- LH, OT.24.We, 2R: St. Augustine, Sermon on Pastors 46, 6–7: CCL 41, 533–534 – Shepherds who take advantage of their flock seek milk (sustenance) and wool (honors) and then neglect the sheep. St. Paul tended the sheep, and had God for his sustenance and honor. He received sustenance and honor from his flock, but he did not seek these things, but the things of Christ (HOLY ORDERS: *Symbols*: Shepherd).
- LH, OT.24.Th, 2R: St. Augustine, Sermon on Pastors 46, 9: CCL 41, 535–536 – Wicked shepherds kill the sheep through their bad example and their wicked lives. A wicked shepherd is a murderer, just as he who lusts after a woman in his heart is an adulterer (HOLY ORDERS: *Symbols*: Servant; Shepherd).
- LH, OT.24.Fr, 2R: St. Augustine, Sermon on Pastors 46, 10–11: CCL 41, 536–538 – The wicked shepherd neglects to strengthen the weak, by not preparing them for temptations and the cross for fear of giving offense. Some wicked shepherds even promise worldly prosperity. This is building on sand, and will lead to ruin. To build on rock is to build on Christ, which means persecution and suffering (HOLY ORDERS: *Symbols*: Shepherd).
- LH, OT.24.Sa, 2R: St. Augustine, Sermon on Pastors 46, 11–12: CCL 41, 538–539 – God chastised his only Son; if we are adopted sons, he will chastise us as well. A shepherd who strengthens the weak does so by preparing them for suffering and temptations and trials by speaking of God's fidelity and love; he binds up the broken by promising him God's mercy when he is held back by fear (HOLY ORDERS: *Symbols*: Physician; Shepherd).
- LH, OT.25.Su, 2R: St. Augustine, Sermon on Pastors 46, 13: CCL 41, 539–540 – The weak sheep must be strengthened so as to not break under temptation and so as to be able to endure suffering. They can still do good works. The ill sheep, however, have already given in to evil desires, and have no strength to do good works, like the paralytic. The shepherd is called to open the roof and lower him down to Christ (HOLY ORDERS: *Symbols*: Physician; Shepherd).
- LH, OT.25.Mo, 2R: St. Augustine, Sermon on Pastors 46, 14–15: CCL 41, 541–542 – Oftentimes sheep who are lost do not want to be found. The shepherd must seek them out anyway for God does not want them to be lost (HOLY ORDERS: *Symbols*: Shepherd).
- LH, OT.25.Tu, 2R: St. Augustine, Sermon on Pastors 46, 18–19: CCL 41, 544–546 – The Catholic Church is shepherd of the sheep. She is a vine.

Some sheep stray, and some branches fall off, or are cut off to prune the vine. But the Church, especially through her shepherds, who are not and will never be lacking, seeks out the lost sheep, and knows that God can graft back on the separated branches (HOLY ORDERS: *Symbols*: Shepherd).

• LH, OT.25.We, 2R: St. Augustine, Sermon on Pastors 46, 20–21: CCL 41, 546–548 – Shepherds have the duty to warn the sheep about sin. In the case of unfaithful shepherds, Christ will still shepherd the sheep as long as they do what the shepherds say and not what they do (HOLY ORDERS: *Symbols*: Shepherd).

• LH, OT.25.Th, 2R: St. Augustine, Sermon on Pastors 46, 24–25.27: CCL 41, 551–553 – Christ shepherds the sheep through the Scriptures, which are healthy and green pastures, and he judges rightly what each sheep needs. (HOLY ORDERS: *Symbols*: Shepherd).

• LH, OT.25.Fr, 2R: St. Augustine, Sermon on Pastors 46, 29–30: CCL 41, 555–557 – All good shepherds are united in Christ, the Good Shepherd, who shepherds the flock through them. To St. Peter in a special way Jesus entrusted the unity of the flock, and Christ is especially united to him (HOLY ORDERS: *Symbols*: Head of the Body; Shepherd).

• LH, OT.25.Sa, 2R: St. Hilary, Discourse on Psalm 64, 14–15: CSEL 22, 245–246 – The river of grace (Ezek. 47:1–12) is the Holy Spirit, given in Baptism. The Eucharist is food to prepare us for the life to come (BAPTISM: *Symbols:* Fountain of Water; Second Birth; EUCHARIST: *Symbols*: Bread and Wine / Nourishment).

• LH, OT.26.Tu, 2R: St. Polycarp, Letter to the Philippians 6,1–8,2: Funk 1, 273–275 – The virtues that priests should live.

• LH, OT.27.Su, 2R: St. Gregory the Great, Pastoral Guide, Book 2, 4: PL 77, 30–31 – The ordained priest or bishop is called to silence when discretion requires, and to speak out when words are of service, including words of reproach (HOLY ORDERS: *Symbols:* Shepherd).

• LH, OT.27.Tu, 2R: St. Ignatius of Antioch, Letter to the Trallians 1, 1–3, 2; 4, 1–2; 6, 1; 7, 1–8, 1: Funk 1, 203–209 – How the Church does not exist where there are not bishops, priests, and deacons (HOLY ORDERS: *Symbols:* Father; Servant).

• LH, OT.27.Th, 2R: St. Ignatius of Antioch, Letter to the Philadelphians 1, 1–2, 1; 3, 2–5, 1: Funk 1, 226–229 – The faithful should remain united to their bishop and to the one Eucharist, celebrated by the bishop and his presbyters (EUCHARIST: *Symbols:* Altar / Table; Breaking of Bread; HOLY ORDERS: *Symbols:* Shepherd).

- LH, OT.27.Sa, 2R: St. Gregory the Great, Homily on the Gospels, 17, 3, 14: PL 76, 1139–1140.1146 – The importance of praying for vocations, both for those who are called to the priesthood as well as to those who have already been ordained, and how many ordained ministers neglect their ministry (HOLY ORDERS: *Symbols:* Laborer of the Harvest; Shepherd).
- LH, OT.28.Su, 2R: St. Cyril of Alexandria, Commentary on Haggai, Ch. 14: PG 71, 1047–1050 – Christ and the Church are the true Temple (EUCHARIST: *Types*: Animal Sacrifices).
- LH, OT.28.Mo, 2R: St. Fulgentius, Against Fabianus, Ch. 28, 16–19: CCL 91A, 813–814 – The Eucharist is the memorial of the death and Resurrection of Jesus Christ. Sharing in the Body and Blood of Christ in the Eucharist sanctifies the faithful (EUCHARIST: *Symbols*: Bread and Wine / Nourishment; Cup of Salvation).
- LH, OT.28.Tu, 2R: St. Columban, Instruction on Compunction, 12, 2–3: Opera, Dublin 1957, pp. 112–114 – Prayer that God would enkindle his heart with divine love now and in eternity (CONFIRMATION: *Symbols*: Fire).
- LH, OT.28.Fr, 2R: St. Augustine, City of God, Book 10, 6: CCL 47, 278–279 – How Christians unite themselves to the sacrifice of Christ on the cross, both in their daily works of mercy and in the Mass ("the sacrifice of the altar") (EUCHARIST: *Symbols*: Altar / Table).
- LH, OT.29.Tu, 2R: St. Augustine, Letter to Proba, 130, 11, 21–12, 22: CSEL 44, 63–64 – St. Augustine explains the Our Father (EUCHARIST: *Symbols*: Bread for the Journey / Daily Bread / Viaticum; Bread from Heaven / Bread of Life / Bread of Angels).
- LH, OT.29.Fr, 2R: St. Augustine, Letter to Proba 130, 14, 27–15, 28: CSEL 44, 71–73 – The Holy Spirit intercedes for us, inspiring in us the desire of eternal life, which is the fountain of life that satisfies our thirst (BAPTISM: *Symbols:* Fountain of Water).
- LH, OT.29.Sa, 2R: St. Peter Chrysologus, Sermo 117: PL 52, 520–521 – Christ is the last Adam, and is greater than the first Adam in many ways. Through Baptism ("the virginal font") the Christian is reborn and shares in the last Adam's life (BAPTISM: *Symbols:* Second Birth).

- LH, OT.32.Mo, 2R: From a homily written in the second century, Ch. 3, 1–4, 5; 7, 1–6: Funk 1, 149–152 – It is not enough to call Christ our Lord, we must live as he has taught us, or we will be disqualified from the race (CONFIRMATION: *Symbols*: Seal).
- LH, OT.32.Tu, 2R: From a homily written in the second century, Ch. 8, 1–9, 11: Funk 1, 152–156 – To obtain eternal life one should repent of sin, guard the body as a temple of God, love others, and safeguard the baptismal seal (CONFIRMATION: *Symbols*: Seal).
- LH, OT.33.Th, 2R: St. Gregory of Nyssa, Commentary on the Song of Songs, Ch. 2: PG 44, 802 – Prayer to the Good Shepherd by his bride to find pasture, drink at the living fountain, and sleep in peace (BAPTISM: *Symbols:* Fountain of Water; HOLY ORDERS: *Symbols*: Shepherd).
- LH, OT.33.Fr, 2R: St. John Eudes, On the Kingdom of Jesus, Pars 3, 4: Opera Omnia 1, 310–312 – The mysteries of the life of Christ are brought to fulfillment in the individual Christian and in the Church through the sacraments, through suffering united to Christ, etc. (BAPTISM: *Symbols:* Second Birth).
- LH, OT.34.Tu, 2R: St. Augustine, Treatise on John, Tract. 35, 8–9: CCL 36, 321–323 – Christians are the light compared to unbelievers. But in the light of heaven all intermediate things, including the Scriptures, will be unnecessary (BAPTISM: *Symbols:* Fountain of Water; Illumination / Light / Candle).
- LH, OT.34.We, 2R: St. Macarius (attributed), Homily 28: PG 34, 710–711 – Woe to the soul without Christ! (HOLY ORDERS: *Symbols:* Sea Captain).
- LH, OT.34.Th, 2R: St. John Chrysostom, Homily 33, 1.2: PG 57, 389390 – As long as we are sheep we overcome with the shepherds help. If we turn into wolves we are overcome, for we are without the shepherd. The sheep should be wise and clever like a snake, with that cleverness that is willing to lose anything except the head, that is, faith (HOLY ORDERS: *Symbols:* Shepherd).
- LH, Christ the King, 2R: Origen, On Prayer, 25: PG 11, 495–499 – The Kingdom of God is in his holy ones, where he reigns. By avoiding sin and bearing fruit in the Spirit our souls become a Paradise where God may walk (BAPTISM: *Symbols:* Second Birth).

ADVENT AND CHRISTMAS

• LH, Adv.1.Su, 2R: St. Cyril of Jerusalem, Catechetical Instruction 15, 1–3: PG 33, 870–874 – Comparison of the first and second comings of Christ.

• LH, Adv.1.Tu, 2R: St. Gregory of Nazianzus, Oratio 45, 9, 22.26.28: PG 36, 634–635.654.658–659.662 – The eternal Word became flesh and died to save us (HOLY ORDERS: *Symbols*: Shepherd).

• LH, Adv.2.Tu, 2R: Vatican II, Lumen Gentium 48 – The pilgrim Church journeys toward eternal life (EUCHARIST: *Symbols*: Bread and Wine / Nourishment).

• LH, Adv.2.Th, 2R: St. Peter Chrysologus, Sermo 147: PL 52, 594–595 – How the history of salvation was motivated by God's love, and brought about a response of love (HOLY ORDERS: *Symbols:* Father).

• LH, Adv.2.Sa, 2R: Bl. Isaac of Stella, Sermo 51: PL 194, 1862–1863, 1865 – How Christ unites all the redeemed in his Body, the Church, and how Mary and the Church are similar in so far as they are mother, virgin, receive the Holy Spirit, etc. (BAPTISM: *Symbols:* Second Birth; HOLY ORDERS: *Symbols:* Head of the Body).

• LH, Adv.3.We, 2R: St. Irenaeus, Treatise Against Heresies, Book 4, 20, 4–5: SC 100, 634–640 – God wants men to "see" him. He was seen by the prophets through the Spirit, then by believers in the Son, and will be seen in eternal life, bestowed by the Father (BAPTISM: *Symbols:* Second Birth).

• LH, Dec17, 2R: St. Leo the Great, Letter 31, 2–3: PL 54, 791–793 – Jesus Christ was truly human, and thus made us truly participants of divine life through adoption (BAPTISM: *Symbols:* Second Birth).

• LH, Christmas, 2R: St. Leo the Great, Sermo 1 in Nativitate Domini, 1–3: PL 54, 190–193 – The birth of Christ is an occasion of great joy and praise of God. Christians should live according to their dignity as children of God and temples of the Holy Spirit (BAPTISM: *Symbols:* Illumination / Light / Candle; Second Birth).

• LH, Dec31, 2R: St. Leo the Great, Sermo 6 in Nativitate Domini, 2–3, 5: PL 54, 213–216 – At Christmas we celebrate not only the birth of Christ, but also our birth through Baptism as adopted children in him, and we are called to live in his peace (BAPTISM: *Symbols:* Immersion; Second Birth; HOLY ORDERS: *Symbols*: Head of the Body).

- LH, CT.BE.Mo, 2R (Latin Edition: Jan 2): St. Basil the Great, On the Holy Spirit, Ch. 26, Nn. 61, 64: PG 32, 179–182.186 – How the Holy Spirit works in the Body of Christ, uniting all its members (BAPTISM: *Symbols:* Second Birth; CONFIRMATION: *Symbols:* Seal).

- LH, CT.Epiphany, 2R: St. Leo the Great, Sermo 3 in Epiphania Domini, 1–3.5: PL 54, 240–244 – The Lord has brought salvation to all nations, as he promised to Abraham. This is signified by the adoration of the Magi (HOLY ORDERS: *Symbols:* Father).

- LH, CT.AE.Mo, 2R: St. Peter Chrysologus, Sermo 160: PL 52, 620–622 – Christ reveals his incarnation (i.e. his divinity) in different ways in the visit of the Magi, the baptism of Christ, and in the miracle at Cana (BAPTISM: *Types:* Dove; Anointing of Priests, Prophets, and Kings; *Symbols:* Washing; EUCHARIST: *Types:* Water to Wine; *Symbols:* Cup of Salvation).

- LH, CT.AE.Tu, 2R: St. Hippolytus, Sermon on the Epiphany, 2.6–8.10: PG 10, 854.858–859.862 – Jesus, the river of life, gives his divine life and perfection to our humility in Baptism (BAPTISM: *Types:* Rivers of Eden; *Symbols:* Fountain of Water; Illumination / Light / Candle; Liberation; Second Birth; Washing).

- LH, CT.AE.We, 2R: St. Proclus of Constantinople, Sermo 7 in sancta Theophania, 1–3: PG 65, 758–759 – The baptism of Christ manifests even more wonders than the birth of Christ. Christ sanctified the waters of Baptism with his baptism and gives a new flood to the world, which does not destroy but gives life (BAPTISM: *Types:* Flood; Dove; *Symbols:* Fountain of Water).

- LH, CT.AE.Th, 2R: St. Cyril of Alexandria, Commentary on the Gospel of John, Book 5, Ch. 2: PG 73, 751–754 – Jesus received the Holy Spirit in baptism as a man, in order that, united to his human nature, we might share in the Spirit.

- LH, CT.AE.Fr, 2R: St. Maximus of Turin, Sermo 100, De sancta Epiphania 1, 3: CCL 23, 398–400 – In his baptism, Christ sanctified the waters of Baptism. Like the pillar of fire which preceded the Israelites when they crossed the Red Sea, Jesus precedes us through Baptism, giving us a light to follow (BAPTISM: *Types:* Pillar of Cloud and Fire; *Symbols:* Illumination / Light / Candle; Second Birth; Washing).

- LH, CT.AE.Sa, 2R: Faustus of Riez, Sermo 5, De sancta Epiphania 2: PLS 3, 560–562 – Water changing into wine at Cana symbolizes the transformation of the Old Covenant into the New Covenant, and the transformation of the soul in Baptism (BAPTISM: *Symbols:* Second Birth).

- LH, Baptism of the Lord, 2R: St. Gregory of Nazianzus, Oratio 39 in Sancta Lumina, 14–16.20: PG 36, 350–351.354.358–359 – Jesus sanctifies the waters of the Jordan with his baptism. The Christian is called to be the light of the world (BAPTISM: *Types:* Waters at Creation; Dove; *Symbols:* Fountain of Water; Illumination / Light / Candle; Immersion; Second Birth; Washing).

LENT AND HOLY WEEK

- LH, Lent.AAW.Fr, 2R: St. John Chrysostom, Supp., Homily 6 De precatione: PG 64, 462–466 – Prayer from the heart is a supreme good (CONFIRMATION: *Symbols:* Fire).
- LH, Lent.1.We, 2R: Aphrahat, Dem. 11, On Circumcision, 11–12: PS 1, 498–503 – God renews and changes his covenant and its corresponding law, first with Adam, then Noah, then Abraham, then Moses, and finally with Christ, the eternal covenant. Circumcision was a type of Baptism and faith, which circumcise the heart and lead across the true Jordan into the promised land (BAPTISM: *Types:* Circumcision; Crossing of the Jordan River; CONFIRMATION: *Symbols:* Seal; HOLY ORDERS: *Symbols:* Father).
- LH, Lent.1.Th, 2R: St. Asterius of Amasea, Homily 13: PG 40, 355–358.362 – We should follow the example of Christ, the Good Shepherd. He seeks out the lost sheep, showing us that no one is beyond hope (BAPTISM: *Symbols:* Immersion; Second Birth; CONFIRMATION: *Symbols:* Seal; HOLY ORDERS: *Symbols:* Shepherd).
- LH, Lent.1.Fr, 2R: St. Aelred, From the Mirror of Love, Book 3, 5: PL 195, 582 – Christ as model of brotherly love in his love of his enemies (CONFIRMATION: *Symbols:* Fire).
- LH, Lent.2.Mo, 2R: St. John Chrysostom, Cat. 3, 24–27: SC 50, 165–167 – Christ is a new and greater Moses, Baptism is a new and greater Exodus, and the Eucharist is a new and greater manna (BAPTISM: *Types:* Crossing of the Red Sea; EUCHARIST: *Types:* Manna; Water from the Rock; *Symbols:* Altar / Table; Bread and Wine / Nourishment).
- LH, Lent.2.We, 2R: St. Irenaeus, Against Heresies, Book 4, 14, 2–3; 15, 1: SC 100, 542.548 – Throughout the history of salvation, God foreshadowed

what was to come in Christ (EUCHARIST: *Types:* Animal Sacrifices; Water from the Rock; HOLY ORDERS: *Types:* Levites).

- LH, Lent.2.Sa, 2R: St. Ambrose, On Flight from the World, Ch. 6, 36; 7, 44; 8, 45; 9, 52: CSEL 32, 192.198–199.204 – God is the true treasure. Take refuge from this world in spirit, even if still here in body, entering into his rest and drinking from the fountain of life (BAPTISM: *Symbols:* Fountain of Water).

- LH, Lent.3.Su, 2R: St. Augustine, Treatise on John, Tract. 15, 10–12.16–17: CCL 36, 154–156 – The Samaritan woman foreshadows the coming of the Gentiles into the Church, and the water from the well foreshadows the gift of the Holy Spirit (BAPTISM: *Symbols:* Fountain of Water).

- LH, Lent.3.Th, 2R: Tertullian, Treatise on Prayer, 28–29: CCL 1, 273–274 – The power of prayer (EUCHARIST: *Types*: Animal Sacrifices).

- LH, Lent.4.Mo, 2R: Origen, Homily on Leviticus, 9, 5.10: PG 12, 515.523 – The sacrifice of Christ brings about true propitiation; he is the true lamb of atonement foreshadowed by the Temple sacrifices (BAPTISM: *Symbols:* Turning toward the East; HOLY ORDERS: *Types:* High Priest).

- LH, Lent.4.We, 2R: St. Maximus the Confessor, Letter 11: PG 91, 454–455 – God is merciful, and awaits his children with opens arms when they leave home, and seeks them out like lost sheep when they wander (HOLY ORDERS: *Symbols:* Father; Shepherd).

- LH, Lent.4.Th, 2R: St. Leo the Great, Sermo 15, De passione Domini, 3–4: PL 54, 366–367 – The great victory that Christ won for us by assuming our human nature (BAPTISM: *Types:* Fruit of the Tree of Life; *Symbols:* Second Birth).

- LH, Lent.4.Fr, 2R: St. Athanasius, Easter Letter 5, 1–2: PG 26, 1379–1380 – The feast of the Passover of the Lord, in which he was sacrificed, is celebrated yearly, gives grace, and unites the faithful (EUCHARIST: *Types*: Water from the Rock; *Symbols*: Bread and Wine / Nourishment).

- LH, Lent.5.Su, 2R: St. Athanasius, Easter Letter 14, 1–2: PG 26, 1419–1420 – How the feast of Easter is kept in prayer, faith, and deeds (HOLY ORDERS: *Types:* High Priest; Shepherd).

- LH, Lent.5.Mo, 2R: St. John Fisher, Commentary on the Psalms 129: Opera omnia, edit. 1579, p. 1610 – How Jesus Christ is our eternal High Priest, who entered once for all into the Holy of Holies by the sacrifice of his blood (EUCHARIST: *Types*: Animal Sacrifices; HOLY ORDERS: *Types:* High Priest).

- LH, Lent.5.Tu, 2R: St. Leo the Great, Sermo 8 de passione Domini, 6–8: PL 54, 340–342 – The death and Resurrection of Christ has destroyed death, united all peoples, and brought to fulfillment the prefigurations of the Old Covenant in the Sacraments of the Eucharist and Holy Orders (EUCHARIST: *Types:* Animal Sacrifices; HOLY ORDERS: *Types:* Priesthood; Anointing of Priests, Prophets, and Kings; Levites; Seventy Elders of Moses).

- LH, Lent.5.We, 2R: St. Augustine, Commentary on the Psalms, 85, 1: CCL 39, 1176–1177 – Jesus Christ is head of his Body, the Church, and when the Church prays Jesus Christ prays for her and in her. Christ as man is truly human, in all the humility of our nature (HOLY ORDERS: *Symbols:* Head of the Body).

- LH, Lent.5.Th, 2R: Vatican II, Lumen Gentium 9 – The People of God, the Church, is the visible sacrament of unity (BAPTISM: *Symbols:* Second Birth).

- LH, Lent.5.Fr, 2R: St. Fulgentius of Ruspe, Treatise on Faith Addressed to Peter, Ch. 22, 62: CCL 91 A, 726.750–751 – How the sacrifices of the Old Covenant prefigured the sacrifice of Jesus Christ on the cross, offered up by the Church throughout the world in the sacrifice of bread and wine (EUCHARIST: *Types:* Animal Sacrifices; HOLY ORDERS: *Types*: High Priest; Priesthood).

- LH, Lent.5.Sa, 2R: St. Gregory of Nazianzus, Oratio 45, 23–24: PG 36, 654–655 – About the celebration of the Passover of Christ, the faithful are admonished to keep the Passover in a spiritual sense by following Christ in their lives and to prepare for the eternal Passover (EUCHARIST: *Types*: Passover / Passover Lamb).

- LH, Lent.HW.Su, 2R: St. Andrew of Crete, Oratio 9 in Ramos Palmarum: PG 97, 990–994 – How Christ enters Jerusalem meek and without glory, and with what attitudes we should go out to meet him (BAPTISM: *Symbols:* Washing; White Garment / Wedding Garment).

- LH, Lent.HW.Tu, 2R: St. Basil, On the Holy Spirit, Ch. 15, 35: PG 32, 127–130 – Through Baptism accompanied by conversion we die and rise with Christ (BAPTISM: *Symbols:* Immersion; Second Birth; Washing).

- LH, Lent.HW.We, 2R: St. Augustine, Treatise on John, Tract. 84, 1–2: CCL 36, 536–538 – One who truly loves lays down his life for the other, like Christ did for us. Receiving him in the Eucharist, we should be willing to do the same, as were the martyrs (EUCHARIST: *Symbols*: Altar / Table; Banquet; Bread and Wine / Nourishment).
- LH, Lent.HW.Th, 2R: St. Melito of Sardis, Easter homily, 65–71: SC 123, 95–101 – Christ is the Passover Lamb, who was slain to destroy the power of sin. Abel, Isaac, Jacob, Joseph, Moses, David, and the prophets all foreshadowed his coming (BAPTISM: *Types*: Crossing of the Red Sea; EUCHARIST: *Types*: Passover / Passover Lamb).
- LH, Lent.HW.Fr, 2R: St. John Chrysostom, Catecheses 3, 13–19: SC 50, 174–177 – The blood of the Passover lamb sprinkled on the door is a type of the Eucharist on the lips of Christians; the water and blood from Christ's side symbolize Baptism and the Eucharist, from which the Church is born; as Eve was born from Adam's side, so the Church was born from the side of Christ, the Second Adam (BAPTISM: *Types:* Water from the Side of Christ; *Symbols:* Second Birth; EUCHARIST: *Types:* Passover / Passover Lamb; Blood from the Side of Christ; *Symbols*: Bread and Wine / Nourishment).
- LH, Lent.HW.Sa, 2R: From an ancient homily on Holy Saturday: PG 43, 439.451.462–463 – Jesus Christ descends into Hades and awakes Adam, and, having healed the wound of Adam's sin by his suffering and death, he invites him to the eternal paradise (HOLY ORDERS: *Symbols*: Shepherd).

EASTER TIME

- LH, ET.1.Mo, 2R: St. Melito of Sardis, Easter Homily, Ch. 2–7, 100–103: SC 123, 60–64.120–122 – Jesus Christ fulfills the prefigurations of the Passover and of the Passover lamb (EUCHARIST: *Types*: Passover / Passover Lamb).
- LH, ET.1.We, 2R: Easter homily by an ancient author, Sermo 35, 6–9: PL 17 [ed. 1879], 696–697 – Christ has brought salvation to mankind through his Resurrection. Christians share in his Resurrection through Baptism and the sacraments (BAPTISM: *Symbols*: Illumination / Light / Candle; Second Birth).
- LH, ET.1.Th, 2R: St. Cyril of Jerusalem, Jerusalem Catecheses, 20:4–6, Mystagogica 2, 4–6: PG 33, 1079–1082 – In Baptism not only are our

sins forgiven and we are adopted as children of God, but we also share in the death and Resurrection of Christ, symbolized by the triple immersion (BAPTISM: *Symbols:* Illumination / Light / Candle; Immersion; Second Birth; Washing).

- LH, ET.1.Fr, 2R: St. Cyril of Jerusalem, Jerusalem Catecheses, 21:1–3, Mystagogica 3, 1–3: PG 33, 1087–1091 – The anointing with oil in Baptism / Confirmation signifies and brings about the gift of the Holy Spirit (BAPTISM: *Types:* Anointing of Priests, Prophets, and Kings; *Symbols:* Second Birth; White Garment / Wedding Garment; CONFIRMATION: *Symbols:* Anointing; Seal).

- LH, ET.1.Sa, 2R: St. Cyril of Jerusalem, Jerusalem Catecheses, 22, Mystagogica 4, 1.3–6.9: PG 33, 1098–1106 – The bread and the wine are truly transformed into the Body and Blood of Christ. This is a mystery to be believed by faith (EUCHARIST: *Types:* Bread of the Presence / Cereal Offerings; *Symbols*: Bread and Wine / Nourishment; Bread from Heaven / Bread of Life / Bread of Angels; Cup of Salvation).

- LH, ET.2.Su, 2R: St. Augustine, Sermo 8 in octava Paschae 1.4: PL 46, 838.841 – The baptized have been reborn and clothed with Christ. They have received new life and the forgiveness of their sins, and participate in Christ's death and Resurrection (BAPTISM: *Types:* Circumcision; *Symbols:* Immersion; Second Birth; White Garment / Wedding Garment; CONFIRMATION: *Symbols*: Seal).

- LH, ET.2.Mo, 2R: Pseudo-Chrysostom, Ancient Easter Homily: PG 59, 723–724 – The Passover was a type of the death and Resurrection of Christ, into which we enter through Baptism (BAPTISM: *Symbols:* Immersion; EUCHARIST: *Types:* Passover / Passover Lamb; HOLY ORDERS: *Symbols:* Father).

- LH, ET.2.Tu, 2R: St. Fulgentius of Ruspe, Book addressed to Monimus, 2, 11–12: CCL 91, 46–48 – The Mystical Body of Christ is built up through the Eucharist and through the Holy Spirit who sanctifies and unifies her in charity (EUCHARIST: *Symbols*: Breaking of Bread).

- LH, ET.2.We, 2R: St. Leo the Great, Sermo 12 de Passione, 3, 6–7: PL 54, 355–357 – How the risen Christ nourishes and builds his Church (BAPTISM: *Symbols:* Immersion; Second Birth; EUCHARIST: *Types:* Passover / Passover Lamb; *Symbols:* Bread and Wine / Nourishment; HOLY ORDERS: *Symbols:* Father; Shepherd).

- LH, ET.2.Th, 2R: St. Gaudentius of Brescia, Tract. 2: CSEL 68, 30–32 – How the redeeming sacrifice of Christ is made present in the Eucharist in order to continue his presence, to strengthen, to unite, and to sanctify. Those who have escaped the power of Egypt and of Pharaoh can share in this banquet (BAPTISM: *Types:* Crossing of the Red Sea; CONFIRMATION: *Symbols:* Fire; EUCHARIST: *Types*: Passover / Passover Lamb; *Symbols:* Bread and Wine / Nourishment; Bread for the Journey / Daily Bread / Viaticum; Gift of Finest Wheat).

- LH, ET.2.Sa, 2R: Vatican II, Sacrosanctum Concilium 5–6 – The salvation which Christ gives was brought about in the Paschal Mystery. Through Baptism we enter into that Paschal Mystery, and in the Eucharist we celebrate and proclaim it (BAPTISM: *Symbols:* Immersion; EUCHARIST: *Types*: Passover / Passover Lamb).

- LH, ET.3.Su, 2R: St. Justin Martyr, First Apology, 66–67: PG 6, 427–431 – How the first Christian communities celebrated the Eucharist (BAPTISM: *Symbols:* Second Birth; Washing; EUCHARIST: *Symbols*: Bread and Wine / Nourishment*).*

- LH, ET.3.Mo, 2R: St. Bede the Venerable, Commentary on 1 Pet., Ch. 2: PL 93, 50–51 – The Church is a chosen race, a royal priesthood, and a consecrated nation, redeemed by Christ according to the typology of Israel freed from Egypt (BAPTISM: *Types:* Crossing of the Red Sea; Pillar of Cloud and Fire; Anointing of Priests, Prophets, and Kings; *Symbols:* Illumination / Light / Candle; Liberation; Washing).

- LH, ET.3.We, 2R: St. Justin, First Apology, 61: PG 6, 419–422 – Baptism brings about rebirth in the Holy Spirit, washes away sin, and enlightens our intellect (BAPTISM: *Symbols:* Illumination / Light / Candle; Second Birth; Washing).

- LH, ET.3.Th, 2R: St. Irenaeus, Against Heresies, Book 5, 2, 2–3: SC 153, 30–38 – We are saved and incorporated in the Body of Christ through the Eucharist (EUCHARIST: *Symbols*: Bread and Wine / Nourishment; Breaking of Bread).

- LH, ET.4.Su, 2R: St. Gregory the Great, Homily on the Gospels 14, 3–6: PL 76, 1129–1130 – How Christ is the Good Shepherd and how we should go and graze in his pastures (HOLY ORDERS: *Symbols*: Shepherd).

- LH, ET.4.Mo, 2R: St. Basil the Great, On the Holy Spirit, Ch. 15, 35–36: PG 32, 130–131 – Being born of water and Spirit means the baptized die in the water and are reborn through the Spirit (BAPTISM: *Symbols:* Illumination / Light / Candle; Immersion; Second Birth).

• LH, ET.4.Tu, 2R: St. Peter Chrysologus, Sermo 108: PL 52, 499–500 – Through his love, Christ draws mankind to himself. The Christian shares in Christ's priesthood, and is called to offer himself as a living sacrifice in Christ (CONFIRMATION: *Symbols:* Sign of the Cross; EUCHARIST: *Types:* Animal Sacrifices; HOLY ORDERS: *Symbols:* Father).

• LH, ET.5.Su, 2R: St. Maximus of Turin, Sermo 53, 1–2.4: CCL 23, 214–216 – Through Christ's Resurrection, he has opened the doors to heaven. He is the day, the eternal light (BAPTISM: *Symbols:* Illumination / Light / Candle).

• LH, ET.5.Mo, 2R: St. Gregory of Nyssa, Oratio 1 in Christi resurrectionem: PG 46, 603–606.626–627 – The Resurrection of Christ brings about a new creation, conceived in faith, born in Baptism, and matured in the Church through her teachings, the Eucharist, and the practice of virtue. Different elements of nature symbolize different aspects of this new life (v.gr. sun = a pure life, stars = virtues, etc.). (BAPTISM: *Symbols:* Second Birth; EUCHARIST: *Symbols:* Bread and Wine / Nourishment; Bread from Heaven / Bread of Life / Bread of Angels).

• LH, ET.5.Th, 2R: St. Gaudentius of Brescia, Tract. 2: CSEL 68, 26.29–30 – The Eucharist is the Passover of the Lord and bread from heaven (EUCHARIST: *Types:* Passover / Passover Lamb; Water to Wine; *Symbols:* Bread and Wine / Nourishment; Bread from Heaven / Bread of Life / Bread of Angels).

• LH, ET.5.Fr, 2R: Blessed Isaac of Stella, Sermo 42: PL 194, 1831–1832 – How we participate sacramentally in the mysteries and in the divinity of Christ being members of his Body and adopted children through Baptism (BAPTISM: *Symbols:* Second Birth; HOLY ORDERS: *Symbols:* Head of the Body).

• LH, ET.6.Mo, 2R: Didymus of Alexandria, On the Trinity, 2, 12: PG 39, 667–674 – How the Holy Spirit brings about and perfects the new creation given in Baptism (BAPTISM: *Symbols:* Baptism of Fire; Second Birth; HOLY ORDERS: *Symbols:* Father).

• LH, ET.6.We, 2R: St. Leo the Great, Sermo 1 de Ascensione, 2–4: PL 54, 395–396 – Summary of the encounters and graces during the days between the Resurrection and the Ascension (Eucharist: *Symbols*: Breaking of Bread).

- LH, ET.6.Sa, 2R: St. Augustine, Treatise on St. John, Tract. 124, 5, 7: CCL 36, 685–687 – How St. Peter and St. John represent the active and the contemplative lives respectively.
- LH, ET.7.Mo, 2R: St. Cyril of Jerusalem, Catechetical Instruction 16, De Spiritu Sancto 1, 11–12.16: PG 33, 931–935.939–942 – The Holy Spirit is like living water. All things depend on it, and its effects are different in each (Baptism: *Symbols:* Fountain of Water).
- LH, ET.7.We, 2R: Vatican II, Lumen Gentium 4.12 – The Holy Spirit gives life to sinners, enriches the Church with gifts, transforms Christians into temples of God, and gives charisms (Baptism: *Symbols:* Fountain of Water).
- LH, Pentecost, 2R: St. Irenaeus, Treatise Against Heresies, Book 3, 17, 1–3: SC 34, 302–306 – The Holy Spirit, like rain or dew from above, gives new life through Baptism and Pentecost (Baptism: *Symbols:* Second Birth; Washing; Baptism: *Symbols:* Dew from Above).

Proper of Saints

- LH, St. Raymond of Penyafort (Jan 7), 2R: St. Raymond of Penyafort, Letter, Monumenta Ord. Praed. Hist. 6, 2, Romae 1901, pp. 84–85 – Persecutions are the lot of all true Christians (Eucharist: *Symbols*: Cup of Salvation).
- LH, St. Fabian (Jan 20), 2R: St. Cyprian and the Roman Church, Letter 9, 1 and 8, 2–3: CSEL 3, 488–489.487–488 – St. Cyprian and the Roman Church reflect on the example of Pope St. Fabian, and the Church of Rome explains the merciful but firm attitude to be had toward those who fall into serious sin after Baptism, urging them to penance to be reconciled with God and the Church (Holy Orders: *Symbols*: Shepherd).
- LH, St. Blase (Feb 3), 2R: St. Augustine, Sermo Guelferbytanus 32, De ordinatione episcopi: PLS 2, 639–640 – A shepherd shows his love for Christ by feeding his sheep and suffering for them (Holy Orders: *Symbols*: Servant; Shepherd).
- LH, Our Lady of Lourdes (Feb 11), 2R: St. Marie Bernadette Soubirous, Ep. Ad P. Gondrand, 1861: *cf.* A. Ravier, Les écrits de sainte Bernadette,

Paris 1961, pp. 53–59 – St. Bernadette tells the history of her visions of the Virgin Mary at Lourdes (CONFIRMATION: *Symbols:* Sign of the Cross).

- LH, St. Cyril and Methodius (Feb 14), 2R: From an Old Slavonic Life of Constantine, Ch. 18: Denkschriften der kaiserl. Akademie der Wissenschaften, 19 [Wien 1870], p. 246 – How St. Cyril died praying fervently for the flock he had served throughout his life (HOLY ORDERS: *Symbols:* Servant).

- LH, Chair of Peter (Feb 22), 2R: St. Leo the Great, Sermo 4 de natali ipsius, 2–3: PL 54, 149–151 – St. Peter professed his faith in Jesus as Messiah. Jesus made St. Peter the rock on which he would build his Church and entrusted him with the keys of the kingdom (HOLY ORDERS: *Symbols:* Shepherd).

- LH, St. Polycarp (Feb 23), 2R: Letter on the Martyrdom of St. Polycarp by the Church of Smyrna, Ch. 13, 2–15, 2: Funk 1, 297–299 – The story of the martyrdom of St. Polycarp (EUCHARIST: *Types*: Animal Sacrifices; *Symbols*: Cup of Salvation).

- LH, Saints Perpetua and Felicity (Mar 7), 2R: From the story of the death of the holy martyrs of Carthage, Chap. 18, 20–21: edit. van Beek, Noviomagi, 1936, pp. 42.46–52 – The death of the martyrs of Carthage, thrown to the lions (BAPTISM: *Symbols:* Washing).

- LH, St. Frances of Rome (Mar 9), 2R: Mary Magdalene Anguillaria, Life of St. Frances of Rome, Ch. 6–7: Acta Sanctorum Martii 2, *185–*187 – How St. Frances of Rome lived many virtues, and served those in need spiritually and physically (EUCHARIST: *Symbols:* Medicine of Immortality; PENANCE: *Symbols:* Medicine for the Soul; HOLY ORDERS: *Symbols:* Physician).

- LH, St. Cyril of Jerusalem (Mar 18), 2R: St. Cyril of Jerusalem, Catechetical Instruction 3, 1–3: PG 33, 426–430 – Through Baptism the Christian enters into the Wedding Feast as bride of Jesus Christ (BAPTISM: *Symbols:* Washing; White Garment / Wedding Garment; CONFIRMATION: *Symbols:* Seal).

- LH, St. Turibius de Mongrovejo (Mar 23), 2R: Vatican II, Christus Dominus 12–13.16 – The qualities of a holy bishop (HOLY ORDERS: *Symbols:* Father; Servant; Shepherd).

- LH, St. Vincent Ferrer (Apr 5), 2R: St. Vincent Ferrer, Treatise on the Spiritual Life, Ch. 13: ed. Garganta-Forcada, p. 513–514 – The preaching of a priest should be that of a compassionate and loving father, not dry and abstract. In Confession, the priest should be warm and charitable. He should ask God for the gift of charity (HOLY ORDERS: *Symbols:* Father).

- LH, St. Stanislaus (Apr 11), 2R: St. Cyprian, Letter 58, 8–9.11: CSEL 3, 663–666 – The spiritual armor of the Christian (in reference to Eph. 6:10–20) to be able to come out victorious from the battle (CONFIRMATION: *Symbols:* Sign of the Cross).
- LH, St. Martin I (Apr 13), 2R: St. Martin I, Letter 17: PL 87, 203–204 – Having been exiled, Pope St. Martin reflects on his sufferings and loneliness, and prays for the universal Church, expressing his trust in Jesus Christ (HOLY ORDERS: *Symbols:* Shepherd).
- LH, St. George (Apr 23), 2R: St. Peter Damian, Sermo 3, De sancto Georgio: PL 144, 567–571 – St. George was an example of a soldier of Christ. Through Baptism we are cleansed of our sins and reborn, entering into the Tent of the Church, in which we journey toward the Temple of heaven (BAPTISM: *Symbols:* Second Birth; Washing; White Garment / Wedding Garment; CONFIRMATION: *Symbols:* Fire).
- LH, St. Fidelis of Sigmaringen (Apr 24), 2R: From a eulogy for St. Fidelis of Sigmaringen – St. Fidelis brought relief to the poor and sick in peace and war, as well as zealously witnessing to the faith (ANOINTING OF THE SICK: *Symbols:* Anointing).
- LH, St. Catherine of Siena (Apr 29), 2R: St. Catherine of Siena, Dialogue on Divine Providence, Ch. 167, Gratiarum actio ad Trinitatem: ed. lat., Ingolstadii 1583, f. 290v–291 – Praise to the Holy Trinity and his infinite perfections, in which he allows us to share (CONFIRMATION: *Symbols:* Fire).
- LH, St. John of Avila (May 10), 2R: St. John of Avila, Talk sent to Fr. Francisco Gómez, SJ: BAC 304, Obras completes del santo maestro Juan de Ávila, 3, p. 364–365.370.373 – Reasons why a priest is called to holiness (HOLY ORDERS: *Types:* Priesthood).
- LH, St. Nereus and St. Achilleus (May 12), 2R: St. Augustine, Commentary on the Psalms, 61, 4: CCL 39, 773–775 – Christ is the head of the Body, and because of that we can share in his sufferings and fill up what is lacking of the sufferings of Christ (HOLY ORDERS: *Symbols:* Head of the Body).
- LH, St. Pancras (May 12), 2R: St. Bernard, Sermo 17 in psalmum Qui habitat, 4, 6: Opera Omnia 4, 489–491 – God accompanies those who are in tribulation (CONFIRMATION: *Symbols:* Fire).

- LH, Our Lady of Fatima (May 13), 2R: St. Ephrem the Syrian, Sermon 3, De diversis: Opera Omnia, III, syr. et. lat., Romae 1743, 607 – Since the Incarnation took place through Mary, she is the temple of the Son of God, the new mystical heaven, the branch bearing sweet fruit, and the fountain from which living water flowed. She was prefigured by Eve (BAPTISM: *Symbols:* Fountain of Water).

- LH, St. Cristopher Magallanes (May 21), 2R: St. Caesarius of Arles, Sermo 225, 1–2: CCL 104, 888–889 – Every Christian can be spiritually united to the martyrs by living the virtues (CONFIRMATION: *Symbols:* Seal; Sign of the Cross).

- LH, St. Gregory VII (May 25), 2R: St. Gregory VII, Letter 64 extra Registrum: PL 148, 709–710 – How the Church is Mother and takes care of her children even in the midst of persecutions with the grace of God (HOLY ORDERS: *Symbols:* Father; Shepherd).

- LH, St. Mary Magdalene de Pazzi (May 25), 2R: St. Mary Magdalene de Pazzi, On Revelation and On Trials, Mss. III, 186.264; IV, 716: Opere di S. M. Maddalene de Pazzi, Firenze, 1965, 4, pp. 200.269; 6, p. 194 – The Holy Spirit comes into the soul like a fountain, giving it his riches and virtues (BAPTISM: *Symbols:* Fountain of Water; CONFIRMATION: *Symbols:* Seal).

- LH, St. Philip Neri (May 26), 2R: St. Augustine, Sermo 171, 1–3.5: PL 38, 933–935 – Rejoice in the Lord, not in the world.

- LH, St. Boniface (June 5), 2R: St. Boniface, Letter 78: MGH, Epistolae, 3, 352.354 – The Church is like a ship, steered by the bishops through their teaching and defense of the faith. This is a terrifying responsibility, but the bishop must trust in God's grace (HOLY ORDERS: *Symbols*: Sea Captain; Shepherd).

- LH, St. Ephrem (June 9), 2R: St. Ephrem, Sermo 3, de fine et admonitione, 2.4–5: ed. Lamy, 3, 216–222 – How the spiritual life, received in Baptism and nourished in the Eucharist, is superior to the earthly life (CONFIRMATION: *Symbols*: Seal; EUCHARIST: *Symbols*: Altar / Table; Bread for the Journey / Daily Bread / Viaticum).

- LH, St. Peter and St. Paul (June 29), 2R: St. Augustine, Sermo 295, 1–2.4.7–8: PL 38, 1348–1352 – Peter alone among the apostles represents the entire Church. He represents the unity and universality of the Church. He was entrusted with feeding the sheep. Let us look to the examples of St. Peter and St. Paul (HOLY ORDERS: *Symbols*: Shepherd).

- LH, St. Anthony Zaccaria (Jul 5), 2R: St. Anthony Zaccaria, Sermon to fellow members of his society, J.A. Gabutio, Historia Congregationis Clericorum Regularium S. Pauli, 1, 8 – How we should imitate St. Paul, who through faith brought good out of persecutions and suffering (HOLY ORDERS: *Symbols*: Father).
- LH, St. Camillus de Lellis (July 14), 2R: S. Cicatelli, Vita del P. Camillo de Lellis, Viterbo 1615 – How Christ should be served in the sick and suffering (CONFIRMATION: *Symbols*: Fire).
- LH, St. Bonaventure (July 15), 2R: St. Bonaventure, Journey of the Mind to God, Ch. 7, 1.2.4.6: Opera Omnia, 5, 312–313 – How the Holy Spirit can lead the person who leaves behind the world and desires God into deep mystical union with him (CONFIRMATION: *Symbols*: Fire).
- LH, St. Mary Magdalene (July 22), 2R: St. Gregory the Great, Homily on the Gospels 25, 1–2.4–5: PL 76, 1189–1193 – How Mary Magdalene revealed her burning love for the Lord when she stayed behind after not finding the body (CONFIRMATION: *Symbols*: Fire).
- LH, St. Bridget (July 23), 2R: St. Bridget, Oratio 2: Revelationum S. Birgittae libri, 2, Romae 1628, p. 408–410 – Honor and blessing to Jesus Christ for his Paschal Mystery (EUCHARIST: *Types*: Passover / Passover Lamb).
- LH, St. Peter Julian Eymard (Aug 2), 2R: St. Peter Julian Eymard, La Présence réelle, vol. 1, Paris, 1950, pp. 270–271 and 307–308 – The Church is united as the Body of Christ through the Eucharist, source of life for souls and societies (BAPTISM: *Symbols:* Fountain of Water; EUCHARIST: *Symbols*: Altar / Table; Bread and Wine / Nourishment; Bread from Heaven / Bread of Life / Bread of Angels; Breaking of Bread).
- LH, Dedication of St. Mary Major (Aug 5), 2R: St. Cyril of Alexandria, Homily delivered at the Council of Ephesus, 4: PG 77, 991.995–996 – How much the Virgin Mary should be praised, for salvation came because of her and she is the holy temple of God (CONFIRMATION: *Symbols:* Anointing).
- LH, St. Cajetan (Aug 7), 2R: St. Cajetan, Epist. ad Elisabeth Porto: Studi e Testi 177, Città del Vaticano 1954, p. 50–51 – How Elisabeth should give herself completely to Jesus Christ, who has won eternal life for her (EUCHARIST: *Symbols*: Altar / Table).
- LH, St. Lawrence (Aug 10), 2R: St. Augustine, Sermo 304, 1–4: PL 38, 1395–1397 – St. Lawrence partook of a gift of self at the Lord's table and

then practiced that gift in his martyrdom (EUCHARIST: *Symbols*: Altar / Table).

- LH, St. John Eudes (Aug 19), 2R: St. John Eudes, On the Admirable Heart of Jesus, Book 1, 5: Opera Omnia 6, 107.113–115 – The Christian is member of Christ's Body through Baptism. All he is and does should be animated by Christ. This union is strengthened through Confirmation and is perfected in the Eucharist (HOLY ORDERS: *Symbols*: Head of the Body).
- LH, St. Louis (Aug 25), 2R: St. Louis, From a spiritual testament to his son: Acta Sanctorum Augusti 5 (1868), 546 – Love God above all else. Prefer to die rather than to commit a mortal sin. Live united to the Church and promote goodness and virtue (HOLY ORDERS: *Symbols*: Father).
- LH, St. Monica (Aug 27), 2R: St. Augustine, Confessions, Book 9, 10–11: CSEL 33, 215–219 – St. Augustine and his mother, St. Monica, speak about eternal life shortly before she dies (EUCHARIST: *Symbols*: Altar / Table).
- LH, Beheading of John the Baptist (Aug 29), 2R: St. Bede the Venerable, Homily 23: CCL 122, 354.356–357 – John the Baptist witnessed to Christ and to the truth with his words and martyrdom (CONFIRMATION: *Symbols:* Seal).
- LH, Triumph of the Cross (Sep 14), 2R: St. Andrew of Crete, Oratio 10 in Exaltatione sanctae crucis: PG 97, 1018–1019.1022–1023 – The cross is the greatest of treasures. On it Christ won our salvation, opened the stream of immortality from his pierced side, opened the gate of paradise, and shared the fruit of the tree of life. It is a sign of suffering and a trophy of victory (BAPTISM: *Types:* Fruit of the Tree of Life; Water from the Side of Christ; EUCHARIST: *Types:* Blood from the Side of Christ).
- LH, St. Cornelius and St. Cyprian (Sep 16), 2R: St. Cyprian, Letter 60, 1–2.5: CSEL 3, 691–692.694–695 – St. Cyprian rejoices in the fidelity of Pope St. Cornelius and of the entire Roman Church in the face of persecutions.
- LH, St. Januarius (Sep 19), 2R: St. Augustine, Sermo 340, 1: PL 38, 1483–1484 – A bishop ought to live for his flock, and be the servant of his flock (HOLY ORDERS: *Symbols*: Laborer of the Harvest; Servant; Shepherd).
- LH, St. Cosmas and St. Damian (Sep 26), 2R: St. Augustine, Sermo 329, 1–2: PL 38, 1454–1455 – Christ on the cross paid the price for the world. The martyrs, by the grace of God, drink the cup of suffering and testify

to Christ's blood (EUCHARIST: *Symbols*: Banquet; Bread and Wine / Nourishment; Cup of Salvation).

- LH, St. Jerome (Sep 30), 2R: St. Jerome, Prologue of the Commentary on Isaiah, 1.2: CCL 73, 1–3 – Ignorance of Scripture is ignorance of Christ. Jerome will explain the book of Isaiah, which contains all the mysteries of the Lord Jesus Christ from his birth to his death and Resurrection (CONFIRMATION: *Symbols:* Seal).
- LH, St. John Leonardi (Oct 9), 2R: St. John Leonardi, Letter to Pope Paul V: in archivo Ordinis Clericorum Regularium Matris Dei – To reform the Church, it is important to promote the holiness of bishops and priests and the education of the faithful (HOLY ORDERS: *Symbols*: Head of the Body; Shepherd).
- LH, St. Hedwig (Oct 16), 2R: Life of St. Hedwig, Acta Sanctorum Octobris 8 (1853), 201–202 – How St. Hedwig lived the fire of divine love (CONFIRMATION: *Symbols:* Fire).
- LH, St. Margaret Mary Alacoque (Oct 16), 2R: St. Margaret Mary Alacoque, Letter, Vie et Oeuvres 2, Paris 1915, 321.336.493.554 – The Sacred Heart of Jesus is a fountain of mercy, charity, love, and light. The faithful should unite themselves to the Sacred Heart (EUCHARIST: *Symbols*: Altar / Table).
- LH, St. Ignatius of Antioch (Oct 17), 2R: St. Ignatius of Antioch, Letter to the Romans, Ch. 4, 1–2; 6, 1–8, 3: Funk 1, 217–223 – St. Ignatius of Antioch desires to be a martyr for Jesus Christ (EUCHARIST: *Symbols*: Gift of Finest Wheat).
- LH, St. Luke (Oct 18), 2R: St. Gregory the Great, Homily on the Gospels, 17, 1–3: PL 76, 1139 – The Lord follows after the work of his preachers, who prepare the way for him. Pray for priests that they may be true laborers who preach and who live charity (HOLY ORDERS: *Symbols:* Laborer of the Harvest).
- LH, St. Paul of the Cross (Oct 19), 2R: St. Paul of the Cross, Letter 1, 43; 2, 440.825 – The importance of praying about the cross of Jesus Christ in order to grow in love and union with God (CONFIRMATION: *Symbols:* Fire).
- LH, St. Isaac Jogues and St. John de Brébeuf (Oct 19), 2R: St. John de Brébeuf, Spiritual Diary: The Jesuit Relations and Allied Documents, The Burrow Brothers CO, Cleveland 1898, 164,166 – How St. John de Brébeuf desires to suffer martyrdom for love of Christ and for the glory of God and

the conversion of the Native Americans (EUCHARIST: *Symbols*: Cup of Salvation; HOLY ORDERS: *Symbols:* Father).

- LH, St. John of Capistrano (Oct 23), 2R: St. John of Capistrano, Mirror of the Clergy, Pars 1, Venetiae 1580, 2 – It is important for priests to live what they preach, to truly be salt of the Earth and light of the world (EUCHARIST: *Symbols*: Altar / Table).

- LH, St. Anthony Claret (Oct 24), 2R: St. Anthony Mary Claret, L'egoismo vinto, Romae 1869, 60 – The love of Christ is the source of apostolic zeal (CONFIRMATION: *Symbols:* Fire).

- LH, All Saints (Nov 1), 2R: St. Bernard, Sermo 2: Opera Omnia, Edit. Cisterc. 5 (1968), 364–368 – The feast of All Saints lifts our hearts and minds to heaven and inspires in us the desire to be with them and to live united to Christ our head, who will come again (HOLY ORDERS: *Symbols*: Head of the Body).

- LH, St. Martin de Porres (Nov 3), 2R: St. John XXIII, Homily at the Canonization of St. Martin de Porres, May 6, 1962: AAS 54 (1962), 306–309 – The example of St. Martin de Porres' love for God and for his neighbor (EUCHARIST: *Symbols*: Bread and Wine / Nourishment).

- LH, St. Charles Borromeo (Nov 4), 2R: St. Charles Borromeo, Sermon given during the last synod he attended, Acta Ecclesiae Mediolanensis, Mediolani 1599, 1177–1178 – If a priest wants to grow in his interior union with God, he must foment interior silence, study, practice what he preaches, take care of himself, and make time for prayer and the sacraments (CONFIRMATION: *Symbols:* Fire).

- LH, Dedication of St. John Lateran (Nov 9), 2R: St. Caesarius of Arles, Sermo 229, 1–3: CCL 104, 905–908 – Christians are reborn in Baptism through the ministry of the Church, and become living temples of Christ (BAPTISM: *Symbols:* Second Birth).

- LH, Leo the Great (Nov 10), 2R: Leo the Great, Sermo 4, 1–2: PL 54, 148–149 – Through the Sacraments of Baptism, Confirmation, and Holy Orders, Christians share, in different degrees, in the one priesthood and kingship of Christ (BAPTISM: *Types*: Anointing of Priests, Prophets, and Kings; CONFIRMATION: *Symbols:* Sign of the Cross; EUCHARIST: *Symbols*: Altar / Table; HOLY ORDERS: *Symbols:* Anointing).

- LH, St. Martin of Tours (Nov 11), 2R: Sulpicius Severus, Letter 3, 6.9–10.11.14–17.21: SC 133, 336–344 – How St. Martin foresaw his death, and how he was willing to continue faithfully serving his flock up to the moment of his death (HOLY ORDERS: *Symbols:* Father; Shepherd).

- LH, St. Josaphat (Nov 12), 2R: Pope Pius XI, Encyclical Letter Ecclesiam Dei: AAS 15 (1923), 573–582 – St. Josaphat worked faithfully for the unity of the Church (HOLY ORDERS: *Symbols*: Shepherd).

- LH, St. Albert the Great (Nov 15), 2R: St. Albert the Great, Commentary on Luke 22, 19: Opera Omnia, Paris 1890–1899, 23, 672–674 – There is nothing more profitable, more pleasant, more beneficial, more desirable, and more similar to eternal life than the Eucharist (EUCHARIST: *Types:* Fruit of the Tree of Life; Passover / Passover Lamb; Manna; *Symbols*: Bread and Wine / Nourishment).

- LH, Dedication of the Churches of Peter and Paul (Nov 18), 2R: St. Leo the Great, Sermo 82, in natali apostolorum Petri et Pauli 1, 6–7: PL 54, 426–428 – How the martyrdom of St. Peter and St. Paul give splendor to the Church and how we can hope in their intercession (HOLY ORDERS: *Symbols:* Head of the Body).

- LH, St. Clement I (Nov 23), 2R: St. Clement, Letter to the Corinthians, Ch. 35, 1–5; 36, 1–2; 37, 1.4–5; 38, 1–2.4 – How great are the the the gifts given to us by God through Jesus Christ! In him we have been made one Body (HOLY ORDERS: *Types:* High Priest).

- LH, St. John Damascene (Dec 4), 2R: St. John Damascene, Statement of Faith, Ch. 1: PG 95, 417–419 – How God created, redeemed, loved, and called St. John Damascene to serve him and shepherd his flock; petition of help and guidance (CONFIRMATION: *Symbols:* Fire; EUCHARIST: *Symbols:* Bread and Wine / Nourishment; HOLY ORDERS: *Symbols:* Shepherd).

- LH, St. Nicholas (Dec 6), 2R: St. Augustine, Treatise on John 123, 5: CCL 36, 678–680 – Shepherds must tend the sheep even to the point of martyrdom for them, remembering that they are Christ's and not their own (HOLY ORDERS: *Symbols*: Shepherd).

- LH, St. Ambrose (Dec 7), 2R: St. Ambrose, Letter 2, 1–2.4–5.7: PL (edit. 1845) 879, 881 – The bishop must guide the ship of the Church though the storms of the sea, and must drink the waters of Jesus Christ, and share those waters through his words (BAPTISM: *Symbols:* Fountain of Water; HOLY ORDERS: *Symbols*: Sea Captain).

- LH, St. Peter Canisius (Dec 21), 2R: St. Peter Canisius, Epistulae et Acta (edit. O. Brunsberger), I, Friburgi Brisgoviae, 1896, pp. 53–55 – St. Peter

Canisius feels called to evangelize Germany, and drinks waters from the side of Christ, receiving the gifts of peace, love, and perseverance (BAPTISM: *Symbols:* Fountain of Water).

- LH, St. Thomas Becket (Dec 29), 2R: St. Thomas Becket, Letter 74: PL 190, 533–536 – The great responsibility that a bishop has, how important it is for him to stay united to the pope, and how he must fight to the end to win the crown (HOLY ORDERS: *Types*: High Priest; *Symbols*: Head of the Body; Laborer of the Harvest; Sea Captain; Shepherd).

COMMONS

- LH, Common of the Dedication of a Church, 2R: Origen, Homily on Joshua 9, 1–2: SC 71, 244–246 – Christians are living stones of a spiritual building (EUCHARIST: *Symbols*: Altar / Table).
- LH, Common of One Martyr, 2R: St. Augustine, Sermo 329, 1–2: PL 38, 1454–1456 – Christ on the cross paid the price for the world. The martyrs, by the grace of God, drink the cup of suffering and testify to Christ's blood (EUCHARIST: *Symbols*: Banquet; Bread and Wine / Nourishment; Cup of Salvation).
- LH, Common of Pastors, 2R, For a pope: St. Leo the Great, Sermo 3 de natali ipsius, 2–3: PL 54, 145–146 – The mission and role of the pope (HOLY ORDERS: *Symbols:* Sea Captain; Shepherd).
- LH, Common of Pastors, 2R, For a bishop: St. Fulgentius of Ruspe, Sermo 1, 2–3: CCL 91A, 889–890 – The bishops are servants and stewards of Jesus Christ (HOLY ORDERS: *Symbols*: Servant; Shepherd; Steward).
- LH, Common of Pastors, 2R, For a priest: Vatican II, Presbyterorum ordinis Ch. 3, 12 – Priests have a special obligation to seek holiness (HOLY ORDERS: *Types*: High Priest; *Symbols*: Anointing; Head of the Body; Servant; Shepherd).
- LH, Common of Pastors, 2R, For a missionary: Vatican II, Ad gentes 4–5 – The Church received from Jesus Christ the missionary mandate to go and spread the faith to all nations (HOLY ORDERS: *Symbols*: Shepherd).

Related Christological Titles
or Antiphons of the Psalms and Canticles
from the Liturgy of the Hours

TITLE (CHRISTOLOGICAL READING) OR ANTIPHON	PSALM OR CANTICLE	SUMMARY OF PSALM	LITURGY OF THE HOURS
They are happy who, putting all their trust in the cross, have plunged into the water of life (from an author of the second century).	Ps. 1	Blessed is the man who delights in the law of the Lord.	Psalter.1.Su, OR, Title1
In the fullness of time, God sent his Son, born of a woman, that we might become his adopted children.	Ps. 2	You are my Son. This day I have begotten you.	Mar25, OR, Ant1
The rulers of the earth joined forces to overthrow Jesus, your anointed Son (Acts 4:27).	Ps. 2	You are my Son (God's Anointed). This day I have begotten you.	Psalter.1.Su, OR, Title2
Now the reign of our God has begun and power is given to Christ, his anointed, alleluia.	Ps. 20	Prayer for victory for the king, the anointed.	Psalter.1.Tu, EP, Ant1
The Lamb himself will be their shepherd and will lead them to springs of living water (Rev. 7:17).	Ps. 23	The Lord is my shepherd, there is nothing I shall want.	Psalter.2.Su, DP, Title1; Psalter.4.Su, DP, Title1

In you is the fountain of life; we drink from the streams of your goodness.	Ps. 36	The sinner does not fear God and dies, but the just drinks from the source of life, found in God.	Sacred Heart, OR, Ant1
If anyone thirsts, let him come to me and drink from the ever-flowing streams.	Ps. 42	My soul longs for God like a deer for running water.	Corpus Christi, OR, Ant2
Let all who thirst come; let all who desire it, drink from the life giving water (Rev. 22:17).	Ps. 42	My soul longs for God like a deer for running water.	Psalter.2. Mo, MP, Title1
As a deer longs for flowing streams, so my soul longs for you, my God, alleluia.	Ps. 42	My soul longs for God like a deer for running water.	ET.Psalter. 2.Mo, MP, Ant1
Your inmost being must be renewed, and you must put on the new man (Eph. 4:23–24).	Ps. 51	David's humble petition to God that he wash away his sin.	Psalter.1.Fr, MP, Title1; Psalter.2.Fr, MP, Title1; Psalter.3.Fr, MP, Title1; Psalter.4.Fr, MP, Title1
The soldier baptizes his king, the servant his Lord, John his Savior; the waters of the Jordan tremble, a dove hovers as a sign of witness, and the voice of the Father is heard: This is my Son.	Ps. 63:2–9	My soul longs and thirsts for God.	Baptism of the Lord, MP, Ant1

Clothed in white robes, they will walk with me, says the Lord, for they are worthy.	Ps. 63:2–9	My soul longs and thirsts for God.	Holy Innocents (Dec 28), MP, Ant1
Let all the earth adore you, Lord, and let it be joyful; for a new light has dawned upon the ages.	Ps. 66	Praise God for his wondrous deeds, including bringing us relief after passing through water and fire.	Baptism of the Lord, OR, Ant2
These events are recalled as a warning to us (1 Cor. 10:6).	Ps. 78:1–39	The wonders God worked in the Exodus: crossing of the Red Sea, water from the rock, bread of angels.	ET.Psalter. 4.Fr, OR, Title1 CT.Psalter. 4.Fr, OR, Title1
The children of Israel ate the manna and drank from the spiritual rock which followed after them.	Ps. 78:1–39	The wonders God worked in the Exodus: crossing of the Red Sea, water from the rock, bread of angels.	ET.Psalter. 4.Fr, OR, Ant2 CT.Psalter. 4.Fr, OR, Ant2
Live as children born of the light. Light produces every kind of goodness and justice and truth (Eph. 5:8–9).	Ps. 112	The just man is happy. Light rises in the darkness for the upright.	Psalter.4.Su, EP2, Title2
In the Jordan river our Savior crushed the serpent's head and wrested us free from his grasp.	Ps. 112	The just man is happy. Light rises in the darkness for the upright.	Baptism of the Lord, EP, Ant2

You too left Egypt when, at baptism, you renounced that world which is at enmity with God (St. Augustine).	Ps. 114	God worked marvelous wonders when he brought Israel out of Egypt.	Psalter.1.Su, EP2, Title2
He will save his people from their sins (Matt. 1:21).	Ps. 130	A trusting cry from the depths for forgiveness of sins.	NP.We, Title2
He has won us for himself . . . and you must proclaim what he has done for you. He has called you out of darkness into his own wonderful light (cf. 1 Pet. 2:9).	Ps. 135 Ps. 135:1–12	Praise the wonderful things God does for us.	Psalter.3.Fr, EP, Title1 Psalter.4. Mo, MP, Title3
Zion, prepare your wedding chamber to receive Christ the King.	Ps. 147:12–20	God showers down his blessings upon Zion.	Presentation of the Lord (Feb 2), EP, Ant2
You burned away man's guilt by fire and the Holy Spirit. We give praise to you, our God and redeemer.	Ps. 149	The joy of God's holy people.	Baptism of the Lord, MP, Ant3
Blessed be the God and Father of our Lord Jesus Christ, who in his great love for us has brought us to a new birth (1 Pet. 1:3).	Tob. 13:1–8	In the exile God scourged Israel for its iniquities, but he will again gather them from among the Gentiles.	Psalter.1.Tu, MP, Cant
If anyone thirsts, let him come to me and drink (John 7:37).	Isa. 12:1–6	With joy you will draw water at the fountain of salvation.	Psalter.2.Th, MP, Cant

I will pour cleansing water upon you, alleluia.	Ezek. 36:24–28	I will sprinkle clean water upon you and give you a new heart.	ET.Psalter. 4.Sa, MP, Ant2
With your whole heart turn to God and he will blot out all your sins (Acts 3:19).	Dan. 3:26–27, 29, 34–41	Humble petition for the forgiveness of sins.	Psalter.4.Tu, MP, Title2
Springs of water are made holy as Christ revealed his glory to the world. Draw water from the fountain of the Savior, for Christ our God has hallowed all creation.	Dan. 3:57–88, 56	Invitation to all creation to bless the Lord.	Baptism of the Lord, MP, Ant2
Jesus Christ loved us, and poured out his own blood for us to wash away our sins.	Hab. 3:2–4, 13a, 15–19	The Glory of the Lord who saves his anointed one.	Lent. HW.Fr, MP, Ant2
Christ is baptized, the world is made holy; he has taken away our sins. We shall be purified by water and the Holy Spirit.	Luke 1:68–79	Canticle of Zechariah.	Baptism of the Lord, MP, CantZech
Christ Jesus loved us, poured out his blood to wash away our sins, and made us a kingdom and priests for God our Father. To him be glory and honor forever.	Luke 1:46–55	Magnificat.	Baptism of the Lord, MP, Magn
A wondrous mystery is declared to us today: the Creator of the universe has washed away our sins in the waters of the Jordan.	Rev. 15:3–4	All nations shall come and worship in the presence of the Lord.	Baptism of the Lord, EP, Ant3